INSIDE THE FINANCIAL
FUTURES MARKETS

WILEY FINANCE EDITIONS

INSIDE THE FINANCIAL FUTURES MARKETS
Third Edition

Mark J. Powers
Mark G. Castelino

JOHN WILEY & SONS, INC.
New York • Chichester • Brisbane • Toronto • Singapore

To Jo and Leonie

Copyright © 1991 by Mark J. Powers and Mark G. Castelino.
Published by John Wiley & Sons, Inc.

Library of Congress Cataloging-in-Publication Data:

Powers, Mark J.
 Inside the financial futures markets / Mark J. Powers, Mark G. Castelino.
— 3rd ed.
  p.   cm.
 Includes index.
 ISBN 0-471-53674-1
 1. Financial futures. I. Castelino, Mark G., 1946–   . II. Title.
HG6024.A3P68   1991
332.64′5—dc20   91-9210

Printed in the United States of America

10 9 8 7 6 5 4 3 2 1

Contents

Part One

Introduction to
Futures Trading

1
Introduction

This book is about one of the most exciting new financial products to be developed in several decades—futures contracts on financial instruments. These new futures contracts include contracts on Treasury bills, Treasury bonds, Treasury notes, Eurodollars, stock indexes, and foreign currencies.

It's fair to say that very few new financial products have been as quickly accepted. During the 1980s futures contracts completely reshaped our capital markets. By 1990 most chief financial officers of major corporations were familiar with the concepts of hedging interest rates. Most major borrowers, every major lender, major underwriters, and every major portfolio manager find it necessary to have morning reports detailing how the firm's hedged positions have changed from the previous day.

PURPOSE OF THIS BOOK

This book introduces, explains, and illustrates the basic concepts of trading interest rate futures contracts, the economic purpose of the trading, and its operational characteristics. The book also focuses on the concepts of hedging and helps the reader through the basics of developing a corporate hedging plan.

This is not a book designed to make the reader wealthy through successful speculation. It does cover, however, some of the basic aspects of trading.

ORGANIZATION OF THE BOOK

The book is divided into five parts. Part One introduces the reader to the economics and social purposes of futures trading and the basic concepts of futures trading. It explains the elemental aspects of getting started in trading, including the selection of a broker and the entering of orders to buy and sell.

Part Two is a brief description of the two basic approaches to price analysis and forecasting—technical and fundamental. The technical analysis portion covers chart building and interpretation as well as statistical analysis of price movement. Fundamental analysis refers to the study of some of the basic economic data reflecting the supply and demand for funds in the capital markets.

Part Three begins with a description of the role of money in the economy and then explains the concepts of risk and return, their definitions, and techniques for measuring them. The basic concepts of financial calculations are covered including duration, convexity, discounted cash flow, bond equivalent yields, and so on. Yield curves, what they are, why they take on the shape they do, and what they reveal are also discussed.

The remainder of Part Three discusses the cash markets and the characteristics of money market and debt instruments, including Treasury bills, Eurodollar deposits, bonds, notes, and mortgage-backed securities. Market characteristics, methods of valuation, how to determine the cheapest to deliver, and payment provisions, are covered.

Part Four explains the foreign exchange markets, stock indexes, and options. The relationships between interest rates and foreign exchange values are discussed, along with the economic factors affecting foreign exchange rates. In addition, a number of foreign exchange hedging examples are provided. Stock index futures, portfolio insurance, and program trading are discussed and reviewed, and, finally, two complete chapters are devoted to options and option strategies.

Part Five is devoted entirely to hedging. Hedging theory and practical concepts are covered in-depth. All of the concepts discussed in earlier chapters are combined in the illustrations of hedging and rising rate markets and declining rate markets. The concepts of basis estimation, cross-hedging, dollar equivalency, under-value and over-value, cost of carry, as well as other important elements are discussed and illustrated. A number of special problems and situations in which hedging is used by banks, insurance companies, savings and loans (S&Ls), mortgage bankers, and industrial corporations are presented. This part also contains a chapter on arbitrage. It ends with a short chapter on hedge accounting issues.

2

The Role of Futures Markets

THE SOCIAL AND ECONOMIC PURPOSES OF FUTURES TRADING

The major difference between an economy guided by the market mechanism and one directed centrally is that the former is controlled primarily by two influences—consumer demands and relative costs of production. When markets operate with few imperfections, such as monopolistic pressures, the forces of competition tend to lead the economy to serve consumer demands effectively and efficiently. For this reason it is generally considered desirable to take steps that will reduce those market imperfections that limit competition and to encourage those activities that foster competition. Interest rate futures contribute on both scores.

An Aid to General Competition

Supreme Court Justice Louis D. Brandeis made the point best in the early part of this century, when he noted that the organization of an exchange is a society's attempt to capture the economist's concept of perfect competition. He said that the purposes to be accomplished by trading through such institutions are good in that they tend toward (1) greater equality of opportunity, (2) greater efficiency in physical markets, and (3) improvement in the flows of information. All of these are part and parcel of effective competition.

An Aid to Capital Formation

Financial futures not only add to the general competitiveness of the economy by reducing barriers to competition, but they also aid in capital formation by helping to improve our savings and investment flows. The long-run significance of this should not be underestimated. The lack of sufficient savings and investment has been a major contributor to a rampant increase in inflation, the decline in productivity, and the decrease in international competitiveness. Personal savings rates in the United States rank among the lowest of industrialized countries.

Financial futures help improve our savings and investment flows by providing strong and more stable commercial banking, investment banking, and brokerage industries. In today's uncertain times that is not an insignificant benefit. The maintenance of an efficient savings and investment process depends on investment banking and brokerage firms who can take the risk of carrying inventory of securities for periods of time while awaiting the resale and distribution of these securities to long-term investors.

No longer do the fortunes of a firm that is "making a market" in money instruments depend solely on a trader's ability to outguess the market. Now the risk of owning, building, and disposing of an inventory of bonds or commercial paper can be kept at a tolerable level while the market-making activities can continue apace.

During the 1980s brokerage firms or dealers in credit instruments learned how to use the financial futures markets to a competitive advantage as an integral part of serving their customers and in their market-making activity.

An Aid to New Product Development

Financial futures aid in the mobilization of savings by spawning a wide array of new savings products offered by local banks, savings and loans (S&Ls), leasing companies, insurance companies, and others. These new products could not come into being without the financial futures markets. In the long run, the experience should not be too unlike that in other areas where futures are an integral part of the pricing process. In those industries a rich variety of risk repackaging services are now available. Indeed, many of the forward contracting devices used throughout the agribusiness, metals, and food industries could not exist today were it not for futures markets. For example, certainly meat packers, who are faced with very sharply veed short-run cost curves for operating their slaughter plants, would not be able to offer farmers forward contracts with open pricing dates if the futures for hogs and cattle did not exist.

Metals firms would likewise find it difficult to attract capital to carry inventories if the futures did not facilitate cash-and-carry business.

During the 1980s we saw innovative new financial products offering forward rates to lenders and borrowers alike. Often the products included options providing both sides great flexibility in structuring their investment activities. In short, financial futures have stimulated the growth of financial intermediation services, with a resultant increase in the flow of funds between savers and investors.

ECONOMIC FUNCTION OF FINANCIAL FUTURES

The basic economic functions performed by financial futures markets are competitive price discovery, hedging of price risks, financing of inventory, and the allocation of resources.

Price Discovery

The prices of money generated by the interest rate futures markets reflect the combined views of a large number of buyers and sellers as to the current supply/demand situation and the relationship of prices 12 to 18 months hence. This does not mean that a futures price is a prediction that will hold true for all times. Instead, it is an expression of opinions concerning *today's* expectations about the level of interest rates and the shape of the yield curve at some point in the future. As conditions change, opinions change and, of course, so will rates. These changes do not make the markets' pricing function less useful. On the contrary, keeping the supply/demand equation current makes the system more useful than a one-time prediction. By coalescing all the diverse and scattered opinions into one readily discernible number, interest rate futures prices provide a consensus of knowledgeable thinking on the price of money in coming weeks or months. Price discovery is the raison d'être for futures markets.

Risk Shifting

The second major function of interest rate futures is risk shifting. A futures market allows the separation of the risk of price change from risk arising from other normal business functions similar to the separation of theft or fire risk from other business risks. Separating these risks allows them to be "packaged" in special ways and transferred from those who have them but may not want them (hedgers) to those who do want them (speculators).

The risk of price change is ever present and represents costs that must be borne by someone. In a competitive atmosphere those costs are passed on to consumers. If the mortgage banker has to assume the risk, he will offset it by paying less for the securities, charging more for them when selling them, or a combination of the two. If on the other hand, the banker can transfer the risk to someone else through a hedge, he can lower the cost of doing business.

Hedging Function

Hedging refers to action taken to neutralize price risk. In this regard it's obvious that the futures markets are not the only means one can use to hedge. This book, however, focuses on hedging as a futures trading technique. As such hedging flows from the natural pricing functions performed by the futures exchanges.

The best way to visualize a hedge is to think of it as a temporary substitute for a transaction one will make at a later time in another market. The concept is understood easiest through an example. Assume you are a corporation. It is December 1, and you know that as a regular part of your seasonal cash flow you will have approximately $1 million in excess cash available for short-term investment next June. Further, assume that you expect interest rates to decline between now and June. You can on December 1 establish, within a small margin of error, the rate you will receive on the funds you will invest in June by buying a futures contract for June Treasury bills. When June arrives you simply purchase the T-bills through your normal channels and offset your futures contract by selling the contract you previously bought. The futures contract served as the temporary substitute during the December to June period. If interest rates have indeed fallen since December and if that fall was also reflected in futures prices, the gain on the futures contract will help make up for the lower rate of return on the T-bills. If interest rates have risen in the interim, the "loss" on your futures position is similarly offset by the greater return on the T-bills you buy.

The converse example may be a situation where you know on December 1 that you will need to borrow funds during June to finance inventories for 90 days. If you expect rates to be higher in June than rates currently reflected in the futures market you can protect yourself from paying the higher rate by selling a 90-day T-bill contract. If rates do go up, the gain on the futures contract will help offset the increased cost of borrowing. In the meantime the futures contract acts as a temporary substitute for the actual borrowing transaction you will make in June.

The foregoing example demonstrates the very simplest concepts of hedging. More sophisticated considerations come into play in actual practice. Such concepts as basis pricing, exchange of futures for physicals, and dollar equivalency are all refinements in hedging that will be explored in later chapters.

Suffice it to say for now that the great benefit one gets out of hedging is the flexibility in timing purchases, sales, and anonymity.

It's important to note also that there are many other ways of hedging interest rate costs. Using the futures market is only one of those ways. Generally a manager will find it is the cheapest, easiest, and most efficient method available and that it fits nicely into a mix of strategies.

Market Efficiency—Reduced Monopoly Power

A futures market acts as a focal point where buyers and seller can meet readily. This improves overall market efficiency by reducing search costs. Buyers automatically know where the sellers are and vice versa. They do not need to search each other out. Accessibility is maximized.

A futures market in interest rates reduces segmentation in the market. It fosters competition by unifying diverse and scattered local markets. Local monopolists have a difficult time maintaining control when national markets easily accessible to all people offer their customers other alternatives. Integrated national markets mean that prices in all local markets tend to move more closely in unison with the national markets. Price relationships for a larger number of locations and a larger number of related products become more stable. This makes for more efficient and effective hedging of a wider number of risks.

Informational Benefits

The futures market has become an economical and efficient mechanism for improving the flows of information in the marketplace. It is those flows of information relative to prices, volume, and market expectations of participants that allow the futures market to make an overall contribution to competition. The futures market reflects more fully the scope of market information available and embeds this information in a way spot markets are unable to do. Some of this advantage flows from the fact that participation in futures markets is usually larger than in the spot markets. Given the same capital the futures trader can control about three times more government securities than his cash market counterpart who faces higher money requirements. Also, a futures trader can sell short in futures markets without the need first to borrow the securities and pay a fee.

Economist Dr. Jacob Grossman has gathered preliminary evidence suggesting that the implied yield curves in futures markets anticipate the shape of the future spot yield curve far better than the spot yield curve does for the six-month forecast. His evidence suggests that futures increase the efficiency of the cash Treasury bills market because they help strengthen the relationships between the short-term rates and the long-term rates.

How much is the service of the futures markets worth to the consumer? That is hard to say. Some studies of the use of futures markets have shown that those who use futures for hedging purposes over several seasons have a more stable income pattern than those who do not. They do not always get the peak prices, but they do not often get the bottom prices either. The futures market provides them with the opportunity to stabilize their incomes and allows them to lower their operating margins to obtain a competitive advantage. In a competitive industry, these benefits ultimately get passed on to customers.

Of course, a futures market cannot do all things for all people, but if it functions properly it should foster an improved competition throughout the marketplace, thus encouraging more efficient use of resources.

HISTORY OF FINANCIAL FUTURES

The history of financial futures is closely intertwined with the growth of inflation in the United States and the relaxation of interest rate regulations.

Many of the interest rate restrictions and regulations that had been put in place during and immediately after the Second World War remained in existence into the early 1960s. But starting with the early and mid-1960s, as inflation rates began to creep up, interest rate regulations were relaxed. State usury laws came into question. The 4.25% coupon ceiling on Treasury bonds was removed. Regulation Q on large commercial accounts was relaxed. The prohibitions against interest paid on demand deposits were relaxed. And more recently automatic savings/checking account transfers have become usual. This relaxation of interest rate restrictions culminated in the action on October 6, 1979, when the Federal Reserve essentially switched their monetary policy to one of controlling the monetary aggregates from one of controlling interest rate levels directly.

The lessening of interest rate restrictions was born of necessity, principally the necessity of maintaining a strong housing sector in the face of higher interest rates, which in turn were caused by higher rates of inflation. The surge of inflation experienced in the United States in the late 1960s and early 1970s had its roots in the monetary and fiscal policies followed by the Johnson administration, when it decided to fight the Vietnam war by pumping up the money supply instead of raising taxes.

This underlying trend toward higher interest rates and increased volatility in rates was obvious in 1970 but not generally viewed as a permanent phenomenon. The sector of society that felt the undercurrents more directly than any other group was probably the commodity traders. Underlying commodity prices were becoming more volatile but, most important, price relationships between different time periods began to reflect interest rate volatility.

Contributing to the volatility of interest rates in 1971 was President Nixon's decision to devalue the dollar and withdraw the United States from the Bretton Woods agreement, an international agreement designed to maintain fixed exchange rates for the major currencies of the Western world. The impact of President Nixon's action was reflected immediately in higher and more volatile rates as countries adjusted interest rates to protect the value of their currencies.

The turmoil in the international monetary system and in interest rates, as noted earlier, was most obvious to the commodity people because the demand for hedge services in commodities began to grow rapidly. It was suddenly also obvious that a whole new market for hedge services was emerging. The risks that banks, borrowers, and lenders had were precisely the same sorts of risks that a grain exporter or a lumber wholesaler had. One was pricing credit instruments, the other pricing bushels of grain or board feet of wood.

So it was that in 1972 the first futures exchange in the world designed exclusively to trade financial futures contracts came into being—the International Monetary Market (IMM). At the announcement of the organization of the exchange, it was noted that the intent was to make the exchange a center for trading a wide variety of financial instruments, including government debt securities. The first contracts listed for trading were futures in foreign exchange. They caught on quickly.

Also, during the early 1970s the Government National Mortgage Association's (GNMA) cash market in mortgage certificates began to grow rapidly. The GNMA market had been established by the government in order to facilitate the flow of funds into the housing industry. Rising interest rates and inflation had created the fear that the demand for housing would decrease and the housing market, a very important segment of the economy, would collapse causing a severe recession and unemployment. As these markets in GNMA certificates began to grow there emerged a forward contract market in the certificates. These forward contracts became the precursor to the formalized futures contracts in GNMAs that emerged a few years later.

By 1975 the economy had been through severe shocks from the Russian wheat deals and the increase in oil prices and was just coming out of the

1974 recession. In October of 1975 the Chicago Board of Trade offered the first interest rate futures contract, the Government National Mortgage Association pass-through certificate futures contract. It caught on immediately and during the first three months of its existence traded 20,000 contracts.

A few weeks after the GNMA contract began trading the International Monetary Market began trading in the Treasury bill futures. And 10 years after the first financial futures were offered, Kansas City began the trading in stock index futures.

Today a whole array of financial futures contracts are offered for trading. In foreign exchange they include contracts in the Swiss franc, the deutsche mark, the Mexican peso, the French franc, the Italian lira, the Canadian dollar, the pound sterling, and the Japanese yen. On the interest rate side there are contracts in 30-day commercial paper, 90-day Treasury bills, Eurodollars, Treasury notes, mortgage-backed securities, certificates of deposit, and long-term government bonds. In stock indexes these are the Value Line Index, S&P 500, S&P 100, CBOE 100, NYSE, and a range of others. We also have futures contracts on the Commodity Research Bureau futures index (CRB) and the trade-weighted index of the dollar (USDX).

In summary, the financial futures markets emerged out of economic necessity. As the underlying volatility and the risk associated with the holding of inventories or the borrowing or lending of money increased, the capitalistic system responded with the development of the financial futures contracts for hedging. To date, the growth in volume of trading has been phenomenal, but it is only a small percentage of the volume that will exist 10 years from now.

3

The Institutional Aspects
of Futures Trading

Futures trading is not a new endeavor. Its roots go back to the medieval fairs and beyond. But in all its history, few more exciting growth periods have existed than the last decade. This section provides the reader with a quick overview of the futures industry, its institutions, and its participants. These include exchanges, clearinghouses, brokers, government regulatory bodies, and trading participants. Each will be explained briefly.

THE EXCHANGES

In a legal/economic sense, exchanges are an attempt to capture the economists' concept of perfect competition. Justice Brandeis in the early part of this century noted that the exchanges are a set of rules that assure open access to many sizes and kinds of buyers and sellers; exchanges provide equal opportunity for participation, foster information flows, and in general restrict certain liberties in the marketplace in order to expand certain larger liberties that maximize the overall contribution of the marketplace to society.

From a practical standpoint exchanges are defined as meeting places. They actually serve as communication centers and can be likened to a giant funnel. The sides of the funnel are composed of the communication lines that go out all around the world and collect orders from buyers and sellers located in various places and collect and disseminate information relevant to the supply/demand factors affecting price. Inside the funnel is the exchange floor where the trading takes place in the hubbub of an auctionlike atmosphere. And out the neck of the funnel come the prices one after another as the trades are consummated.

Basic Functions

The basic functions of an exchange are:

1. To furnish the facilities for the buyers and sellers to meet and conduct their business.
2. To set and enforce the rules under which this trading will be conducted.
3. To collect and disseminate information relative to the market and to the factors affecting prices.
4. To provide an institutional framework for arbitrating disputes and settling differences that may arise in the conduct of the trading.

Locations

Commodity exchanges offering financial futures are located around the world. The first exchange to open its doors to financial instruments trading was the International Monetary Market (IMM) established in 1972. Trading began in foreign currencies on May 16, 1972. Although the first contracts dealt only with foreign currency, the IMM initiated trading in Treasury bill futures in January 1976.

The first interest rate futures contract was developed on the Chicago Board of Trade (CBT) in October of 1975 when the contract calling for delivery of Government National Mortgage Association certificates was listed for trading.

In 1978 the American Stock Exchange established a subsidiary called the American Commodities Exchange (ACE). It was the first exchange located in New York devoted exclusively to the trading of financial instruments. Shortly thereafter, the New York Stock Exchange announced its intentions to open the New York Futures Exchange (NYFE) as a subsidiary, also devoted solely to trading financial futures contracts. NYFE opened its doors in August, 1980, and in September absorbed the struggling ACE.

Several foreign countries have established such exchanges in their parts of the world. The most notable of the recent start-ups have been in Great Britain, Switzerland, Japan, Germany, Canada, Australia, Singapore, and Hong Kong.

Internal Organization

Commodity exchanges are membership organizations. Membership is usually, though not always, limited to individuals, who may assign their membership privileges to a corporation. Only members of the exchange are allowed to conduct the actual trading in the futures contract. Members are also allowed to participate in the management of the exchange through their voting privileges.

Obtaining a Membership

Changes in membership occur only as privately held exchange seats become available for purchase on a bid and offer basis. Exchange memberships are bought and sold just like any other asset. Recent prices of memberships range from several thousand dollars to more than a half million. Memberships are broadly held both occupationally and geographically. Bankers, investment bankers, mortgage bankers, money market dealers, commercial manufacturing firms, brokers, futures commission merchants, and individuals such as lawyers, dentists, farmers, and shopkeepers own memberships. Memberships at U.S. exchanges may be held by U.S. or non-U.S. citizens.

There are generally two reasons for owning a membership. The first is to obtain physical access to the floor or, in the case of electronic exchanges, to the computers, where one can participate directly in the trading. The second is to reduce the cost of trading, but this reason is less important now that commission rates are no longer fixed by the exchange and are instead negotiated. The former reason is particularly important if one wants to establish a brokerage business. Probably the reason most professional speculators desire physical access to the floor, however, is because it gives them immediate communication access to the market. They have no time lag between making a decision to buy or sell and entering the order into the pit.

Although memberships are held by individuals, many memberships are controlled by corporations. Many members are employees of firms whose business involves futures trading. The companies sponsor the applicant, loan him the money to purchase the membership, and get agreements for surrender of the membership if the employee leaves the company. The member in turn assigns his privileges to the company. Memberships may also be leased.

The principal requirements for membership are that the applicants be of good character and financially responsible. Obtaining a membership is not complicated or difficult. The exchanges are relatively open. A new worth of slightly more than the price of the membership and the absence of a bad reputation appear to be all that is required for exchange membership. Of course, exchange membership alone does not qualify one to execute trades on the trading floor. One must also obtain a personal financial guarantee. That aspect is discussed in the section on clearinghouses.

Exchange Management

The exchange is governed by a board of directors elected or appointed from a slate of nominees selected from the membership and, on most exchanges, from several nonmember candidates who represent the public at large or the various commodity interests affected by the contracts traded on the exchange. The board is responsible for establishing major operating policy and for making and amending the exchange's rules. In addition, it may act in a judicial capacity in conducting hearings involving member misconduct.

Daily administration of the exchange is in the hands of an appointed and salaried president employed with the approval of the exchange board. The president as chief executive officer of the exchange is assisted by such other officers and staff as he deems necessary. The staff functions include (1) auditing and investigating the activity of member firms, (2) reviewing the conduct of the member firms in their daily trading, (3) collecting and disseminating information about the markets and the trading, (4) conducting feasibility studies into new areas of business the exchange might develop, and (5) providing educational materials and services to the various segments of the public concerned with or interested in the function and operation of the market.

Usually the exchange members play an important role in the governing of the exchange by serving on committees. Certain committees are common to almost all exchanges. These include arbitration committees, membership committees, rules committees, business conduct committees, public relations and marketing committees, floor practice committees, floor broker qualifications committees, and contract specifications committees. Their titles reflect their functions and responsibilities.

The Trading Floor

The most visible and exciting part of an exchange is the trading floor or, in the case of an electronic exchange, the computer screens. This chapter describes traditional open outcry exchanges. Electronic trading is conducted by video display terminals tied to a central processor. Electronic trading attempts to duplicate the process of pit trading. The clearing process is identical, but instantaneous. The central points of the trading floor are the trading pits or rings—specified areas in which the floor brokers and floor traders do their buying and selling. All bids and offers are made by open outcry and by hand signals in the trading pit.

To the casual observers standing in the visitors' balcony of the Chicago Mercantile Exchange or Chicago Board of Trade on any given day there is a mystery about the markets. The trading floor looks to be the size of a football field. As one views it from above one can see several thousand people. A few are sitting or standing at small cubicles with telephones. Others are on their feet and there is a constant motion of coming and going, some walking casually and others with great intensity. Where the action is frantic there are concentrations of people, with men and women shouting and waving their arms and signaling with their fingers simultaneously. They are trading. To the first-time visitor it seems chaotic. But history has shown it to be an efficient means of arriving at competitive prices for the purchase and sale of futures contracts.

As bids and offers are made and trades are consummated, prices are reported by an observing reporter (an employee of the exchange) and posted on the quotation board, which may be a huge electronic scoreboard located on the ends and side walls of the exchange or large television monitors located above the pit. This price information is also carried instantaneously via ticker and telex to other markets and trading centers throughout the world.

Most floor brokers have telephone, telex, and other communication lines adjacent to the trading areas. From these they receive customer orders for trades and send confirmations of executed trades back to customers.

Execution of Trades

When someone decides to trade on the exchange (having first opened an account with a member firm—a simple procedure explained below), he places the order with a registered representative of a member firm. A proper order should specify whether to buy or sell, what contract, the number of contracts, and at what price and length of time the order is to remain open. When the account executive accepts the order, he confirms it orally and later in writing through the mail. This enables the customer to double-check the accuracy of the order and also confirms in writing that the representative has accepted responsibility for it. The order is immediately time-stamped and sent by wire to the floor of the exchange where it is time-stamped again. Upon receipt on the floor it is sent via a "runner" to the floor broker in the pit. After execution the floor broker endorses the price on the order form, returns it via runner to the floor telex operator who in turn verbally confirms the trade to the account executive.

The NYFE experimented with a substitute for the runners by establishing an electronic means of delivering orders directly to the pit through a system called Order Execution and Retrieval (OER). This was supposed to provide the small trader more direct access to the pit than he enjoys at any other commodity exchange. The small one- or two-lot order was expected to get faster transmission to the pit and faster confirmation of the execution price through OER than might be the case where a runner is used. The system was discontinued due to lack of use.

According to federal regulation all exchanges and registered persons eligible to accept orders from the public must maintain a record-keeping system requiring each handler (except the pit broker) of an order to record the time at which he receives the order. Such a time record makes it easier for the exchange, the federal government, or any customer (who believes a broker has taken advantage of an order by trading ahead of it or by some other abusive practice) to reconstruct the life history of that order and to determine with a high degree of certainty whether the complaint is valid. Such a time-stamping system protects the brokers as much as the customers.

At the end of each trading day the member firm reports all transactions to the clearinghouse, which reconciles (or matches) the trades and assumes the opposite side of the trade for both the original buyer and seller. This assumption of responsibility by the clearinghouse as the second party to each contract greatly simplifies the settlement and delivery process and facilitates the offsetting of futures positions by traders.

THE CLEARINGHOUSE

When bank robber Willy Sutton was asked why he robbed only banks, he replied, "Because that's where they keep the money." Precisely for that reason anyone who desires to become familiar with commodity trading should spend a good deal of time becoming familiar with the clearinghouse, because that's where they keep the money. Most of us are familiar with the clearinghouse operations our nation's banking system uses to expedite the flow and transfer of funds from one bank to another within the system. In the case of a futures exchange the clearing operation exists to perform a similar function. It facilitates the flow and transfer of funds resulting from its member firms' execution of trades. As is true in the case of the bank depositor, the individual commodity trader has no direct contract with the clearing organization. This organization serves simply as a central point for depositing and dispensing funds to be credited or debited to the accounts of member firms.

In addition, the exchange clearinghouse acts as the guarantor of contract performance. The fulfillment of contract obligations of a clearing member is guaranteed through the collective financial resources of the clearinghouse, regardless of what happens to the original individual member parties of the contract.

Furthermore, the exchange clearinghouse performs the important function of assigning and overseeing the deliveries of futures contracts when they mature.

Membership in the clearinghouse is normally confined to exchange members. Those exchange members who are not clearinghouse members must have their trades cleared (verified and guaranteed) by another member who is part of the clearinghouse. Put another way, each exchange member who executes trades must either be a member of the clearinghouse or affiliated with a clearing member.

The Clearinghouse Guarantee

As noted, the clearinghouse becomes the guarantor of the contract to both the buyer and the seller. After the transaction is completed in the trading pit the two parties cease to deal with each other and instead deal with the clearinghouse. Hence, to the person trading on the exchange a most important element in the financial integrity of his transaction is the financial soundness of the clearinghouse.

Although there are individual differences among clearinghouses, there are three major elements that help assure financial security of the transactions. These are:

1. The collection of a security deposit from both the buyer and the seller.
2. Daily settlement in cash by both buyers and sellers of all changes in contract value.
3. The capital resources of the clearinghouse corporation and of its shareholders or members, if they are assessable.

The first two of these elements are explained in detail below. The assessability aspect of the third element refers to any assessments that might be made against clearing members as a result of a financial failure by one of the members. For example, at the IMM a classs A clearing member could be assessed up to $500,000 based upon the proportion of the open interest the clearing member held prior to the occurrence of the financial difficulty. Any remaining loss after the initial assessment of $500,000 per clearing member would be further assessed against the clearing members based upon their proportion of the total number of contracts cleared during the period six months prior to the day the financial difficulty was declared by the clearinghouse. Since the capital requirements to be a clearing member are quite large at most exchanges, it is evident that in the case of an assessable clearinghouse the total financial resources to back the integrity of the futures contracts are quite large.

The Clearinghouse Function

The function of the clearinghouse begins after the trade is executed. Clearinghouse members submit trade confirmation cards for each trade executed. These cards are then matched or verified by the clearinghouse. Once that process is completed the member brokers cease to deal with one another directly. Now, they each deal exclusively with the clearinghouse. In effect, they are now long or short to the clearinghouse, since it has assumed the position of second party to each member's transaction. The liquidation of the contracts is facilitated through this system, because a trader can now offset a contract without the necessity of obtaining the agreement of the original second party to it. The clearinghouse merely notes that the original obligation is canceled through a countervailing position. The clearing member, not the individual customer, is ultimately responsible for fulfillment of a contract with the clearinghouse. The customer's responsibility lies solely with his clearing member. The brokerage firm, after executing the trade, then deals exclusively with its clearing member, who deals with the clearinghouse.

Margin or Security Deposit

Whenever a transaction is made in the market, both parties to the trade are asked to post a "good faith bond" in the form of cash, T-bills, listed securities, or letters of credit. This "good faith" money is referred to as "margin." It is really a security deposit, a term that much more accurately describes it and distinguishes it from margin in the securities market.

The clearinghouse establishes and maintains strict control over these minimum security deposits (margins) both for initiating and for maintaining positions. Member firms are required to collect these minimum amounts from customers. Brokers may and frequently do charge customers more than the minimum but they may not collect less. Clearing member firms must in turn deposit and maintain a specified level of funds in the clearinghouse to back up either their aggregate or their net market positions. Some clearinghouses margin positions on a net basis (100 long and 100 short in the same month is net zero) and others require margin on a gross basis (100 long and 100 short in the same month is 200 contracts).

Requiring these funds ensures performance under the terms of the futures contract. It is a safeguard or surety bond to both buyer and seller (and to the carrying broker) that there will be funds available to make proper settlement when the contract is terminated. When the contracts are offset or delivered upon, this money is returned to the trader along with the profit on the transaction, or it is applied toward his debts if he has lost money.

A trader who has a paper profit on a transaction may usually withdraw the gain over and above the minimum security deposit required at any time before he offsets his position. On the other hand, if the transaction shows a paper loss, his account will be debited accordingly. If the loss causes the equity in the account to fall below 75% of its original margin, the trader may be asked to deposit additional funds to maintain the value of his account at the required minimum amount. These additional deposits are called "variation margin deposits."

Daily Settlement

The clearinghouse requires daily settlement in cash for all price variations in every contract traded. This means that each day the clearinghouse credits the accounts of the clearing members showing a net gain due to favorable price movements during that day's trading and requires immediate payment from those members showing a net loss on their positions. Since there is a buyer for every seller, the monies paid out must equal the monies collected and the clearinghouse must show neither a gain nor a loss. It must balance before a new trading day begins. Brokers use the cash payments received from the clearinghouse to pay out trading profits to customers. Conversely they have to pay additional money to the clearinghouse to cover losses sustained by customers.

As noted above, margin in the commodities markets is a different concept from margin in the securities market. When an investor buys a stock on margin, the margin represents an equity interest in the security and the investor owes the unpaid balance as debt. In futures the trader is not buying or selling the commodity but only agreeing to buy or sell it at a later date. In one sense you could look at the purchase or sale of a futures contract as a purchase or sale of the right to participate in the price change. The margin payment is considered a "sign of good faith" or "earnest" money such as might be used in acquiring a piece of property. The purchaser and the seller promise to fulfill their contracts during the delivery month.

Margins on securities are set by the Federal Reserve Board and their purpose as stated in the Securities and Exchange Act is to prevent the excessive use of credit for the purchase or carrying of securities. New purchases of stock on margin generate credit in a way that adds to the national money supply. When stock is bought the entire purchase price is paid to the seller a few days after the transaction. If the purchaser is buying the stock on margin the balance of the purchase price must be borrowed in order to make his full payments. Ordinarily this balance is borrowed from the broker or from a bank and in either case the effect is to expand the national total of bank credit leading to an expansion of the national money supply by at least the amount borrowed. This points up a major distinction between margin in commodities and margin in the stock market. Margin in commodities does not in and of itself involve the borrowing of money nor does it affect the money supply.

With the advent of financial futures trading, and especially stock index futures, the old issue of control of futures margins was revived. Historically, the futures exchanges have established futures margins without any intervention or oversight by government agencies. Indeed, the 1974 legislation process that created the Commodity Futures Trading Commission (CFTC) specifically left the setting of margins in the hands of the exchanges. This was not especially to the liking of the Securities and Exchange Commission (SEC) or Federal Reserve.

But when the 1987 and 1989 stock market crashes occurred, a lot of political attention was focused on the linkages between the futures on stock indexes and the trading of stocks with special emphasis on the differences in margin requirements and regulation. As of this writing, 1990, it appears that considerable political support is building to regulate margins on financial futures, especially stock index futures, in the same manner, if not at the same level, as margins on individual stocks.

Margins and Leverage

One of the great myths about commodity trading is that commodity prices fluctuate much more than stock prices. This is simply not true. Take a look at the stock tables in your daily newspaper. It is not hard to find a stock that fluctuates more than 50% in value within the same year. Compare that to the commodity prices and you will find that very few commodity prices fluctuate from the high to the low by more than 50% in any single year.

The point to be made here is that the volatility of commodity prices is not the reason for the great risk associated with commodity trading. That risk arises from the use of leverage. Leverage is defined as the amount of money needed to control a given amount of resources. Leverage is high in futures markets because margins are low. In the stock market margins are currently at 50%. In futures markets the margins are usually less than 10% and in some instances less than 1% of the market value of the futures contract. Because of the low futures margins, one can control large amounts of resources with small amounts of capital. Hence, a slight change in the value of the total contract results in a substantial change in the amount of money in your account. For example, a 1% change in $10,000 invested in the stock market via a nonmargined account will equal a 1% change in equity, or $100. A 1% change in a futures contract valued at $10,000 is equal to a $100 change in account equity also. But to control that $10,000 futures contract you probably needed to put only $750 down as your initial margin, and a $100 change in that $750 is equal to a 13% change in your equity. It is this leverage factor that causes commodity futures to be considered a high-risk investment. Of course there is nothing that says you must use all that leverage. You can arbitrarily set your personal margin higher, say at 30%. This would reduce your leverage and render your trading more conservative.

MARKET PARTICIPANTS

Participants in the market can be divided into four groups: commission houses or futures commission merchants, floor traders and floor brokers, speculators, and hedgers.

Futures Commission Merchants

A futures commission merchant (FCM) is precisely what the name implies. It is a business that acts as an intermediary and stands between the brokers in the pit and their customers who are the real principals to the trade. In a legal sense an FCM obtains its license to do business from the Commodity Futures Trading Commission, which monitors and oversees the activity of the FCM.

Most FCMs own their own exchange memberships or have working relationships with members of all of the active commodity exchanges. Some are integral parts of large brokerage or investment-banking houses. And some are affiliates with or subsidiaries of firms that conduct most of their business in the cash market.

The services provided by an FCM include a communications system for transmittal of orders, research, trading strategy suggestions, trade execution, and record-keeping services. In selecting an FCM the following areas should be examined.

Communications Systems

One of the most important services an FCM, acting as agent for its customers, provides is a fast and efficient communication system that links the customer as quickly as possible with the auction system on the floor of the exchange. Usually this link is accomplished by telex or direct telephone, the latter being faster.

Research

One will find a good deal of variation in the quality and extent of the research available from various FCMs. Some FCMs concentrate on price forecasting and provide intraday, weekly, and long-term price forecasts. Others concentrate their efforts on market interpretations, such as analyses of who is buying and who is selling in the market. Almost all FCMs provide news and "rumor" analysis. Probably the greatest amount of market research concentrates on technical analysis of the market. Technical analysis, as explained elsewhere in this book, refers to the study of market activity itself; for example, quantitative research relating to changes in trading volume, open interest, and price activity. The last is usually accomplished through the observation and study of various chart patterns.

Trading Strategy Suggestions

In addition to providing the types of market research suggested above, FCMs generally provide their customers with recommendations on trading strategies. These strategies may relate to spreads and straddles or may identify overvalued contracts and undervalued contracts. Some recommendations concentrate on arbitrage strategies designed to take advantage of temporary differences between the cash yield curve and the futures prices.

Trade Executions and Record Keeping

Of all the services, this is probably the most important one an FCM provides its customer. Most FCMs maintain offices scattered throughout the country and sometimes overseas. Most of them maintain large staffs on the floors of the exchanges and in the "back office." The sole function of these floor personnel is to facilitate and expedite the customer's order, and to see that it gets executed at the best possible price and that accurate paper work recording the transaction is accomplished quickly. One will find great diversity among FCMs with regard to the ability to perform in this area. Some are better organized than others.

Floor Traders/Floor Brokers

Trading on the floor of the exchange is conducted as a continuous auction where every person in the pit is his own auctioneer. Orders can be executed only by open outcry. The people who specialize in executing orders for others are called "floor brokers." They get a small fee—usually a couple of dollars—for each transaction they execute. Floor brokers are members of the exchange, and, if they themselves are not clearing members, they are affiliated with a clearing member.

Also participating in the trading in the ring are "floor traders." Floor traders are speculators who, as members of the exchange, trade for themselves. Some of them can be classified as "scalpers." A scalper is a person who stands ready either to buy at a price slightly below the last price or to sell at a price slightly above the last price. He or she attempts to predict the very short-run direction of price changes and to profit from them. A scalper is usually not worried about major moves. A scalper who is an astute trader can make a lot of money on very small changes on price. From an economic standpoint the scalper provides good trade-to-trade liquidity in the market. Indirect evidence suggests that the scalper is well compensated for the liquidity he provides.

Some floor traders are "position traders." These persons tend to carry the positions for longer periods of time. They may attempt to take advantage of the spread between prices for different delivery months for the same commodity, or the price spread between different commodities with the same delivery date when such price differences cannot be explained. They add to the liquidity of the market just as scalpers do and help to lower the cost of hedging.

Speculators

Speculators deal with changes in the expected price levels over time. They usually do not own or use the cash commodity in which they deal. Profit on their futures position is their only motive. Speculators help assume price risk. They also help produce information about future events that may be important in affecting the price of the commodity. Speculators also act as arbitrageurs. Arbitrage refers to the simultaneous purchase and sale of the same instrument in different markets to profit from unequal prices. The arbitrageurs ensure that cash and futures prices converge at delivery. When the futures price differs from the spot price by more than the cost of arbitrage, the opportunity for risk-free profit occurs, and arbitrageurs will act to buy in the low market and sell in the high market, thus forcing the prices toward their proper equilibrium. The arbitrageur also keeps a close watch on the differences between near and distant futures for a given commodity. If the spread moves beyond the "cost-of-carry," again an opportunity for risk-free profit is created. Actual response to these price discrepancies must be quick, since there are others also paying attention to the profit possibilities. Thus, the prices are forced back into line with carrying costs in a relatively short time.

SELECTING A BROKER

There is probably no decision, related to getting started in trading, that puzzles people more than selecting a broker. In truth it is difficult to know in advance, without a good deal of independent research, what kind of service one will get from an individual broker and the broker's firm. To minimize this risk consider the following guidelines.

First, visit the prospective broker in his office. A face-to-face meeting with him at his place of business, where you can observe the surroundings and the people associated with him, can provide you with valuable information about the character of the individual and firm with whom you are dealing.

Second, find out if the broker is registered with the Commodity Futures Trading Commission in Washington, D.C. According to federal law both brokers and firms must be registered with the Commission. If the individual or the firm have any outstanding charges against them as a result of allegations relating to fraud or misfeasance, a check with the Commission will reveal that information.

Third, one must look beyond the broker to the firm. Does the brokerage firm provide good communications facilities for keeping posted on up-to-the-minute prices? Do the facilities provide for direct relay of your orders to the floor of the exchange? What sort of research facilities does the firm have and how good are they? How good is the firm's back office? Can they provide fast and accurate record keeping? There are no precise answers to these questions. They are value judgments you must make on your own. You can probably best judge a firm by comparing it with other firms and by talking to customers who deal with the firm you are considering.

It goes without saying that a broker cannot be all things to you. He can't promise you profits and spend all his time pondering your account or discussing it with you on the phone, and he can't be right all the time. Further, some brokers take a very short-run view of things and are more interested in getting the immediate order than in giving proper thought to whether or not that particular transaction is appropriate for the strategy the customer wishes to follow. The encouraging aspect of this situation, however, is that those people gradually are eliminated by the natural market forces.

If misunderstandings should arise or mistakes should be made by one party or another, the first place to go to complain about a broker is to his immediate superior. Most complaints are settled there. If you are right, a settlement of the dispute will be made to compensate you. If further action is necessary, both the exchange on which the transaction was made and the Commodity Futures Trading Commission have departments to receive and investigate complaints about broker activities. They need evidence, however, to do the job and the burden of proof is on the customer.

In summary, finding a good broker is not difficult if you know what you are looking for. A true professional interested in providing quality service and who has a strong brokerage organization behind him can strongly enhance the profitability of your trading.

MANAGED ACCOUNTS: CTAs AND CPOs

Speculators have a variety of vehicles available for participation in futures trading. They may of course do it by opening their own account with a broker and managing it themselves. Other alternatives include having their accounts managed by a Commodity Trading Advisor (CTA) or joining a commodity limited partnership organized by a Commodity Pool Operator (CPO). CTAs and CPOs must be registered as such by the CFTC.

Commodity Pools are entities which act as organizers of vehicles through which funds are solicited for the purpose of trading in futures and options markets.

Most Commodity Pools are organized as limited partnerships, giving the limited partner investor the protection that limits a loss to the amount of his investment.

Multiple owner single accounts, or groups of accounts, formed expressly for the purpose of trading with common management, and with all participants sharing in the profits or losses according to their proportionate investments, also would be considered commodity pools.

CTAs in the futures world are similar to investment advisers in the securities world. By definition, they are individuals or entities that have some sort of discretionary authority to enter orders and make transactions for accounts owned by someone else. With few exceptions, the assets under management by CPOs are traded by CTAs.

Collectively, CPO and CTA activity is referred to as the managed money element of the futures and options industry, and the vehicle through which the CPOs and CTAs operate are referred to generically as futures funds.

CTAs and CPOs operating in the United States are required to register with the Commodity Futures Trading Commission (CFTC).

Growth and Structure of the CPO/CTA Industry

The growth of the managed futures business during the decade of the 1980s was explosive in the United States. In the 1990s, the major growth is occurring in Europe and Asia—that trend is likely to continue as today the industry in Europe and Asia is approximately at the same level of relative development as it was in the United States in 1980.

Figure 3.1 shows the equity growth in public futures funds operating in the United States between 1980 and 1990. The growth is spectacular. The data show that in 1980 the equity in domestic public funds in the United States was about $154,000,000. Ten years later, in 1990, it is $2,902,000,000—that's about a 35% annualized compounded rate of growth, which is spectacular by any standard. These numbers do not include private pools, offshore pools, or individual managed accounts. If such private monies were included, the total would add up to about $18 Billion, or about 60% of all segregated commodity funds at Futures Commission Merchants (FCMs).

In 1979, there were only a dozen public futures funds. Today there are hundreds.

In the early stages of the development of the commodity managed money industry, nearly all of the participants were individual speculators, who for one reason or another, did not want to manage their own account. Oftentimes speculators find it difficult to manage their trading accounts for any of the following reasons:

1. They are inexperienced in trading and feel more comfortable hiring a professional to do it.

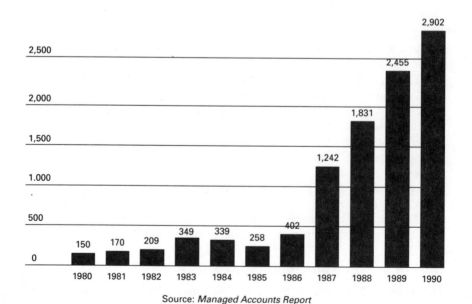

Source: *Managed Accounts Report*

FIGURE 3.1 Equity growth of public futures funds (domestic).

2. They do not know and understand proper money management techniques, especially how to conserve capital.
3. By banding together into a pool, they can reap economic efficiencies in the form of reduced trading costs, better use of margin monies, and so on, than could be obtained by them individually through smaller single accounts.
4. The legal entity of a limited partnership gives them comfort that they will not lose more than the amount they invested.
5. They lack access to timely information or do not have the time and opportunity to manage their individual accounts. Most people are busy with day-to-day work activity and earning a living.

As the decade of the 1980s unfolded, and financial engineering exploded, the major international banks, investment banks, and pension funds discovered that well-managed commodity funds can add significant value to portfolios. Historically, commodity funds have been poorly, or in some cases, even negatively correlated with stocks and bonds. This meant that one could enhance materially the performance of large-scale portfolios of stocks and bonds such as those managed by major industrial, commercial, and financial institutions by including portfolios of managed commodity futures products.

This discovery was helped tremendously by the advent of stock index futures trading. Stock index futures and options gave the Wall Street houses their entree into futures trading, and provided a completely new product, which would allow the application of hedging principles so long practiced in the agricultural area, to the professional money management for portfolios of stocks, bonds, and currencies. As the data in Table 3.1 show, in 1980 neither Stock Index, nor Petroleum Futures, trading existed.

Table 3.1 Relative Volume of Contracts Traded (U.S. Exchanges)

	1979	1990
Interest Rates	7.4	44.6
Agricultural	61.7	20.6
Energy	0	12.8
F/X	2.9	10.5
Metals	26.9	6.1
Stock Indices	0	5.3
Other	1.1	.1
	100%	100%

Today they account for nearly one-fifth of all futures trading in the United States.

As financial futures grew, it became clear to banks that they could be organizers, sellers, and traders of commodity funds and could offer such products without fear of violating the Glass Steagal Act in the United States and with no real limitations to selling internationally. CitiBank and Chase Manhattan Bank are two of the largest firms engaged in the commodity managed money business.

Futures and options trading is growing more rapidly outside the United States than inside the United States The data in Table 3.2 show that Japan and Europe now account for approximately twice as much trading as they did just three years ago. This growth has been due almost entirely to trading in financial futures.

As further evidence of the growth of managed futures trading, consider the following:

1. As of December 1989, five Japanese firms were involved in offering funds totaling about $300 Million. Today, two years later, there are nearly three times that many funds with equity in excess of $1 Billion. It is estimated that by the end of 1991, the Japanese could have $2 Billion, or perhaps, $3 Billion invested in managed futures products.
2. In the United States, the industry face was changed considerably when, in 1987, Eastman Kodak and AMP, Inc. put small portions of their employees' pension funds in commodity trading strategies. It was reported that Eastman Kodak committed $50 Million to a trial invest-

Table 3.2   International Financial
Futures and Options Volume
(% Attributable by Country)

	1987	Jan. 1990
U.S.	84.2	66.0
Japan	6.9	12.1
U.K.	4.1	7.1
France	1.6	7.2
Singapore	.7	1.2
Australia	—	3.8
Other	2.5	2.6
	100.0	100.0

ment and AMP, Inc., $10 Million. It has also been reported that by early 1990, Kodak had increased its investment in such funds fourfold.

3. The Detroit Fireman's & Policeman's Beneficial Association invested its first $5 Million in managed commodity monies in 1986, and by the first quarter of 1990, was reported to have $22.5 Million invested in two funds.
4. The Frank Russell Company, one of the largest and most prestigious pension consulting firms in the United States, has developed several commodity private limited partnerships to facilitate pension investing.

Despite the statistical and anecdotal evidence demonstrating rapid growth in the managed futures area, and the growth and participation by both individuals and institutions, it is clear that the surface has hardly been scratched in penetrating the market for these products. It is likely that less than 1% of institutions in the United States are participating. Only a handful of employee retirement programs have investments in managed futures. Most of the money invested in managed futures products is emanating from private individual investments. Nevertheless, the trend is clearly toward rapid growth and increased participation by institutions, especially pensions.

There are many reasons why institutions are taking a go-slow attitude toward investments in managed futures products. Among them are:

1. The public image of the commodity futures industry is not good. Generally, the industry as a whole is held in low esteem.
2. Only a few academic studies have been conducted of sufficient rigor to demonstrate the potential advantages of investments in managed futures funds as a separate asset class and, therefore, a diversification technique.
3. Institutions, in particular pension funds, compare the assets they invest in any single asset class against a particular asset class. There is very little experience by which decision makers can draw historical parallels and comfort with respect to the performance of these investments relative to their traditional standard performance measures.
4. In some countries there are unresolved legal questions regarding investments in managed futures; for example, "prudent man rules," fiduciary responsibilities, and taxation issues.
5. Institutions and pension funds especially are notoriously slow in adopting new technology, especially new technology of the financial engineering type. Their adoption is slowed even further when the products are sold by untrained, uninitiated, and sometimes, poorly motivated salesmen, who are unwilling, or unable, to understand the pension manager's problems and objectives in allocating assets.

Hedge Pools for Small Hedgers

Hedging is one of the major economic benefits emanating from futures trading. Oftentimes the small producer is the one who most needs hedging. It is that same small producer who is most ill-equipped to use futures because he:

1. Does not have trading skills and knowledge to do the hedges.
2. Does not have the time to do it.
3. Does not have access to timely information.
4. Finds it very expensive.
5. Produces such a small amount as to not make it worthwhile to expend the effort.

Pooled hedge accounts help solve that problem. The CFTC has recently approved the first bona fide hedge pool allowing small farmers to buy hedge units in a commodity fund, organized by a CPO, and operated by a CTA, which will conduct the hedging for the farmers.

The introduction of such a concept may provide a very viable means for hundreds of small producers and smaller commercial firms to utilize the existing futures contracts and may make the potential benefits of hedging finally available to the sector that needs it most.

Number of Participants

The National Futures Association (NFA) is responsible in the United States for the registration and supervision of CPOs and CTAs. NFA took over this registration and supervision activity from the CFTC in 1985. The data in the Table 3.3 below illustrate the growth in the industry during the decade of the 1980s.

The numbers showing registrations probably overstate the size of the CPO/CTA industry. Many of the registrations are held for convenience, or are filed as part of another filing such as an FCM registration. To provide a more realistic count of registrants, the NFA further refines the

Table 3.3 Number of Registrants

Registrant	1979	1991	Primary Registrants 1991
CPO	717	1278	1000
CTA	1216	2516	1013

categories by identifying registrants as either primary or secondary. Under that approach, the number of registrants whose primary business is acting as a CTA dropped to 1013 as of February 1991, only about 40% of all CTA registrants.

Even these numbers probably overstate the size of the industry. Reviews of public records indicate that only about 225 CTAs have any substantive activity in managing money. Of these, about 50 of them manage about 80% of the monies under management.

Open Interest and Volume of Business

A recent study completed by the CFTC provides insight into the volume of business done by CPOs, Pools, and CTAs. Their study reflects data collected in 1988 from a sample of large CPOs, Pools, and CTAs. It reports only on activity on U.S. Exchanges. The study reports the following:

1. On average, CPOs accounted for about 4.3% of the long position open interest, and about 4% of the short position open interest, for all commodities traded on U.S. Exchanges.
2. For individual commodities the per cent of open interest, long or short, accounted for by CPOs had a very wide range—approaching a daily average of 20% in some commodities. The maximums reached on any single day, during the survey period, sometimes exceeded 50% for some commodities.
3. On average, CPOs accounted for about 3.7% each of the average daily long volume and short volume of trading in all U.S. futures during the survey period. Again considering individual futures, the volume of trading accounted for by CPOs regularly reached levels exceeding 25% of daily volume. This was particularly true in some of the less active commodities. In the most heavily traded commodities such as bonds and stock indexes, CPOs usually accounted for less than 4% of the daily volume.

While these figures are indicative of CPO activity as a part of total trading, they probably seriously understate the relative importance of managed money trading as a per cent of non-member trading at the Exchanges. Studies conducted by the Exchanges show that in general 30 to 50% of all trading in individual contract markets is accounted for by members represented on the floor of the Exchange. If one adjusts these CFTC data to reflect CPO activity as a per cent of non-member trading, then it is clear that CPOs are accounting for a much higher percentage of the public participation in these markets.

Another qualifying factor that should be taken into account in interpreting these data is the trend in individual trading through personal accounts. Many FCMs in recent years have reported their individual account trading is down substantially, and that participation by individuals in their pools has exploded. In other words, many fewer people are opening individual accounts at brokerage houses and instead are opting to participate in the futures as individuals who own shares in unit trusts, limited partnership units, or other individual elements as part of a pool.

Lastly, as noted above, the CFTC study date was for 1988 and focused entirely on the U.S. industry. As previously noted, the most rapid growth in the managed money area has occurred outside the United States in recent years. It is likely, therefore, that the volume of trading accounted for by CPOs, Pools, and CTAs on the non-U.S. Exchanges is at least as great as at the U.S. Exchanges.

Turning your money over to a professional CTA is not a surefire way to make money. Oftentimes the fees charged for organizing the pool, paying the manager, and so on, are high. However, the investor gets the benefit of not having to spend time and emotional energy worrying about what futures to trade, when, where, and at what price. A hired professional will do it for him. Some CTAs have regularly provided extraordinary returns. It pays therefore to analyze carefully their track records and methods of trading. Indeed, several firms have sprung up that specialize in evaluating money managers, creating commodity fund portfolios, and monitoring investment performance.

4
The Order

One of the most elementary, yet most important, aspects of commodity futures trading is learning about the different types of orders that may be given to brokers and how, why, and under what conditions such orders should be used.

An "order" is by definition an instruction given to your broker directing him to take certain action for your account. There are seven basic parts of the commodity order, and each part is a specific instruction. These instructions are:

1. To buy or to sell.
2. The quantity involved, for example, one contract or ten contracts.
3. The month involved, for example, March or June.
4. The commodity involved, for example, T-bills or Treasury bonds.
5. The exchange on which the order should be executed, for example, Chicago Board of Trade or NYFE.
6. The price, for example, a market order or a limit order.
7. The time limit in which the order is in effect, for example, one day or "Good till Canceled."

Although these elements are part of every order, the fact that each element can vary independently gives the trader a wide latitude in the types of orders he can enter. It will be readily apparent from the following examples that a fairly substantial number of order types can be used, with each designated to cover a special situation.

Here are some caveats and reminders before we review the individual orders. First, some futures contracts are traded for more than one year ahead. When you give an order, it is important that you indicate the year in which the contract matures as well as the trading month. Second, in the absence of any specified time limit entered as a part of the order, all commodity orders entered are considered day orders. That is, they are effective only during the specific trading session in which, or immediately prior to which, they are entered. Third, all orders in which a price is not specified are considered market orders and are to be executed immediately at the best price possible. Finally, it is illegal for a broker or a customer to enter opposing orders to buy and sell the same futures contract for the same customer simultaneously. Such a transaction would be considered fictitious and is known as a "wash sale."

When placing orders with your broker, be sure that your instructions concerning each of the seven elements are clear and complete. It is surprising how many misunderstandings result from failure to ensure that the broker knows exactly what the customer wants done.

SOME ILLUSTRATIONS OF COMMODITY ORDERS

One can categorize orders into four basic groupings. These groupings are not mutually exclusive, but for illustrative purposes they help one understand the versatility and flexibility of entering orders. The groupings used in what follows include time orders, price orders, combination orders, and stop orders. The examples listed under each group attempt to illustrate a major characteristic of the order type.

1. Time Orders

1a. Time Order:
"At 1:30 A.M. Chicago time BUY 4 June IMM T-bill MKT"
"BUY 3 June CBOT 10-year T-notes 84.12 GTC"
"SELL 3 June CBOT T-bonds 78.00 GTW" (or "GTM")
"BUY 2 Sept IMM T-bills 92.20 GT Mar 10"

We have already noted that, in the absence of specific instructions to the contrary, all commodity futures orders entered expire at the close of the trading session following or during which they are entered. Futures orders, however, can also be entered good at or good through (GT) specified time periods. For example, a specific time order, as in the first illustration, must be entered by the floor broker as close to the exact time specified as possible. The symbol "GTC" used at the end of an order directs that the order be kept open until it is canceled. A "GTW" order expires at the close of the trading *week* following or during which it is entered. A "GTM" (Good Through *Month*) order expires at the close of the trading session on the last trading day of the current month. Time orders, such as GTC, GTW, GTM, and GT orders, that continue in effect for a specified time beyond the trading session during which they are entered are also known as "open orders."

1b. Market-on-Close Order:
  "SELL 10 Dec NYFE Composite Index MKT on Close"

The market-on-close order must be executed only during the official closing of the market on the day it was entered and the execution price must fall within the range of closing prices for that specified contract month.

1c. Fill or Kill (FOK) Order (also called a "Quick Order"):
  "SELL 3 Dec CBT T-bonds 85.63 FOK"

An FOK order instructs a floor broker to execute the order immediately at the price stated or, if such an execution is not possible, to cancel or "kill" the order. An FOK order can be filled either in whole or in part. Any part remaining unfilled is immediately canceled. A report on the part executed must come back immediately.

1d. Opening (OPG) Only Order:
  "BUY 20 June IMM T-bills 89.40 OPG Only"

Such an order is to be executed only during the official opening of trading on the day for which the order is placed. If the floor broker is unable to execute it during that time period, the order is immediately canceled. If the order happened to be a market order for execution on the opening only, the actual execution need not be the exact opening sale as long as the execution falls within the range of prices that took place during the official opening of the exchange for the delivery month involved.

2. Price

2a. Market (MKT) Order:
  "BUY 1 Sept CBT T-bond MKT"

Such an order is executed at the best possible price immediately following the time it is received by a floor broker on the trading floor.

2b. Limit Order:
  "BUY 1 June IMM T-bill 89.00"
  "SELL 1 Sept IMM T-bill 89.50"

A limit order is used when the customer wishes to buy or sell at a specified limit price or better. On a BUY order, a limit order may be filled at the price specified or at a price below it. On a SELL order, a limit order may be filled at the limit price or at a price above it. A limit order never becomes a market order.

2c. Market If Touched (MIT) Order:
  "SELL 10 Dec IMM T-bills 89.40 MIT"

The use of the acronym MIT gives that particular order some priority that enables it to be executed when the price limit is reached by the market even though only one contract may have traded at the limit price. It should be understood, however, that when the market reaches the specified limit price, an MIT order becomes a market order for immediate execution. As a result, the actual execution may or may not be at the limit price. The advantage obtained from using MIT orders is that the trader is usually assured of getting an execution somewhere near his limit price. An MIT sell order is placed at a price above the existing market. An MIT buy order is placed at a price below the existing market. This is in contrast with the buy-stop (sell-stop) order placed at a price above (below) the existing market.

2d. Not Held (NH) Order:
  "SELL 3 June CBOT T-bonds 86.63 NH"

Such an order gives the floor broker some discretion in execution. If, for example, the market is trading close to 86.63 but looks strong, the floor broker can elect to try for a better price than 86.63 if he wishes. In the event that he does so and misses, however, he cannot then be held to an execution at 86.63.

2e. Scale Order:
  "BUY 5 Dec CBOT 10-year T-notes MKT and 5 each 20 points lower, total 30 GTC"
  "SELL 5 Dec IMM T-bills 89.60 and 5 each 20 points Up, Total 30, GTC"

Both illustrations represent a form of contingent order. The floor broker is instructed to buy or sell additional contracts on a scale, provided he is able to execute the first part of the order. Scale orders to BUY or SELL may also be entered, with the contingent part(s) of the order to be executed only on stop orders, for example "SELL 1 June IMM T-bill 89.60 and STOP-SELL 1 Each 20 points down, total 4." Note that the first order in the preceding examples could just as well have been entered with a limit price, 89.60 for example, for the first part of the order, instead of "MKT," and could have been a day order instead of a Good till Canceled order.

2f. Discretionary Order:
  "BUY 1 March IMM T-bill 89.00 with 4 pts. Disc."

Such an order may be executed by a floor broker as high as 89.04, or at any price lower than 89.04. In the case of a Discretionary BUY order, the amount of discretion given is used at a price "above" the limit price, while in the case of a SELL order, the discretion given is used at a price "lower" than the limit price.

3. Stop Orders

If there is an art to commodity trading it is probably knowing where to place stop orders. Just as in the stock market, you can use stop orders to automatically get out of losing positions or automatically get into desired positions if the price moves to the level you specify. A stop order does not guarantee you will get the price you stipulate, but it does ensure that the broker will do the best he can to get it when the market moves to the appropriate level. This order does help limit risk. Stop orders are a must if you can't be in constant contact with the market.

3a. Stop Order:
     "SELL 3 June CBT T-bonds 79.10 Stop"
     "BUY 2 Sept NYFE Composite Index 80.10 Stop"

A sell-stop order becomes effective only when the contract trades at or below, or is offered in the trading ring at or below, the stop price. A buy-stop order becomes effective only when the contract trades at or above, or is bid at or above, the stop price. If either of these things happens, then an existing stop order becomes a market order in the hands of a floor broker and is filled immediately thereafter at the best possible price, which may or may not be the trigger price. A sell-stop order is used to limit losses or protect a profit on long futures positions. A buy-stop order is used to limit losses or protect a profit on open short futures positions. Stop-orders are also used by some traders to initiate or liquidate positions when the market penetrates key support or resistance points. Stop orders may be entered as day orders, as Good till Canceled (GTC) orders, or as orders good for a limited time span.

3b. Stop-Limit Order:
     "BUY 1 June IMM T-bill 89.10 Stop Limit"
     "SELL 25 Sept IMM T-bills 89.40 Stop Limit 89.15"

A stop-limit order is used in much the same way as a regular stop order except that its execution is restricted to the limit price specified or a better price. In the first example, if June IMM T-bill contracts trade at or above 89.10, or are bid at or above 89.10, the stop-limit order becomes effective. The floor broker with such an order in hand must try to buy one contract of June T-bills at 89.10 or less. He may not pay more. In the second example, when and if September 1984 T-bills trade or are offered at or below 89.40, the sell stop-limit order becomes effective. The floor broker must sell 25 September T-bill futures at the market, provided he can do so at a price not lower than 89.15, the limit price. Note that because the execution price is limited with a stop-limit order, there is a risk that in a very fast-moving market the broker may not be able to execute it. Thus, the trader who wishes to protect his position against the possibility of a disastrous loss may want to consider using regular stop orders rather than stop-limit orders for protection against loss.

3c. Enter Open Stop (EOS) Order:
   "SELL 2 Dec IMM T-bills MKT Enter Open Stop 61.50"

Most brokers accept EOS orders only on a "not held" basis; that is, the broker cannot be held for failure to enter or execute the "stop" part of the order. Just as with a regular stop order an EOS BUY order has a limit price above the prevailing market. An EOS SELL order has a limit price below the prevailing market.

4. Combination Orders

4a. Contingent Order:
   "If March CBT T-bonds trade 87.20 or higher, BUY 20 December CBT T-bonds MKT"

Contingent orders are entered with the understanding that the execution of one order depends upon another element. Brokers who accept such orders usually assume no responsibility for simultaneous or exact price execution, since it is physically impossible for them to be in two places at the same time.

4b. Cancel Former (CFO) Order:
   "SELL 1 March CBT T-bond 69.10 GTC, CFO SELL 1 June CBT T-bond 70.10 GTC entered (date)"
   "BUY 10 Sept IMM T-bills 89.10, CFO BUY 10 Sept 1984 IMM T-bills 89.00 entered today"

The identification of former orders to be canceled may also be made by referring to the brokerage firm's original internal entering number of the order as well as the date on which it was entered. When entering a CFO order, it is important to make sure that the new order includes a complete identification of the former order that is to be canceled.

4c. Give-Up (GU) Order:
   "BUY 10 Dec IMM T-bills MKT, give up XYZ & Co. J. Doe (account number)"

In this example, J. Doe, a customer of XYZ & Co., may have been traveling and presumably was in a city where XYZ & Co. did not have an office. To accomplish his desire to BUY 10 Dec IMM T-bills, he utilized the office of one of the competitor firms and asked an account executive at that firm to buy 10 Dec 1984 IMM T-bills for his account at XYZ & Co. The account executive would likely ask J. Doe for identification, or check with XYZ to be sure that Mr. Doe has an account with the firm. Assuming that all is well, the order would then be executed and the trade turned over to an XYZ & Co. representative on the exchange floor for clearance by that firm. In return for the service performed, the out-of-town broker would bill XYZ & Co. a "wire toll charge" for the use of its wires in entering the transaction.

4d. Intermarket Order (Same Commodity):
   "BUY 20 March IMM S&P Index SELL 20 March 1984 NYFE Composite Index, N.Y. 2 point premium"

This order represents a spread order executed between the Stock Index futures contracts traded on the NYFE and on the IMM. Both sides of such an order are usually communicated to a floor broker on one of the two exchanges involved. It is then his job, through interexchange communication by phone or wire with a floor broker on the other exchange, to arrange for the execution of both ends of the spread as nearly simultaneously as possible, but in any event at a difference not less favorable than that specified by the customer. Only a few brokerage firms accept these orders regularly except from very large customers.

4e. Limit or Market on Close Order:
   "BUY 5 Dec IMM T-bills 89.40 or Market on close"

This order directs the floor broker to buy December IMM T-bills at 89.40. If, however, the broker is unable to fill the order at 89.40 or lower during the trading day, he is instructed in any event to buy five December IMM T-bills at the market during the official closing period of trading for December T-bills that day.

4f. One Cancels the Other (OCO) Order:
   "SELL 1 Sept IMM T-bill 89.10 or 88.60 Stop, OCO"

This type of order provides the customer with two or more alternatives. In the OCO order above, the floor broker is directed to sell one contract of Sept IMM T-bills at 89.10 or at 88.60 stop, whichever comes first. If he has not yet sold at 89.10 and the market drops so that the September contract either trades at or is offered at or below 88.60, then the broker is instructed to sell the contract "at the market" and cancel the other half of the order. The price received may, in fact, be less than 88.60.

4g. Spread or Straddle Orders:
    "Spread   SELL 50 Dec CBT bonds
                     BUY 50 March CBT bonds Dec 20 points or less
                     premium"
    "Straddle   BUY 8 March IMM T-bills
                     SELL 8 Dec IMM T-bills even"
    "Straddle   BUY 3 Dec IMM T-bills
                     SELL 3 June IMM T-bills, June 50 pts or more
                     premium"
    "Spread   BUY 1 June IMM T-bills
                     SELL 1 June CBT T-bonds market"
    "Straddle   BUY 1 March CBT cert. deposit
                     SELL 1 March IMM cert. deposit Market"

The first three examples illustrate the most popular type of spread order; that is, where both sides are in the same commodity and exchange. (Note that straddle or spread orders may be placed at specified limit differences as well as "at the market.") The fourth illustration portrays an intercommodity spread order; the fifth one illustrates an intermarket straddle order.

4h. Switch Order:
    "Switch BUY 2 June IMM T-bills SELL 2 Dec IMM T-bills, June 100 pts premium or less"

A switch order is used to move an existing long or short commodity futures position from one delivery month to another or from one market to another. In appearance and in handling on the floor such an order closely resembles a straddle order but the effect is different. Some brokers give reduced commissions on switch orders.

4i. Exchange For Physicals (EFP) Order or an Against Actuals (AA) Order:
    "SELL 5 June IMM T-bills 90.00 EFP to XYZ Co. vs. cash"

An EFP or AA order represents one of the two types of orders that can legally be communicated to an exchange trading floor and does not require competitive pricing. Such an order would be used, for example, by a dealer who has just made a sale of T-bills in the spot market to the XYZ Co. Presumably the XYZ Co., prior to the spot market transaction, had an open long hedge in June futures. By using an EFP order the dealer eliminates the short hedge he had in June T-bill futures and transfers the

June futures sale to the XYZ Co., which, when received, offsets the XYZ Co.'s long hedge in June futures. Obviously the use of an EFP order requires some advance negotiations between the two principals to the related spot market transaction. Note that any transaction completed ex-pit—that is, outside the trading ring—must be reported to and be approved by the proper exchange officials.

Part Two

Price Analysis

5

Price Forecasting through Technical Analysis

In 1912 a Jesuit library in Verona, Italy, sold an ancient volume to Wilfred Voynich, a dealer in antiquities. The book, reputed to have been written in the 13th century by Roger Bacon, a Franciscan monk with a fascination for cryptography, contains page after page of what appears to be Arabic handwriting.

For the past 70 years or so cryptographers have attempted to decipher the text. Even the legendary William F. Friedman, captain of the team that broke the purple Japanese diplomatic code just before Pearl Harbor and considered by most to be the greatest cryptographer who ever lived, has tried. None has succeeded. Today the Voynich manuscript lies in a museum vault, a silent challenge to cryptanalysts the world over seeking to uncover the secret of its message.

Technical analysts approach commodity price analysis in much the same manner that cryptographers attempt to decipher a code. They have no less expectation that written in those squiggly lines is a message containing the ultimate secret to forecasting commodity prices—if only the code could be broken.

Technical analysis refers to the study of market activity itself—prices, trading volume, open interest, and other numerical data that can be derived from those three statistics. Technical analysts prefer to study the market itself rather than the supply/demand factors that affect the price for a given commodity. They believe that even if one knew where to find all the fundamental information about the supply and demand for a particular product, one still wouldn't be able to predict market response to that information. Technical analysts believe that the only place where all the factual supply and demand data—plus the mass moods, hopes, fears, estimates, and guesses of everyone in the market—are crystallized is in a commodity's price, volume, and open interest.

They believe that by studying *how* prices have acted you can obtain more insight about future price movement than you can by studying *why* prices have acted a certain way. The basic assumption underlying the technical approach to the market is that by studying statistics generated by the market it is possible to come to meaningful conclusions about future prices. In short, they believe that the way the market behaved yesterday may indicate how prices will behave tomorrow.

Technical analysts do not believe futures prices represent a purely random walk. They point to the futility of trying to know and understand all the factors that affect supply and demand and argue that there are so many fundamental elements in play at any one time that it is easy for an important one to be overlooked or improperly weighted.

But the most likely reasons that technical analysis is so popular is that it is easy, efficient, and esoteric. Only three series of data are required— price, volume, and open interest. These data are easy to get and to store in computer models. The models used to massage the data are relatively simple and straightforward. Thus, decision making is efficient and easy.

Technical analysts usually approach their market analysis task by using one or a combination of the following basic approaches:

1. Analysis of pattern on price charts.
2. Moving average and statistical analysis.
3. Analysis of market composition.

We will describe briefly each of these approaches.

PATTERNS ON PRICE CHARTS

Probably the oldest method of technical market analysis known is the interpretation of patterns of movements on price charts. There are two basic types of price charts used in technical analysis: bar charts and point and figure charts. Both kinds of charts are easily constructed. All you need is the price information, volume, open interest, some graph paper, and a pencil.

If you don't want to be bothered or don't have the time to build and maintain your own charts there are numerous chart services available to provide ready-made charts for a fee. Some of these services provide only one type of chart, but others provide a combination of various types of charts and also offer interpretations of the price patterns.

The first step in constructing any chart is to decide on the frequency of the prices to be plotted; that is, daily, weekly, or monthly. Normally, commodity charts are kept on a daily basis, but many analysts also keep weekly and monthly price charts to get a longer-term perspective.

Bar Charts

Figure 5.1 is a typical bar chart. In standard procedure, each day's price activity is represented by one vertical bar (line) in the open area on the graph. The top of the line marks the point of the day's highest price. The bottom of the line marks the day's lowest price. The closing price is shown by a short horizontal "tick" mark extending to the right.

Across the bottom of the chart is a daily calendar with the weekends left out. Each square contains only a five-trading-day week. This prevents the two-day weekend "gap" in the chart between two sets of weekly data.

The numbers running up the right side of the chart are the prices. Each day is plotted to the right of all preceding days.

Below each price plot on the chart another vertical bar is frequently drawn from the bottom up to indicate volume of trading for that day. And a dot is usually placed to indicate the total open interest on that day.

A number of variations are possible in this standard procedure. Some technicians chart only the closing prices. Others enter a midrange that consists of the high plus the low divided in half. The opening price is sometimes shown as well. All these procedures have advantages and disadvantages and each technician must decide which he considers most useful.

As the data is recorded, the analyst will begin to observe price formations or patterns that, according to traditional chart lore, are recurring and have forecasting significance. This chapter will not attempt to detail all of the different patterns that various technicians have discovered during the years, but Figure 5.2 contains the most publicized patterns. For those interested in a more definitive source of information on chart patterns and their analysis, *Technical Analysis of Stock Trends,* by Robert D. Edwards and John Magee (Springfield, Mass.: John Magee Inc., 1948), is recommended.

Point and Figure Charts

Point and figure charting of futures prices has its roots in securities analysis, just as bar chart analysis does. The construction of a point and figure chart is relatively simple. As with bar charts the vertical axis of the point and figure chart shows prices. (See Figure 5.3.) The major difference is

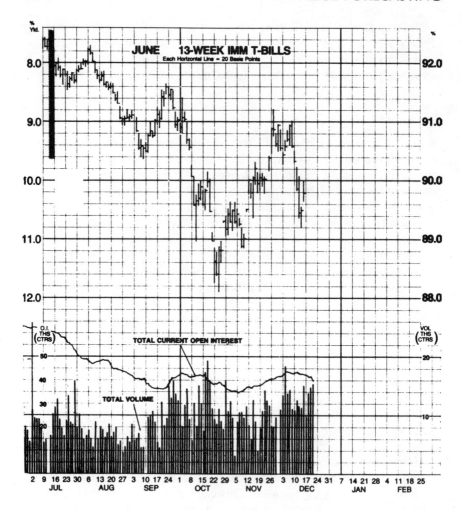

FIGURE 5.1   June: 13-week IMM T-bills.

that a point and figure chart has no calendar along the bottom. Entries on point and figure charts are triggered by price changes without regard to when they occur.

Entries are made on a point and figure chart by putting Xs and Os in boxes whenever a predetermined price change occurs. The general rules for developing such a chart are:

1. Xs represent price increases; Os represent price decreases.
2. The range of the day (difference between the high and the low) is the important datum to use in making the point and figure chart.

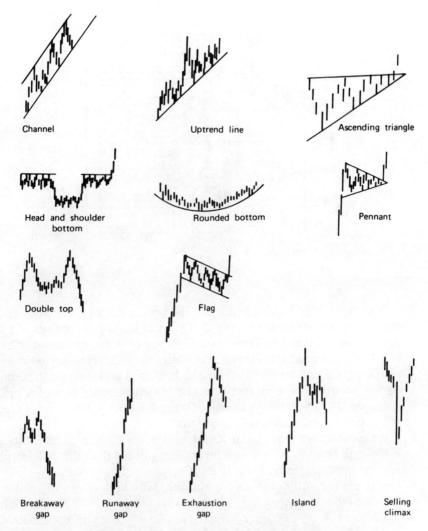

FIGURE 5.2 Typical chart patterns. The mirror image of most of these patterns has an opposite implication.

3. To start the chart, begin with a day in which the range represents at least the minimum number of boxes you are using as your basis for making buy/sell decisions. If three boxes are used, the chart is referred to as a three-box reversal chart. If four boxes are used, it is a four-box reversal chart. If the day's close is above the midpoint that day, the first column is marked with Xs; if below, the first column is Os.

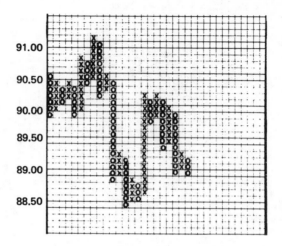

FIGURE 5.3   Point and figure chart.

The size of the box is important. Normally each box should represent some convenient number that reflects small price moves. This may be the equivalent of one "point" in the contract value or it may be more. Most good chart services optimize their charts by periodically reviewing the effectiveness of various box sizes and reversal criteria. As the volatility of a market changes, the appropriate size of a box and reversal distance also change. Optimizing helps keep the charts reflective of current market conditions.

4. If the most recent entry is an X (O), review the daily high (low) first. If the high (low) is at least one box higher (lower) than the last entry, add the appropriate number of Xs (Os).

5. If you are currently plotting Xs and the daily high does not require drawing more Xs, then consider the low. If the day's low is lower than the highest X by the agreed upon number of boxes to constitute a reversal, begin a column of Os one box below and one box to the right of the highest X. Otherwise, no additional entry is made for that day.

6. If you are currently plotting Os and the daily low does not require drawing more Os, then consider the high. If today's high is higher than the lowest O by the reversal criterion or more, begin a column of Xs one box above and one box to the right of the highest O. Otherwise, no additional entry is made that day.

7. A simple buy signal occurs when the current column of Xs rises one box higher than the top box in the immediately prior column of Xs.

8. A simple sell signal occurs when the current column of Os falls one box lower than the lowest O in the immediately prior column of Os.

Point and figure charts can be used to follow intraday price moves or long-term trends. As in bar charts, one will find various chart patterns revealed in point and figure charts.

(See Figure 5.4 for a sampling of some of the typical patterns identified in financial instrument futures.)

SETTING PRICE OBJECTIVES

Bar Charts

It is one thing to be able to identify price direction; it is another to be able to identify the price objective. A well-disciplined trader has a price objective in mind at the time he enters the trade. This objective may be stated as a percentage of return on margin desired or it may be obtained from an analysis of the price activity. The most logical price objective for a trade is the major support or resistance level established from previous market activity. For example, in attempting to set a price objective when entering a long position, one should look at the most well-defined resistance level above the purchase point. If the market tests that level by a price move, there is a possibility you will see one of the top formations described earlier and shown in Figure 5.2. A conservative trader would locate the price objective a reasonable distance below the prior major resistance level and use intermediate resistance levels as a means of adding to his positions on technical setbacks. A more aggressive trader might wait to see how prices deal with the major resistance level, in the hope of a breakthrough to new highs.

If one were entering a short position, one would set the downside objective in precisely the same manner, except one would be considering major support levels.

It is important to keep in mind that there are no rigid rules to be applied in setting price objectives. Support and resistance, trend lines, price formations, mathematical rules of thumb—all can be utilized to help estimate the distance a price move will travel before it is exhausted.

Point and Figure Charts

Generally, point and figure chartists set their price objectives by horizontal and vertical counts of the boxes comprising a particular chart formation. The theory behind this technique is that the amount of price activity at a particular level is important in determining the extent of the following price move. The logic is similar to the "support and resistance" logic used in bar charting. Previous contract highs or lows should always

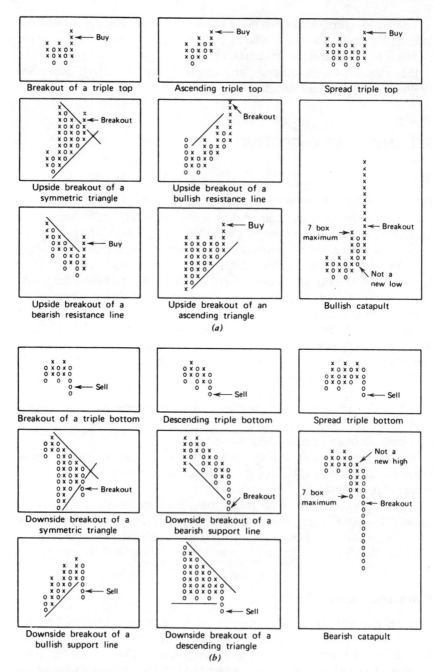

FIGURE 5.4 (a) Compound point and figure buy signals; (b) compound point and figure sell signals. (Courtesy P. J. Kaufman)

be used as a substitute objective if another technical method indicating potential strength or weakness causes a test of the highs or lows.

As tempting as it is to rely on such techniques as the counting of boxes or the width of a rectangular consolidation pattern on a bar chart as a means of setting price objectives, one needs to be warned of the dangers inherent in relying too heavily on such rote methods. Keep in mind that there are many ways of determining an objective of a trade and that there are no precise rules that are completely reliable.

For the reader desiring a more complete and sophisticated discussion of the methods of technical analysis, chart building, interpretation and price objective analysis, Perry Kaufman's book *The New Commodity Trading Systems and Methods* (New York: Wiley, 1987) is highly recommended.

6

Statistical Analysis Approach

Prices can do only one of three things. They can go up, they can go down, or they can go sideways. What they are doing at any one time is identified as the "trend." There are a wide variety of ways to determine a trend in a series of prices. One can do it by simply drawing two lines connecting the successive major lows and successive major highs on a chart to get a price "channel," or one can do it statistically through a variety of econometric techniques, such as regression analysis.

In any event, free market prices do not normally move in a straight line from one point to another. Instead there is usually a good deal of backing and filling in price movement. This backing and filling reflects the diversity of influences on prices, such as government programs, political events, short-term changes in supply and demand, emotions, hopes and fears, and just plain trading activity. This is referred to by statisticians as "noise."

To make the most efficient use of the data, the technical price analyst needs to be able to smooth out some of that "noise" occurring around the trend. By eliminating as much of it as possible without distorting the underlying trend information embodied in the price movement, an analyst can improve the probability of developing an effective and profitable trading system.

Probably the simplest and best-known technique for eliminating "noise" and smoothing a price series is the moving average.

MOVING AVERAGES

The moving average is best explained by an example. A three-day moving average of closing prices is calculated by summing three successive days of prices. To calculate the average for the fourth day, one drops the closing price for day one from the calculation and adds the closing price for day four. To calculate the moving average for the fifth day, one drops the closing price for day two from the calculation and adds the closing price for day five, and so on. The same procedure holds for calculating moving averages of other spans, such as 10 days or 20 days, and for other prices, such as daily highs or lows.

Daily closing prices	3-day moving average
89.00	
89.10	
89.50	89.20
88.20	88.93
88.00	88.57

The choice of whether one should use a three-day, five-day, ten-day, or whatever length moving average is related to several elements. The first is the sensitivity desired. The more days one uses in a moving average the more smoothing will occur and the less effect short-term fluctuations will have on the average price. (See Figures 6.1 and 6.2.) The more sensitive one wants the average to be in reflecting turning points in the trend, the shorter the averaging period should be.

Second, in selecting the average, one needs to keep in mind the uses to which it will be put. The financial executive who is making weekly decisions on a portfolio would want to wait as long as possible while prices continue to trend before making the buy or sell decision. In such a situation, a 3-day moving average won't aid decision making very much, but a 20-day moving average may.

What Prices to Use

In calculating the moving average one obvious question is, Should one use opening prices, closing prices, an average for the day, the high price, or the low price for the day? The answer is that one can use any of these but each of them may serve a different purpose. Most people use the closing price. Some calculate separate averages for the high and the low independently, thus obtaining a "band" representing the daily trading range or volatility.

Other Types of Moving Averages

Perry Kaufman, in his book *The New Commodity Trading Systems and Methods,* reviews a wide variety of other types of moving averages. The accumulative moving average, weighted moving averages, and exponen-

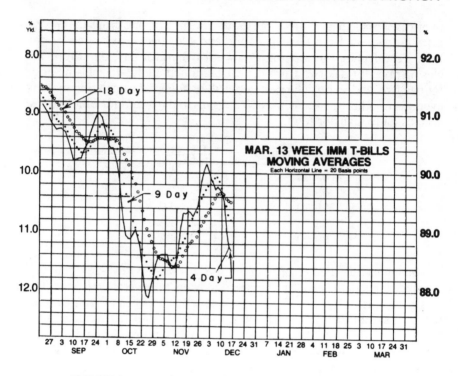

FIGURE 6.1 March: 13-week IMM T-bills moving averages.

tially smoothed moving averages are discussed as additional ways of obtaining a smoothing of price series. Exponential smoothing has a lot of intellectual and theoretical appeal, but the user needs to have a thorough understanding of statistics to make the fullest use of it as a trading tool. An important feature of exponentially smoothed averages is that all previously used prices are part of the new result, but with decreasing importance as they go back in time. There is a dilution effect based on time elapsed and on the smoothing constant. Hence, such averages react slower than most linear moving averages.

Leads and Lags in Plotting

Moving averages can also be plotted in different ways, with each having a major impact on their interpretation. Most analysts plot them the conventional way by placing the moving average value for that day on the same vertical line on the chart as the price for that day. If prices have been trending higher over the period of calculation, this will cause the moving average value to lag behind or below the actual prices. And when

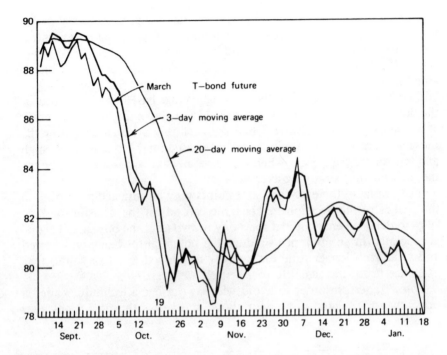

FIGURE 6.2 March T-bonds versus 3-day moving average and 20-day moving average.

prices are declining, the moving average will be above the actual prices. One can adjust for this by plotting the moving average with a lead or lag of several days. In this way the turning point in the moving average and in the actual price series can be put in phase and will coincide more closely on the chart.

RULES FOR USING MOVING AVERAGES

As is obvious from the preceding discussion, there are so many possible combinations of moving average techniques that the rules for applying these techniques can be extremely challenging. The goal here is to cover only some of the very basic rules.

Regardless of which of the moving averages one uses, the value of an unadjusted moving average will lag behind the actual market price. As pointed out above, this lag will cause the moving average to be below the market price when prices are rising, and it will cause the moving average to be above the market price when prices are falling. When prices change direction the moving average and the actual commodity prices will cross. When this crossing occurs a basic trading signal is generated. If the rising price line crosses the moving average, it is considered a buy signal. If the declining price crosses the moving average, it is a sell signal. (See Figure 6.3.)

Of course, if one has built the moving average based on closing prices, the buy signal refers to the rising price closing above the moving average and a sell signal is generated when the declining price closes below the moving average. If the moving average is based on the average daily high and low then signals occur when the new daily average is above or below the previous day's moving average.

The timing of the entry and exit points may be adjusted according to the wishes of the decision maker. One can adjust the decision-making rules to delay an entry or exit for a day or two after the buy or sell signal is generated in an attempt to reduce the potential for being whipsawed and to allow a longer time for a newly developed trend to confirm its existence or for the signal to reveal itself as false.

Some traders, in order to avoid whipsaw, utilize a technique called a price "band." A band is an area above and below the price track that

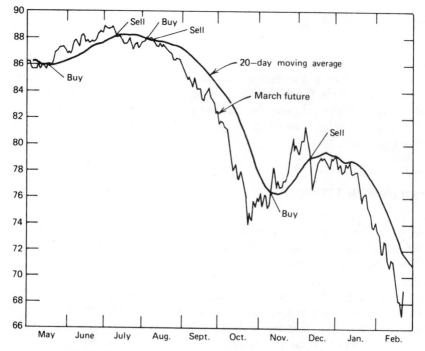

FIGURE 6.3 March T-bonds versus 20-day moving average.

acts as a buffer zone for the trader in making decisions. For example, a trader may decide to close out his long position when a moving average is penetrated from the upside by a price but not to enter the short position until price exits the lower boundary of the band. Most traders create bands by developing a percentage of the current price or of the current trend value. Others use an absolute point value, for example, 30 points. (See Figure 6.4.)

MULTIPLE MOVING AVERAGES

By combining various moving averages into a system, one can develop a means of timing trading decisions. For example, a 3-day moving average combined with a 20-day moving average allows one to use a 3-day moving average as a timing technique while retaining the 20-day moving average for defining the long-term trend. This way a trader can be more comfortable entering the market when he sees a recent short-term surge of prices in the direction in which he intends to establish new positions.

Two different rules that can be followed in applying multiple moving averages are:

1. Buy when the shorter moving average crosses the longer moving average going up, or sell when the shorter moving average crosses the longer moving average going down, as shown in Figure 6.4. This rule keeps one always in the market, going from long to short and back again as the long-term trend is violated by the short-term trend.
2. Buy when the current price crosses above both moving averages and close out your long position when the current price crosses below either moving average, or sell when the current price crosses below both moving averages and close out the short position when the price crosses above either moving average. For example, one would have gone short

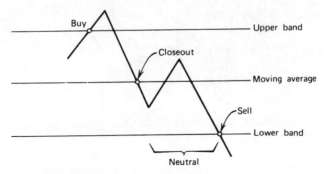

FIGURE 6.4   Trend line value. (Courtesy P. J. Kaufman)

at point A in Figure 6.5 and remained short until point B, at which level one would take a neutral position. The short position would have been reinstated at point C. Following this rule allows one to remain neutral when closing out a current position even if the long-term trend has not been penetrated. One does, however, suffer the potential for possible whipsaw as a result of being too close to the current price.

Kaufman demonstrates a number of these multiple moving average systems and tests several of them. His book is well worth reading by anyone seriously interested in technical trading systems.

The 5- and 20-day multiple moving average system of trading is quite popular. One of the best known of these systems is the Donchian method, which uses volatility-penetration criteria relative to a 20-day moving average. Donchian personalizes the system by adding judgmental factors relating to the extent to which the 20-day moving average must be penetrated and the day of the week on which the signals occurred.

As you can see, the combination of different factors and criteria one can put into a moving average trading system are multifold and dependent very much on choice and experience.

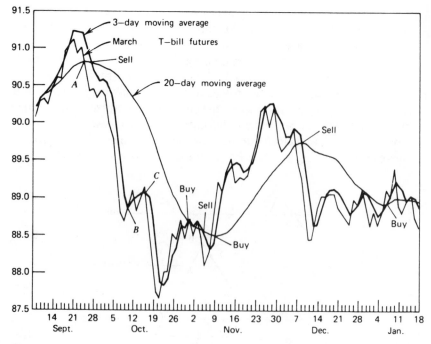

FIGURE 6.5 March T-bills versus 3-day moving average and 20-day moving average.

OSCILLATORS AND THE MEASUREMENT OF MOMENTUM

For many commodity analysts, merely being able to discern a trend in market prices is not sufficient refinement or understanding of the price activity to give them confidence in making decisions. Consequently, they want not only to know what the trend is but also to obtain a measurement of the *rate* of change in price. Or, to put it another way, they want to know the slope of the trend line.

Momentum is usually calculated by taking the difference between prices for fixed time intervals. For example, today's three-day momentum value would be the average difference between today's price and the price three days ago. If the price of T-bills has changed 60 points during the past three trading days the momentum measurement would be 20 (60/3 = 20).

Another popular method of measuring momentum is to calculate the difference between a 3-day and a 10-day moving average, or some other set of short- and longer-term moving averages. The rationale behind this procedure is to take advantage of the smoothing effect of moving averages; if the analyst uses the same moving averages for generating buy/sell signals, some calculations are already completed.

One will note as momentum calculations are plotted that a trend may continue up, but in smaller and smaller increments. As the increment of increase lessens, it suggests a decrease in momentum and an approaching turning point in the trend—or at the very least a flattening out of the trend line.

At that point the momentum index achieves its greatest value in determining whether a market is "overbought" or "oversold." When the momentum index is high and begins to slow its ascent or turns down, the market is considered oversold and a downward price reaction is expected. Conversely, when the momentum index is low and starts to slow its decline or turns up, the market is considered oversold and ready for an upward move. (See Figure 6.6(a) and (b)).

There are some significant risks in developing trading rules around momentum indicators. For example, to use a rule that considers crossing of the "zero" line by the momentum index as a change in price trend, requiring you to buy when the momentum index crosses the zero line going up and to sell when it crosses the zero line going down, creates risk of being whipsawed. See Figure 6.6 for examples of whipsaw action where the zero line (rate of change in price is zero) is used for determining trend changes. You could easily find yourself selling into an upward market at the time the market is strong; and, if you don't get an immediate reversal of the price trend, you might need substantial margin reserves to hold

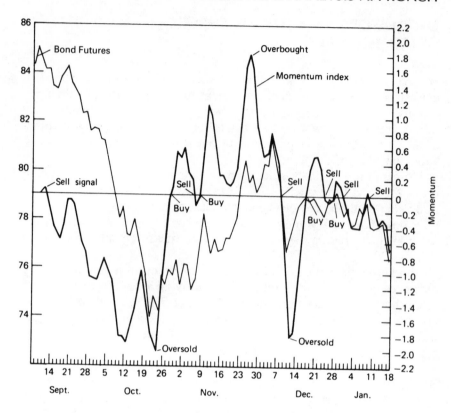

FIGURE 6.6(a) March T-bonds versus (3-day–10-day) momentum.

your position. The important thing is that you must realize you are essentially trading against the trend and making an informed guess that you will be able to identify very closely the turning point in the trend.

The terms "oscillator" and "momentum index" are frequently used interchangeably. Although they are calculated differently, for all practical purposes they measure the same thing. Perhaps the most popular type of oscillator is one that compares the daily highs and lows to the previous day's close. It is calculated by subtracting the previous day's close from today's high and dividing that number by the absolute difference between the high and the low for today. The extreme values will be +1 and −1, with the former indicating an overbought condition and the latter an oversold condition. The middle of the scale, zero, would imply a sideways price trend. For example, if yesterday's close for March T-bills was 89.00 and today's high and low were 89.40 and 89.90, respectively, the oscillator value would be +0.80 (89.40 − 89.00 = 0.40; 0.40 ÷ 0.50 = 0.80).

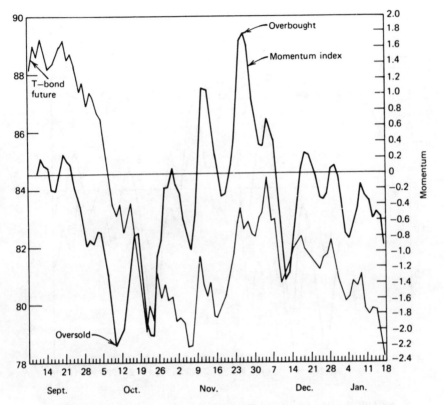

FIGURE 6.6(b)   March T-bonds versus (3-day–10-day) momentum.

MARKET COMPOSITION APPROACH

The composition-of-market approach is a technical approach to market analysis and price forecasting that is supplementary to other approaches. Alone it does not provide much of a basis for refined forecasting.

Traditionally technical analysts have studied the basic structure of the market by analyzing its volume and open interest activity. When these two pieces of information are combined with other available information they heighten the sense of what's happening in the markets.

"Volume" refers to the total number of contracts traded during a given time period. It represents the total of purchases or of sales, not of purchases and sales combined. So each time a transaction is completed (whether it involves the establishment of a new position or the offset of an old position), the volume is increased by one.

"Open interest" refers to the futures contracts that have been entered into and not yet liquidated. It is the total purchase or sale commitments

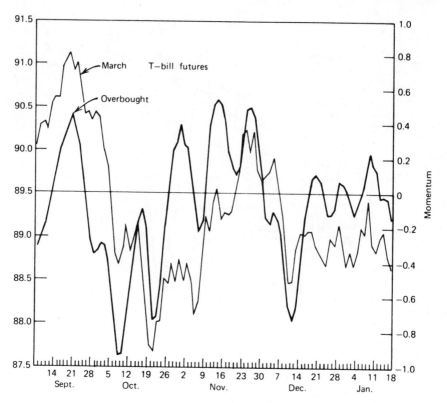

FIGURE 6.6(c)   March T-bills versus (3-day–10-day) momentum.

or the number of contracts outstanding. As with volume, the open interest figure is for one side of the market only—not for the long and short sides combined. However, unlike volume, the effect of a transaction upon open interest depends on whether new positions are being established or old ones closed out.

Open interest increases only when new purchases are matched with new sales. Decreases in open interest occur only when old longs close out their positions by selling to old shorts, who are buying to cover. Open interest also decreases when a short makes a delivery of actuals on a futures contract. There is no change in open interest when a new purchase is matched with an offsetting transaction (sale of a previous purchase), or if a new sale is matched with an offsetting transaction (purchase of a previous sale).

All open contracts must ultimately be closed out in one of two ways—by an offsetting futures transaction or through delivery of the physical commodity. Table 6.1 summarizes the effect of a particular transaction on open interest.

TABLE 6.1 Effect of Transaction on Open Interest

Transaction	Effect on Open Interest
Purchases by old sellers from old buyers	Reduced
Purchases by old sellers from new sellers	Unchanged
Purchases by new buyers from old buyers	Unchanged
Purchases by new buyers from new sellers	Increased
Sales by old buyers to new buyers	Unchanged
Sales by old buyers to old sellers	Reduced
Sales by new sellers to old sellers	Unchanged
Sales by new sellers to new buyers	Increased

To illustrate the concept of open interest and the impact of a transaction on the open interest, consider the following. Assume that you now have no position in the market but decide today to buy one futures contract of bonds. If the seller on the other end of your transaction was closing out a previous long position in bonds, the open interest would not change. You have in effect "replaced" the seller in the market. He was long. Now he isn't and you are.

On the other hand, if your seller was initiating a new short position there would be a new long (you) and a new short (him) in the market and open interest in bonds would go up by one.

If sometime later you have a profit in your bond position and decide to sell and take those profits, you close out your long position. If the buyer on the other end was closing out a short position to stop losses, your transaction would reduce the open interest by one, as the bond positions outstanding would be reduced by one long (you) and one short (him). On the other hand, if his was a new long position, the buyer would "replace" you and the open interest in bonds would remain unchanged.

Statistics on open interest and volume of trading are easily available from the exchanges, your local broker, and many major metropolitan newspapers. In addition, the Commodity Futures Trading Commission

(CFTC) publishes monthly statistics on open interest and volume of trading for all of the commodities. The commission also provides information about the nature and size of traders who hold the open contracts and whether they are generally classified as large and small speculators or hedgers. (See Table 6.1.) Some traders follow this information on the belief that it provides a good indication of the relative buying or selling strength of the people in the market.

INTERPRETING CHANGES IN VOLUME AND OPEN INTEREST

Most technical analysts believe the changes in open interest and volume of trading have forecasting value only when considered in connection with price changes. Almost any book on technical analysis provides a summary of rules of thumb for relating changes in open interest in volume to price action. Generally these rules of thumb and their rationale are stated as follows:

1. If the open interest is up and prices are also up, this indicates new buying and a technically strong market. The increase in open interest means new contracts are being created, and since prices are advancing, buyers must be more aggressive than sellers.
2. If open interest is going up while prices are going down, short selling or hedging is taking place and the market is technically weak. Again, the increase in open interest means that new contracts are being established. However, since prices are decreasing, sellers must be more aggressive than buyers.
3. If the open interest is going down and prices are also declining, this comprises liquidation by longs rather than new selling pressure and implies a technically strong market.
4. If the open interest is going down and prices are going up, this suggests short covering rather than new buying, and a technically weak market.
5. If the volume of trading follows the price—that is, if volume expands on price strength and declines on price weakness—the market is in a technically strong position and should go higher. By the same token but to a lesser extent, if the volume of trading expands on price weakness and declines on price strength, the market is considered to be in a technically weak position and ready to go lower.

Like all rules of thumb, however, there are many pitfalls in their rote application. Further, there's very little statistical evidence indicating that these rules of thumb are actually successful in generating trading profits.

7

Fundamental Price Analysis

Fundamental price analysis is the process of forecasting the supply of and demand for credit and the resultant prices of fixed income securities. It involves the simultaneous evaluation of economic information, political forces, and investor attitudes as they interact with each other.

This chapter presents a review and enumeration of the economic factors that affect the economy and interest rates. The chapter does not attempt an in-depth evaluation of credit availability or flow of funds in the economy, nor does it attempt subjective evaluation of investor attitudes and political forces.

The chapter does provide the reader with a checklist of economic information and gives a preliminary sense of the importance of each piece. The list is not exhaustive or all-inclusive. Whole books have been devoted to this subject and it is impossible in the short space provided here to do justice to the topic. The hope, though, is that the reader will get sufficient flavor from what is written here to appreciate the scope and complexity of the topic and will thus be motivated to delve further.

ECONOMIC INFORMATION

A market analysis is constantly bombarded with information relating to the state of the economy, changes in prices, indicators of future economic activity, and facts and figures relating to monetary growth. Success as an analyst depends on the ability to sort out the relevant from the irrelevant and give proper weight to the relevant.

Table 7.1 shows a schedule of various economic reports released by the federal government during the month of July. These reports provide

TABLE 7.1 Announcement Dates of Economic Indicators—July 1990

MONDAY	TUESDAY	WEDNESDAY	THURSDAY	FRIDAY
2 N.A.P.M. Index (10:00 EDST) May: 50.7% Jun: ___ Construction Spending (10:00 EDST) Apr: −0.7% May: ___ FOMC Meeting	**3** Factory Orders (10:00 EDST) Apr: −2.3% May: ___ FOMC Meeting	Independence Day **4** U.S. Markets Closed	Monthy Auto Sales **5** May: 6.7 ml (SAAR) Jun: ___	**6** Unemployment (8:30 EDST) May: 5.3% Jun: ___ FOMC Minutes Release May Meeting (4:15 EDST)
9 Consumer Credit (Target Date) Apr: +1.0% May: ___	**10**	**11** End of Maintenance Period Treasury Auction: 7-Year Note	**12**	**13** Retail Sales (8:30 EDST) May: −0.7% Jun: ___ Producer Prices (8:30 EDST) May: +0.3% Jun: ___ 10-Day Auto Sales

16	17	18	19	20
Business Inventories (10:00 EDST) Apr: +0.1% May: ——	U.S. Trade Balance (8:30 EDST) Apr: –$6.9 bl May: ——	Housing Starts (8:30 EDST) Jun: —— Consumer Prices (8:30 EDST) Jun: —— Industry Production & Capacity Utilization (9:15 EDST) Jun: ——		
23	**24**	**25**	**26**	**27**
Treasury Budget (2:00 EDST) Jun: ——	Employ. Cost Index (8:30 EDST) 1990–Q1: +5.5% Q2: —— 10–Day Auto Sales	Durable Goods (8:30 EDST) May: +3.9% Jun: —— End of Maintenance Period Treasury Auction: 2-Year Note	Treasury Auction: 52–Week Bill	Real GNP (8:30 EDST) 1990–Q1 (F): +1.9% Q2 (P): ——
30	**31**			
Personal Income (10:00 EDST) May: +0.3% Jun: ——	New Home Sales (10:00 EDST) May: —— Jun: ——			

an excellent source of information on the factors that affect the performance of the economy and thus determine the supply and demand for credit. The elements that make up these reports can be categorized into leading, concurrent, and lagging indicator groups.

Leading Indicators

Leading indicators provide advance signals about the health of the economy during the coming months. They reflect coming changes in the business cycle and consequently provide the interest rate analyst with an early warning system for identifying changes in interest rate trends.

Certain pieces of economic information relating to various sectors of the economy act as leading indicators in measuring the underlying health of the economy and the strength of business. The federal government has combined a number of these statistical series into a single index called the Leading Indicator Index. These leading indicators, while helping to predict some of the other variables, are themselves sometimes difficult to predict. One reason for this is that they are, in general, highly sensitive to disturbances of all kinds and are particularly volatile. Many of them are tied to expectations that change rather rapidly.

The components of the Leading Indicator Index are:

1. Average work week of production and manufacturing workers.
2. Manufacturing layoff rate.
3. New orders for consumer goods and materials.
4. Vendor performance-percent of companies reporting slower deliveries.
5. Net business formation.
6. Contracts and orders for plants and equipment.
7. New building permits for private housing units.
8. Net change in inventories on hand and on order.
9. Changes in sensitive prices.
10. Changes in total liquid assets.
11. Stock prices of 500 common stock.
12. Money supply—M-2.

These elements reflect changes in the early stages of the production and investment processes in our economy. For example, increased output calling for additional labor input is likely to be met first by manufacturers lengthening the work week and only later by manufacturers hiring new workers. Similarly, reductions in hours worked will precede layoffs in times of falling demand. Thus, cyclical changes in average hours worked precede those of changes in employment, particularly in manufacturing. The components of the Leading Indicator Index are selected by the federal government on the basis of their economic significance, their statistical adequacy, and their usefulness in identifying turning points in the business cycle.

As these indicators are released throughout the month, traders tend to give immediate reactions to the numbers. This frequently results in some short-term volatility in prices. If the indicator shows signs of a weakening economy, lower rates are likely to follow as the market begins to discount the expectation of a weaker economy ahead.

Concurrent and Lagging Indicators

Concurrent and lagging indicators show the general direction of the economy and confirm or deny a trend or change in the trend implied by the leading indicators. These indicators show the degree of change that has taken and is taking place in the economy. Often the release of a report on one of these indicators causes the market to adjust rapidly as investors are made aware that the declining or advancing activity has confirmed earlier signals of the leading indicators. Thus, concurrent and lagging indicators are often used to forecast the slope and the direction of business cycles.

Some of the key indicators in these groups are:

- **Unemployment.** Released at the beginning of the month, this report reflects the change in employment for the immediately preceding month and shows current economic activity.
- **Trade Balances.** Released monthly, these figures are very important to the strength of the dollar. The dollar's health is often followed very closely by the market as an indicator of potential foreign buying of securities. A strong dollar draws private foreign buying, but often causes selling by foreign central banks.
- **Domestic Car Sales.** This monthly figure shows the seasonally adjusted and annualized number of cars sold during the past month. It is a good indicator of consumer confidence and overall economic activity, since the auto industry is such a big part of our economy. Statistics on 10-day car sales are released during the month.
- **Consumer Credit.** Released monthly, this report provides a clue to the attitude of consumers toward spending. It is an indicator of the demand for credit from a large and important sector of the economy.
- **Retail Sales.** Released monthly, this report reflects the total of past retail activity and credit purchases, as well as cash. It is another good indicator of consumer confidence and overall economic activity.

- **Producer Price Index.** Released at the beginning of the month, this report covers the immediate past month. This replaces the old Wholesale Price Index. It reflects the cost of resources needed to produce manufactured goods and is a good indicator of future consumer price increases, because it shows the rate of inflation for raw materials.
- **Business Inventories.** This is an important key indicator, as it reflects the demand for short-term credit by businesses. As inventories build, they are usually financed through bank loans or commercial paper. Increases or decreases usually signal changes in the demand for credit. Inventory levels are generally good indicators of the duration and intensity of a business slowdown or speedup. If inventories are high when a slowdown begins, the recession is usually expected to be longer and more severe because factories will run at reduced levels until inventories are sold off. High inventories may also act as a short-term support for interest. Demand for credit to finance inventories could keep interest rates higher longer than they normally would be if inventories were low and if the economy were still in a business slowdown.

  Low levels of inventories going into an upturn in the business cycle may result in a short inflation spurt and a quick acceleration of business activity. The process of rebuilding inventories creates jobs and ultimately causes consumer demand to increase. This consumer demand often cannot be met by existing inventories, so prices climb, economic activity increases, and factories open to meet the new demands.
- **Housing Starts.** This report is released monthly. The levels of economic activity in the whole economy are greatly affected by the level of home construction. Housing starts are a good indicator of the demand for long-term mortgage money and short-term construction loans. They also give indicators of the number of GNMAs and other types of mortgage-backed securities that will need to be supplied in the near future.
- **Industrial Productions.** This indicator concerns the level of factory output in the previous month. It is a good lagging indicator that shows the depths of recessions and the highs of booms.
- **Personal Income.** This indicator reflects consumers' buying power. It measures potential demand for goods and services and reflects general levels of economic activity.
- **GNP.** This figure is usually regarded as past history. It confirms direction and amplitude of economic change. It is not a useful item for making trading decisions.
- **Consumer Price Index.** This is the measure of inflation. It is a key factor in bond prices, as investors usually demand a real rate of return of at least 2% for government bonds over the long term. The CPI is usually released during the third week of the month. Market participants watch these numbers very closely as indicators of future changes in long-term bond rates and money market rates.

WHERE TO FIND THIS INFORMATION

All of this economic information is reported in daily newspapers as it is released to the public during the month. Because market experts make forecasts of the data prior to their actual release, the market frequently begins to "discount" or react to the news before it is actually announced. A schedule of release dates and forecasts similar to those in Table 7.1 is usually available from your brokerage firm. It should not only give the dates of release but also a synopsis of recent numbers and an estimate of the new numbers. This type of information is vital for making short-term trading decisions and timing long-term investments.

Which Piece of Economic Data Is the Most Important?

No single economic indicator will permanently dominate the market. As times change, indicators replace each other as the "most important" factor in the market. Sometimes the market will concentrate on one or two elements and pretty much ignore all others for a short while. It is the job of the trader to identify which factor is of most concern at present and key off that factor for short-term trading. For example, during most of 1982 most market analysts watched the money supply and ignored other indicators. The feeling was that the Federal Reserve was going to dominate the market and that the Fed was making policy decisions based on money growth and inflation rates. Later in the year and early in 1983 the money supply and inflation began to be downplayed as other economic indicators showed the economy was in a general downward slide and the Fed indicated it was going to pay less attention to the money supply in policy-making. Money numbers hardly caused a ripple in this environment.

In summary, watch all the economic factors but try to identify what the market perceives to be the most important at that time. What is most important can be ascertained by reading traders' comments as quoted in the various news media, by consulting your broker, and by watching the market's reaction to indicators as they are released.

The Calendar of New Debt Offerings

All markets move up or down on expectations but eventually the new supply of securities will bring investors and traders down to earth and force the market to a level justified by the fundamental factors. Newly marketed issues are the acid test. Market prices may deviate from equilibrium on a short-term basis but new supply sets the longer-term levels. Therefore, new supply is a checkpoint through which a market must move to be accepted by investors as a true indicator of value and price trend. A new issue of bonds that cannot be successfully underwritten at current price levels often will cause a general market decline. This happens because market participants come to realize that they may have miscalculated investor demand.

New and abundant supply by itself is not always an indicator of a forthcoming market decline. A new supply of corporate, municipal, or government bonds sometimes brings investors into an underpriced market. This demand often causes all market participants to move higher in price.

There are also times even in bull markets when the supply will temporarily overwhelm the economic fundamentals reflecting the state of the economy. In these situations the market will seek a level at which bonds can be sold to the public and temporarily ignore the longer-run economic conditions. Eventually the new supply will be underwritten and the market will once again react to the economic fundamentals.

In analyzing the supply side of the equation there are two key questions to keep in mind. First, what is the future supply? Second, which new issues coming to market are the "bellwether" issues that will reflect the general near-term price action?

Future Supply

The future supply of new issues can be found every Monday in the *New York Times* and the *Wall Street Journal*. Both of them review the issues scheduled to be brought to market during the coming week and the "street comment" about their likely prices and rates. In addition, both of those papers publish weekly the "visible supply" of corporate and municipal bonds.

The regular financing of the U.S. Treasury can be anticipated by watching the newspaper and learning the financing cycles explained in Chapters 11 and 14. The amount to be issued is usually estimated by professional market analysts and economists. Their estimates can be found in the daily market news releases. Indication of things to come can be found in the monthly Treasury deficits, as budget deficits play an important role in determining future Treasury supply.

The Federal Reserve of New York publishes data on the amount of commercial paper, bankers' acceptances, and certificates of deposit outstanding each week. This information is available as part of the weekly money figures report.

Bellwether Issues

Which issue keys the market's near-term direction? Often a large utility issue such as an AT&T bond or a municipal bond underwriting will set the tone of the market. Sometimes a new issue that follows a significant price change will be the crucial test of a market. In short, there are no hard and fast rules for identifying bellwether issues. One needs simply to remain alert to market needs.

In summary, one needs to be aware of the importance of supply in making short-term trading decisions. But be aware also that supply alone usually will not set the long-term market direction. The real overall direction will be determined by a combination of fundamental economic factors affecting demand and supply.

Federal Reserve Information

The Federal Reserve system provides information that is very helpful in analyzing the economy and predicting Federal Reserve activity.

Weekly reports are issued every Friday at 4:15 P.M. EST. These reports contain information on:

- The money supply growth on a one-week lagged basis. It is often instructive to plot the money growth against the Federal Reserve's monthly growth targets. See Figure 7.1 for a sample chart of money supply superimposed on the Federal Reserve's targets. When the growth rate for money violates the target ranges, the Fed frequently takes corrective action and increases or decreases the money supply. This indicator is a fairly reliable predictor of future Federal Reserve policy changes.
- Loan demand, both nationwide and in major money market banks.
- The average rates for Fed funds.
- Dealer positions in Treasury issues.
- The conditions of the Federal Reserve Bank of New York's account.

On Thursday afternoons, after 4:15 P.M., the Federal Reserve announces its weekly statistics relating to the money supply and credit. These statistics are carefully watched by all traders, because they give indications of changes in federal policy and of potential activities the Federal Reserve may need to undertake in order to accomplish its public policy objectives.

Generally, the Fed announces changes in M-1, which measures checking accounts, cash, and other deposits that are readily available for spending, and M-2 and M-3, which measure other deposits and accounts that are less readily available for spending. These weekly money supply figures are annualized to give an indication of whether the Fed is meeting its money supply growth target rates each year. As new investment vehicles have been developed in recent years, M-1 has become a less important measure of monetary policy, whereas M-2 and M-3 have become more important.

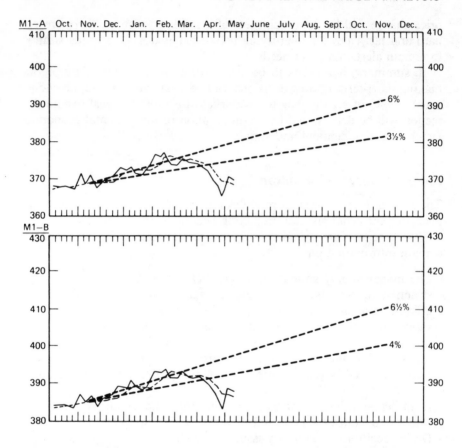

FIGURE 7.1 Monetary aggregates and the Federal Reserve's long-term growth targets (seasonally adjusted, in billions of dollars).

The Fed also reports on the velocity of turnover of money. The same level of monetary aggregates in the economy, but a faster rate of turnover can have similar impact as a constant rate of turnover but an increase in the total amount of money outstanding.

The Fed also reports levels of reserves that the banks are required to maintain at the central bank. Net borrowed reserves result when the banks as an aggregate have to borrow more than they have on deposit with the Fed to meet reserve requirements. Net free reserves is the opposite situation, when banks as an aggregate have more on deposit than they need to meet reserve requirements. These net free reserves give clues as to the Fed's need to enter into securities transactions in order to affect the Fed funds rate.

The Fed funds rate is an interest rate charged among banks for reserves they borrow and lend to each other. It is watched closely as a good indicator of short-term Federal Reserve policy. If the Fed believes the Fed funds rate is getting away from the level it feels is consistent with its reserve policies, it may enter the market and buy or sell government securities to increase or decrease the reserves and thereby affect the Fed funds rate.

The Fed also reports weekly on the total of commercial paper and industrial loans outstanding at financial and nonfinancial institutions. These statistics give one a good idea of the overall demand for credit and the sector of the economy from which that demand is coming.

One of the best sources of fundamental information is the minutes of the Federal Reserve's Open Market Committee monthly meetings. These can be obtained by contacting the Federal Reserve Bank of New York. A most rewarding exercise is to review these minutes by making note of the economic factors the Open Market Committee discussed in its deliberations. After doing this several times you will quickly note how its attention shifts from a certain economic factor one month as a key element in establishing its policy to another factor the next month. With experience the successful market analyst will come to anticipate those factors that are most important to the Fed at any given time.

In summary, the information needed to do good fundamental analysis is vast and complex. It is often advisable to subscribe to a service that presents the information in a timely and orderly fashion.

Treasury Financings and Interest Rates

The Treasury competes in the marketplace for money just like everybody else. The timing, amount, and maturity of Treasury borrowings all have an impact on the demand for money and on the resulting interest rates. Sometimes this impact can be substantial—at other times it may be insignificant. For example, in the fourth quarter of 1982, the Treasury had record borrowings (an annual rate in three months of $230.1 billion, up from $186.8 billion in the previous quarter), yet interest rates fell. A sharp contraction in corporate borrowing as a result of a sharp contraction in economic activity allowed the Treasury to fill its needs without overwhelming the market. Further, investors who had liquid cash bid aggressively in the early auctions for Treasury debt. Evidently, they expected rates to fall and wanted to get the higher rates while they could. That investor activity built on itself and allowed rates to continue falling even as the Treasury auctioned more debt.

The large government deficits are the major reason for large government borrowings. Since the deficits are not expected to decline soon, there is fear that as economic activity begins to build again interest rates will be bid back up as the Treasury competes with business borrowers for the savers' dollars.

The Fed's Credit Guidelines

For anyone interested in understanding interest rate movements, it is a good idea to study the sources and uses of funds in the economy. The Federal Reserve provides a large volume of quarterly information showing the flow of funds in the economy. Generally, the data is adjusted for seasonal variation.

In late 1982 and early 1983, the Federal Reserve moved away from its previous heavy emphasis on the money supply and toward targeting the growth of total credit. The credit guideline is based on the total outstanding debt of all American businesses, individuals, and federal, state, and local governments.

This move toward less reliance on the money supply numbers was made necessary by the introduction of new money market accounts, Super-Now accounts, and other innovations in the financial system. Discrepancies between the growth of the monetary aggregates and the performance of the economy were appearing. The Fed needed another measure of the impact its actions were having, or were likely to have, on the economy. The growth of total credit is closely related to the growth of U.S. economic activity and the relationship has been relatively stable for a couple of decades. Total credit outstanding has hovered near $1.45 for every $1.00 of the economy's GNP. Furthermore, statistical comparisons have shown that both prices and output are as closely related to credit as they are to the supply of money. Last, total credit measurements do not get as easily distorted by the introduction of new financial products. New regulations or financial innovations that merely cause borrowers to substitute one form of debt for another leave total credit unaffected.

Despite this, one shouldn't believe that the Fed's reliance on total credit will necessarily result in a quantum leap in the ability of the Fed to manage monetary affairs. Common sense and recent history caution against relying too heavily on any strict guideline, whether it is total credit or the total money supply. Nevertheless, it is useful to have specific policy tools and to have specific objectives related to them, and the available evidence indicates that current movements of total credit do contain information about future business activity.

All of this suggests then that one of the regular statistics an analyst should watch is Federal Reserve credit creation. That can be monitored through the Federal Reserve's balance sheet. That balance sheet is the record of Fed policy. If the Fed is creating credit, its assets expand. If the policy is stand pat or restrictive, its assets hold steady or decline. Weekly Federal Reserve reports net out the activity for the week and show the end result.

In this regard it is also useful to look at how credit flows have generally acted at various stages of the business cycle. A study by Salomon Brothers, a major investment banking house, found that the volume of transactions in various financial markets did indeed respond to the more general expansion and contraction of the trade cycle. They did not, however, march lockstep—up, then down—with the overall cycle.

Part Three

Cash and Futures Markets for Debt Instruments

8
Money in the Economy

Money is the grease that makes an economy run smoothly. Imagine the economy of a country as one big machine. This machine represents all the mills, factories, farms, offices, and shops that turn out the goods and services consumed in the society. Everyone with a job works on this big machine. Some are repairers, some are operators, but all of them are producing goods and services the people use.

Naturally, all of the workers are paid and these workers use their money to buy things produced by the machine. Thus, a nice smooth circle is completed of people working on the machine, being paid by the machine, and buying their goods and services from the machine.

If the people buy all that is produced, then everything is in balance and the economy for this country is healthy and stable. Sometimes, however, imbalances appear and interrupt the smooth flows of labor, money, and goods and services. When this happens, prices change and we get increases or decreases in economic activity.

These imbalances may arise because of leakages in flows of spending by the machine or by the people. For example, people may decide not to spend all of their money on goods and services but may decide instead to *save* some of their income. Thus, they do not buy as many cars and television sets. Since the flow of money back to the machine is reduced, the machine slows down its production. Fewer people are needed to run the machine, and total income and total buying power are reduced. Economists refer to this set of affairs as a recession.

Usually, however, these savings find their way back to the machine through the hands of businesspeople who borrow the funds from the people and reinject the money back into the spending flow by increasing the size of the machine, that is, building plants, buying new equipment and inventory. Depending on how much of the savings businesspeople want from people, they raise or lower the price (interest rate) they are willing to pay people for the use of their money. These activities, which are analogous to modernizing and expanding the machine, create new jobs and increase total income, thus bringing the flows of spending back toward a balance.

A second imbalance, or drain on the flows, can be caused by taxes collected by the government. Taxes are paid to local, state, and national governments and have the same slowdown effect that savings have. However, just as with savings, the tax money finds its way back into the system because the government hires people and buys goods and services.

Just as increases in savings and taxes can create imbalances in the system through withdrawals, imbalances can also be created by people refusing to save and simply demanding more goods and services from the government. The government can either refuse the demands or pay for them by raising taxes or by printing money, which is then given to the machine in payment for the goods and services. Refusing the demands and raising taxes are not always popular with the people; hence, governments frequently opt to print more money. Frequently, this is more money than is necessary to keep the machine running smoothly. In order to meet this output, the machine forgoes repairs and hires untrained workers. All the income is used to produce goods to meet the current demand and none is used for expanding, rebuilding, and updating the machine. This results in reduced efficiency. Ultimately, costs increase and the machine reaches the limits that it can produce. To alleviate this, consumers need to be convinced to postpone their purchases. This is best done by raising prices. This is referred to as inflation. Hence, when too much money gets into the system, the result is inflation.

MONEY, THE MACHINE, AND THE BANKING SYSTEM

It should be obvious from the above that if the flows of money spending match the flows of goods and services, prices will remain stable and the machine will run smoothly. If imbalances in flows of money occur, the machine slows down or works at such a furious pace it generates more momentum than it can handle. Thus, the amount of money and the smoothness with which it flows from individuals back to the machine through the land, labor, and capital become most important in determining the health of an economy.

To make this all flow smoothly in an economy, every country has a banking system through which they facilitate the flow of funds and adjust the supply of money. Banks serve as depositories for people's savings. They act as intermediaries by making these savings available to businesspeople for investment expenditures and the vital function of furnishing business and government with credit. Through their lending function, banks are able to adjust the money supply to make the flow of spending match the flows of goods and services, land, labor, and capital.

Naturally, most governments do not allow banks to operate willy-nilly in this system. Instead, the governments establish a Central Bank which acts to regulate the actions of commercial banks and to manipulate the expansion and contraction of the money supply. Thus, the ultimate control of the money supply rests with the government.

In the United States, the Federal Reserve Board, through its network of regional federal reserve banks, acts as the Central Bank. Its methods of operation differ only in degree from Central Banks of other countries. The Fed operates to control the money supply by controlling the amount of excess reserves in the banking system. Long ago banks found it prudent to maintain reserves against their deposits in order to meet the normal cash withdrawals of their customers. Current federal law requires them to maintain certain minimum reserves. The amounts over and above the minimums needed are called "excess" and are funds available for lending. The Fed controls excess reserves by:

1. Adjusting the required ratio of reserves to deposits. By lowering the required reserve ratio, the Federal Reserve decreases the amount of reserves that member banks are required to maintain in their accounts and makes additional reserves available to the member banks. Thus, a reduction in the required reserve ratio from 12% to 10% would increase the amount of excess reserves and thereby increase the amount of money available for lending. By raising the required ratio, the opposite would occur.
2. The purchase or sale of government securities, T-bills, bonds, and so on. When the government buys the securities, it pays money to the banks, which increases member bank reserves, and vice versa when the government sells.
3. Lending reserves to member banks.

A commercial bank may be short on reserves relative to its demand for loans and may then borrow from the Federal Reserve. The bank will pay a rate of interest known as the discount rate. The Fed can set the discount rate at whatever level it wants. By raising this rate of interest, borrowing is made more expensive and commercial banks will be less inclined to borrow reserves. They will have to raise the rate of interest to customers, and as the price of credit goes up, usually the demand for such credit will go down. Conversely, by reducing the discount rate, borrowing is made less expensive and banks will be more inclined to borrow reserves and make loans to their customers.

Thus, the Central Bank of the government acts to regulate the actions of the commercial banks and thereby to regulate the supply of money to accomplish specific objectives related to levels of employment, personal income, and price stability.

The extent to which the Central Bank accomplishes these objectives has a great influence on interest rates.

REPOS

"The Fed is doing Repos." Traders hear or read these words daily or at least weekly.

Anybody who trades interest rate futures needs to become familiar with the Federal Reserve's daily activities to affect interest rates. One of these activities is buying and selling securities and doing it through "Repos."

A "repo" is short for a "repurchase agreement." A repurchase agreement is a transaction that involves the sale of a security, usually U.S. government securities, with the simultaneous commitment by the seller that, after a stated period of time, she or he will repurchase the security from the original buyer for the purchase price plus an agreed rate of return on the original value. It is a short-term loan.

The repo provides the temporary seller of securities with a source of borrowed funds that can be used to finance an inventory or cover a deficit cash position. An exception to this is the Fed. When the Fed is said to be doing repos (RPs), it is lending money, that is, increasing bank reserves.

The opposite of a repo is a reverse repo, which is a purchase-resell agreement. It consists of the purchase of a security, usually a U.S. government security, with the simultaneous commitment by the buyer that, after a stated period of time, she or he will resell the security to the original seller for the original price plus an agreed rate of return. Reverses are used by dealers to borrow securities they have shorted. Again, an exception is the Fed. When it is said to be "doing reverses," it is borrowing money; that is, absorbing or decreasing reserves.

In short, a repo is executed by a temporary seller of securities or the borrower of funds, whereas a reverse repo is executed by the temporary buyer of the securities or the lender of funds.

Federal Reserve's Role

One of the ways the Fed controls excess reserves is by the purchase or sale of government securities (T-bills, bonds, and so on). When the government buys securities, it puts more money in the member bank reserves.

When it sells securities, it collects money from the bank, thus reducing member bank reserves and the supply of money available for lending.

If the money market is temporarily tight (demand for loans high relative to the supply of loanable funds) and the Fed needs to supply reserves to the banking system, the Federal Reserve Bank of New York may agree to enter into repurchase contracts with nonbank government securities dealers. These agreements, which are usually made at the discount rate and only at the initiative of the Federal Reserve, are an important complement to regular purchases and sales of government securities in the open market. They are particularly useful when reserves are needed only for a few days.

In such a case, the Federal Reserve may make repurchase agreements scheduled to mature when reserves will probably be more readily available. This procedure makes it unnecessary to buy outright a large block of securities one day and sell them the next or in the very near future. Normally, the "bewitching hours" for the Fed activity is late morning or early afternoon (EST).

Influence on Rates

Repos also have been used by the Federal Reserve when it is making an effort to keep short-term rates up for balance of payments reasons. Their use avoids the direct downward pressure exerted on bill rates when the system buys short-term government securities outright. When repos are used, dealers know that the reserve injection is not permanent and will be reversed shortly.

In the mid-1960s, the Federal Reserve system initiated the practice of using reverse repos to withdraw reserves on a temporary basis. Analogous to the case of the repo, the reverse repo is thought to exert less upward pressure on interest rates than an outright sale, primarily because the technique provides dealers and other market participants with the knowledge that the reserve absorption is only temporary.

The Federal Reserve usually sets a target for the interest rate it calls the Federal funds rate. That's the rate banks charge each other for the overnight loan of reserves. Sometimes the Fed funds rate fluctuates widely within a single trading day. For example, some days the Fed funds rate has fluctuated by as much as 100%. This sort of volatility frequently occurs on Wednesdays. Wednesday is an important day of the week for Fed watchers because it's the last day for banks to meet their reserve requirements for the latest statement week. Hence there are sometimes last minute scrambles for funds. Traders usually ignore the funds rate on Wednesdays.

The volatility may also be due to technical factors. For example, a few years ago during a particularly volatile period, the Fed had been buying securities to add reserves and keep the funds rate close to its target. When the market became volatile, the Fed announced that it planned to add reserves by buying government securities temporarily through four-day and seven-day "repurchase agreements." This had the desired effect on the market of stabilizing the Fed funds rate by providing the needed reserves for the banks. Traders knew, however, that by the following week those securities would be sold back and reserves would be reduced again. Thus, upward pressure was being maintained on interest rates.

The Federal Reserve did not invent repos. Indeed, it was a reaction by the banks to Federal Reserve regulations that resulted in banks developing the repurchase agreements. Repo agreements involving U.S. Treasury and federal agency securities have become the fastest growing source of discretionary funds to commercial banks. The repo interest rate is to a large extent the marginal cost of funds for a bank.

Today many commercial banks regard repos as one of a number of alternative sources of funds that may be used to finance their securities portfolios or their lending activities. The rate paid by commercial banks generally ranges from 10 to 15 basis points below the Federal funds rate but may vary depending on the availability of securities.

Corporate Users

The government and banks are not the only ones involved in repos. A repo can be used by a corporation to temporarily provide cash in lieu of issuing commercial paper, liquidating investments in adverse markets, or borrowing from banks.

One of the reasons for the growing volume of repos done by business corporations has been the recent development of sophisticated cash management techniques. Corporate cash management involves procedures designed to speed the receipt of income and delay disbursement of payments, and reduce the uncertainty about daily cash flow patterns, thus permitting businesses to hold only a minimum amount of funds without explicit interest return.

These procedures have resulted in a more efficient use of corporate funds and have served greatly to increase the availability of funds for investment in money market assets. Corporate treasurers have increasingly used repos as an attractive alternative to maintaining surplus funds in noninterest earning demand deposits.

Repos may be tailored to any short-term maturity and are relatively free of risk. In addition, like money market assets in general, repos may be used not only to invest temporary excess cash but also to earn interest on funds being accumulated for tax or dividend payments and on the proceeds of long-term financing temporarily awaiting disbursement.

In summary, Federal Reserve activity in the cash market is very important to anyone trading interest rate futures. One of the ways the Fed affects interest rates on a daily or even intraday basis is through the purchase or sale of repos.

Fed activity in the market depends very much on how closely the market rate for Federal funds reflects the Fed's target rate for Fed funds and whether the Fed believes any deviation of the market rate from the target is of a temporary or longer-run nature. If Fed officials believe it is temporary, they are more likely to use repos as their method of entering the market; if they do use repos, you know that their activity and impact will be reversed in a day or so.

INFLATION AND INTEREST RATES

Inflation rates become important in forecasting interest rate levels because the expectations about levels of inflation get built into the price for borrowing money. Look at it this way. Four years ago the dollar would buy a newspaper, a gallon of milk, and a package of gum. Inflation (rising prices) has caused the domestic purchasing power of the dollar to decline so that today it takes two dollars to buy the same amount and quality of goods. So, if you loaned someone a dollar 10 years ago and if the average annual rate of inflation was 10%, when he or she pays it back today it is worth only about half as much as when you loaned it. If you had charged 5% per year interest, you would have collected $.50 in interest and, counting that, would find your dollar worth only about three-fourths as much as 10 years ago.

Had you anticipated the 10% average annual inflation rate, you would have asked for at least a 10% interest charge in order to maintain your purchasing power over the 10-year period. More likely you would have asked for 15% interest, reasoning that you expect money to provide a 5% real rate of return after accounting for the 10% expected inflation. It is this latter way that businesspeople and bankers react. Thus, expected inflation rates get built into interest rates. That is what has happened in recent years.

The Inflationary Process

Monetary economists trace the inflationary process through as follows. First, a change in the rate of the growth in the money supply causes a change in people's incomes in the same direction about six to nine months later. This money "burns a hole in the pocket" and people rush out trying to spend their extra income. It usually takes about another six to nine months before this increased demand catches up with the available supply and prices start to rise. Thus, about a year to a year and a half after the money supply increases, one can expect to see a rise in prices. The CPI reflects the general prices of things people buy and thus it becomes the most handy means of measuring inflation. The extent to which the money supply is increased, of course, will affect the extent to which incomes increase, which in turn will affect the amount of money people have to spend and their ability to bid up prices. So a small change in the money supply beyond the amount necessary to maintain economic growth, employment, and stable prices will probably result in small amounts of inflation.

9
Pricing of Money Market and Capital Market Fixed Income Securities

Securities markets may be classified broadly as *money markets* and *capital markets*. The term money market is used to define a market in which short-term securities (maturities of one year or less) are traded. The securities represent debt obligations of the issuers. They are highly marketable and usually (though not always) have negligible default risk. The term capital market defines a market in which long-term securities (maturities greater than one year or no maturity) are traded. The securities may be debt obligations of the issuer as in the case of bonds, or claims of ownership (common stock). They differ from money market securities primarily in terms of their marketability (less) and risk (more). Taken together, the money and capital markets perform the important function of efficiently allocating scarce capital resources in a free market economy.

Following are examples of money market securities and capital market securities:

Money Market Securities

- Treasury Bills
- Commercial Paper
- Negotiable Certificates of Deposit
- Federal Funds

- Bankers' Acceptances
- Eurodollars

Capital Market Securities

- Treasury Bonds and Notes
- Municipal Bonds
- Corporate Bonds
- International Bonds
- Mortgage-Backed Securities
- Preferred Stock
- Convertible Bonds and Preferred Stock
- Common Stock

The term *fixed income* securities derives from the fact that they typically pay their holders a predetermined amount of income in the form of interest paid periodically over the life of the security. The amount of interest paid is based on the face value and the stipulated interest rate or yield on the security. Defined as such one may classify a fixed income security as belonging to either the money market or the capital market.

CHARACTERISTICS OF FIXED INCOME SECURITIES

Fixed income securities characteristically are defined in terms of their face value, maturity date, interest rate, and the periodicity of interest payments. Following are examples of a money market security and a capital market fixed income security.

Money Market Security: 90-Day T-bill Auctioned at a Yield of 10%

The investor in this T-bill will pay a price of $975,000 for each $1 million in face value to be received at the end of 90 days. Hence, the interest earned over 90 days is $25,000. The price and interest is computed as follows:

$$\text{Interest} = [\text{Yield}/100] \times \text{Face Value} \times [\text{Number of Days to Maturity}/360]$$
$$= [10/100] \times \$1,000,000 \times [90/360]$$
$$= \$25,000$$

$$\text{Price} = \text{Face Value} - \text{Interest}$$
$$= \$1,000,000 - \$25,000$$
$$= \$975,000$$

The price can be alternatively calculated without first calculating the interest as shown below:

Price = Face Value × [1 − (Yield/100) × (Number of Days to
    Maturity/360)]
    = $1,000,000 × [1 − (10/100) × (90/360)]
    = $975,000

T-bills are called *discount* securities because they are sold at a discount from their face value. They gradually increase in price over their lifetimes as the interest accrues. At maturity the face value is received. Not all money market securities are sold on a discount basis. Certificates of Deposit (CDs) are an example of what are known as *add-on interest* type securities. They are purchased at their face values. At maturity the interest is added on to the face value and paid by the issuer.

Because an investor collects interest based on face value but pays a price less than the face value, the quoted yield on a discount security understates its true yield. The simple interest terms, or the *simple interest yield,* is computed as follows:

Simple Interest Yield = (Interest/Price) × (360/Number of Days
    to Maturity)
    = ($25,000/$975,000) × (360/90)
    = .1026 (10.26%)

Note that all of the preceding calculations assume a 360-day year. In reality we all know there are more than 360 days in a year. Receiving a year's worth of interest in 360 days is certainly preferable to receiving it over 365 days. Hence, all else remaining the same, a security paying interest on a 360-day basis is preferred to another paying it on a 365-day basis. Bonds pay interest on a 365-day basis.

BOND EQUIVALENT YIELD

To compare yields on different securities then, one must translate yields to a common equivalent basis. A common basis for comparison is the *Bond Equivalent Yield.* Bonds pay interest semiannually and, as just noted, assume a 365-day year. Therefore, to make a common comparison an adjustment must be made to the simple interest yield to convert it into a bond equivalent yield. For T-bills that have a maturity of less than 180 days, the bond equivalent yield is the simple interest yield multiplied by (365/360). Hence, for the 90-day T-bill described in the first example, the bond equivalent yield is 10.4025% (10.26 × 365/360). For discount securities with maturities greater than 180 days, the computation is slightly more complex and is shown in Appendix B.

As short-term investments, money market securities are often held until their maturity and therefore are considered to have little or no interest rate risk. The little interest rate risk they possess arises if they have to be sold prior to maturity, because the price at which they are sold will depend on whether interest rates have changed since their purchase. A rise in interest rates causes the *realized return* to be lower then the *anticipated return* on the security. The reverse is true if interest rates fall.

$$\text{Anticipated Return (\$)} = \text{Face Value} \times \text{Yield at Purchase} \times \frac{[\text{Holding Period}]}{360}$$
$$= \$1,000,000 \times 0.10 \times 30/360$$
$$= \$8,333.33$$
$$\text{Realized Return (\$)} = \text{Selling Price} - \text{Purchase Price}$$

Where: Selling and purchase prices are calculated at yields prevailing at the date of sale and purchase, respectively, of the security using the price formula shown earlier.

Table 9.1 displays the excess return (realized return less anticipated return) measured in dollars on an investment in a $1-million face value 90-day T-bill for different yields prevailing at the end of the holding period of 30 days. The bill is purchased at a yield of 10%.

Table 9.1 reveals that even for relatively large changes in interest rates (yields) the excess returns (positive or negative) measured in dollars are relatively small compared to the size of the investment. This explains why dealers in money market securities can afford to take highly leveraged

TABLE 9.1 Excess Return ($) from Purchasing a
$1-Million Face Value 90-day T-bill for a Holding
Period of 30 Days

Yield at End of Holding Period	Realized Return	Excess Return
8%	$11,667	$3,333
9	10,000	1,667
10	8,333	0
11	6,667	(1,667)
12	5,000	(3,333)

Note: The 90-day bill is purchased at a yield of 10% ($975,000).

positions in several hundred million dollars of such securities through transactions such as repurchase agreements (repos and reverse repos).

For those interested in a more detailed analysis of transactions in money market securities (both discount and the add-on interest type), see *Money Market Calculations: Yields, Break-Evens, and Arbitrage* by Marcia Stigum, Dow-Jones Irwin (Publishers), Homewood, Illinois, 1981.

Capital Market Fixed Income Security: 10%, 20-Year U.S. Government Bond

The investor will receive a semiannual coupon of $5,000 each six months per $100,000 ($100,000 × .10/2) face value for the next 20 years. At maturity the face value will be received. The cash flow an investor will receive if the bond is held to maturity is shown in Figure 9.1.

Common to the two securities described (90-day T-bill and the 10%, 20-year bond) is a well-defined cash flow stream an investor can expect to receive if the securities are held until maturity. There is no event (other than default) that can alter the cash flow stream. However, the value investors are willing to ascribe to either security may change over time because interest rates change; hence, the term "interest rate sensitive" securities. A rise in interest rates will typically cause the price of any fixed income security to fall in order to make it attractive to potential buyers who will demand the higher level of interest. The only way these buyers can be enticed to purchase the lower interest paying securities is if they can be purchased at a lower price. The reverse is true if interest rates fall.

To compute the new price of a fixed income security if interest rates change, the concept of *present value* or *discounted cash flow* is introduced.

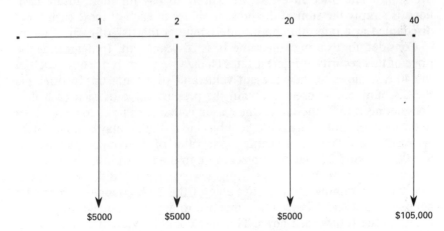

FIGURE 9.1   Illustration of cash flow from a 10%, 20-year U.S. government bond.

PRESENT VALUE AND DISCOUNTED CASH FLOW

Fundamental to the pricing of any security, fixed income or other, is the concept of present value. The concept of present value dates back to the work of the great American economist Irving Fisher on the *Theory of Interest.* Stated simply, it means a dollar today is worth more than a dollar next year, because today's dollars can be invested to earn additional dollars in the future. Alternatively stated, dollars to be received in the future are worth their present value in today's dollars. The connecting link between present and future dollars is the discount rate (or required rate of return). For example, if the discount rate is 10%, the present value of $100,000 to be received next year is $90,909, computed as follows:

$$\text{Present Value} = \text{Future Value}/[1 + \text{Discount Rate}]^{\text{\# of years}}$$
$$= \$100,000/[1 + .10]^1$$
$$= \$90,909$$

Sometimes the reciprocal of the denominator of the preceding expression is referred to as the *discount factor.* It is the present value of $1 to be received in the future. For example, the discount factor at 10% for one year is 0.90909 (1/1.10). Discount factors for different discount rates and number of years to receipt of the future cash flow are readily available in the appendices of many finance texts, thus allowing one to easily determine the present value of any future cash flow.

Price as the Present Value of Future Cash Flow

Fixed income securities can be viewed as a bundle of cash flows dispersed over time. The price investors are willing to pay for these future cash flows is simply the sum of the present values of each of these cash flows discounted at a rate that appropriately reflects the risk of each of them.

Consider, for example, the same 10%, 20-year bond. To determine the price of this security if interest rates change we need to discount each of the 40 cash flows to their present value and sum them up. In principle the discount rate(s) used to obtain the present value of each cash flow does not need to be the same. The reason is that cash flows to be received in the more distant future could be subject to risks that may be nonexistent for earlier cash flows. For example, the value of the coupon payment of $5,000 in period 20 may be subject more to the risk of inflation than the first coupon. In such a case one might wish to use a different discount rate for determining the present value of the 20th coupon than the 1st coupon. However, it is common practice to assume a single rate to discount all the future cash flows. This rate could be viewed as some form of average of the discount rates for each of the cash flows. For bonds this rate is called the *yield to maturity* (ytm). It can be used to compute the price of the bond as follows:

$$\text{Price} = \$5000/(1 + \text{ytm}/2) + \$5000/(1\ \text{ytm}/2)^2 + \ldots +$$
$$\$105,000/(1 + \text{ytm}/2)^{40}$$

Table 9.2 displays prices of the 10%, 20-year bond as the yield to maturity is varied. The wide fluctuation in bond prices revealed in Table 9.2 indicates the substantial (price) risk any long-term fixed income security is subject to as interest rates vary. Typically, the longer the maturity of the security the greater the price fluctuation as interest rates are allowed to vary. Table 9.3 shows how the maturity of a fixed income security influences its price as interest rates vary. All securities are assumed to have a face value of $100,000.

Table 9.3 illustrates an important point about how the market may actually price fixed income securities. It is apparent that the longer the maturity of the security the greater its *price risk* as interest rates vary. If investors are to bear risk (price or other), they would demand a premium in compensation. This premium could come in the form of a higher yield. The commonly observed upward-sloping yield curve, in which longer maturity securities provide higher yields than shorter maturity securities, is consistent with this reasoning.

What Determines the Yield on a Security?

Many factors influence the yield on a security. Before discussing these factors, it is worth pointing out that we only observe *prices* in security markets and not *yields.* Yields can only be inferred from the observed

TABLE 9.2 Prices for the 10%,
20-Year U.S. Government Bond under
Various Interest Rate Scenarios

Yield to Maturity	Price
6%	$146,229.54
8	119,792.77
9	109,200.79
10	100,000.00
11	91,976.94
12	84,953.70
14	73,336.58

TABLE 9.3 Effect of Maturity on Prices under Varying Interest Rates

Yield	90-Day T-bill	10%, 5-Year	10%, 10-Year	10%, 20-Year
6%	$98,500	$117,060	$129,755	$146,229
8	98,000	108,110	113,590	119,792
10	97,500	100,000	100,000	100,000
12	97,000	92,640	88,530	84,954
14	96,500	85,953	78,812	73,337

prices. This is important because in the calculation of yield several simplifying assumptions are made.

In theory there could be as many yields on a security as assumptions underlying its calculation. The best example that comes to mind is the yield on a mortgage-backed security. There are as many yields given the price of a mortgage-backed security as there are prepayment scenarios. The yield for mortgage-backed securities quoted in the financial section in most newspapers, for example, assumes full repayment of the remaining principal balance at the end of 12 years. In actuality prepayment may take place at any time. As a result, such a yield quote could severely overestimate the yield an investor is likely to earn, particularly if the mortgage-backed security carries a high coupon and interest rates have dropped sharply. On the other hand, the quoted yield would tend to underestimate the yield the investor may earn if interest rates rise. For this reason many brokerage houses provide tables of *cash-flow yields* for mortgage-backed securities. A cash-flow yield is the yield on a mortgage-backed security assuming a *constant prepayment rate (CPR)*.

In the case of regular coupon-bearing bond there are at least two yields often quoted. One is the *current yield,* which is obtained by dividing the coupon by the price (coupon/price). The other is the more familiar *yield to maturity.* By discounting every coupon at the same rate the yield to maturity calculation implicitly assumes a flat yield curve even though the yield curve may not be flat. Alternatively, the yield to maturity may be viewed as a complex average of rates used to discount each of the future cash flows such that the sum of those discounted cash flows equals the bond's quoted price.

Since the term *yield on an investment* usually connotes *return on investment,* it is tempting to conclude that the yield to maturity on a bond, or the cash flow yield on a mortgage-backed security, is the rate of return one would earn if either security were held to maturity. Unfortunately, this is almost never true. Only in the special case of a single cash flow security (such as a zero-coupon bond) would such a conclusion be strictly correct.

The foregoing discussion on yields on a security illustrates that any yield inferred from a security's price is only as good as the assumptions underlying the calculation of its value. Despite this apparent shortcoming, yields can be used to maximum advantage, especially in comparisons across different securities.

It is common to view the interest rate (or the yield on a security) as a composite of the real rate plus premiums for inflation (anticipated and unanticipated) and risk (default or other).

Interest Rate = Real Rate + Inflation Premium + Risk Premium

According to the *Classical Theory of Interest,* the real rate of interest is determined by the supply and demand for capital—supply depending on the willingness and ability of people to postpone consumption, and demand depending on the opportunities for productive investment. The intersection of the supply and demand curves is the real rate of interest.

If the suppliers of funds anticipate that inflation will erode the purchasing power of money, they will naturally demand a premium to compensate for the erosion in value. This premium may be viewed as an *inflation premium.* Since inflation is always observed only after the capital has been transferred from borrowers to lenders at a predetermined interest rate, the inflation premium is often referred to as a premium for *anticipated inflation.* In a highly uncertain inflationary environment, it is not uncommon for the suppliers of funds to demand an additional premium for *unanticipated inflation.* Hence, when inflation fears rise bond prices fall.

When one allows for the possibility that money lent may never be recovered because of bankruptcy of the borrower or some other contingency, the concept of a *risk premium* naturally follows. Moody's and Standard and Poor's are two agencies that evaluate the credit quality of thousands of borrowers. U.S. government bonds have a special status because they are assumed free of default risk. All other bonds are classified by their degree of default risk—from AAA, bonds judged to be of the highest quality or "investment grade" bonds, to C, the lowest-rated class of bonds. The lower the quality of the bond the larger is the risk premium demanded by investors. Preserving or raising the rating of bonds is of keen interest to their issuer. This is particularly in evidence when the rating agencies lower the quality of the bonds of state or local governments. It often makes front page news in the newspapers. Politicians start scampering around and start berating the rating agencies. A reduced rating means tens or even hundreds of millions of dollars more in interest payments, with ramifications for the raising of taxes to meet those payments.

Term Structure and Risk Structure of Interest Rates

In viewing interest rates as a composite of several factors, it is easy to see why the yields on securities differ from one another, and consequently their prices. Although it is prices of securities that determine their yields and not the other way around, yields are a much better measure of value. Prices depend on factors other than just yields (maturity, for instance). Thus, making a straightforward price comparison between two securities may be meaningless. Yield quotations, on the other hand, allow for ease of comparison across the quality and maturity spectrum, thus permitting useful explanations for differences in value. The *term structure* and the *risk structure* of interest rates provide such explanations for differences in value.

The term structure of interest rates relates the yield on a security to its maturity. If the term structure is upward sloping it implies that investors are demanding a higher rate of return the longer the maturity of the instrument. The reasons for this higher rate of return could be several. For example, higher anticipated inflation in the future would require the addition of an inflation premium to compensate investors for the lower purchasing power of their future dollars. Another explanation for the premium is the lower liquidity and marketability of longer-time securities vis-à-vis shorter-term securities. Yet another explanation is simply that investors expect short-term rates to rise in the future and are not prepared to go out to the long end of the yield curve without being compensated up front for it.

The risk structure of interest rates relates the yield on a security to its risk of default at various points in the maturity spectrum. The risk structure of interest rates is represented graphically as shown in Figure 9.2. Each curve in the figure is a term structure for a class of securities in the same default risk category. For example, the lowest curve represents U.S. government securities. Since they are assumed to be default free, they carry the lowest interest rate at any prespecified maturity. The higher the position of the curve the greater is the default risk. Hence, at any given maturity the additional premium for default risk can be computed as the spread between the yields of securities in two categories. There is a tendency for the yield spreads to widen as maturity increases in reflection of the increasing default risk with increasing maturity. Also, as interest rates rise, the spreads at any maturity level tend to widen for the same reason.

WHY DO PRICES CHANGE?

Prices of all securities (fixed income or other) change almost continuously. The common explanation for this behavior is that prices reflect information currently available. As new information is generated, traders

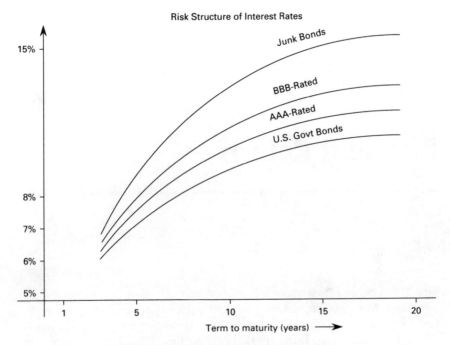

FIGURE 9.2 Risk structure of interest rates.

quickly evaluate it and impound this new information into prices by buying or selling the securities. This is known as the *Efficient Market Hypothesis*. In its extreme form it argues that studying historical information (past series of prices being a subset) is of no value in detecting underpriced or overpriced securities. This view has naturally been challenged by technical analysts who make a living from predicting future price trends from past ones.

Changes in the prices of fixed income securities derive fundamentally from changes in interest rates. As interest rates rise, prices of fixed income securities fall and vice versa. However, prices do not all fall or rise by the same amount. The price sensitivity (or price risk) of fixed income securities to changes in interest rates is a function of several variables such as maturity, level of interest or coupon payment, call features, prepayment features, and so on. Quantifying the price sensitivity of a fixed income security to changes in interest rates is a key step in evaluating the potential risk of portfolios of such securities. More important, it is critical to the design and execution of *effective hedging*. The following chapter deals with the topic of risk and return with a special emphasis on fixed income securities.

10

Risk and Return

One of the major functions of securities markets is to facilitate the efficient allocation of scarce capital resources to various sectors within an economy. The prices of securities provide the requisite signals for the direction of the flow of capital. If the markets are to function effectively, security prices traded in them must closely reflect the risk and reward potential of the real investments the securities represent.

The idea that risks will be taken only if the potential for reward exists is so fundamental that it hardly bears repeating. However, the management of risks to accommodate the diverse needs of investors is an extremely important function and, hence, well worth exploring. This chapter deals with the issue of risk and return as it relates to investments in securities markets.

The first part of the chapter discusses risk and return in a conceptual framework. Concepts of expected return, standard deviation, and correlation are introduced together with their contribution in analyzing the risk-return trade-off. The second part of the chapter focuses on the risk-return characteristics of a particular class of securities, the fixed-income type, because some of the most successful futures markets are based on them. Here the true nature of *interest rate risk* is explored. The concepts of duration and convexity are explained, together with their contributions toward the measurement of interest rate risk. The potential role played by futures and options as a risk management tool is explored in the concluding section of the chapter.

THE CONCEPTUAL FRAMEWORK

An investment derives its return from two sources—income and price appreciation. This return is deemed risky if it deviates from its projected amount. Hence, the risk of an investment derives fundamentally from the unpredictability of either, or both of, the income from and the price at which the investment is sold.

The major difference between fixed income securities (typically debt-based instruments) and non-fixed income securities (typically equity-based instruments) is the predictability of the income portion of their returns. The income portion from fixed income securities (interest payments) is much more predictable than that from equity instruments (dividends). This predictability might seem on the surface to render a huge advantage to fixed income securities, such as bonds, over stocks as investment vehicles. However, predictability of income does not necessarily translate into predictability of return, because prices may change.

Return Defined

It is common to define return on an asset in the context of a single period. The return is comprised of an income portion and a price appreciation portion as shown in the following equation:

Return =

$$\frac{\text{Income} + (\text{End of Period Price} - \text{Beginning of Period Price})}{\text{Beginning of Period Price}}$$

For fixed income securities, such as bonds, it is straightforward to see that in a single period context risk derives primarily from the uncertainty of the *end of period price,* since *income* is well-defined as the promised interest on the bond.

Consider, for example, the returns on a 10%, 20-year U.S. government bond. To keep the calculation simple it is assumed that the bond pays interest annually and is purchased at par, $100 (i.e., its yield to maturity (ytm) is 10%). The return on the bond over the holding period of one year will depend on the level of interest rates prevailing at the end of the year. If interest rates rise, causing the price of the bond to fall to say $92, the return on the bond will be 2% (10% interest less 8% decline in price). The reverse will be true if interest rates rise. Table 10.1 displays the return for various levels of interest rates.

Table 10.1 reveals how the return on a bond is influenced by the level of interest rates prevailing at the end of the holding period. Note how the return is skewed toward positive values rather than negative values. This

TABLE 10.1   Return on a 10%, 20-Year U.S. Government Bond for a Holding Period of One Year

Interest Rates	Beginning Price	Ending Price	Interest Income	Return
8.00%	$100.00	$119.21	$10.00	29.21%
9.00	100.00	108.95	10.00	18.95
10.00	100.00	100.00	10.00	10.00
11.00	100.00	92.16	10.00	2.16
12.00	100.00	85.27	10.00	−4.73

Note: The ending price is calculated for a 19-year bond.

behavior should be expected because interest income acts like a buffer that counters losses from falling prices. In general, the larger the income portion from an investment is, the larger is the buffering action.

Concept of Expected Return

The concept of the *expected return* on an investment borrows from probability theory. Since the future level of interest rates can never be known with certainty at the time the investment is made, return on investment, by definition, is uncertain. However, any subjective forecast of future interest rates implies a forecast of future returns. This forecast is termed as the expected return on the investment. Given the probabilities of future interest rates, the expected return is computed as follows:

$$\text{Expected Return} = \Sigma \text{ Probability} \times \text{Return}$$

The expected return on the 10%, 20-year bond for a sample probability forecast of future interest rates is shown in Table 10.2.

Table 10.2 reveals an interesting facet regarding the expected return on fixed income securities. A quick calculation of the interest rates expected to prevail at the end of the holding period reveals that they are expected to remain at 10%. However, the expected return on the bond is 10.6145% (i.e., 0.6145% higher than the current level of 10%). Why? The answer is revealed in Table 10.1. Note how the change in the price of the bond is larger for a prespecified fall in interest rates compared to an identical rise in interest rates. This is an important property possessed by all fixed income securities, in general. It is called *convexity* and will be discussed in greater depth later in this chapter. At this point it suffices to say that the more convex a security is, the greater is its price change for a downward move in interest rates than for an upward move in interest rates.

TABLE 10.2 Calculation of Expected Return

Probability	Interest Rate	Bond Return	Probability × Bond Return
0.10	8.00%	29.21%	2.92100
0.15	9.00	18.95	2.84250
0.50	10.00	10.00	5.00000
0.15	11.00	2.16	0.32400
0.10	12.00	−4.73	−0.47300
Expected Return = Σ Probability × Return =			10.61450%

The expected return on an investment is useful because it provides a forecast of future investment performance. However, it fails to convey any information on the reliability (risk) of the forecast. Estimates of risk are often obtained through the *standard deviation of returns.*

Standard Deviation as a Measure of Risk

The standard deviation of returns conveys information on the extent to which returns may deviate from their expected returns. As such, it is useful as an estimate of the risk of an investment. Obviously, the greater the probability that the return may deviate from its forecasted value the greater is its risk and vice versa. Given the probability distribution of possible returns from an investment, the standard deviation is easily computed through the formula shown below:

$$\text{Standard Deviation of Return} = \Sigma \text{ Probability} \times [\text{Return} - \text{Expected Return}]^2$$

The calculation of the standard deviation of the returns for the 10%, 20-year U.S. government bond is shown in Table 10.3.

Interpretation of Standard Deviation

Intuitively, the standard deviation is a measure of the spread (or deviation) of possible returns on an investment from its expected return. The larger the standard deviation the greater is the possibility that the actual return will depart from its expected value. Since risk may be viewed as the extent to which actual returns deviate from expected returns, standard deviation is a useful way to quantify it.

A detailed interpretation of the standard deviation requires assumptions regarding the probability distribution of returns from which it is

TABLE 10.3 Calculation of Standard Deviation of Returns

Probability	Return	Return − Expected Return	(Return − Expected Return)²	Probability × (Return − Exp. Return)²
0.10	29.21%	18.60%	345.79	34.58
0.15	18.95	8.34	69.48	10.42
0.50	10.00	−0.61	0.38	0.19
0.15	2.16	−8.45	71.48	10.72
0.10	−4.73	−15.34	235.45	23.55

Variance = 79.46

Standard Deviation = $\sqrt{\text{Variance}}$ = 8.91%

calculated. If a *normal* probability distribution is assumed, a detailed assessment of the risk of the investment can be made. Figure 10.1 provides an example of such an assessment.

Figure 10.1 is a normal distribution of returns from the investment in the 10%, 20-year bond. The expected return is 10.6145% with a standard deviation of 8.91%. The normal distribution resembles a bell-shaped curve, perfectly symmetrical around the expected return. This implies that there is a 50% chance that returns may be greater than 10.6145% and a 50% chance that returns may be less than 10.6145%. The standard deviation for a normal distribution further implies that there is a 68% chance that the actual return will lie between plus or minus one standard

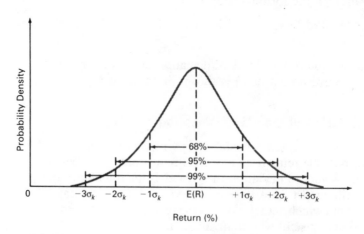

FIGURE 10.1 Normal probability distribution, with ranges.
E(R): Expected Return = 10.6145%   σ: Standard Deviation = 8.91%

deviation from the expected return, a 95% chance for it to lie between plus or minus two standard deviations, and a 99% chance it will lie between plus or minus three standard deviations from the expected return. In fact, many more inferences can be made with the use of tables on the standard normal distribution, which are readily available in any statistics textbook.

The expected return and standard deviation of returns are useful statistics because they enable one to quantify forecasts of investment performance together with the risk associated with those forecasts. More important, they permit comparisons of value across different investments on the basis of risk and return. For example, it is well acknowledged that Treasury bills are less risky than Treasury bonds, which are themselves less risky than common stock. If the investment performance of each of these classes of securities is looked at over the last 15 years, the risk-return trade-off is seen in Table 10.4.

TABLE 10.4 Returns on the Standard and Poor's (S&P) 500 Index, U.S. Government Bonds, and U.S Treasury Bills (1968–1987)

	Annual Returns		
Year	S&P 500 Index	U.S. Government Bonds	U.S. Government T-bills
1973	−14.67%	−1.09%	6.91%
1974	−26.46	4.33	8.02
1975	37.21	9.19	5.78
1976	23.85	16.77	5.08
1977	−7.18	−0.66	5.14
1978	6.57	−1.17	7.22
1979	18.42	−1.22	10.38
1980	32.41	−3.96	11.25
1981	−4.91	1.88	14.72
1982	21.41	40.36	10.53
1983	22.51	0.69	8.80
1984	6.27	15.54	9.78
1985	32.17	30.96	7.73
1986	18.62	24.14	6.08
1987	5.25	−2.67	5.12
Average Return	11.43	8.87	8.17
Standard Deviation	17.95	13.28	2.67

Risk and Return in a Portfolio Context

The concepts of expected return and the standard deviation are useful in comparing value across different classes of securities. However, they can be used to maximum advantage in the construction of portfolios of securities with prespecified risk-return characteristics. Creation of such portfolios requires additional information on the price behavior of the securities, specifically, how their prices move with respect to each other.

Security prices do not move in a perfectly synchronous manner. The fundamental reason for this nonsynchronous price behavior is that securities are structurally different from each other in terms of the timing, certainty, and size of their cash flow receipts. These structural differences cause security prices to respond differently to new information. The relative behavior of security prices to new information and the extent to which that behavior is predictable have formed the basis of portfolio theory. The key to understanding this theory is the concept of *correlation*.

Concept of Correlation

Correlation measures the degree to which security prices move with respect to each other. Two securities are said to be perfectly correlated if given the price change of one security, the price change of the other is known with certainty. Correlation between two securities is said to be perfectly positive if their prices move up or down perfectly in sync. They do not necessarily have to move up or down by identical amounts, only that given the change in price of one, the change in price of the other is known. The securities are perfectly negatively correlated if their price movements are opposite to each other. Once again, the upward movement in one security completely defines the downward movement in the other security. By extension, if predictability of price movement is less than perfect, correlation is less than perfect—positive or negative. The correlation between any two securities is a measurable quantity and is defined as the *correlation coefficient*. It lies between $+1$ and -1. A formula to compute it is available in any introductory statistics text.

Correlation is a powerful concept and extremely useful in portfolio construction because it allows for the possibility of risk reduction in portfolios without affecting expected return. Its risk reduction potential is seen in the following example where two securities are combined into a portfolio whose expected return and standard deviation are calculated for different values of the correlation coefficient between the two securities.

	Security A	Security B
Expected Return	10%	12%
Standard Deviation	8%	10%

Suppose W_A and W_B are the proportions invested in each security, where $W_A + W_B = 1$; then the expected return and standard deviation of the portfolio is given by:

$$E(R) = W_A E(R_A) + W_B E(R_B)$$

where E( ) is the expected value operator;

$$\sigma(R) = W_A^2 \, \sigma^2(A) + W_B^2 \, \sigma^2(B) + 2W_A W_B \, \rho_{A,B}\sigma_A\sigma_B$$

where σ( ) is the standard deviation operator

$\rho_{A,B}$ is the correlation between A and B

Table 10.5 uses the above formulas to compute the expected return and standard deviation of an equally weighted ($W_A = W_B = 0.5$) portfolio of securities A and B for different values of the correlation coefficient.

Table 10.5 illustrates the role played by the correlation coefficient between securities in affecting the standard deviation of return of a portfolio comprising the two securities. As the correlation coefficient declines so does the risk of the portfolio, as defined by the portfolio's standard deviation. Maximum risk reduction results when the correlation coefficient is -1. Just as important, the correlation coefficient has no effect on the expected return on the portfolio; it only affects its risk. Of course, if one chooses to weight the portfolio differently, return will also be affected. In fact, an *efficient frontier* can be drawn by weighting the two securities differently in portfolios. The efficient frontier represents combinations of the securities that provide the highest level of return for any given level of risk, or alternatively, the lowest level of risk for any given level of return.

TABLE 10.5 Expected Return and Standard Deviation of an Equally Weighted Portfolio of Securities A and B for Different Correlation Coefficients

Correlation Coefficient	Expected Return	Standard Deviation
1.00	11.00%	9.00%
0.60	11.00	8.06
0.20	11.00	7.00
0.00	11.00	6.40
−0.20	11.00	5.74
−0.60	11.00	4.12
−1.00	11.00	1.00

The entire discussion of risk and return so far has dealt with the issue in the context of a single period. This is a useful starting point in a more complete analysis of the topic. However, the major shortcoming of any single period type analysis is the extraordinary emphasis on price change as a major component of the total risk of a security. This shortcoming could be a serious one for fixed income securities, particularly if the securities are to be held as long-term investments. Hence, the remainder of this chapter focuses on the risk-return characteristics of this particular class of securities.

RISK AND RETURN IN FIXED INCOME SECURITIES

The predictability of the cash flow from fixed income securities is what makes them attractive investment vehicles for inclusion in many portfolios. At the same time this predictability can adversely affect investment performance by generating uncertainty over the value of the portfolios as interest rates change. Futures markets are useful in managing this uncertainty. Effective use of these markets, however, requires a thorough understanding of how a changing interest rate environment affects the performance of fixed income securities, and an understanding of how to measure the risk associated with performance.

Risk in Fixed Income Securities

A rising interest rate environment clearly has a negative impact on the prices of fixed income securities. However, does this fact necessarily translate into fixed income securities being poor investment vehicles in a rising interest rate environment? The answer is, not necessarily. The reason is that although higher interest rates will almost always lower prices of fixed income securities, they simultaneously imply that the interim cash flows from the securities can be reinvested at higher rates of return. Depending on the length of the investment horizon and the size of the interim cash flows, the reinvestment income will partially or wholly offset the fall in prices. This suggests that when evaluating the attractiveness of a particular fixed income security for inclusion in a portfolio, or when one is considering hedging it, the security's true *interest rate risk* must be properly measured, especially with respect to the investor's goals and the investment horizon.

Interest rate risk may be viewed as consisting of two components: price risk and reinvestment risk.

Price Risk

Price risk is the risk of price change due to changing interest rates. It is commonly observed in the bond market. As interest rates rise, bond prices fall and vice versa. The price sensitivity to changes in interest rates is not the same for all bonds because bonds differ in terms of the coupon payment and maturity. In general, the greater the maturity of the bond or the larger the size of its coupon payment, the greater is its price change for a given change in interest rates. Measuring this price change is useful in evaluating the price risks of entire portfolios and in designing *hedge ratios* to effectively manage the risk of price change. It is easily computed and is commonly referred to as the *value of an 01* (Val01) or the *price value of a basis point* (PVBP). The Val01 or PVBP represents the price change in the bond for a one basis point change in the bond's yield. For example, the Val01 for a 10% coupon bond with 20 years to maturity that is currently selling at par (ytm = 10%) is computed as follows:

$$\text{Val01} = \text{Price (@ ytm} = 10\%) - \text{Price (@ ytm} = 10.01\%)$$
$$= \$0.08573 \text{ per } \$100 \text{ of face value}$$
$$= \$85.73 \text{ per } \$100,000 \text{ of face value}$$

Table 10.6 provides the Val01 for several bonds for face values of $100,000. Table 10.6 reveals the coupon effect and the maturity effect on the changes in prices of bonds for a one basis point change in interest rates. Note the larger Val01 for the 12% coupon bond compared to the 10% coupon bond for any given maturity. Also note how the price change of a bond, given its coupon rate, declines as the bond ages toward its maturity date.

TABLE 10.6 Val01 for Bonds Differing in Coupon and Maturity

Bond	Price	ytm	Val01
10%, 5 Year	$100,000	10.00%	$38.60
10%, 10 Year	100,000	10.00	62.28
10%, 20 Year	100,000	10.00	85.73
10%, 30 Year	100,000	10.00	94.57
12%, 5 Year	107,722	10.00	40.47
12%, 10 Year	112,462	10.00	67.56
12%, 20 Year	117,159	10.00	97.47
12%, 30 Year	118,929	10.00	110.43

Reinvestment Risk

As useful as the measure of the price risk of a bond may be, it is essentially a static measure, because it is an estimate of the price change of the bond for a given change in interest rates at a point in time. If bonds are held in portfolios as long-term investments, statistics such as the Val01 or PVBP will tend to overstate the true interest rate risk of a bond, especially if the investment horizon is several years in the future. One reason for this was mentioned earlier—the effect of higher reinvestment income in a rising interest rate environment. Just as important, price risk declines as a bond ages toward its maturity date. By introducing an investment horizon as a variable into the bond selection process, the role played by reinvestment income (or reinvestment risk) must be considered. The trade-off between price risk and reinvestment risk is best explored through an example.

Consider the purchase of a U.S. government bond with a 10% coupon maturing in 20 years. The bond has a face value of $100,000 and is selling at par. The investment horizon is assumed to be eight years. The terminal value of this investment at the end of eight years will consist of:

     1. Reinvestment of the coupons over eight years.

plus 2. Price of the bond in year eight.

where:

Reinvestment Income   = Future value of an annuity of $5,000 per six months for eight years at the reinvestment rate.

Price of the Bond   = Present value of $5,000 per six months for (in year eight)   the remaining 12 years, plus the present value of $100,000 discounted at the reinvestment rate.

In the computation of the reinvestment income and the price of the bond in year eight it is implicitly assumed that the current yield curve is flat, and any shift in rates that takes place occurs through a parallel shift in the yield curve. This assumption is made only for expositional purposes. In principle, any shape of the yield curve, as well as yield curve reshapings, can be analyzed through simulations.

Table 10.7 displays the terminal value of a $100,000 investment in the bond at the end of the investment horizon (eight years) under different interest rate scenarios. The rate of return is computed as follows:

$$\text{Rate of Return} = \left\{ \left[\frac{\text{Terminal Value}}{\text{Purchase Price}} \right]^{\frac{1}{2 \times \text{Horizon (years)}}} - 1 \right\} \times 2$$

Several noteworthy points are revealed in Table 10.7.

1. The fluctuation in the rate of return over the investment horizon is much less than that of interest rates themselves.
2. Declining prices due to rising interest rates are partially or wholly offset by reinvestment income. Thus, price risk is offset by reinvestment risk.
3. The average return and standard deviation of return for the eight-year investment horizon are both much less than for a one-year investment horizon. (Compare Table 10.7 with Table 10.1.)

The natural ability of bonds, or any fixed income security, to offset price risk against reinvestment risk is an important property and is used extensively to immunize fixed income portfolios against changes in interest rates. This ability is captured in the concept of *duration*.

DURATION

Duration of a bond is measured in years. From an economic point of view, it is the number of years it would take for the (additional) reinvestment income of a bond to exactly offset its change in price, thus leaving its target rate of return intact. Its potential to bond portfolio managers is immediately seen, since managers typically have to deal with well-specified horizons and target portfolio returns. Constructing a portfolio with a duration equal to the investment horizon is a much easier task than forecasting future trends in interest rates.

TABLE 10.7 Terminal Value at the End of an Eight-Year Horizon of a $100,000 Investment in a 10%, 20-Year U.S. Government Bond under Various Interest Rate Scenarios

Interest Rates	Reinvestment Income	Bond Price (Year 8)	Terminal Value	Rate of Return
8.00%	$109,123	$115,247	$224,370	10.36%
9.00	113,597	107,248	220,845	10.15
10.00	118,287	100,000	218,287	10.00
11.00	123,206	93,424	216,630	9.90
12.00	128,363	87,450	215,813	9.85
			Average Return	10.05%
			Standard Deviation	0.19

Duration Defined

The duration of a security is the *weighted average life* of the security. Unlike maturity, which only identifies the time to the final cash flow from the security, duration recognizes the existence of all interim cash flows. The duration of a security is sometimes referred to as the security's half-life (the concept of a half-life is borrowed from physics, in which it is defined as the length of time it takes a radioactive substance to shed half its initial radioactive content).

The concept of duration was developed in 1938 by Frederic Macaulay, who was attempting to obtain a more meaningful measure of the life of a bond as it related to changes in its price. The formula he developed is known as *Macaulay duration*.

$$\text{Macaulay Duration} = [PV(C_1) \times 1 + PV(C_2) \times 2 \ldots \ldots \ldots$$
$$+ PV(C_N) \times N]/P = \Sigma\, W_i \times i$$

where: $PV(C_i)$ is the present value of the cash flow to be received in period "i."

$W_i = PV(C_i)/Price$ is the weight to be applied to period "i."
P = Price of the security.

The formula is easily applied and is shown for calculating the duration of a 10% coupon, 10-year bond in Table 10.8. The bond is assumed to be selling at par. The discount rate used in computing the present value of the cash flows is the yield to maturity on the bond, adjusted for the periodicity of the cash flow payments. For a bond it will be ytm/2.

The duration of a coupon bond is always less than its maturity. It is very rare to find any security with interim cash flows, such as coupon-bearing bonds and mortgage-backed securities, to have durations of more than 10 years, no matter how long their maturity may be. This is because their discounting process causes the weights of distant periods to be so small that they have negligible influence in the computation. The only securities with potentially high durations are zero coupon bonds, since their durations must equal their maturity. This is true because a zero coupon bond has only a single cash flow to be received at maturity, and the weight of this cash flow must be one. All discount-type securities have durations equal to their maturity.

Duration as a Measure of Volatility

Although duration is measured in years and may seem to have little to do with volatility, a slight transformation of it, called *modified duration*, leads to a useful measure of a security's volatility.

Modified Duration = Macaulay Duration/[1 + Yield/# of cash flows per year]

Hence, for the above bond, its modified duration is 6.2311 (6.5427/1.05). The modified duration of a security is always less than its Macaulay duration.

Knowing a security's modified duration, its price sensitivity to changes in interest rates is easily determined. It is given by:

$$\frac{\text{Change in Price}}{\text{Price}} = - \text{Modified Duration} \times \text{Change in Interest Rates}$$

Multiplying both sides of the above equation by the price of the security yields *dollar duration*, which is the dollar change in price for a given

TABLE 10.8 Calculation of the Duration of a 10%, 10-Year Bond Selling at Par

Period (i)	Cashflow (C_i)	PV(Cashflow) ($PV(C_i)$)	Weight (W_i)	Weight (W_i) × Period ($_i$)
1	5	4.7619	0.0476	0.0476
2	5	4.5351	0.0454	0.0907
3	5	4.3192	0.0432	0.1296
4	5	4.1135	0.0411	0.1645
5	5	3.9176	0.0392	0.1959
6	5	3.7311	0.0373	0.2239
7	5	3.5534	0.0355	0.2487
8	5	3.3842	0.0338	0.2707
9	5	3.2230	0.0322	0.2901
10	5	3.0696	0.0307	0.3070
11	5	2.9234	0.0292	0.3216
12	5	2.7842	0.0278	0.3341
13	5	2.6516	0.0265	0.3447
14	5	2.5253	0.0253	0.3535
15	5	2.4051	0.0241	0.3608
16	5	2.2906	0.0229	0.3665
17	5	2.1815	0.0218	0.3709
18	5	2.0776	0.0208	0.3740
19	5	1.9787	0.0198	0.3759
20	105	39.5734	0.3957	7.9147

$$\sum_i \text{Weight (i)} \times \text{Period (i)} = 13.0853 \text{ periods}$$

$$\text{Duration} = 6.5427 \text{ years}$$

change in interest rates. It is identical to the Val01 (or PVBP) if the change in interest rates is one basis point.

Knowledge of the durations of securities is useful because it allows for a comparison of the relative risk of the securities which may differ in terms of the size and timing of their cash flows. For example, a 10 basis point change in yield for the 10%, 10-year bond will result in a percentage price change of 0.6231% (6.2311 × .10%). If the bond was a 20-year bond, its percentage price change for the same 10 basis point change in yield would be 0.82%. Table 10.9 shows the percentage price changes for several bonds with different durations.

Interpreting Duration

It is true that duration is a useful measure of volatility as seen in Table 10.9. However, one must be aware of the many assumptions underlying the computation of its value. Any significant change in these assumptions will also significantly alter its value. For example, duration suffers from the same assumption of a flat yield curve as does yield to maturity; that is, all interest rates (short and long) are equal. The calculation further assumes that any change in interest rates will be constant across the maturity spectrum. Neither of these assumptions are generally true. Most important though, duration will change as interest rates change. Hence, any estimate of volatility derived from duration is valid only to the extent that interest rates do not change by a significant amount. As interest rates rise duration will fall because of the smaller weights in the duration calculation. The drop in duration could be significant if interest rates drop sharply. Duration also changes with the passage of time. One would fully

TABLE 10.9   Price Changes (%) as a Function of Duration and Yield Changes

Bond	Price	Modified Duration	Price Change (%) Yield Change (Basis Points)			
			10	20	30	40
U.S. 10%, 5 Year	$100,000	3.6854	−0.37%	−0.74%	−1.11%	−1.47%
U.S. 10%, 10 Year	100,000	6.2310	−0.62	−1.25	−1.87	−2.49
U.S. 10%, 20 Year	100,000	8.1891	−0.82	−1.64	−2.46	−3.28
U.S. 10%, 30 Year	100,000	9.0344	−0.90	−1.81	−2.71	−3.61
U.S. 12%, 5 Year	107,722	3.5874	−0.36	−0.72	−1.08	−1.43
U.S. 12%, 10 Year	112,462	5.7374	−0.57	−1.15	−1.72	−2.29
U.S. 12%, 20 Year	117,159	7.9472	−0.79	−1.59	−2.38	−3.18
U.S. 12%, 30 Year	118,929	8.8700	−0.89	−1.77	−2.66	−3.55

expect duration to fall as a security ages toward its maturity date. However, it does not decline at the same rate as does maturity. Maturity declines faster. Because the maturity of an instrument must fall with the passage of time, if interest rates fall simultaneously, duration could very well rise, at least temporarily.

Duration of a Portfolio

One very useful property of duration is that it is additive; that is, the duration of a portfolio is the weighted average of the durations of the individual securities in the portfolio, with the weights being the proportion of total funds invested in each security. For example, a $10-million portfolio with $4 million invested in one security with a duration of five years and $6 million invested in another security with a duration of eight years would have a weighted average duration of 6.8 years $(5 \times .4 + 8 \times .6)$.

It should be pointed out that although two portfolios may have the same weighted average duration (implying they have the same price risk), one must realize that the price one is talking about is really instantaneous price risk, that is, the price change for a sudden change in interest rates. Depending on the durations of the securities in the portfolios, the passage of time could significantly alter the durations of the portfolios and, therefore, their price risks. For example, it is possible to construct two portfolios with the same duration from assets with widely differing durations. One portfolio could consist of securities with durations of one year and seven years. The second portfolio could consist of securities having a four-year duration. The passage of time will significantly alter the duration of the first portfolio (and its price risk) compared to the second portfolio. The important point here is that one must be careful in giving too much emphasis to averages. A single average number fails to reflect the extremes from which the average is derived.

Despite the assumptions underlying its calculations, duration clearly possesses a huge advantage over maturity in describing the price sensitivity of a security to changes in interest rates. The advantage derives fundamentally from the recognition that the size and timing of the interim cash flows play a significant role in determining the size of the price change for any given change in interest rates. However, the estimate of price change that duration provides is valid only for a small change in interest rates. As mentioned earlier, if the change in interest rates is large, duration itself changes, and so does its estimate of volatility. The question that naturally crops up is, How large is large where interest rate changes are concerned? The answer is provided through the concept of *convexity*.

Convexity

To use an analogy to describe convexity, one can say that if duration represents velocity then convexity represents acceleration. Duration defines the percentage change in price for a small change in interest rates. Convexity defines the speed at which the percentage price changes occur. Alternatively stated, convexity measures the rate of change of duration as interest rates change. One can visualize convexity conceptually. A price/yield curve is typically sloping. The steepness of the slope varies along the curve. The greater the curvature, the greater the convexity.

The value added by convexity over that of duration is seen when interest rates change by a large amount. By recognizing that some securities change in price much faster than others as interest rates change, knowing a security's convexity provides valuable information to accurately estimate the price change. The best example of the effect of convexity is seen in comparing the performance of mortgage-backed securities to those of coupon bonds in a falling interest rate environment. If interest rates fall dramatically, a homeowner may prepay his or her old mortgage prior to maturity and take out a new mortgage at a lower rate. This phenomenon works to the disadvantage of the holder of high coupon-bearing mortgage-backed securities because prepayments force reinvestment of the proceeds at lower interest rates. The "capping-out" or "stabilization" of prices of mortgage-backed securities as rates fall is a reflection of this prepayment phenomenon. No such capping-out is seen for regular coupon-bearing noncallable bonds. If interest rates rise, on the other hand, there is no incentive for the homeowner to prepay and so mortgage-backed securities display price behavior similar to securities that do not allow prepayment. This behavior of high coupon mortgage-backed securities is a reflection of their low (or even negative) convexity. Negative convexity means that prices could actually fall as rates dropped.

Just like duration, convexity is easily measurable. A formula to compute it is shown in Appendix B. Rules of thumb regarding the convexity of securities are:

1. Longer the maturity—greater the convexity.
2. Smaller the coupon—greater the convexity. Zero coupon bonds are highly convex.
3. Prepayments, as in the case of mortgage-backed securities or callable bonds, lower convexity.

Application of Convexity

Knowledge of a bond's convexity leads to a more accurate estimate of the percentage change in its price than an estimate given only by its duration. Specifically, the percentage price change is given by:

$$\frac{\text{Change in Price}}{\text{Price}} = \begin{aligned}&-[\text{Modified Duration}] \times [\text{Change in Yield}]\\&+ 1/2[\text{Convexity}] \times [\text{Yield Change}]^2\end{aligned}$$

The convexity of the 10%, 20-year U.S. government bond selling at par is computed as 117.47. Its duration is 8.1891. Using the preceding formula, the percentage price change in the price of the bond for a 100 basis point drop (-1% or -0.01 change in yield) in interest rates is:

$$= - [8.1891 \times (-.01)] + 1/2(117.47)(-0.1)^2$$
$$= 0.0819 + 0.0059$$
$$= 0.0878 \ (8.78\%)$$

Hence, the 8.78% rise in the price of the bond comprises 8.19% due to duration and 0.59% due to convexity. The contribution of convexity to the overall percentage price change is small. However, its contribution increases with the size of the interest rate change. Table 10.10 provides estimates of the percentage price change for larger changes in interest rates.

Hedging Implications

Hedging is a process that is intimately related to risk management. Typically, hedging vehicles such as futures, options, or combinations of both are used for such a purpose. The role played by the hedging vehicles can be seen within the conceptual risk-return framework as well as in the management of risk of fixed income securities.

In the conceptual framework, the role of correlation between securities is critical in realizing risk reduction. Risk can be sharply reduced or possibly even eliminated through the introduction of securities negatively correlated with those in the portfolio. By taking positions in futures and

TABLE 10.10 Contributions of Duration and Convexity to Percentage Price Changes for a 10%, 20-Year U.S. Government Bond Selling at Par

Yield Change	Percentage Price Change		
	Due to Duration	Due to Convexity	Total Change
-4.00%	32.76%	9.40%	42.15%
-3.00	24.57	5.29	29.85
-1.00	8.19	0.59	8.78
0.00	0.00	0.00	0.00
1.00	-8.19	0.59	-7.60
2.00	-16.38	2.35	-14.03
3.00	-24.57	5.29	-19.28
4.00	-32.76	9.40	-23.36

options opposite to the securities held, the effect of negative correlation is artificially introduced. In so doing, the risk-return characteristics of a portfolio can be altered dramatically according to the specifications of the portfolio manager. Just as important, this risk reduction can be accomplished at a much lower cost than can be achieved with just the cash securities.

In managing the risk of fixed income securities it is essential to obtain as accurate an estimate as possible of the price sensitivity of the securities to changes in interest rates. For small changes in interest rates, duration provides an accurate estimate of price change. For larger changes in rates, the contribution from convexity needs be added to the contribution from duration. Taken together, the price change estimates provided by duration and convexity play a major role in the decision of how large or small a position needs to be taken in the hedging vehicles to provide for an effective price offset.

11
Yield Curves

A few years ago a young man fresh out of college walked into the office of an older gentleman who was revered for his knowledge of the government securities markets. The young man nervously explained that he had become interested in the T-bill futures market and wanted to learn how to trade them. How, he asked the older gentleman, should he learn to identify opportunities?

The older gentleman sat and looked at the floor and said nothing. The young man began to feel embarrassed. Just as he was about to repeat the question, fearing the old fellow hadn't heard him or had forgotten it already, the old gentleman looked up and said, "Study yield curves."

The young man rose, thanked him, and left feeling disappointed. Nine months and $25,000 of profit later, the young man realized how valuable the old man's advice had been. For indeed the yield curve reveals all.

LOOK AT RETURN

If you want to do an intelligent job trading interest rate futures, spend your time studying yield curves.

In the fixed income securities market, yield refers to the annual rate of return from holding the security. It is determined by interrelating the interest rate, the price paid, and the remaining life of the security. For example, if you loan someone $100 for one year at 7% interest, the yield on that investment is 7%. If you paid $100 for a $100 face value bond with a coupon of 8% maturing in one year, the yield would be 8%. However, the picture in bonds, or any other debt instrument competitively

123

bought and sold in the marketplace, is complicated by the fact that their prices change. If you bought the same $100, 8% bond for say, $95, its yield would be approximately 13.26%, or the sum of the 8% coupon and 5.26% (5/95 = 0.0526). Yield adjusted in this way for market price and time to maturity is called *yield to maturity*. This is the figure plotted on the yield curve.

Yields are important because they reflect interest rates in the various money and capital markets. These interest rates reflect powerful linkages between the money market, the bond market, the stock market, the mortgage market, the commodity market, and the foreign exchange market. Money moves rapidly from one market to another seeking the highest possible return. A *yield curve* refers to the shape of the line you get when you plot yields of various Treasury securities, or any other homogeneous group of securities, against their various maturities. When a number of issues are plotted on a graph with yield on the y axis and maturity on the x axis, a pattern emerges from the placement of the dots. A smooth curve drawn such that the dots are evenly distributed on either side of the curve reveals the yield curve. Figure 11.1 displays the yield curve obtained from data on U.S. Treasury issues on October 1, 1990.

UNDERSTANDING YIELD CURVES

There are several reasons why one should understand yield curves. First, it focuses one's attention on the cash market. Cash market activity provides clues to pricing relationships in the futures markets. Second, it helps one to view securities by their relative values. Hence, the yield curve becomes the general standard by which to measure individual value. Because of the inverse yield/price relationship for fixed income securities, securities with yields above the yield curve are relatively underpriced, whereas those below the yield curve are relatively overpriced. If the yield on a particular security appears to be sharply out of line with other securities of similar maturity, it may be a candidate for a buy/sell decision. However, an explanation of this seemingly aberrant behavior usually exists. For example, well-*seasoned* issues trade closer to the yield curve than less well seasoned issues. Seasoning refers to how long the issue has been trading actively. A well-seasoned issue trades in a more active and liquid market. Also, differences in coupon rates for bonds of similar maturity are subject to different degrees of interest rate risk. Given this risk factor, one would expect a divergence between yields on bonds with similar maturity but different coupons.

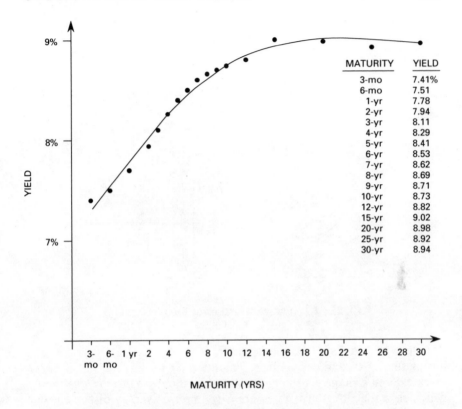

MATURITY	YIELD
3-mo	7.41%
6-mo	7.51
1-yr	7.78
2-yr	7.94
3-yr	8.11
4-yr	8.29
5-yr	8.41
6-yr	8.53
7-yr	8.62
8-yr	8.69
9-yr	8.71
10-yr	8.73
12-yr	8.82
15-yr	9.02
20-yr	8.98
25-yr	8.92
30-yr	8.94

FIGURE 11.1   Yield curve for U.S. Treasuries (October 1, 1990).

The Different Shapes of the Yield Curve

It is not sufficient to know how yield curves are derived. One also needs to know why they take on different shapes. Figure 11.2 shows several different shapes of the yield curves that have been observed historically.

Panel A displays the so-called *normal* or upward-sloping yield curve where short-term rates are lower than long-term rates. Traders refer to this as a *positive carry* market. One can borrow short term and lend long term to earn the spread between the two rates. The usual explanation for the upward-sloping shape is that lenders demand an additional premium or higher interest rates in compensation for tying up their money for longer periods. The reasons for the additional premium vary from inflation, which reduces the purchasing power of money, to higher interest rate risk, to the lower liquidity and marketability of the longer maturities.

Panels B, C, and D describe yield curve shapes that confound the explanations given for the normal upward-sloping curve. The downward

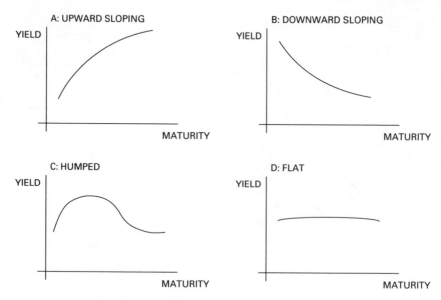

FIGURE 11.2 Different shapes of the yield curve.

sloping curve in Panel B, for instance, was observed at several times during the 1970s and early 1980s. Traders refer to it as a *negative carry market.* Such a shape is usually explained by the *expectations hypothesis,* which says that long-term rates are a geometric average of the current short-term rate and expectations of future short-term interest rates. Hence, if the current short-term rates are high but are expected to decline over time, current long-term rates should be below current short-term rates. Panel C (humped yield curve) and Panel D (flat yield curve) are unusual and are more reflective of the transition of the yield curve from a downward-sloping curve to upward sloping, or vice versa.

Shifts in the Yield Curve

Yield curves not only change shape but also shift from one level to another. This suggests that predicting the final shape of the yield curve is not in itself sufficient to generate trading profits. The level must also be predicted. Figure 11.3 provides an example in point.

Suppose the yield curve is presently described as curve A, which is downward sloping, that is, short-term rates are higher than long-term rates. It is further believed that over time the curve will revert to its normal upward-sloping shape with long-term rates being higher than short-term rates. Curves B and C represent two possible scenarios where the final upward-sloping shape is finally realized. However, the realization

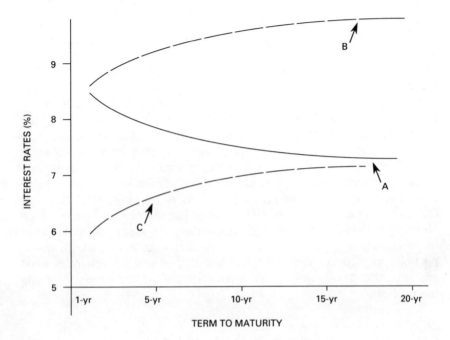

FIGURE 11.3   Shift in yield curve.

of the final upward-sloping shape was the result of sharply contrasting events. In curve B it was long-term rates that rose relative to short-term rates. In curve C short-term rates dropped relative to long-term rates. It is easy to see that profiting from either of these final shapes would have required significantly different trading strategies.

Interest Rate Volatility

Interest rates constantly change. Even though short-term interest rates are generally more volatile than long-term interest rates, the price effects of this difference in volatility are substantially different for securities of varying maturities. Long-term securities show much greater swings in prices for a given change in interest rates than short-term securities.

Perhaps the best way to show the relationship between price change and interest rate changes is to consider a bond with one year to run paying a 6% coupon and priced at par. If the yield rises to 7%, the price of the bond falls to 99.05 (i.e., 99$2/32$). If the yield drops to 5%, its price rises to 100.96 (100$31/32$).

Thus, a swing of 1% in either direction causes an approximately 1% change in price. The reason the change in price is not exactly 1% is because of the compounding effect of the semiannual coupon payments.

Now, if the bond had five years to run, a 1% rise in yield would cause the price to drop to 95.84 (95^{27}/$_{32}$). The change in price approaches but does not equal (again because of compounding effects) five percentage points, which would be expected by multiplying the one-year result five times.

In principle, the longer the maturity of the bond the greater the price change for a given change in interest rates. One useful measure of the relative volatility of bonds with different maturities is known as the *yield value of* ^{1}/$_{32}$. It measures the change in yield required for a ^{1}/$_{32}$ change in price. Table 11.1 provides values for a ^{1}/$_{32}$ for bonds of different maturities.

Table 11.1 reveals how large the relative changes in yield must be to effect identical changes in prices for bonds of varying maturities. For example, the yield on a 1-year bond would have to change by more than 10 times that of the 30-year bond to produce the identical (^{1}/$_{32}$) change in price. Hence, any decision to alter the composition of a fixed income portfolio as a consequence of a forecast of changing interest rates must recognize the varying interest rate sensitivities of the securities composing the portfolio.

Deriving Forward Rates from the Yield Curve

The yield curve is often used as a predictor of interest rates. In fact, some people claim it is a better predictor of interest rates than some of the widely publicized econometric models, including those used at the Fed. The logic underlying the predictive value of the yield curve is simple. Since investing over a given horizon can be achieved by either purchasing a long-term security or a sequence of short-term securities, it is possible to extract implied (forward) rates from the yield curve. For example,

TABLE 11.1   Yield Value of ^{1}/$_{32}$ Change in Price

Bond	Yield Value of a ^{1}/$_{32}$ (Basis Points)
10%, 1 Year	3.360
10%, 2 Year	1.762
10%, 5 Year	0.808
10%, 10 Year	0.502
10%, 20 Year	0.364
10%, 30 Year	0.330

Note: All bonds are priced at par.

suppose the yields on a one-year and two-year Treasury security are 10% and 10.25%, respectively. The implied forward rate on a one-year security to be purchased one year hence is obtained as follows:

$$\text{Implied Forward Rate} \atop \text{(1-Year Treasury)} = \frac{[1 + 2\text{-Year Rate}]^2}{[1 + 1\text{-Year Rate}]^1} - 1$$

$$= \frac{[1 + .1025]^2}{[1 + .10]^1} - 1 = .1050 \ (10.50\%)$$

The 10.5% may be viewed as the market's consensus of a one-year interest rate expected to prevail next year based on current information. Naturally, as new information arrives interest rates will change and so will the forward rate. However, being able to compute implied forward rates from the yield curve is useful, particularly when compared to quotes obtained from an independent source such as the interest rate futures markets. As we shall see later, the futures markets can be used in conjunction with the cash market to exploit unjustifiably wide interest rate differentials.

THE FUTURES YIELD CURVE

Just as one can develop a yield curve from issues traded in the cash market, a yield curve can be obtained from the interest rate futures markets. If futures prices are viewed as prices expected to prevail at the time of delivery, then a yield curve derived from futures prices can be viewed as the embodiment of yields expected to prevail in the future.

The major difference in constructing a yield curve from futures prices is that one must use data from several different futures markets (T-bills, T-notes, T-bonds, etc.). When constructing the curve it is important to use the same contract month for each futures instrument, because each different contract month represents a different future time period and therefore reflects different expectations. If one mixed different contract months (e.g., June and December) in the same yield curve, one would be mixing apples with oranges by mingling expectations for June with those for December. For example, a yield curve expected to prevail in December 1990 could be constructed from the following futures prices (yields) on October 9, 1990 (see Table 11.2). For comparison purposes the cash market yields are also displayed. It is apparent from Table 11.2 that if futures yields reflect expectations, then the short-term rate (90-day T-bills) is expected to fall, and the intermediate and long-term rates are expected to rise between October and December.

TABLE 11.2   Futures Yields for December
1990 Contracts

| Futures Contract | December 1990 | | Cash Yield |
	Futures Price	Futures Yield	
90-Day T-bill*	93.18	7.034%	7.21%
2-Year T-note	100¹/₃₂	7.982	7.92
5-Year T-note	98⁴/₃₂	8.460	8.46
10-Year T-note	94⁷/₃₂	8.884	8.84
15-Year T-bond	89⁵/₃₂	9.195	9.07

* The yield for the 90-day T-bill is the bond-equivalent yield.

The Strip Curve

Another useful curve that can be obtained from futures prices is the *strip curve*. A strip curve is obtained, for example, from a series of successive T-bill futures contracts. If you were to purchase the December, March, June, and September T-bill futures contracts, you would own a one-year strip. Owning a one-year strip would be equivalent to owning a one-year T-bill purchased in December, because the series of futures contracts provides the owner the rights to purchase a 90-day T-bill every three months. The four separate bills would cover a total maturity span of 12 months.

To obtain the equivalent coverage, you simply take delivery on the December futures, thus receiving a 90-day T-bill that matures in March. Money from the maturing March bill is then used to take delivery on the March futures contract, which is a 90-day T-bill maturing in June. Similarly, delivery is taken on the June and September contracts to realize a one-year investment.

The Strip as a Measure of Value

Knowing the value of a strip provides a benchmark against which to measure the value of an alternative investment. For example, suppose the Treasury is auctioning 360-day bills and you are considering entering the auction. You could compare the price you would need to pay in the auction with the price you would pay if you bought the nearby cash bill plus three consecutive futures contracts; you could then select the cheaper alternative.

To illustrate, assume that on September 15 you can purchase a 360-day T-bill at a yield of 7.07%. Assume also that a futures strip is selling at yields shown as follows. All yields are bond equivalent yields.

Cash bill maturing in December	7.36%
December T-bill futures	7.03%
March T-bill futures	6.80%
June T-bill futures	6.94%

The preceding strip would yield approximately 7.03%, that is four basis points below the cash 360-day T-bill. Even though the strip yields less than the cash bill by straightforward comparison of yields, it has a major advantage in terms of flexibility. Since you are always carrying an actuals position on the front end of the strip, you can move from T-bills to CDs or Eurodollars or whatever instrument will provide the best short-term yield while keeping the latter part of the strip intact. This flexibility provides the opportunity to increase the yield above the guaranteed yield of 7.03%. The price paid for this flexibility is the up-front cost of four basis points (below the 7.07% yield of the cash bill).

The risks of the strip strategy are minor but need to be considered nevertheless. If rates change significantly, you could receive margin calls on the futures positions. The opportunity costs of such calls must be considered.

Further, when rolling over from one cash position to another, one incurs transactions costs. These costs will tend to reduce the effective yield of the strip. Last, if short-term rates drop sharply, you would be rolling over from an instrument with a high yield to one with a low yield. Although this low yield would be offset by gains in the futures positions, the tax effect of the gains may reduce the offset.

The message here is quite simple: To use the strategy effectively, you need to monitor the markets continuously and be able to make your calculations instantaneously. Learn to understand the yield curve for futures as well as the actuals. Once you learn it, you will possess the beginnings of a standard of value. This standard then becomes the means of identifying many profitable opportunities.

THE ECONOMY AND THE SHAPE OF THE YIELD CURVE

To conclude the discussion of yield curves, a few words on the underlying economic reasons for the shape and changes in the yield curve are in order. This is important for those interested in trading interest rate futures, since they are concerned with how the realization of a recession or a boom in the economy will influence the shape and level of the yield curve.

The yield curve changes shape as monetary and fiscal policies change and the economy moves through the business cycle. A slowdown in business activity results in a decrease in the demand for short-term loans to finance consumer purchases. Consumer expenditures account for approximately two-thirds of GNP. In a recession, particularly for an economy where high oil and gasoline prices hurt new car sales, overall retail sales tend to fall. Consumers find themselves in a tighter and tighter squeeze between income growth and the cost of living. As consumer spending falls businesses begin reducing inventories. Unemployment starts to climb, putting an even further squeeze on consumer income. Inflation and the burden of past debts cause consumers to cut back even more and to be very cautious in making major purchases such as automobiles, major appliances, and other durable goods. All of this further reduces the demand for short-term loans. As a consequence, short-term rates fall sharply. Shortly thereafter, business investment in plant and equipment falls, causing intermediate and long-term rates to fall but not as sharply as short-term rates.

As an economic slowdown becomes apparent, one should expect to see two basic changes in the yield curve. First, any inversion of short-term rates over long-term rates should disappear. A normally shaped upward-sloping yield curve should appear. Second, the overall level of interest rates should fall. The extent of the fall depends on the severity of the recession.

When the economy is at the beginning of a new business cycle the yield curve should be normally shaped and money should be readily available. As consumer spending and income start to increase, people find themselves able to increase their purchases through borrowing. Businesses begin to expand their production to meet the new demand. As the borrowing pressure builds up, short-term interest rates start rising. New business investment and creeping inflation begin to push long-term rates up but slower than short-term rates. As the business cycle matures, the yield curve begins to flatten out or even invert.

Finally, one must realize that the yield curve is essentially made by professionals who trade on the basis of assessments of the current and future states of the economy. To the extent that the yield curve embodies expectations, it does partially reflect a consensus forecast of the future state of the economy. The fact that the yield curve is continuously changing does not imply errors in such forecasts but rather that events that were inherently unpredictable occurred, thus forcing a reassessment of forecasts. The result of the reassessment is a new yield curve and a revised estimate of the future state of the economy.

12

The U.S. Treasury
and Debt Instruments

As noted in Chapter 8 the government may create imbalances in the economy through excessive spending. The government pays for the goods and services it obtains by raising taxes or by borrowing from the people through the sale of various debt securities. These debt instruments are created by the Treasury Department and various government agencies. Collectively, the U.S. government is the largest borrower of money in the economy and the Treasury is the single most important issuer of debt.

To finance the huge U.S. national debt the Treasury issues several types of securities. Those of most interest for this exposition are T-bills, T-notes, and T-bonds.

TREASURY BILLS

T-bills are U.S. debt securities with a maturity of one year or less. They are direct obligations of the U.S. treasury and are sold to investors through the Federal Reserve System acting as agent for the U.S. Treasury. T-bills do not bear interest. Instead, they are sold at a discount to par and are redeemed at face value at maturity. The difference between the discounted selling price and the par or face value received at maturity comprises the yield or the interest earned. Thus, the amount of the discount and the length of time the bills have to maturity implies a specific annualized yield on the bill if held until maturity. For example, a 90-day bill sold for $977,250 would yield 9%.

T-bills are good indicators of money market conditions. They are widely held by many different types of investors. The economic factors that affect their prices also affect the prices of other money market instruments. Their price movements are closely correlated with commercial paper, bankers' acceptance, certificates of deposit, discount notes of the Federal National Mortgage Association (FNMA), Federal Home Loan Bank (FHLB), and Federal Farm Credit (FFC) agencies, and, to a lesser extent, the prime rate.

T-bills are currently issued in three-month, six-month, and one-year maturities. The bills are issued by the U.S. Treasury Department and the discount is established through an auction held by the Federal Reserve each Monday afternoon, with the bills going to those bidders offering the highest price; that is, the lowest interest cost to the Treasury. This auction technique allows the Treasury to let the prevailing market conditions establish the yield with each new bill issue sold.

The Auction

As mentioned, the Federal Reserve banking system acts as the agent for the Treasury in the auction. All bids must be submitted to a Federal Reserve bank by 1:00 P.M. (New York time) on the day of the auction.

The U.S. Treasury accepts two types of bids in the bill auctions—competitive bids and noncompetitive bids. Competitive bids are submitted by money market banks, dealers, or other institutions who buy large quantities of bills. They express their bids as discounted prices on the basis of par (one hundred). For example, a dealer who wants to buy three-month bills may pay a price of 96.199, equivalent to a yield of 15.037% on a discount basis.

Large investors who submit competitive tenders usually wait until the last minute before submitting their bids. They survey the various primary dealers to get the latest "feel" for the market. Just before the deadline they phone in their final prices and quantities to an agent who is in close proximity to a Federal Reserve branch. That agent has the customer's forms already filled out and signed. The agent inserts the prices and amounts and runs the bid into the Federal Reserve bank at the very last moment. Only the agile stand at the front door of a Federal Reserve bank at 12:59 EST on a Monday.

Noncompetitive bids emanate from agencies of the U.S. government, the Federal Reserve banks, and small investors who are generally not prepared to make the precise calculations required by the competitive bids. The minimum denomination is $10,000 and the absolute maximum is $500,000. In the sequence of awarding bids, a sufficient amount of the issue is set aside at the start of the auction to fulfill the noncompetitive awards first. All noncompetitive awards are made at the average price of the auction. Governments and Federal Reserve banks who make non-competitive bids are awarded their bids in full. Noncompetitive tenders by private investors are then accepted in multiples of $5,000 (above $10,000) up to the individual limit permitted. The remainder of the issue is then allocated among competitive bidders, beginning with those who bid the highest and ranging down in price until the total amount is issued. The lowest price accepted by the Treasury is called the "stop-out" price. If there are a number of bids that have been entered at the "stop-out" price, the Treasury may award each of the bidders a proportionate share of the amount requested.

After the auction is completed, the amount and price range of accepted bids are announced and the bidders are advised of the acceptance or rejection of their tenders. Competitive bidders pay their bid price while the noncompetitive bidders pay the weighted average price of the accepted competitive bids.

As noted above, at these weekly auctions, the Treasury sells bills with 90- and 180-day maturities. Thus, not only is the Treasury selling new bills every week, but it also has bills maturing as a result of auctions held 90 and 180 days previously.

Three- and Six-Month Treasury Bill Cycles. T-bills originally sold with 180 days to maturity eventually become 90-day bills. Thus, the auctioning of new 90-day bills is in a sense a "reopening" of the old 180-day bill auction. The Treasury reopens that auction to adjust more closely its need for funds during the next 90 days. Knowing that the U.S. Treasury has a six-month cycle in its issuing of bills, with the opportunity for reopening that issue as time passes, is important in evaluating the po-tential deliverable supply of bills for a futures contract. Since the 180-day bills will ultimately become 90-day bills available for delivery on the futures contract, one can track the potentially deliverable supply of T-bills 90 days prior to settlement. The supply of 90-day bills available to satisfy futures contracts includes the newly issued bills as well as the old 180-day T-bills auctioned 90 days earlier.

The One-Year Bill Cycle. The Treasury does not auction 360-day or one-year bills every week. Instead, the Treasury sells 360-day bills once every 28 days. Unlike the 180-day bills, this group of bills is not reopened before maturity. The 28-day cycle allows for 13 auctions each calendar year.

At one time the 360-day bill was reopened after 90 days and a "nine-month" bill was created. This practice was abandoned several years ago and has not been reinstated.

Cash Management Bills

Cash management bills are sold periodically by the Treasury to smooth out short-term cash flow problems. Generally, these bills are sold in the third and fourth quarter when cash receipts are low and disbursements high. The bills are then paid off in the second quarter when tax receipts are higher. The dates of the maturities for cash management bills usually coincide with three-month maturities and fall just after tax collection dates.

These bills are very similar to the Tax Anticipation Bills (TABs) that were once sold. When the Treasury ceased leaving the proceeds of T-bill sales in Treasury tax and loan accounts at commercial banks, they also stopped selling TABs and began to sell cash management bills.

The Federal Reserve in the Auction

The largest single holder of any maturing bill will almost always be the Federal Reserve Bank of New York and its customers. The Bank's customers are usually foreign monetary authorities. The Bank acts as their agent in making new purchases and in rolling over existing T-bill holdings that are maturing. It is not unusual for this group to control 50% of maturing T-bills.

The amount of bills owned by the Federal Reserve Bank of New York is an important consideration for anyone entering a competitive bid, because the Fed can, through its priority status, reduce the bills available to the public by 50%. Further, the Bank may not roll over or replace all the bills that are maturing. The Federal Reserve Bank cannot purchase more bills in the auction than they have maturing.

Sometimes the Bank will use the auction to subtly drain reserves from the banking system by allowing bills to mature and refusing to purchase new bills to replace them; this difference between maturing bills and new purchases must then be bought by the public. When the public pays for the bills, money leaves the commercial banking system and goes into the Treasury's account at the Federal Reserve, where it is effectively withdrawn from circulation. Such activity frequently means that the price of the auctioned bill will be cheaper than would otherwise be the case. So, going into an auction, it is important to know if the Federal Reserve Bank of New York is in a reserve "adding" or "withdrawing" position before the auction.

Evaluating the Auction Results

The day following the auction the Federal Reserve system (Fed) publishes the auction results providing the high, low, and average prices; the percentage of the total awarded at the lowest price; the amount of the non-competitive tenders; and the total amount tendered.

The auction results frequently provide clues in advance about the secondary market. Some of the things to watch for are:

1. The size of the noncompetitive tender. A large noncompetitive tender suggests that the investing public, and the Fed, have taken a large portion of the bills and "put them away"; that is, taken them out of the secondary market. A small noncompetitive tender means the dealers may hold a large percentage of the newly auctioned bills, and thus the floating supply is quite large.
2. The auction results compared to the general range of preauction "talk" or expectations. As mentioned previously, there is usually a guesstimate of what prices will be necessary to clear the market in the auction. If the actual results reflect those early estimates, this situation usually indicates a good underwriting from institution buyers. Prices lower than those anticipated prior to the auction usually reflect less institutional interest than expected. In these situations, dealers underwriting bids will win more bills than anticipated and will increase the supply in the secondary market.
3. The auction "tail." The tail is the difference between the average price and the lowest price. The difference between the highest price and the average price is usually ignored because it is likely to reflect a misinformed bid. A long tail shows the issue was poorly underwritten and investor interest was not great.

When the difference between the average and lowest accepted bid is less than two basis points, this usually reflects a strong underwriting with aggressive bidding. A tail of more than two basis points suggests the underwriting was weak with no really strong demand. In this latter situation many of the underwriting bids of primary dealers will be hit or awarded, and one should expect that there will be an overabundance of supply when the bill opens for trading in the secondary market.

THE SECONDARY MARKET

Trading Characteristics of the Treasury Bill Market

The trading characteristics of the secondary market for T-bills can best be understood by breaking the market into three distinct sectors—each sector reflective of a different time frame in the life cycle of a bill. Sector 1 of the market represents the one-year bills; that is, those having seven months to one year to maturity. Sector 2 represents those with a remaining life between three and seven months. And Sector 3 represents those bills with less than three months (see Figure 12.1). The prices for the bills in each of these categories respond to different factors and key off different points on the yield curve.

Perhaps the best way to explain this process is to follow a one-year bill through its life cycles as it moves from issue to maturity a year later. For purposes of our illustration we will assume a normal, positively sloped yield curve.

Sector 1

As noted above, Sector 1 of this yield curve runs from about 180 to 360 days. Thus, this area of the curve reflects the prices, and yields on the current year bill and all previous year bills auctioned in the past five months.

Once a new 360-day bill begins trading in the secondary market it is quoted on the daily "run." The run refers to a quotation of the bid and ask price of the three currently most actively traded bills.

These will almost always be the latest three-month, six-month, and one-year bills. Primary dealers automatically quote the run as an indication of the relative values of the various sections of the yield curve throughout the trading day. Those bills not on the run are also quoted, but the quotes usually must be requested.

Actively traded bills will trade on a 0.02% bid to ask spread, and an "off the run" bill will trade on a 0.04% to 0.10% spread depending on maturity. The average size trade is quite large, with $1,000,000 being the minimum. Five-million-dollar trades are usual and easily transacted without negotiation. Trades of large size are easily transacted with little negotiation and only slight price concessions.

A newly auctioned one-year bill will be actively traded and quoted on the run for the first month of its life. But after it is 28 days old, a new auction occurs and a new star is born. The new one-year bill replaces the old one on the run. Once no longer quoted actively on the run, that one-

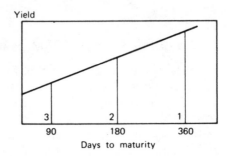

FIGURE 12.1   Hypothetical yield curve.

year bill begins to trade less actively. This is due partly to the fact that it is no longer on the run, but also because a distribution process takes place and the floating supply in the secondary market decreases rapidly. That bill begins to trade on a yield spread differential to the newest year bill. The spread between the bid and asked price starts to increase.

Gradually the trading in that bill becomes less influenced by the most recently auctioned one-year bill and begins to fall under the pricing influence of the six-month bills. (See Sector 2 in Figure 12.1.) When the bill finally gets into the same month as the newly auctioned six-month bill, it will then begin to trade in direct relation to the current six-month bill.

It is important to keep in mind that bills originally issued as one-year bills are not deliverable on 90-day T-bill futures contracts traded on the IMM. They are deliverable only on the market basket one-year T-bill futures contract traded on the IMM.

Sector 2

This area of the T-bill yield curve is dominated by the six-month bills. The newly auctioned six-month bill begins to trade actively right after the end of the auction period on Monday, until it takes a back seat the next Monday when a new six-month bill is auctioned. During this first week in the life of a six-month bill, there is heavy trading as the distribution process takes place. The bills change hands and gradually many of them end up in the hands of ultimate lenders. Thereafter, that bill begins to trade less actively and soon its value is affected by its growing distance from the latest six-month bill. Gradually the spreads widen and the daily volume begins to decrease.

When the six-month bill gets to be two or three weeks away from having only 90 days left until maturity, its price begins to reflect the trading in the current three-month bill. Eventually it becomes a three-month bill and goes back "on the run" as the 90-day bill.

Sector 3

This is the portion of the bill market dominated by the three-month bill. In general, it encompasses all bills with less than three months to maturity. Thus, this sector will include the new three-month bill and the old one-year and six-month bills that now have three months to run. The 90-day bill is the most liquid trading of all T-bills. This is mostly because of the large amounts outstanding and the relatively smaller price changes as yields change. Recently auctioned three-month bills trade on a "spread" or roll value against the newest three-month bills. The "roll" refers to the relative value in basis points per week between different issues of bills. This roll, or price spread per week, can reflect either a positive yield pickup when the yield curve is positive, or a give-up of yield when the yield curve is negative. It is not unusual for roll spreads to range from +5 basis points to −5 basis points over an interest rate cycle.

As the bill moves toward maturity, its value begins to be more influenced by the short-term cost of overnight money and less by the 90-day values. Thus, 60-day T-bills will trade at yields closely approximating 60-day repurchase agreements. Thirty-day bills will trade at yields approximating those for 30-day money. And during the final days they will trade roughly equal to overnight money.

The spread between the bid and ask also tends to widen as the bill approaches maturity. This widening in the spread results from the decreasing value of a basis point as maturity approaches. To compensate, dealers try to maintain a constant dollar margin by increasing the bid/ ask spread.

Some General Trading Guidelines

T-bills have no credit risk between issues. They are all government guaranteed and any bill is a perfect credit substitute for any other. But all T-bills do not trade equally. Some are more equal than others. For example, three- and six-month bills tend to have more liquid trading than one-year bills partly because their supplies are larger.

Some T-bills have more attractive maturity dates than others and therefore trade at slight premiums to bills with other maturity dates. For example, the first bill of a new fiscal quarter will generally trade at a slight premium to its neighbors because of its value as window dressing for balance sheet purposes. These bills can be used to effect certain tax benefits that also add to their attractiveness. Late December and late June bills in particular have value for financial statement and tax reasons.

Bills that mature on or near corporate dividend dates also generally trade at a premium to other bills as corporations hold in a T-bill the cash they are accumulating to pay the dividend.

Last, the six-month bill that corresponds to the IMM delivery dates for 90-day T-bills generally begins to outtrade the rest of the bills as the 90-day bill auction that corresponds with an IMM delivery date approaches.

The Role of Primary Dealers

The primary dealer has three basic functions in the T-bill market. First, he has an unwritten obligation to participate in the bill auctions. A dealer does not necessarily have to purchase in every auction but must submit bids to assure that the bills will be sold.

Second, he must make an active two-sided market under all market conditions and stand ready to buy or sell at the prices he quotes. Of course, a good deal of latitude exists in the prices and amounts he is willing to buy or sell at any one time.

Third, the dealer acts as a conduit for tenders from the public to the Federal Reserve, both in the primary auction bids and when the Fed is buying or selling bills for its own account. To avoid confusion and speed up response time, the Federal Reserve Open Market Desk uses only the 30 Primary Government Bond Dealers, who in turn use their resources to contact other large institutional customers who may want to buy or sell to the Fed.

The Role of the Federal Reserve Open Market Desk

The Open Market Desk plays a very large role in the secondary market. It conducts part of its monetary policy through the T-bill market when it buys or sells Treasury bills for its own account. Such purchases and sales may be outright or through repurchase and reverse-repurchase agreements.

When the Fed buys bills it adds money to the banking system and reduces the floating supply of bills, thus temporarily strengthening bill prices. When the Fed does repurchase agreements, it temporarily reduces the supply of bills in the market and adds money to the banking system. This also effectively reduces the short-term cost of financing dealer positions. When it sells T-bills or does reverse repos, the effect is the opposite.

The Fed is usually in the market once or twice a week in one of the four ways mentioned—outright buys, outright sells, repos, or reverse repos.

Second, the Fed also acts as an agent, buying and selling for customers. If the Fed fulfills its customer's needs from its own account, there is no immediate change in the supply of bills, but reserves in the banking system are impacted. Conversely, if the Fed fills customers' needs from the marketplace, it affects the supply and demand for bills but has no impact on reserves in the banking system.

Delivery of Cash Treasury Bills

All T-bills sold for regular or normal delivery settle (are delivered) the day following execution. Bills sold for cash delivery settle the same day as the transaction. The Federal Reserve, whether trading repos, reverses, or actuals, almost always trades for cash settlement.

Nearly all deliveries of cash bills occur through the "book entry" system operated by the Federal Reserve. This system is simple and relatively straightforward. Under the book entry system banks that are members of the Federal Reserve hold their securities at the Fed in accounts for which the record keeping is computerized. Thus, each bank has an account at the Fed, and as the transactions occur those accounts are adjusted accordingly. The actual engraved pieces of paper never move from one location to another. If First of Chicago were, for example, to sell bills to Citibank, it would make delivery by sending a wire message to the Fed instructing its computer to debit the First of Chicago's account for x number of bills and credit Citi's account for the same number. Simultaneously, the Fed's computer would automatically transfer money equal to the purchase price of the bills out of Citi's reserve account at the Fed and into First of Chicago's reserve account. Almost all transactions in government securities are settled in this way, through simple adjustments of accounts kept at the Federal Reserve.

Individual commercial banks have subaccounts for each of their clients. When they receive notification through the Fed wire that their accounts have been credited with the appropriate bills, they then, through their internal computerized record-keeping systems, credit their customers' accounts with the appropriate bills and debit their accounts for the correct funds. If one were to buy a T-bill, the customer's bank would charge the account or honor the check and issue a receipt of ownership saying the customer owns a specific number of T-bills, which the bank holds for him in its account at the local Federal Reserve Bank.

13

The U.S. Treasury Bill and Eurodollar Markets

THE TREASURY BILL FUTURES CONTRACTS

T-bill futures were first listed for trading on the IMM in January 1976. That first contract called for delivery of Treasury bills with 90 days left until maturity. The contracts were traded for delivery in the months of March, June, September, and December.

Since that time the contracts have been revised to reflect a "market basket" contract. That is, the delivery unit is not restricted to 90-day bills only, but also includes a bill originally issued as a year bill as a deliverable bill into its 90-day bill contract. The purpose of expanding the number of issues eligible for delivery is to relieve the pressure on the cash market at futures delivery time and assure that a sufficient supply of bills is available for delivery.

The "price" of the future is quoted in terms of an exchange-devised index representing the actual annualized T-bill interest yield subtracted from 100. Hence, if you want to know the annual interest yield being represented by a particular futures quote, subtract the quote from 100. For example, an index number of 94.5 represents an annual yield of 5.5%. In contrast to interest rates, the index goes down as the contract loses value and vice versa. Almost all newspapers carrying T-bill futures quotes carry the interest yield price as well as the index price. Bids and offers in the trading pit at the exchange must be made in terms of the index, so be sure that you give your orders to your broker in terms of the index. The minimum price fluctuation of the contract is 0.01 of the index or one basis point of annual yield. This is equivalent to $25 on a standard $1,000,000 T-bill futures contract.

As noted earlier, the Fed holds T-bill auctions every week. The last day of trading in T-bill futures for any particular month is the second day following the third T-bill auction of that month. Delivery is the following day.

Delivery is accomplished through banks that are registered with the exchange and are members of the Federal Reserve System. Through them you can have the T-bills delivered to your account in any major city. Futures delivery is a relatively simple procedure and mirrors the action taken when deliveries are made in the cash market.

The futures contract on 90-day T-bills calls for the delivery of bills having 90 days of life remaining. Thus, on delivery you obtain an instrument that will earn interest over the next 90 days. At the time you buy Treasury bills, you pay something less than face value—the difference between what you pay and the face value will be equal to the accrual of the interest during the remaining 90 days.

Keep in mind as you consider trading in financial instruments that there is an inverse relationship between prices and yields. If you expect interest rates to go up, take a short position in the market. If you expect interest rates to go down, take a long position in the market.

Delivery of Treasury Bill Futures

As described in the section on the cash market for T-bills, delivery is made through the "book entry" system. To accomplish delivery on the IMM, the following steps must be completed (delivery is accomplished similarly on the other exchanges):

1. On notice day, the last trading day, notice must be made by the seller to the clearinghouse of intent to deliver.
2. "Order to expect" instructions are given to the bank of the seller. The seller instructs his bank that he has sold bills through the exchange clearinghouse. The seller also instructs them to be ready to wire the T-bills and to accept payment from the clearinghouse via the Fed money wire.
3. The official settlement price on the exchange is converted to a discount yield and from that an actual dollar price is calculated. For example,

Settlement (Index) Price = 94.00
100 − 94 = 6%   (6%, 91 Days to Maturity)
$984,833.33 = Invoice Price (see the next section for formula)

4. The exchange clearinghouse contacts the seller's bank to confirm the value of the bills being delivered.
5. Delivery is made. See Figure 13.1 for a diagrammatic presentation of the delivery process.

T-Bill Formula

1. Calculating the actual dollar price from the quoted yield prices.
$ price =

$$\$1,000,000 - \frac{(\text{Days to Maturity} \times \text{T-bill Yield} \times \$1,000,000)}{360}$$

For example, 6% bills, 91 days to maturity:

$$1,000,000 - \frac{91 \text{ Days} \times 0.06 \times 1,000,000)}{360} = \$984,833.33$$

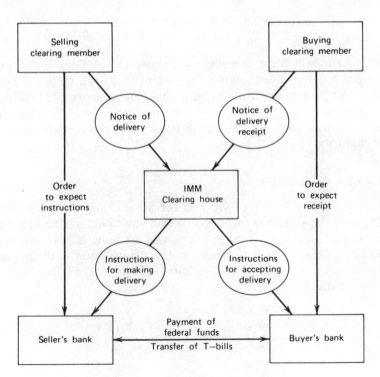

FIGURE 13.1   Delivery of Treasury bills.

2. Determining yield when T-bill face value, days to maturity, and actual issue price are known.

$$\frac{(\text{T-bill Face Value} - \text{Actual Issue Price}) \times 360}{\text{Days to Maturity} / \text{T-bill Face Value}} = \text{T-bill Yields}$$

for example, $1,000,000 \times 91$ days:

$$\frac{(\$1,000,000 - \$984,833.33)}{\$1,000,000} \times \frac{360}{91}$$

3. Calculating equivalent bond yield. This is a much misunderstood number. It relates the yield on T-bills to the yields on coupon-bearing securities, taking into consideration the amount of the discount from face value and the time until maturity. T-bill yields are calculated on a 365-day basis.

$$\frac{(\text{T-bill Face Value} - \text{Actual Dollar Price})}{\text{Actual Dollar Price to Maturity}} \times \frac{365}{\text{Actual Days}}$$

For example, 6% yield, $1,000,000 worth of T-bills, with 91 days to maturity:

$$\frac{(1,000,000 - 984,833.33)}{984,833.33} \times \frac{365}{91} = 6.18$$

This formula will cause a slight overstatement of T-bill yield versus coupon-bearing investments when comparisons are made of T-bills over 180 days to maturity, because the coupon instrument will have a coupon interest payment to reinvest after six months. Treasury bills make no six-month interest payments; they only pay 100% of face value at maturity.

Value of a Basis Point

A basis point is a 0.01% of yield. If the yield changes from 9.00% to 9.02%, then the yield has increased by two basis points. The value of a basis point (Val01) is the change in price for a one basis point change in yield. For a Treasury bill it changes in direct proportion to the maturity of the bill. For example, for a $1-million face value T-bill the Val01 for different maturities is as follows:

Maturity of T-bill	Val01
90-day	$25.00
180-day	50.00
360-day	100.00

Since the T-bill futures contract is based on a $1-million face value 90-day T-bill, a change in the yield of the futures contract implies a $25 change in its price. This translation of a change in yield to a change in price is important for hedging applications of a cash market instrument other than 90 days. For example, if a 180-day CD is to be hedged with the T-bill futures contract, then for every $1 million of face value of the 180-day CD two T-bill futures contracts would be required to offset identical changes in yields in the CD and the T-bill contract. In general, the number of contracts required to offset price changes in the instrument hedged with those on the T-bill contract (assuming identical changes in yields) is given by the *maturity adjustment*.

$$\text{Maturity Adjustment} = \frac{\text{Maturity of Instrument Hedged (Days)}}{90 \text{ Days}}$$

Hence, the maturity adjustment would be 2.00 for a 180-day CD. It would be 4.00 for a 360-day CD.

THE EURODOLLAR FUTURES MARKET

The great growth of the Eurodollar market and its increasing use by corporations as well as financial institutions prompted the introduction in the summer of 1981 of a contract on Eurodollar time deposits.

A Eurodollar is defined as any U.S. dollar on deposit outside of the United States. This generally means dollar balances on the books of London branches of major world banks. Since these deposits lie outside the United States, they do not fall under U.S. jurisdiction and, therefore, the regulations such as reserve requirements and maximum interest rate restrictions that govern domestic deposits do not apply to Eurodollars.

The trading of Eurodollar time deposits involves several risks that are not present in the government securities market. First, obviously, Eurodollar deposits reflect private credit, whereas government securities reflect public credit; hence, the credit risk associated with the trading of the underlying cash instrument is greater for Eurodollars than for Treasury bills. Generally, banks involved in the Eurodollar market place a limit on the size of Eurodollar deposits they will accept from other banks. They analyze each other's credit standing and allocate an internal line of credit for each bank with which they deal. These lines are based on their perceptions and analyses of the size, financial strength, and reputation of the other party. Another risk that arises in the cash market for Eurodollars is a sovereign risk. That risk is independent of the bank with which the funds are placed and relates instead to the country under whose regulation that bank operates. There is always the risk that a particular country may establish regulations that would affect the movement of bank deposits into or out of the country. This happens particularly when a country's currency is under pressure.

The Eurodollar cash market also includes a forward market in which banks quote rates from today's (spot) date to a future date (forward) for deposits or placements. A typical transaction for a bank interested in improving its yield would be:

1. To borrow dollars from another bank for six months.
2. Lend those dollars to a third party for three months—thus creating a three-month gap between their asset and their liability.
3. After the initial three-month investment matures, reinvest the principal and the interest received for the remaining three months.

Generally, when the bank knows what the initial three-month investment will be, it is then able to calculate the rate it needs on the last three-month segment in order to achieve its break-even rate. It is then in the position to evaluate the alternatives for its second three-month investment. It may decide that the second three-month investment should be a loan to a corporate customer to which it will commit today for drawdown three months hence. It may also decide to close out the position by making a forward deposit commitment, or it could simply wait and take its chances that interest rates will move in its favor and will be higher at the end of the first 90-day period.

One thing that happens in these types of forward transactions is that a bank uses up its lines of credit with other banks. This type of transaction also inflates the balance sheet of the participating bank.

Another way of accomplishing the same objective without using up valuable lines of credit, or inflating the balance sheet, is to use the Eurodollar futures.

For example, assume that in September a bank wanted to price in advance the last three-month portion of a six-month asset that would be funded by a six-month Eurodollar liability. The bank would be interested in protecting against a fall in interest rates from the period beginning the middle of December through the middle of March and would make the following transactions:

1. In September, borrow six-month Eurodollars and, simultaneously, make a three-month loan.
2. In September, buy one IMM Eurodollar contract for delivery in December.
3. In December, receive the money from the maturing asset (loan) and relend that money for three months at the then current interbank rate; and, simultaneously, sell (offset) one Eurodollar contract on the IMM.

The proceeds from the futures should be applied to the new asset to get the net investment rate.

Settlement in the Eurodollar Futures Market

The Eurodollar futures contract traded at the IMM is based on the London Interbank Offer Rate (LIBOR) for time deposits of a duration of three months. Unlike CDs, these time deposits are nonnegotiable and thus the Eurodollar futures contract became the first futures contract based on the concept of cash settlement.

At the end of each trading day, a large number of randomly selected prime London banks are polled to determine their offered rates for 90-day dollar-denominated deposits. After discarding the high and the low, the average of the remaining rates is used to determine the settlement cash price. This procedure is followed twice on the day the contract expires—once at a randomly selected time in a 90-minute window prior to closing and then at closing. The procedure is intentionally complicated to prevent any market participant from unduly influencing the final settlement price.

The effectiveness of the cash settlement procedure is confirmed by the great success of the futures contract. On October 29, 1990, the open interest on the Eurodollar contract was 689,619 contracts with a volume of sales of 108,495 contracts—a success by almost any measure.

Comparing a T-bill Futures Quote with a Eurodollar Futures Quote

Both the T-bill futures contract and the Eurodollar futures contract are quoted in a similar manner. The cash price equals 100 minus the annualized yield. However, the annualized yield for 90-day T-bills is a discount yield, whereas that for Eurodollars is an add-on interest yield. The distinction needs to be borne in mind especially when comparing prices (or yields) of the two futures contracts.

For example, suppose the T-bill futures contract is priced at 92.00 and the Eurodollar futures is priced at 91. The annualized yields implied by these prices are 8% for the T-bill contract and 9% for the Eurodollar contract. To compare these yields with each other they need to be put on an equivalent basis. Either convert the discount yield (T-bill futures) to an add-on interest yield (Eurodollar futures) or vice versa.

The conversion from the discount yield of the T-bill futures to the add-on interest yield of the Eurodollar futures is as follows:

$$\text{Add-on Interest Yield} = \frac{\text{Discount Yield} \times 90/360}{[1 - \text{Discount Yield} \times 90/360]} \times \frac{360}{90}$$

$$= \frac{0.08 \times 90/360}{1 - 0.08 \times 90/360} \times \frac{360}{90}$$

$$= 0.08163 \ (8.163\%)$$

Thus, the 8% yield quoted on the T-bill futures contract is equivalent to 8.163% when quoted on an add-on interest yield basis.

Spreads between CD, T-bill, and Eurodollar Rates

As noted earlier, Eurodollar and CD rates reflect private credit, whereas T-bill rates reflect public credit. Generally, because of the credit characteristics of Eurodollars, rates on Eurodollars will exceed rates on CDs. Further the spread between Eurodollar rates and CD rates does not remain constant. It responds to a variety of market forces, most of which are unpredictable, and many of which involve political decisions of the United States and foreign governments. The spread also reacts to changes in currency relationships. A strong dollar will generally result in a narrowing of the spread between Eurodollar rates and domestic CD rates. An increase in Federal Reserve requirements on domestic CDs will also cause the spread to increase. Last, the liquidity of the Eurodollar time deposit market is frequently less than it is for domestic CD deposits. This is because Eurodollar deposits are usually nonnegotiable time deposits, whereas domestic Certificates of Deposit are negotiable. Depositors are willing to receive less interest to gain the ability to raise needed cash in the secondary market, if necessary, prior to the deposit's maturity.

Figure 13.2 displays the add-on interest yields on 90-day T-bills, 90-day CDs, and 90-day Eurodollar deposits over the years 1988 to 1989. Figure 13.3 displays the yield spreads—Eurodollars minus CDs, and CDs minus T-bills over the same period.

Figure 13.2 clearly displays that all three interest rates are correlated with each other. They tend to rise and fall in tandem. However, the relationship is much more predictable between CDs and Eurodollars than between CDs and T-bills. This is confirmed in Figure 13.3 where the yield spread between CDs and Eurodollars is much more stable than between CDs and T-bills.

(90-day CDs, T-bills, and LIBOR)

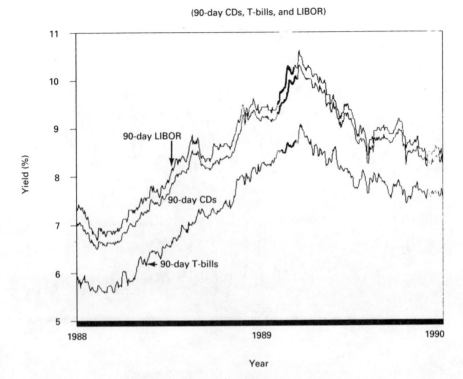

FIGURE 13.2   Yield levels (1988–1989).

HEDGING WITH THE T-BILL AND EURODOLLAR FUTURES CONTRACTS

Both the T-bill and Eurodollar futures contracts can be used in a variety of ways to hedge other money market instruments such as CDs, commercial paper, bankers' acceptances, and so on. For example, a large corporation could use either contract to lock in the rate on anticipated future borrowing. Another example would be for a bank to use the contracts to facilitate the repricing of its CDs. Yet another example would be for a Treasurer to lock in the yield on a future inflow of cash slated for investment in money market securities.

Designing effective hedges requires an understanding of the pricing relationships between the instrument hedged and the instrument underlying the futures contact. Correlation provides such a measure. If the correlation between the yields of CDs and LIBOR exceeds that between CDs and T-bills, it is an indication that the Eurodollar contract might

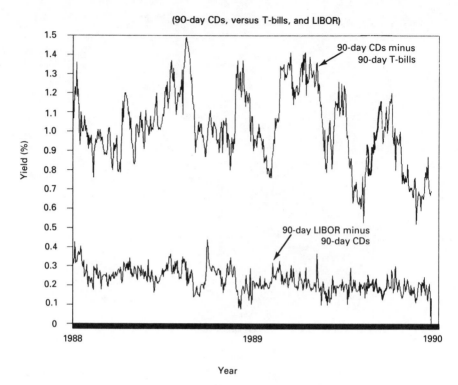

FIGURE 13.3 Yield spreads (1988–1989).

be more effective for hedging CDs than the T-bill contract—at least on a pure risk reduction basis.

Another important factor is basis risk. Since hedging is often viewed as an exchange of price risk (absolute risk) for basis risk (relative risk), one must realize that hedges seldom, if ever, result in the total elimination of risk. Basis risk tends to be higher for hedges where the correlation, mentioned earlier, is lower. More on basis risk is discussed in Chapter 20 on the concept of hedging.

Finally, if futures markets are to be used to effectively reduce risk, there is an implicit price charged for its reduction. The price is built into the basis. It is best seen in the case of an anticipatory hedge. Consider a borrower whose borrowing cost is tied to 90-day LIBOR. Suppose the rate on 90-day LIBOR is currently 10% with the Eurodollar futures for delivery two months hence at 89.90 (10.10%). The spot rate implies that if borrowing is undertaken immediately then the cost would be 10% (spot LIBOR). On the other hand, if borrowing is undertaken two months hence, a rate of 10.10% could be locked in with certainty through the sale of Eurodollar futures. The 10 basis point premium may be viewed as a price paid to get rid of the risk that LIBOR could be much higher than the current rate of 10%.

In viewing the size of the basis between a futures contract and its underlying instrument as a price paid to get rid of risk in an anticipatory (borrowing) hedge raises the interesting question as to which contract (T-bill versus Eurodollar) is the preferred hedging vehicle. As mentioned earlier, correlation between the yield on the instrument hedged with that of the instrument underlying the futures contract is an important factor, but only from a risk reduction perspective. For example, it is well known that the correlation between CDs or commercial paper and LIBOR is generally higher than their correlation with T-bills. So from a pure risk reduction perspective the Eurodollar contract should be the preferred hedging vehicle. However, if the basis between Eurodollar futures and LIBOR is consistently higher than the basis between 90-day T-bills and T-bill futures, the risk premium in Eurodollar futures is also higher. Therefore, the choice of one contract over another should ultimately be decided on the trade-off between the size of the premium and the residual risk from using each hedging vehicle.

14

The Treasury Note and Bond Market

TREASURY NOTES

Treasury notes are coupon-bearing securities issued by the government with maturities of not less than one year and not more than ten years. The timely payment of interest and principal on such notes is fully guaranteed by the government. Interest is paid twice each year in six-month intervals.

Note Cycles

Notes are sold in a variety of cycles similar to the T-bill auction cycles noted earlier.

Two-Year Note Cycle. Notes are issued each month with a 24-month maturity. Every month, a week or so before the month's end, the Treasury offers a new two-year note for sale that is dated to mature at the end of the month 24 months hence.

Four-Year Note Cycle. In the last week of the quarter, the Treasury sells a note that is dated and matures at month's end 48 months hence. These notes eventually become two-year notes and trade in consonance with newly issued two-year notes.

Five-Year Note Cycle. In April, July, October, and January the Treasury auctions five-year notes. These notes are auctioned at the end of the month and are dated and mature on the 15th of the month.

Refunding Cycle. In addition to the note auctions mentioned above, the Treasury engages in fund raising and refundings in the middle month of each quarter, February, June, September, and December. During these periods the Treasury sells a short note of three to four years maturity and another note with a maturity between five years and ten years. The exact maturities depend on market conditions. A long-term bond, usually maturing in 15 to 30 years, is also sold during these refunding periods.

All of the note cycles were begun in the middle 1960s when William Simon was Secretary of the Treasury. They were part of an effort to regularize the issuance of debt and minimize the market impact of concentrating the selling of a huge amount of debt.

TREASURY BONDS

Treasury bonds are coupon-bearing securities issued and guaranteed by the U.S. government. Bonds are issued in two different cycles.

Fifteen-Year Bond Cycle. Each January and July, at month's end, 15-year bonds are auctioned with settlement and maturities on February 15 and August 15.

Refunding Cycle. Every quarterly refunding recently has included a long-term bond with maturities from 25 to 30 years. These bonds usually have a call protection feature that is five years less than maturity. Consideration has also been given to issuing even longer bonds, with 40-year maturities, if market conditions permit.

Treasury Bond Authority

By statute Treasury bonds are limited to a maximum coupon of 4.25% and a maturity of not less than ten years. Originally everything over five years had to be a bond and fell into the 4.25% limitation. This limitation was changed to seven years in 1967 and ten years in 1976. In 1971 Congress authorized the Treasury to sell 10 billion dollars of bonds without regard to coupon rate. This authority is to be reviewed annually by Congress and a new amount authorized. Although Congress has always provided the new authority, it has sometimes delayed the authorization, thus raising concern that it may not always continue to grant blanket increases in the future. Fear of "crowding out" the private sector from the long-term debt market by the Treasury is often cited by Congress as a reason for the foot-dragging.

METHOD OF SALE FOR BONDS AND NOTES

The Auctions

Auctions for bonds and notes are held in much the same manner as auctions for T-bills. The Federal Reserve System acts as agent and bids must be submitted by 1:00 P.M. EST on the day designated as auction day. Bids are submitted differently, however, as notes and bond bids are denominated by yield. The Treasury accepts the yield bids, awards the noncompetitive tenders, then allocates bonds to the highest yield bids until all have been awarded. After that the weighted average competitive bid is calculated and used as the noncompetitive award price. This average price (yield) also becomes the basis for setting the coupon rate on the new issue. The coupons are set to the nearest one-eighth of a point, which allows the average price to be less than par. For example, if the average price were 11.65%, the coupon would be 11.625%. The high, low, and average *dollar* price are then calculated from this coupon price based upon the high, low, and average yields bid in the auction.

The Dutch Auctions. In recent years the Treasury on two occasions used the Dutch auction method to sell Treasury bonds. This method allocated to all successful bidders bonds at the lowest accepted price. Bidding is carried on in the same manner as before but after the high, low, and average bids have been determined, all bids, including noncompetitive, are confirmed at the low price.

Subscription Issues

In 1976 and early 1977, the Treasury sold issues on a subscription basis only. It set a coupon rate, which was a concession to the market, and allowed everyone to subscribe to a maximum amount of $500,000. The higher rate attracted many individuals and smaller institutions and kept dealers from buying large amounts to cover shorts they had created. The issues were heavily subscribed and the after-markets were very active. This method of sale is used to attract money from individuals and small institutional investors who would not be willing to purchase all the new debt issues at then current prices.

Rights Issues

Rights issues of new securities were very popular in the early 1970s when budget deficits were relatively small. In order to participate, however, an investor had to hold a maturing note or bond. Payment for new refunding purchases could be made only by presenting maturing notes or bonds. In this type of refunding the coupon was designated by the Treasury when the refunding plans were disclosed.

Although all three of these methods of sales were used in the 1970s, it is unlikely that they will be used in the very near future unless the market stabilizes and the size of the deficit is reduced.

The Secondary Market

The secondary market for Treasury notes and bonds is broad and deep. Unlike the T-bill market, there are, in the secondary market, many dealer participants from other than the Primary Dealers Association. The primary dealers are a majority of the active market makers but many corporate bond dealers are also actively involved in the long and intermediate government bond markets.

The growth of the secondary market began in the middle 1970s with the regular issuance of long-term debt with current coupons. The market had previously consisted of flower bonds and an occasional small issue. When investors became aware of the availability of a strong, secondary market they began to purchase government bonds on a regular basis. This added a great deal of liquidity to the market for long-term securities.

Over $3 billion in long-term bonds are traded every day by the primary dealers alone.

Pricing and Delivery

Prices for notes and bonds are quoted in dollars, with increments of one thirty-second of a dollar being the norm. Spreads between bid and ask prices are usually two thirty-seconds on short notes, and four thirty-seconds on longer bonds. Each thirty-second is worth $31.25 per one hundred thousand dollars of notes or bonds.

When delivery of any note or bond is made, the dollar price quoted is multiplied by the face amount to get principal amount or price. Then a calculation is done to figure how much accrued interest is owed to the seller. Since the Treasury pays interest every six months, adjustment must be made when a note or bond is sold between coupon dates. The seller must always deliver a bond that has all outstanding coupons attached. If the notes and bonds are in book entry form, then the coupons are already attached. The method of computing the seller's accrued interest is to figure total interest earned from the last coupon date.

The formula is as follows:

$$\text{Accrued Interest} = \frac{\text{Number of Days from Last Coupon Payment} \times \text{Coupon Rate} \times \text{Face Amount}}{365 \text{ days}}$$

The accrued interest is added to the principal amount to determine the total invoice price. This method of accrued interest calculation is the same for futures as it is for cash.

The Bank Range

The bank range is that part of the yield curve where commercial banks usually concentrate their purchases of Treasury notes. This range encompasses the notes in the two- to seven-year range. Because the liabilities of banks tend to be very short, it is prudent for banks to tend to concentrate their fixed income investments in this relatively short maturity range. Therefore, the note market from two to seven years usually reflects the capabilities and attitudes of commercial banks. When bank "liquidity" is low, this area of the market suffers disproportionately from tight money policies.

THE TREASURY BOND FUTURES CONTRACT

The CBT T-bond contract is the most actively traded of all futures. The T-bond futures contract trades on the basis of a hypothetical bond issue created by the contract specifications.

The exchange constructs this hypothetical bond issue by:

1. Setting a standard coupon rate of 8%.
2. Establishing a minimum maturity date. The CBT can use any bond that is not callable for at least 15 years from the *date of delivery,* if callable; or if not callable, bonds that do not mature for at least 15 years from date of delivery. Because of the Treasury settlement dates of February 15 and August 15, the most recently issued 15-year T-bonds fall just short of deliverable specification for the CBT March and September contracts. No maximum is set on maturity for bonds that may be delivered into the contracts.

The futures are traded on dollar prices as any other security would be traded. The yield of the security is set by the forces of a free market and the dollar price resulting is the dollar price quoted on the exchange.

Converting T-bond Futures Prices to Equivalent Cash Prices

The CBT uses a *factor method* for converting futures price quotes to equivalent prices for deliverable bonds. The factor for a specific bond is computed as the present value of future coupons and principal discounted at a yield of 8%, divided by 100. The factors can also be obtained from the CBT.

The CBT publishes a list of factors covering possible deliverable coupons (see Table 14.1) for use in adjusting different coupon rates and maturity dates to equate with the 8% exchange standard. This ensures that every coupon, regardless of whether it is higher or lower than 8%, will receive an equivalent price if it is delivered for settlement of a contract.

To understand how this method works, consider two different bonds when the CBT T-bond futures price is 80.00 ($80,000) for the March 1991 contract:

1. U.S. 11¼ of 2/15/2015. The time from delivery of the March 1991 contract to maturity is 23¾ years. The factor is 1.3429.
2. Issue 10⅜ of 11/15/2007–12. The time from delivery of the March 1991 contract to the call date is 16½ years. The factor is 1.2155.

The equivalent price for each bond is obtained by multiplying the factor by the futures price. Thus, for the 11¼ of 2/15/2015, the equivalent price is 107¹⁴/₃₂ (80 × 1.3429). For the 10⅜ of 11/15/2007–12 the equivalent price is 97⁸/₃₂ (80 × 1.2155). These equivalent prices are then adjusted for a face value of $100,000. Accrued interest is next added on to obtain invoice prices.

To illustrate how the coupon and maturity affects the (equivalent) prices of the cash bonds, assume that the above bonds were to be delivered against the June 1991 contract instead of the March 1991 contract. Since the time from delivery to maturity (or call) has shrunk by three months, the factors get correspondingly reduced. For example, the factor for the 11¼ of 2/15/2015 is now 1.3419. This translates to an equivalent price of 107¹¹/₃₂ (80 × 1.3419).

Delivery of Treasury Bond Futures Contracts

Delivery of Treasury bonds takes place through the Federal Reserve book entry wire transfer system in the same manner as delivery for Treasury bills.

TABLE 14.1   Prices to Yield 8.000% Conversion Factor for Invoicing

Term	Coupon Rates							
	7%	7¹/8%	7¹/4%	7³/8%	7¹/2%	7⁵/8%	7³/4%	7⁷/8%
15	0.9135	0.9243	0.9352	0.9460	0.9568	0.9676	0.9784	0.9892
15-3	0.9126	0.9235	0.9344	0.9453	0.9562	0.9671	0.9780	0.9889
15-6	0.9121	0.9231	0.9340	0.9450	0.9560	0.9670	0.9780	0.9890
15-9	0.9112	0.9222	0.9333	0.9444	0.9555	0.9666	0.9776	0.9887
16	0.9106	0.9218	0.9330	0.9441	0.9553	0.9665	0.9777	0.9888
16-3	0.9098	0.9210	0.9323	0.9435	0.9548	0.9660	0.9773	0.9885
16-6	0.9093	0.9206	0.9319	0.9433	0.9546	0.9660	0.9773	0.9887
16-9	0.9084	0.9198	0.9313	0.9427	0.9541	0.9655	0.9770	0.9884
17	0.9079	0.9195	0.9310	0.9425	0.9540	0.9655	0.9770	0.9885
17-3	0.9071	0.9187	0.9303	0.9419	0.9535	0.9651	0.9766	0.9882
17-6	0.9067	0.9183	0.9300	0.9417	0.9533	0.9650	0.9767	0.9883
17-9	0.9059	0.9176	0.9294	0.9411	0.9528	0.9646	0.9763	0.9881
18	0.9055	0.9173	0.9291	0.9409	0.9527	0.9645	0.9764	0.9882
18-3	0.9047	0.9166	0.9285	0.9404	0.9522	0.9641	0.9760	0.9879
18-6	0.9043	0.9163	0.9282	0.9402	0.9521	0.9641	0.9761	0.9880
18-9	0.9035	0.9156	0.9276	0.9396	0.9517	0.9637	0.9757	0.9878
19	0.9032	0.9153	0.9274	0.9395	0.9516	0.9637	0.9758	0.9879
19-3	0.9024	0.9146	0.9268	0.9390	0.9511	0.9633	0.9755	0.9876
19-6	0.9021	0.9143	0.9266	0.9388	0.9510	0.9633	0.9755	0.9878
19-9	0.9014	0.9137	0.9260	0.9383	0.9506	0.9629	0.9752	0.9875
20	0.9010	0.9134	0.9258	0.9381	0.9505	0.9629	0.9753	0.9876
20-3	0.9004	0.9128	0.9252	0.9377	0.9501	0.9625	0.9749	0.9874
20-6	0.9000	0.9125	0.9250	0.9375	0.9500	0.9625	0.9750	0.9875
20-9	0.8994	0.9119	0.9245	0.9370	0.9496	0.9621	0.9747	0.9873
21	0.8991	0.9117	0.9243	0.9369	0.9495	0.9622	0.9748	0.9874
21-3	0.8984	0.9111	0.9238	0.9364	0.9491	0.9618	0.9745	0.9871
21-6	0.8981	0.9109	0.9236	0.9363	0.9491	0.9618	0.9745	0.9873
21-9	0.8975	0.9103	0.9231	0.9359	0.9487	0.9614	0.9742	0.9870
22	0.8973	0.9101	0.9229	0.9358	0.9486	0.9615	0.9743	0.9872
22-3	0.8967	0.9095	0.9224	0.9353	0.9482	0.9611	0.9740	0.9869
22-6	0.8964	0.9093	0.9223	0.9352	0.9482	0.9611	0.9741	0.9870
22-9	0.8958	0.9088	0.9218	0.9348	0.9478	0.9608	0.9738	0.9868
23	0.8956	0.9086	0.9217	0.9347	0.9478	0.9608	0.9739	0.9869
23-3	0.8950	0.9081	0.9212	0.9343	0.9474	0.9605	0.9736	0.9867
23-6	0.8948	0.9079	0.9211	0.9342	0.9474	0.9605	0.9737	0.9868
23-9	0.8942	0.9074	0.9206	0.9338	0.9470	0.9602	0.9734	0.9866
24	0.8940	0.9073	0.9205	0.9338	0.9470	0.9603	0.9735	0.9868
24-3	0.8935	0.9068	0.9201	0.9334	0.9466	0.9599	0.9732	0.9865
24-6	0.8933	0.9066	0.9200	0.9333	0.9466	0.9600	0.9733	0.9867
24-9	0.8928	0.9061	0.9195	0.9329	0.9463	0.9597	0.9730	0.9864

(continued)

TABLE 14.1   (Continued)

Term	\multicolumn{8}{c}{Coupon Rates}
	7%	7¹/₈%	7¹/₄%	7³/₈%	7¹/₂%	7⁵/₈%	7³/₄%	7⁷/₈%
25	0.8926	0.9060	0.9194	0.9329	0.9463	0.9597	0.9731	0.9866
25-3	0.8921	0.9055	0.9190	0.9325	0.9459	0.9594	0.9729	0.9863
25-6	0.8919	0.9054	0.9189	0.9324	0.9460	0.9595	0.9730	0.9865
25-9	0.8914	0.9050	0.9185	0.9321	0.9456	0.9592	0.9727	0.9863
26	0.8913	0.9049	0.9184	0.9320	0.9456	0.9592	0.9728	0.9864
26-3	0.8908	0.9044	0.9180	0.9317	0.9453	0.9589	0.9725	0.9862
26-6	0.8906	0.9043	0.9180	0.9316	0.9453	0.9590	0.9727	0.9863
26-9	0.8902	0.9039	0.9176	0.9313	0.9450	0.9587	0.9724	0.9861
27	0.8900	0.9038	0.9175	0.9313	0.9450	0.9588	0.9725	0.9863
27-3	0.8896	0.9034	0.9171	0.9309	0.9447	0.9585	0.9722	0.9860
27-6	0.8895	0.9033	0.9171	0.9309	0.9447	0.9585	0.9724	0.9862
27-9	0.8890	0.9029	0.9167	0.9306	0.9444	0.9583	0.9721	0.9860

THE 10-YEAR TREASURY NOTE FUTURES CONTRACT

High and increasingly volatile interest rates in the late 1970s and early 1980s caused investors to be reluctant to commit funds to the purchase of long-term fixed income securities. Instead they preferred to keep their investments liquid and in short-term securities to maximize return at minimum risk. Consequently, the U.S. Treasury and large corporations had an increasingly difficult time in selling long-term debt. They turned to issuing more intermediate-term debt of a 7- to 10-year maturity.

Over the years U.S. Treasury notes have seized an increasingly larger share of marketable Treasury debt. As of 1986 U.S. Treasury notes accounted for as much as 60% of the Treasury's debt, compared to 15.5% for Treasury bonds and 26.5% for Treasury bills. Comparable figures in 1972 were 42.7% for T-notes, 22% for T-bonds, and 35.3% for T-bills.

The CBT's 10-year Treasury note futures contract is based on a security with a face value of $100,000 (par amount) maturing in 6¹/₂ to 10 years. Its 8% coupon corresponds to that on the CBT's Treasury bond contract.

Converting T-note Futures Prices to Equivalent Cash Prices

Although the CBT's 10-year Treasury note contract is based on a nominal 8% coupon, in reality other coupons with maturities ranging from 6¹/₂ years to 10 years can also be delivered on the contract. Each auction of 7- to 10-year notes brings a new list of deliverable notes with different coupons. Just as in the case of the Treasury bond contract, the CBT uses "conversion factors" to obtain equivalent prices for coupons other than the 8% standard.

In any deliverable month each deliverable issue has a specific conversion factor that reflects its coupon and maturity. It is obtained in a manner identical to that described for the Treasury bond contract. Factors in each deliverable month are published by the CBT. Table 14.2 displays a sample of factors for different Treasury notes deliverable on the March 1991 futures contract.

THE FIVE-YEAR AND TWO-YEAR TREASURY NOTE FUTURES CONTRACTS

In addition to the ten-year Treasury note futures contract, a five-year Treasury note contract and two-year Treasury note contract also trade at the CBT. Trading in the latter opened on June 22, 1990.

The deliverable instrument for the five-year contract is any Treasury note with a maturity of no more than five years and three months and no less than four years and three months as of the first business day of the delivery month. The deliverable instrument for the two-year contract must have a maturity of more than one year and nine months from the first business day of the delivery month. Also its original maturity must not be more than five years and three months.

Both the five-year and the two-year note contracts use the same conversion factor procedure as in the T-bond and the ten-year T-note contracts to determine invoice prices for notes with varying coupons and maturities. The par value of the contracts is $100,000.

The minimum price fluctuation for both contracts is $15,625. This translates into a tick value of one-half of 1/32 for the five-year note and one-quarter of 1/32 of the two-year note.

PRICING OF THE T-BOND AND THE T-NOTE FUTURES CONTRACTS

Since the T-bond and the T-note futures contracts allow any of several different T-bonds or T-notes to be delivered against the respective futures contracts, the price at which the futures contract trades must be influenced by the security that is deemed *cheapest to deliver*.

TABLE 14.2 Conversion Factor to Yield 8.000%

Years-Months	9%	9 1/8%	9 1/4%	9 3/8%	9 1/2%	9 5/8%	9 3/4%	9 7/8%
2-0	1.0181	1.0204	1.0227	1.0250	1.0272	1.0295	1.0318	1.0340
2-3	1.0200	1.0225	1.0251	1.0276	1.0301	1.0326	1.0352	1.0377
2-6	1.0223	1.0250	1.0278	1.0306	1.0334	1.0362	1.0390	1.0417
2-9	1.0240	1.0271	1.0301	1.0331	1.0361	1.0392	1.0422	1.0452
3-0	1.0262	1.0295	1.0328	1.0360	1.0393	1.0426	1.0459	1.0491
3-3	1.0279	1.0314	1.0349	1.0384	1.0420	1.0455	1.0490	1.0525
3-6	1.0300	1.0338	1.0375	1.0413	1.0450	1.0488	1.0525	1.0563
3-9	1.0316	1.0356	1.0396	1.0436	1.0475	1.0515	1.0555	1.0595
4-0	1.0337	1.0379	1.0421	1.0463	1.0505	1.0547	1.0589	1.0631
4-3	1.0352	1.0396	1.0441	1.0485	1.0529	1.0573	1.0618	1.0662
4-6	1.0372	1.0418	1.0465	1.0511	1.0558	1.0604	1.0651	1.0697
4-9	1.0387	1.0435	1.0484	1.0532	1.0581	1.0629	1.0678	1.0727
5-0	1.0406	1.0456	1.0507	1.0558	1.0608	1.0659	1.0710	1.0760
5-3	1.0420	1.0472	1.0525	1.0578	1.0631	1.0683	1.0736	1.0789
5-6	1.0438	1.0493	1.0548	1.0602	1.0657	1.0712	1.0767	1.0821
5-9	1.0452	1.0508	1.0565	1.0622	1.0678	1.0735	1.0792	1.0848
6-0	1.0469	1.0528	1.0587	1.0645	1.0704	1.0763	1.0821	1.0880
6-3	1.0482	1.0543	1.0603	1.0664	1.0724	1.0785	1.0845	1.0906
6-6	1.0499	1.0562	1.0624	1.0687	1.0749	1.0811	1.0874	1.0936
6-9	1.0512	1.0576	1.0640	1.0704	1.0768	1.0833	1.0897	1.0961
7-0	1.0528	1.0594	1.0660	1.0726	1.0792	1.0858	1.0924	1.0990
7-3	1.0540	1.0608	1.0675	1.0743	1.0811	1.0879	1.0946	1.1014
7-6	1.0556	1.0625	1.0695	1.0764	1.0834	1.0903	1.0973	1.1042
7-9	1.0567	1.0638	1.0709	1.0781	1.0852	1.0923	1.0994	1.1065
8-0	1.0583	1.0655	1.0728	1.0801	1.0874	1.0947	1.1020	1.1092
8-3	1.0593	1.0668	1.0742	1.0817	1.0891	1.0965	1.1040	1.1114
8-6	1.0608	1.0684	1.0760	1.0836	1.0912	1.0988	1.1064	1.1141
8-9	1.0619	1.0696	1.0774	1.0851	1.0929	1.1006	1.1084	1.1161
9-0	1.0633	1.0712	1.0791	1.0870	1.0949	1.1029	1.1108	1.1187
9-3	1.0643	1.0723	1.0804	1.0885	1.0965	1.1046	1.1126	1.1207
9-6	1.0657	1.0739	1.0821	1.0903	1.0985	1.1067	1.1149	1.1231
9-9	1.0666	1.0750	1.0833	1.0917	1.1000	1.1083	1.1167	1.1250
10-0	1.0680	1.0764	1.0849	1.0934	1.1019	1.1104	1.1189	1.1274
10-3	1.0688	1.0775	1.0861	1.0947	1.1034	1.1120	1.1206	1.1292
10-6	1.0701	1.0789	1.0877	1.0965	1.1052	1.1140	1.1228	1.1315
10-9	1.0710	1.0799	1.0888	1.0977	1.1066	1.1155	1.1244	1.1333
11-0	1.0723	1.0813	1.0903	1.0994	1.1084	1.1174	1.1264	1.1355
11-3	1.0731	1.0822	1.0914	1.1005	1.1097	1.1188	1.1280	1.1372
11-6	1.0743	1.0836	1.0929	1.1021	1.1114	1.1207	1.1300	1.1393
11-9	1.0750	1.0845	1.0939	1.1033	1.1127	1.1221	1.1315	1.1409
12-0	1.0762	1.0858	1.0953	1.1048	1.1144	1.1239	1.1334	1.1429
12-3	1.0770	1.0866	1.0963	1.1059	1.1155	1.1252	1.1348	1.1445
12-6	1.0781	1.0879	1.0976	1.1074	1.1172	1.1269	1.1367	1.1465
12-9	1.0788	1.0887	1.0985	1.1084	1.1183	1.1282	1.1380	1.1479

(continued)

TABLE 14.2 (Continued)

Years-Months	9%	9¹/₈%	9¹/₄%	9³/₈%	9¹/₂%	9⁵/₈%	9³/₄%	9⁷/₈%
13-0	1.0799	1.0899	1.0999	1.1099	1.1199	1.1299	1.1398	1.1498
13-3	1.0806	1.0907	1.1008	1.1109	1.1210	1.1310	1.1411	1.1512
13-6	1.0816	1.0919	1.1021	1.1123	1.1225	1.1327	1.1429	1.1531
13-9	1.0823	1.0926	1.1029	1.1132	1.1235	1.1338	1.1441	1.1544
14-0	1.0833	1.0937	1.1041	1.1146	1.1250	1.1354	1.1458	1.1562
14-3	1.0839	1.0944	1.1049	1.1154	1.1260	1.1365	1.1470	1.1575
14-6	1.0849	1.0955	1.1061	1.1168	1.1274	1.1380	1.1486	1.1592
14-9	1.0855	1.0962	1.1069	1.1176	1.1283	1.1390	1.1497	1.1604

Cheapest to Deliver (CTD)

The seller of a T-bond or T-note contract has the option of delivering any of the several securities that meet the specifications of the futures contracts. Typically, more than 20 securities meet delivery specifications. These securities trade in the cash market at different yields due to the wide variation in their coupon rates and maturities. The conversion factor procedure has a built-in bias because it invoices each deliverable security as if it were yielding 8%. As a consequence, the equivalent price of a deliverable security is often different from the price at which that security trades in the cash market. The security with the lowest cash market price relative to its equivalent price is called cheapest to deliver.

In addition to being able to deliver any qualified bond or note of his choosing—the *wild card option*—the seller of the T-bond or T-note contract is also in possession of several *timing options*. One of these is called the *implied put option*. This option arises because trading in the futures contract terminates at 2:00 P.M. (CST) while cash market trading continues beyond 2:00 P.M. The short has until 8:00 P.M. (CST) to notify the Clearing Corporation of the intent to deliver. This creates a six-hour time window wherein prices in the cash market may fall relative to closing (deliverable) futures prices to the advantage of the short.

Another advantage possessed by the short is the choice of making delivery until the last business day of the month at prices determined on the last trading day of the futures contract (eighth to last business day of the delivery month). If prices fall, the short benefits.

Influence on Futures Prices

The existence of the aforementioned wild card and timing options possessed by the shorts is an obvious disadvantage to the longs. The effect on the price of the futures contract is obvious. The futures contract must be bid down from the theoretical value it would possess in the absence of the options. The theoretical value may be defined as the cash price of the cheapest to deliver security plus the net cost of carrying (coupon income less financing cost) it for delivery. It is discussed in more detail in Chapter 20, "The Concept of Hedging."

HEDGING WITH TREASURY BOND AND TREASURY NOTE FUTURES

The Treasury bond and Treasury note contracts provide the opportunity to manage price risk not only in underlying positions in Treasury securities but also in other fixed income securities, such as corporate bonds and mortgage-backed securities.

Successful hedging strategies require appropriately weighting a hedge (i.e., the number of futures contract to buy or sell) to lock in a price (or yield) for the future purchase or sale of a current or anticipated cash position.

The most common procedure used for weighting a hedge is the conversion factor procedure. For example, if a cash position of $10-million face value of U.S. Treasury bonds, with a conversion factor of 1.5, is to be hedged, then 150 T-bond futures will be sold (1.5 × $10,000,000/ $100,000). Since the currently quoted futures price together with the conversion factors guarantee prices for cash positions at delivery, risk is effectively eliminated if delivery is undertaken. If delivery is neither desired nor feasible (as in most cases), the hedge will be subject to residual or basis risks.

There are additional dimensions to basis risk in hedging with Treasury bond or Treasury note futures compared to hedging with T-bill or Eurodollar futures. These additional dimensions derive from the options the short possess with respect to delivery. The effect of these delivery options is to reduce the predictability of the basis relationship between the cash and futures positions. In general, the predictability of the price relationship between the cash position hedged and the cheapest to deliver security the lower is the basis risk.

Several other weighting procedures other than the conversion factor method are also widely used today. Some of them are the price value per basis point (PVBP), weighting through regression analysis, and duration-based weighting. These are discussed in Appendix B. The underlying theme of all of these methods is how best to determine the number of contracts to buy or sell such that gains (losses) in the cash position are best offset by losses (gains) in the futures position.

15

Mortgage-Backed Securities

The market for mortgage-backed securities has seen astonishing growth ever since it came into existence less than twenty-five years ago. In 1975, the total principal amount of mortgage-backed securities was around $8 billion. Today it exceeds $500 billion, representing around 35% of the total stock of 1–4 family residential mortgages outstanding in the U.S. Mortgage-backed or mortgage pass-through securities, as they are sometimes called, are backed by a pool of mortgages. The holders of the securities receive interest and principal from the mortgages underlying the securities. The income and principal are guaranteed by either of one of three U.S. government agencies—Government National Mortgage Association (GNMA or Ginnie Mae), the Federal National Mortgage Association (FNMA or Fannie Mae), and the Federal Home Loan Mortgage Corporation (FHLMC or Freddie Mac). A fourth type of pass-through security also exists—the Private Pass-Through Security, a security issued by independent companies or commercial banks but without any guarantee.

The enormous growth of the mortgage-backed securities market has been paralleled by the growth in the complexity of the securities. For example, the Government National Mortgage Association issues several different types of securities—GNMA I, GNMA II, GNMA ARMs, GNMA GPMs, GNMA midgets, and still others. A major innovation in the mortgage-backed securities market occurred in June of 1983 when the Federal Home Loan Mortgage Corporation issued the first Collateralized Mortgage Obligation (CMO). Since then several private issuers have issued CMOs. A CMO derives its cash flow from pools of residential mortgages. It differs from a typical mortgage-backed security in that the cash flow from the collateral (mortgages) is allocated to several classes (tranches) of bonds. The tranches carry a coupon and are retired successively from the regular payment (and prepayment) of the principal of the underlying mortgages. The effect of this sub-division is the creation of securities with risk-return characteristics substantially different from those of the mortgages underlying them.

Mortgage-backed securities are so varied and complex that it would be beyond the scope of this book to attempt a comprehensive coverage of them. Hence, the purpose of this chapter is to provide the reader with a basic understanding of the security, its institutional characteristics, and the principles underlying its valuation.

THE MORTGAGE PASS-THROUGH SECURITY

A mortgage pass-through security is created when issuers of mortgages create a "pool" of mortgages and issue securities backed by the pool. A pool may consist of several hundred to several thousands of individual mortgages. The cash flow to the security holders consist of interest and principal derived from the monthly payments on the underlying mortgages.

Mortgage originators (typically, savings and loan associations, commercial banks, and mortgage companies) file the necessary documents with a guarantor to issue the mortgage pass-through security. Depending on the type of underlying mortgages the guarantors are either the Government National Mortgage Association, the Federal Home Loan Mortgage Corporation, or the Federal National Mortgage Association. Of the three agencies, only those securities guaranteed by the Government National Mortgage Association are backed by the full faith and credit of the U.S. government. As a consequence, GNMAs typically sell at yields lower than FNMAs and FHLMC-PCs (Participation Certificates).

The minimum face value of mortgage-backed securities at the time of their issuance is $25,000, with increments of $5000 for those backed by GNMA and FNMA. The increment is $25,000 for securities backed by Freddie Mac. The minimum sizes of the pools also varies with the guarantor. For GNMA I and II it is $1 million and $7 million, respectively. For FHLMC PCs it is $100 million except for the Guarantor's Program ($5 million). For FNMA's the minimum pool size is $1 million.

When an investor purchases a mortgage-backed security, he is provided with a certificate that specifies in detail the obligations of the issuer and the guarantor. The following is a descriptive example of a GNMA certificate.

THE GNMA CERTIFICATE AND ITS CHARACTERISTICS

1. *Face Value.* The certificate states the original principal value of the pool or individual investment. All GNMA pools must have at least $1,000,000 of mortgages in them, but a pool may be distributed among many different investors. The minimum investment is $25,000 and rises in increments of $5,000.
2. *Factor.* The factor is the *percentage* of unpaid principal still remaining on the mortgages that compose the pool backing the GNMA certificate. The factor is multiplied by the face value to determine the current principal balance of the pool.
3. *Current Principal Balance.* The current principal balance is the aggregate amount of unpaid principal outstanding on mortgages in a certain pool. To obtain the dollar value of a GNMA, the current principal is multiplied by the dollar price, and divided by 100.
4. *Coupon.* The coupon on the GNMA is the rate of interest that the purchaser will receive. The coupon is automatically 0.5% less than the standard FHA/VA rate in effect at the time of issuance. This 0.5% is paid to the servicing organization (0.44%) and to GNMA (0.06%) for a guarantee fee. As the mortgage rate for FHA/VA mortgages changes, the coupons on new GNMA pass-throughs change. Thus, there are GNMAs outstanding with different coupon rates.
5. *Pool Number.* Each certificate has a pool number that identifies the exact pool of mortgages backing the certificate.
6. *Date.* The certificate also gives the date the pool was originated and the date the pool will mature.

Payment Provisions

Payments of principal and interest to the certificate holder or "owner of record" are made monthly. GNMA guarantees payment in case of a default by the borrowers. The first payment is made 45 days after the initial issue date. Subsequent payments of principal and interest are made no later than the 15th calendar date of the month following the month in which collection from the borrowers was made.

Any prepayments are also made to the certificate holders on a pro rata basis upon their receipt by the servicer. Prepayment occurs when mortgages are prepaid by borrowers or when borrowers default on their loans. When FHA/VA loans go into default, the loan is repaid in full by the FHA/VA agencies. Any shortfalls resulting from delay in payments between default and repayment are paid by GNMA. This gives a GNMA certificate a double government guarantee: FHA/VA guarantees the mortgages and GNMA guarantees timely payment of principal and interest.

All payments are accompanied by a remittance notice that states the amount of principal being paid, the amounts of prepayments being made, and the amount of interest being paid.

Record date for payment on a GNMA certificate is the last day of each month.

PRINCIPLES UNDERLYING VALUATION OF MORTGAGE-BACKED SECURITIES

Among fixed income securities, the mortgage-backed security (MBS) is probably one of the most complex and difficult to value. The complexity arises from the unpredictability of the cash flow from unscheduled payments of principal (prepayments) on the underlying mortgages. These prepayments complicate the price-yield relationship for the security. One can always obtain a price quote on an MBS. Agreeing on the yield implied by that price quote is an entirely different matter. As mentioned in the chapter on the pricing of fixed income securities, any yield quoted on a fixed income security is based on a given set of assumptions. In principle, there could be as many yields as there are assumptions. Obtaining the yield on an MBS is an exemplary illustration of this principle—there are as many yields on an MBS as there are prepayment assumptions.

Any attempt to comprehensively price an MBS is clearly beyond the scope of this book. Thus, we limit our objective to conveying only some of the basic principles underlying its pricing. For example, how do interest rates affect the price of an MBS? How does one infer the yield on an MBS given its price? How does the prepayment assumption affect the price-yield relationship? What is the logic underlying option-based pricing models for MBSs? What is an *option-adjusted yield,* and how does one compute it? We conclude with some suggestions on how to approach the problem of hedging MBSs.

To illustrate some of the basic principles underlying the pricing of an MBS, consider the following generic mortgage-backed security: MBS 12%, 30-year with a face value of $100,000.

Computing the Monthly Payment and Remaining Principal Balance

The *monthly payment* on an MBS is computed in a manner analogous to that of a regular 30-year fixed-rate mortgage. The face value of the mortgage must equal the present value of 360 monthly payments. For the MBS 12%, 30-year security it is computed as follows:

$100,000 = Monthly Payment × (PV of an Annuity of $1/Month,
360 Months, @ 1% per Month)

Using a present value table or a financial calculator, the monthly payment is obtained as $1028.61. Once the monthly payment is obtained, the *remaining principal balance* at any time during the life of the mortgage is obtained as the present value of the remaining payments. For example, after five years of monthly payments, the remaining principal balance is computed as follows:

Remaining Principal Balance = $1028.61 × (PV of an Annuity of
$1/Month, 300 Months, @ 1% per
Month)
= $97,663.22

Calculating the Yield on an MBS

Calculation of the yield on an MBS, given its price, is straightforward if the cash flow from the security is well defined. For example, if the MBS is anticipated to prepay in full at any given time without any prior (partial) prepayment, its yield is computed in a manner analogous to that of a coupon bond. For instance, assuming full prepayment in five years, the yield on the MBS for a price of 108 ($108,000) is the rate of return that equates the present value of the cash flow of $1028.61 per month for 60 months plus a balloon payment of $97,663.22 at maturity (five years) to the current price. For comparison purposes Table 15.1 provides the yield on the MBS assuming several different prepayment scenarios. The price of 108 is assumed in each scenario.

Table 15.1 illustrates the sensitivity of the yield on the MBS to the prepayment assumption. For a given price of 108, five different yields

TABLE 15.1 Yield on $100,000 Face Value 12% Coupon, 30-Year MBS at a Price of 108 under Several Prepayment Scenarios

Full Prepayment	Remaining Principal Balance	Yield
5 Years	$97,663.22	9.94%
8 Years	95,424.06	10.49
12 Years	90,870.82	10.77
20 Years	71,694.83	10.96
30 Years	0.00	11.00

may be inferred based on the five different prepayment assumptions. Second, the variation in the computed yields is substantial, implying that the prepayment assumption will be critical in pricing. Third, the yield for the 30-year scenario is close to that for a 12%, 30-year Treasury bond priced at 108 (ytm = 11.07%). This suggests that, in the absence of prepayments, the yields on an MBS would closely track those of Treasuries. In theory they should. Abstracting from quality considerations, the structural difference in the cash flow should account for the slight difference in yields. Finally, since quality differences between MBSs and Treasuries preclude the yields on the former being less than the latter, one should expect the price behavior of an MBS to be substantially different from those of Treasuries for a given change in interest rates.

In practice, yields on MBSs are quoted in several ways, depending on the prepayment assumption used. The yields are termed as *cash flow yields,* since they depend on the cash flow predicted by the prepayment assumption. One assumption often used is 12-year prepayment, that is, the mortgage will prepay fully in the 12th year with no prior prepayment. Another assumes the FHA prepayment experience rate. The FHA provides tables that provide the probability of survivals based on the age of a mortgage. Yet another assumption uses a *constant prepayment rate* (CPR). The CPR assumption provides the yield on an MBS assuming a constant fraction of the mortgage is paid down each month. Tables providing yields based on a given CPR are widely available.

As useful as these different methods are in computing the yield on an MBS, they are all variations on a theme—an assumed prepayment structure. More important, they are all essentially static measures of yield; that is, the methods do not recognize that interest rates will change in the future, and that change will be accompanied by an alteration of the prepayment pattern. A major advance in MBS pricing came with the development of option-based pricing models. These models attempt to dynamically derive the future cash flows of an MBS from the future course in interest rates. The yield implied by these cash flows is termed the *option-adjusted yield.*

Option Pricing Model/Option-Adjusted Yields

Since the price of an MBS is affected by the option of the homeowner to prepay, it is useful to view an MBS as a composite security. One part of the security is called the "option-free" component, and the other the "call-option" component. The option-free component may be viewed as an MBS that promises the holder of the security the scheduled payments on the mortgage at the scheduled times. The call-option component represents the (call) option possessed by the homeowner who can repurchase the mortgage at any time at par. Hence, the price of the MBS can be modeled as follows:

Price of MBS = Option-Free Value − Call Option

The relationship could alternatively be stated in terms of yield as:

Yield of MBS = Yield on Treasuries + Option-Adjusted Spread

The option-free component is computed in a straightforward manner by discounting the scheduled future monthly payments at the rate prevailing for securities of similar risk. For example, if it is viewed that, in the absence of prepayment, MBSs should sell at a yield spread of +50 basis points over Treasuries, the option-free price for MBS 12%, 30-year at a yield of 10.50% should be 112^{14}/$_{32}$, assuming the yield on Treasuries is 10%. If the security actually sells in the market at a price of 107^{11}/$_{32}$, then the value placed on the call option (by the market) is 5^{3}/$_{32}$ (112^{14}/$_{32}$ − 107^{11}/$_{32}$). Alternatively, given an independent estimate of the call option, the yield on the MBS can be computed from the given market price. Obtaining an independent estimate of the call option is, however, the crux of the problem—one handled implicitly by the option-based pricing models.

The basic approach in option-based modeling is to simulate paths for future interest rates. This is typically accomplished by using a random number generator that uses an interest rate volatility estimate supplied by the user to provide several different interest rate scenarios for the coming month. Each interest rate scenario in the coming month will, in turn, generate several additional interest rate scenarios in the subsequent month. In this manner a whole series of different interest rate paths are generated. Each path represents a scenario of interest rates that will prevail in each month during the life of the mortgage. Given a specific interest rate path, a prepayment function generates the interest and principal paydown on each node (month) a path. These cash flows are then discounted at a given spread over Treasuries to obtain a price of the MBS for the particular interest rate path. The average price for all the paths is the option-adjusted price of the MBS. Alternatively, given the market price of the MBS, an option-adjusted yield can be computed.

Option-based pricing models have a major advantage over the traditional valuation methods because they dynamically link prepayments to interest rates. Hence, the yield obtained from an option-pricing model is, in principle, superior to traditional cash flow yields that typically assume a prepayment function based on the current level of interest rates. However, option-based models are not without problems. Apart from the sophistication of algorithms required for the price (yield) computation, some critical assumptions are still required. Estimates of interest rate volatility and a prepayment function are critical inputs into the model. An overestimate of volatility will overprice the call option and thus underprice the security. An oversensitive prepayment function will overestimate prepayments in a falling rate environment and thus underestimate the price of the security. These problems notwithstanding, the option approach to MBS valuation does represent a significant advance in the pricing of a truly complex security.

Price Sensitivity of MBSs and Hedging

Obtaining an accurate estimate of the price sensitivity of an MBS to changes in interest rates is critical to effective hedging. The asymmetric response of prepayments to interest rate changes, once again, poses a challenge. The effect of prepayments is best explored through an example. Consider our hypothetical 12% coupon, 30-year MBS priced at par. Assume, further, that the MBS will always sell at a yield spread of +50 basis points over that of a 12%, 30-year Treasury. Table 15.2 displays prices of the two securities under various interest rate (and prepayment) scenarios. The prepayments naturally only apply to the MBS.

Table 15.2 reveals in dramatic fashion the effect of changes in interest rates on the prices of an MBS. The prices of the MBS are far less sensitive to changes in interest rates than those for the Treasury security. The divergence in price sensitivity between the two securities is much greater

TABLE 15.2   Prices of a 12% Coupon, 30-Year MBS, and Treasury Bond under Various Interest Rate and Prepayment Scenarios

Treasury Yield	Full Prepayment (MBS)	Prices	
		MBS 12%, 30-Year	U.S. 12%, 30-Year
8.00%	1 Year	103.34	145.24
9.00	2 Years	104.52	130.96
10.00	4 Years	104.85	118.93
11.00	8 Years	102.57	108.72
12.00	12 Years	96.97	100.00
13.00	12 Years	91.32	92.48
14.00	12 Years	86.15	85.96
15.00	12 Years	81.40	80.26
16.00	12 Years	77.05	75.25

Note: Yield assumed for MBS = Treasury yield + 50 basis points.

when interest rates fall than when interest rates rise relative to the coupon rate. In fact, a continuing drop in interest rates could result in an actual fall in prices of MBSs—a property known as *negative convexity*. All MBSs possess this property to varying degrees, depending on the level of interest rates relative to their coupons. Additionally, negative convexity causes a phenomenon known as *price compression,* that is, a reduction in the price spreads of MBSs with different coupons in a falling rate environment.

One useful measure of a security's price sensitivity is its *effective duration*, that is, the percentage change in the price of a security for a given change in interest rates. An option-based pricing model is particularly useful in estimating the effective duration of an MBS, because it captures the cumulative effect of the price change of the option-free component and the call-option component of the MBS. Hedging the MBS then reduces to taking an opposite position in a synthetic MBS with the same effective duration. The synthetic MBS is created by combinations of futures contracts and/or option contracts on Treasury securities. One way to accomplish this task is to design a position that is short T-bond futures and long T-bond call options. The short T-bond position will offset the risk of the call-free component of the MBS, while the long T-bond call option offsets the call-option component of the MBS. The appropriate positions in the contracts must be such that the effective duration of the hedging vehicles equals that of the MBS.

Finally, the ability to compute an option-adjusted spread, as well as the effective duration of an MBS, invites arbitrage opportunities not only across MBSs with different coupons but also between MBSs and Treasury securities. In the former case, long positions in the underpriced coupons combined with short positions in the overpriced coupons could lead to trading profits. In the latter case, if MBSs are selling at unjustifiably large discounts (too high an option-adjusted spread), arbitrage profits could be realized by combining a long position in the MBS with a simultaneous short position in Treasuries and long T-bond call options.

Part Four

Foreign Exchange Futures, Stock Index Futures, and Options

16

The Foreign Currency
Futures Market

As noted in one of the opening chapters in this book, the first financial futures contracts developed were those for foreign currencies on the IMM. At the same time plans were laid for trading interest rates, and with very good reason, as there is a very close relationship between fluctuations in interest rates and fluctuations in the value of currencies. Thus, if you have a good understanding of interest rate futures, you will find ready application of the same concepts to foreign exchange futures. This chapter introduces the reader to some of the basics of trading in foreign exchange futures contracts offered on the IMM and the NYFE.

THE PRICE OF MONEY

The price of a currency is determined in the same way as the price for any other commodity—by the forces of supply and demand. If the people in the United States begin to demand more English-made products, the demand for pounds sterling goes up; as the demand for pounds sterling increases, Americans will have to pay higher prices to induce holders of sterling to sell. Conversely, if the British developed an overwhelming taste for U.S. goods, they would have to sell more and more pounds

Most of the material in this chapter has previously appeared in *Getting Started in Commodity Futures Trading* by Mark Powers, published by Investor Publications, 219 Parkade, Cedar Falls, Iowa. Reprinted with permission.

sterling for the U.S. dollars to pay for the products they bought. This increase in the supply of sterling being offered for sale would cause the price to drop relative to dollars assuming stable demand for sterling.

RECENT HISTORY OF INTERNATIONAL MONETARY SYSTEM

Cash or spot foreign exchange transactions are usually done through a foreign exchange trader located at a bank, and it has been so down through history. Foreign exchange dealings became relatively common with the development in 11th-century Europe of the Champaigne fairs where merchants bought and sold goods in their counterparts' currencies. Bankers attended the fairs to act as money changers, the modern-day equivalent of the foreign exchange trader. But even before then foreign exchange was traded—and not always on "free market" principles. The Persians in the sixth century attempted to thwart the basic forces of supply and demand by fixing an immutable gold/silver ratio. They failed.

A more recent attempt to fix prices was made in 1944 when a group of economic and finance experts from 47 Western nations met in a New Hampshire resort town called Bretton Woods. Their purpose in meeting was to develop a postwar plan for reconstruction of world trade and national economies. Out of that meeting came a plan for an international monetary system. It had four key points.

1. The establishment of a supernational agency called the International Monetary Fund whose purpose was to oversee the international monetary system and to assure its smooth functioning.
2. The establishment of par values or fixed exchange rates for currencies and an agreement among the countries that they would manipulate the supply and demand for their currencies in such a way as to maintain that rate. They did this by entering the market to buy their currency when its price fell 1% (in practice, 3/4 of 1%) below the declared par and by selling their currency when the price rose 1% (in practice, 3/4 of 1%) above the par value.
3. Agreement that the U.S. dollar would be the kingpin of the system and other countries would accept and hold it for payment of international debts.
4. Agreement that the U.S. dollar was as good as gold and that any time a foreign government wanted to exchange its dollars for gold it could do so at the U.S. Treasury at the rate of $35 an ounce.

This system was in effect from 1944 to 1971, and world trade did indeed expand during those years. It expanded largely because the United

States was willing to run its international business affairs at a loss. The United States continually imported more than it exported. It paid for its imports by running the printing presses and printing dollars. As long as others were willing to accept paper dollars, the United States received fine wines, nice automobiles, radios, televisions, and so on, in return.

Ultimately, however, there were a lot more dollars held by foreigners than the United States held gold. Foreigners had from time to time turned in their dollars for gold and gradually the United States gold supply had disappeared until clearly the dollar was overvalued in terms of gold.

On August 15, 1971, President Nixon declared that the United States would no longer abide by the Bretton Woods agreement of 1944. Accordingly, he said that the dollar was no longer convertible into gold; that is, that foreigners would no longer be able to turn their dollars in to the U.S. Treasury and obtain gold. Further, he said that the exchange rate for the dollar would no longer be fixed, instead it would be allowed to "float"; that is, it would be determined by free market forces.

The dollar floated just like a rock—straight down. It was devalued. Since that time, except for a brief period in 1972 when fixed rates were again reinstated, the value of the dollar has been determined more or less by free market forces with some governmental intervention.

The result of the devaluation of the dollar was that the relative purchasing power of the U.S. dollar was changed dramatically. Imports into the United States suddenly cost more (it took more dollars to buy the same amount of deutsche marks), and exports from the United States were lower priced (fewer deutsche marks would equal the dollar price). For example, between 1972 and 1973 the value of a bushel of wheat at Rotterdam increased by 122% in U.S. dollars, 117% in yen, 185% in deutsche marks, and 129% in sterling. Thus, it took about one-third fewer deutsche marks to buy the same bushel of U.S. wheat in 1973 than it took in 1972. Put another way, the same number of deutsche marks would buy one-third more U.S. wheat in 1973 than in 1972.

THE SPOT MARKET

The buying and selling of spot currencies (for immediate delivery or use) is accomplished through banks. Banks all over the world have accounts with each other in order to serve their customers, many of whom are multinational companies that deal in many different currencies. Every day these banks make deposits and withdrawals for their customers. These deposits or withdrawals result in transfers of funds from one country to another and, therefore, the conversion of one currency into another.

Hence, banks worldwide are constantly buying and selling currencies and providing a ready spot market.

This buying and selling is done by telephone and teletype. If a dealer in Frankfurt, Germany, wants to buy dollars and sell deutsche marks, he will probably call several New York banks and ask each for its rate. When a dealer finds a bank with a suitable rate, the parties agree to the trade and exchange specially coded telegrams confirming the transaction. The bank in Frankfurt will then credit the account of the New York bank with a proper amount of deutsche marks.

If a businessperson desires to convert dollars into deutsche marks to pay a bill, he can simply notify his banker and, after receiving proper information, the banker will see that the proper German bank account is credited. For example, if a businessperson imports German bicycles and needs deutsche marks to pay for them, he simply notifies his banker who, in turn, contacts other bankers in Germany or elsewhere in the world to buy the deutsche marks for the importer and have them deposited in the German bank account of the bicycle manufacturer. The U.S. bank will then deduct the dollar cost of the deutsche marks from the U.S. account of the importer. The importer will never see the deutsche marks; the bankers will simply debit and credit the appropriate accounts.

EVALUATING FOREIGN EXCHANGE RATES

What makes foreign exchange rates fluctuate from day to day? Why did the U.S. dollar buy less in Germany in 1976 than it did in 1966? Would an increase in the general level of interest rates in England be bullish or bearish? For whom?

These questions and many more are of great importance to anyone dealing in foreign exchange. And, as you may have guessed, the answers are not easily determined. Fundamental analysis of the money markets is more difficult than fundamental analysis in other commodities. There is a definite lack of good data, and the markets are highly sensitive to political elements. Yet, over the long run, fundamental economic factors will be the dominant considerations in determining the value of currency.

It is not possible to cover all of the factors in detail here; however, we will touch on some of the highlights of each of them.

INTERNATIONAL TRADE AND CAPITAL BALANCES

The single most important long-run indicator of impending exchange rate changes today is the country's trade balance, also called the balance of goods and services. It reflects the relative value of merchandise imports and exports.

If exports are greater than imports, there is a trade surplus. This is a sign of currency strength. A shift in the trade balance to a deficit (imports greater than exports), on the other hand, is an indication of currency weakness.

A second important indicator is the official monetary reserves of a country, including gold, special drawing rights (SDRs) on account at the International Monetary Fund, and foreign currency holdings. These reserves indicate the ability of the country to meet its international obligations—for example, its ability to repay loans, to finance imports, and to intervene in the foreign exchange market to support (manipulate the value of) its currency. Official reserves should be building up when there is a trade surplus. Official reserves may, but not necessarily will, be falling when there is a trade deficit.

A third important international economic indicator is the capital balances of a country, including the direct foreign investment and the short-term speculative funds that flow to or from a country. Capital movements are very sensitive to short-term interest rates.

With the almost instantaneous speed of the world's financial system, funds may be transferred nearly anywhere in the world. These funds move in response to changes in the interest rates. Capital flows can have tremendous impact on short-term exchange rates. If three-month interest rates in Canada increase to 1% over U.S. rates, people will send their money to Canada. As they do so, they must sell U.S. dollars and buy Canadian dollars. An increase in a country's capital account reflects an increase in demand for assets denominated in that currency, such as time deposits or T-bills. This increased demand indicates fundamental strength in the currency. Conversely, a deficit in capital accounts indicates a weakening in the demand and an expectation that the price of the currency will fall.

DOMESTIC ECONOMIC FACTORS

The underlying influences of the balance of trade, official reserves, and capital flows are the domestic interrelationships among income, prices, and interest rates.

Among the factors to consider in evaluating the domestic health of a country are:

1. The rate of real (after adjustment for inflation) growth in gross national product. Steady growth is an overall indicator of good economic health for an economy.
2. The rate of growth in money supply and interest rate levels. These are important indicators of future economic conditions. The short-term

interest rate differential is important in short-term capital flows. Such flows directly affect the demand for a currency.

3. The rate of inflation relative to the index of industrial capacity utilization. Differing rates of inflation in different countries are another very important factor affecting the price of a particular currency. The end result of inflation is an erosion of purchasing power, which ultimately means a weakening of the currency if other countries are not experiencing the same amount of inflation. High inflation with high utilization suggests that inflation is likely to stay high because "the machine" is already working at capacity, yet the people are demanding more goods. This would suggest a weak currency.

The general price level of a country affects the exports of that country. The United States is a good example. It has nearly priced itself out of the international market in some goods while Japan, on the other hand, making many similar goods, is able to sell them at lower prices. This reduces the exports of the United States and increases the imports to the United States from Japan, creating an outflow of dollars and what economists call an "unfavorable" balance of trade.

Each country should be studied individually and then one country compared against another. Since the futures contracts reflect other currencies relative to the U.S. dollar, other countries' expected and actual economic conditions should be compared to the United States. If the conditions seem more favorable to other countries relative to the United States, buy the futures. If the conditions favor the United States, sell the contract.

POLITICAL AND GOVERNMENTAL INFLUENCES

Political and governmental activities affect exchange rates by helping or hindering the international trade of a country and thus its balance of trade. Study carefully such things as import taxes, negative interest rates (a favorite of the Swiss, this means you pay them interest on savings accounts instead of the other way around), interest equalization taxes, embargoes, and so on.

The internal political stability of a country also bears on the issue. Even in the more well-established industrial nations of the world, the unsettling influence of political elections is reflected in the foreign exchange market. Major economic policy changes, as well as revaluations or devaluations, are often made with an eye to the next election. A change in the political party in power very often brings a change in economic policy. Even the anticipation of a new party being elected to power can affect exchange rates, which leads us to the significance of what people think is going to happen.

EXPECTATIONS

Timing is all important. Expectations about changes in price level and the timing of such changes can have a great impact on the market. Many observers, for example, expected the British pound to be devalued toward the end of 1972, just before Britain entered the Common Market. Early in the year numerous money interests began to act in anticipation of the event and the British government was forced to float the pound in early summer, probably months before they would have liked to. Similarly, many people expected the Mexican peso to be devalued during the latter part of 1976 because a change of political administration would make it a convenient time to do so. The market anticipated the event, although not the exact magnitude, long in advance. The peso was devalued by about 40% on September 1, 1976.

EXPECTED INTEREST RATES AND FOREIGN EXCHANGE SPREADS

Money moves almost instantaneously from one part of the world to another, continuously seeking the highest return available. Thus, if interest rates change in one country relative to another, capital flows from the country of lower interest rates to the country with the higher interest rates.

In the years ahead, investment managers and advisers will need to be skillful at moving funds around the world to various security markets and financial centers. That sort of operation will require an understanding of foreign exchange markets and the concept of interest arbitrage.

Interest arbitrage refers to the purchase and sale of spot and futures in money to take advantage of differences in interest rates between the two countries. This illustrates a very important principle in using the foreign exchange markets: There's a very strong relationship between exchange rate movements and interest rate changes in different countries. The basic rule of thumb is: at equilibrium, the currency of the higher (lower) interest rate country should be selling at a forward rate discount (premium) in terms of the lower (higher) interest rate country's currency.

Thus, if interest rates in Canada tend to be 3% below U.S. interest rates, one would expect a forward U.S./Canadian exchange rate to reflect a 3% discount for U.S. dollars. Market forces will assure this result (assuming certain other factors to be discussed below) because if the exchange rates don't reflect interest rate differentials (plus transactions costs) exactly, arbitrageurs can make money by borrowing funds in the high interest rate country, transferring them to the low interest rate country, and hedging them with a transaction in the forward exchange market. If enough money moves from one country to another in this manner, the spot prices of the two currencies will change relative to the forward price until the spread between spot and futures exactly reflects the difference in interest rates between the two countries. At that point, the arbitrageur's profit opportunities in transferring funds from one country to another will have disappeared and the exchange rate between the two countries will be at what is called "interest rate parity."

The explanation for this relationship is most easily understood through an example. Suppose 90-day interest rates were 11% in Canada and only 9% in the United States. Investors would send money to Canada in order to obtain the 2% greater yield. As they did so they would need to sell U.S. dollars and buy Canadian dollars. Assuming the supply of Canadian dollars remains constant, the increase in demand for them would cause their price to rise slightly.

Now most investors who would move their dollars to Canada in order to gain the 2% greater interest rates will not leave their exchange risk uncovered, since only a small change in the exchange rate will cause the 2% advantage in interest rates to disappear. To hedge they will, at the same time they buy the spot, sell the forward contract until it precisely mirrors the 2% difference in interest rates between the United States and Canada.

Some important assumptions have been made to show how interest rate arbitrage is conducted. It works only under certain conditions:

1. Free flows of funds between the two countries concerned must be possible. In recent years, more and more countries have been instituting certain barriers and controls on the movement of capital into or out of their countries. Obviously, if the controls are effective, great disparities between interest rate differentials and exchange rates may exist for long periods of time and interest arbitrage will not be possible nor will exchange rates reflect interest rate differentials.

2. Expectations of a devaluation, revaluation, or imposition of capital controls on the currencies must be such that they do not outweigh the interest rate differential factor. Sometimes, people hold such strong expectations of changes in the exchange rate due to factors other than interest differentials that interest rate parity considerations are simply overwhelmed.

Hedged interest arbitrage transactions, like those described above, are virtually risk free. The only major risk you take in those transactions is that a country will introduce strong capital controls that could prevent the fulfillment of the futures contract or the repatriation of the funds.

The theory of interest rate parity suggests a strategy for trading spreads based on expected changes in interest rate differentials. Spreads between futures contract months for a currency reflect expectations about interest rate differentials at a future point in time. Therefore, if interest rates today on three-month paper in Germany are at 4% and in the United States are at 10%, the differential is 6% under interest rate parity and one should expect the forward discount on U.S. dollars to be about 6% (i.e., if the spot rate or exchange is 50¢ per deutsche mark, then the 90-day forward rate should be about 50.75). If tomorrow 90-day interest rates in Germany rise to 5% with no change in U.S. interest rates, then the 90-day forward exchange rate will change to about 50.625¢ for each deutsche mark. The difference between the December deutsche mark futures and the March deutsche mark futures reflects *expectations* about what this three-month interest rate differential between the United States and Germany will be in December.

The correct guidelines to follow in implementing the spread strategy are:

1. If the forward prices are at a premium and you expect interest rate differentials to decline, then you should buy the nearby futures, and sell the distant futures.
2. If the forwards are at a discount and you expect the interest rate differentials to increase, then buy the nearby futures, and sell the distant futures.
3. If the forwards are at a premium and you expect interest rate differentials to increase, then buy the distant futures, and sell the nearby futures.
4. If the forwards are at a discount and you expect interest rate differentials to decrease, then buy the distant futures, and sell the nearby futures.

How would this strategy work in practice?

Consider the following. On February 16, 1979, the interest rate differential between the United States and Germany was 6.5%. The forward discount for the U.S. dollar reflected in the June/September futures was 6.2% annualized.

On May 18, 1979—about three months later—the interest rate differential between Germany and the United States was 5.5% annualized. The forward discount for the U.S. dollar reflected in the June/September spread was 4.3% annualized.

Had you followed the above-suggested trading strategy and correctly anticipated a narrowing of the interest rate differentials, you would have gained 27 points on the spread and at $12.50 per point the profit would have been $337.50. The margin requirement for such a spread was at $500 on February 16, 1979.

In summary, paying attention to the interest rates differentials between countries is important to successful foreign exchange trading. During recent years these differentials have been the single most important influence in affecting short-run exchange rate trends.

HEDGING A FOREIGN CURRENCY

In Chapter 20 we discuss the concept of hedging and demonstrate its application to interest rate sensitive assets and liabilities. These same concepts apply to foreign currency hedging.

The following examples illustrate some potential hedging situations available to different sectors of the economy.

The Buy Hedge

Assume a Chicago tractor maker has a Canadian plant that is doing very well and has a certain amount of cash on hand in the form of Canadian dollars. The plant has no need for those funds until Canadian taxes are due in six months. Assume also that the same Chicago tractor maker has an engine plant in Milwaukee that has need of a short-term loan to meet operating expenses. The best move for the tractor maker may be to transfer those funds from the Canadian plant to the Milwaukee plant for six months. In the interim, he would sell the spot Canadian dollars for U.S. dollars and buy Canadian dollars for future delivery, thus establishing a buy hedge. The summary of the transaction would look like this:

Cash market	Basis	Futures market
March 1		
Sell 500,000	100	Buy 5 September
Canadian dollars for		Canadian dollar
$0.84600 =		futures, 100,000 CD
$423,000		each at $0.84500 =
		$422,500

Cash market	Basis	Futures market
September 1		
Buy 500,000	10	Sell 5 Canadian dollars
Canadian dollars at		futures contracts,
$0.84900 =		100,000 CD each at
$424,500		$0.84890 = $424,450
Loss = 300 points	90	Gain = 390 points
($1500)		($1950)

In this example the hedger had a $1,500 loss in the cash market that was more than offset by a $1,950 gain in the futures market. The basis declined from 100 points to 10 points for a net decline of 90 points. Each point is worth $1.00 or $90 for each contract for a total of $450.

The Sell Hedge

Suppose a Chicago bank has excess funds to invest in the short term, and the highest short-term interest rate currently being paid is in Canada. Let's say 91-day Canadian T-bills are yielding 10%, and U.S. T-bills are yielding only 9%. The Chicago banker will buy Canadian dollars in the spot market, transfer them to his Canadian banking correspondent with instructions to purchase 91-day Canadian T-bills. At the same time he will sell Canadian dollars in the futures market for delivery three months hence. The amount of the Canadian dollars he sells in the futures market will include the original number plus enough to cover the interest that will accrue.

The advantage of this hedge is that the banker will have fixed his selling price for the Canadian dollars 91 days from now to be assured that the interest in T-bills will not be lost in the conversion back to dollars if the price of Canadian dollars goes down during the period.

TO HEDGE OR NOT TO HEDGE

In any hedging decision the manager must answer certain basic questions:

1. What is the net risk exposure?
2. What is the probability of a loss as a result of this risk exposure?
3. Which of the alternative methods available for managing this risk will provide the optimum coverage?

What Is the Net Risk Exposure?

Net risk exposure refers to the amount of money that would be lost if the exchange rate for a currency changes. It is an objective measure of the impact a devaluation or revaluation will have on the value of a firm's assets and liabilities. If a currency is devalued, any liability (such as loans) a foreign firm owes in that currency can be paid back with cheaper money. Conversely, if it has been revalued, the currency needed to pay back that loan will cost more.

There are a variety of ways by which the net risk exposure can be calculated. Current assets minus current liabilities is one very simple but probably incomplete way. Most firms today use a more sophisticated procedure that takes account of such things as receivables booked, liabilities incurred, and the method by which the balance sheet values are converted from one currency to another. This is a very complex topic on which whole books can be and have been written. Suffice it to say, before you venture into this area, get your accountant's advice. A thorough understanding of accounting rules and tax laws is of key importance here.

What Is the Probability of Loss on Net Exposure?

This is a subjective evaluation that should be based on an analysis of the economic and political information available about a country. The same sort of information was covered in the preceding chapters. In making this determination, the manager should first estimate the probability that there will be a change in the exchange rate. Is there a 50% chance that the peso will be devalued this month? This year? An 80% chance? And, second, estimate the probability of the size of change in the exchange rate. Will it be 10%, 20%, 30%, or even 40%?

Hedge Yes, Hedge No

Armed with these three pieces of information—net exposure, probability of loss, and probability of size of loss—you can then calculate the expected value of a loss to the firm by multiplying the probability of a loss times the probability of the size of the loss. (See steps a, b, c, and d in Table 16.1.) Once you have that answer, you are then in a position to compare the expected value of the loss (this is calculated by multiplying the probability of a loss by the probable size of the loss) to your cost of hedging.

To estimate the cost, a manager needs to ask, Which of the alternative methods available, singly or in concert with another alternative, will provide the most complete coverage of the risk at the least cost? Generally, a number of alternatives are available. A manager can self-protect through various management techniques; he can hedge by going to the bank and obtaining a forward contract; or he can hedge on a futures contract on the IMM or the NYFE. In making this determination, he must examine the cost of each alternative.

TABLE 16.1   A Hedging Model

a.	Net exposure	10,000,000
b.	Probability of loss	50%
c.	Probable size of loss	10
d.	Mathematical expectation of loss (b × c)	5
e.	Cost of hedge	3
f.	Decision—compare d to e. If d is greater than e, hedge. If d is less than e, do not hedge.	

To the foreign exchange trader, the cost of the hedge includes not just the commission cost, the interest on the margin for the futures contract, and the bid-ask spread but also any premium or discount that is reflected between the futures contract and the expected spot price. For example, if your expected spot price is 3% under the six-month forward price, the "cost of the buy hedge" includes that 3% premium. If the cost of the hedge is less than the expected loss, hedge. If that cost is greater, do not hedge.

A caveat—one should not enter into a hedging transaction without considering the tax implications and the effects on cash flows. Any business firm engaged in foreign exchange transactions would do well to integrate its hedging transactions and its accounting decision to assure it gets the maximum *net* benefit of its risk management efforts.

DELIVERY POINTS FOR THE FUTURES CONTRACTS

Delivery of a currency contract can be made to any bank selected by the buyer located in the country that issued that currency. The seller of the futures contract instructs its bank to contact and follow the instructions of the buyer's clearing member at the exchange regarding the bank and the name of the account to which the delivery is to be made. Choice of the delivery point, specific bank, and account is the responsibility of the buyer.

CONCLUSION

In summary, the world monetary system is in a continual state of transition. As a result, the risk of doing business internationally is increasing right along with the increased demands for international trade. As more and more businesses and banks seek means of protecting themselves from currency losses due to exchange fluctuations, the role of the foreign currency futures will undoubtedly grow in importance.

The currency futures markets can be used by a wide variety of commercial interests. The following are just a few categories in which futures hedging could be helpful:

1. Companies building plants abroad.
2. Companies financing subsidiaries.
3. Manufacturers importing raw materials and exporting finished products.
4. Exporters taking payment in foreign currency.
5. Companies dealing in goods bought and sold into foreign countries.
6. Companies abroad financing operations in Euro-currencies.
7. Stock purchases or sales in foreign countries.
8. Purchases or sales of foreign securities.

The possibilities are virtually limitless. Everyone who deals in or with foreign countries has a need for a hedging mechanism to avoid major losses due to exchange rate fluctuations.

Additionally, through the open, competitive futures market, the general public has an opportunity to make known its hopes, fears, and beliefs about the value of a currency. And with daily reports from a futures exchange of trading volume and price fluctuations, there is a public weathervane providing daily signals of the true value of a currency—giving the public a clearer insight into the effect that political actions, monetary policies, balance of trade, and other factors have on the economics of world commerce. All of this, of course, provides for differences of opinion and trading opportunities.

17
Stock Index Futures

The old Wall Street saying that you can't buy the market averages isn't true anymore. Now if you have an opinion on the market as opposed to an individual stock, you can buy or sell the whole market. Stock index futures provide the means to do so. A futures contract on a stock market index allows you to get in on the price action of a broad group of stocks with or without actually owning any of them. Additionally, options on stock index futures are also currently traded. Taken together, the initiation of trading in options and futures on stock market indices has opened up enormous opportunities for managers of equity portfolios to fine-tune their holdings with far greater economy and efficiency than was possible without them.

Trading in stock index futures began in February 1982 at the Kansas City Board of Trade. The futures contract was based on the Value Line Index. For several years prior to that time the Kansas City Board of Trade had been working actively on the concept of trading futures contracts on a stock market index but, due to regulatory problems, had been unable to make it a reality.

The last major regulatory hurdle was crossed in mid-1981 when the Commodity Trading Futures Commission finally granted approval to the concept of cash settlement of futures contracts. Cash settlement means exactly what it suggests. At the time of delivery, the seller of the futures contract does not have to deliver to the buyer the security underlying the futures contract, but rather will exchange cash equal to the difference between the price of the futures contract originally agreed upon and the price of the underlying security. Thus, in the case of stock index futures, there is no need to scurry around at the time of delivery to collect, in

191

the correct proportion, the shares of the various companies composing the index.

Ever since the Kansas City Board of Trade inaugurated trading in the Value Line Index, other exchanges have followed suit. Table 17.1 displays some of the most actively traded futures and option contracts on stock market indices.

The enormous success of stock index futures has prompted the rapid development of a variety of new indices on other stock groupings, including some highly specialized selections in utility indices, financial indices, consumer staples indices, oil and gas indices, and so on.

TABLE 17.1   Most Actively Traded Stock Index Futures and Option Contracts, and the Exchanges on Which They Are Traded

Exchange	Stock Market Index	Futures Contract Value
Index and Option Market	S&P 500 Futures S&P 500 Options (Futures)	$500 × Index 1 S&P 500 Futures
Chicago Board of Trade	Major Market Index Futures	$250 × Index
New York Futures Exchange	NYSE Composite Index Futures NYSE Composite Index Options (Futures)	$500 × Index 1 NYSE Futures
Kansas City Board of Trade	Value Line Index Futures	$500 × Index
Chicago Board of Options	S&P 100 Options (Actuals) S&P 500 Options (Actuals)	$100 × Index $500 × Index
American Stock Exchange	Major Market Index Options (Actuals)	$250 × Index
Philadelphia Exchange	Value Line Index Options (Actuals)	$500 × Index

WHAT IS A STOCK MARKET INDEX?

A stock market index represents some form of average of the prices of stocks that compose the index. It is a useful measure by which to gauge the effects of events, political or economic, on the performance of the stock market.

Stock market indices can be constructed in a variety of ways. The selection of the stocks comprising the index and the manner in which the average is computed is a function of the information the index is intended to convey.

There are many stock market indices in existence today. The various indices measure performance of the overall market(s) to highly selective segments of it. A perusal of the stock market data bank printed every day in *The Wall Street Journal* will reveal at least 26 different indices for the U.S. equity markets. There are five different Dow Jones averages, five Standard and Poor's indices, five New York Stock Exchange indices, six NASDAQ indices, and five other indices. This by no means covers all indices in existence, but these are the most widely publicized. Following is a brief description of some of the major indices.

Dow Jones Industrial Average (DJIA)

The Dow Jones Industrial Average (DJIA) is composed of 30 actively traded blue-chip stocks with large capitalizations representing the industrial sector of the U.S. economy. The total market value of these stocks is far smaller than that of the entire stock market. Nonetheless, the DJIA is probably the most widely known indicator of performance of the U.S. stock market.

The DJIA is an example of a *price-weighted* index. It is computed by summing the prices of all stocks in the index and dividing by a divisor that maintains continuity in the average in the face of stock splits, stock dividends, mergers, acquisitions, bankruptcies, and so on. Hence, the divisor changes over time. The values of the divisor can be seen daily in *The Wall Street Journal* at the bottom of the table displaying the various Down Jones Averages. For example, the divisor at the end of trading on August 10, 1990, was 0.505. In December 1986, the divisor was 0.889.

Since the divisor in the DJIA changes over time one must be cautious in making statements about returns computed from the average observed at two different points in time. For example, if the DJIA was at 2500 at the start of the year and was 3000 at year end, one cannot conclude from this information that the capital gain portion of return on a portfolio comprising all stocks in the average was 20%. Only if the divisor was the same at the start and end of the year would the return of 20% be strictly correct.

A price-weighted index allows stocks with larger prices to influence the index much more than stocks with smaller prices.

Standard and Poor's 500 Index (S&P 500)

The Standard and Poor's 500 Index (S&P 500) includes prices of stocks of 500 different companies from all major segments of the stock market. There are 400 industrial companies, 40 utilities, 20 transportation companies, and 40 financial institutions. The market value of the S&P 500 Index represents approximately 80% of the entire capitalization of the New York Stock Exchange. As such it represents the performance of the stock market as a whole more than the DJIA does.

The S&P 500 Index is an example of a *capitalization-weighted* index. The weight given to each stock in the index is such that its contribution to changes in the index is proportional to that company's market value relative to the market value of all the companies in the index. It is computed specifically in the following manner. The price of each stock in the index is multiplied by the number of shares outstanding to obtain the total market value of the company. The market value of all companies are then summed together and divided by the average market value of the stocks in the index over the period 1941 to 1943. The result is multiplied by 10 to obtain the value of the index.

A capitalization-weighted index allows stocks that are relatively more important than others (in size and market value) to have a larger influence on the index.

New York Stock Exchange (NYSE) Composite Index

The NYSE Composite Index is also a capitalization-weighted index. It is computed in a manner analogous to the S&P 500 Index. The base date for the index is December 31, 1965, and the base value is set at 50. All stocks traded on the New York Stock Exchange are included in the index. Hence, it represents aggregate stock market performance more accurately than either the DJIA or the S&P 500 Index.

Major Market Index (MMI)

The Major Market Index is composed of 20 blue-chip stocks, 17 of which are included in the Dow Jones Industrial Average. Like the DJIA, the MMI is also a price-weighted index. It is computed by adding the prices of individual stocks in the index and dividing by a special divisor that maintains continuity in the index in the face of stock splits, stock dividends, and so on.

The great similarity of stocks included in the MMI and the DJIA, as well as the method of computation of each index, has resulted in changes in the MMI that closely mirror changes in the DJIA. The historical correlation between the two indices is in excess of 0.98. Hence, the MMI is a near-perfect substitute for the DJIA, thus allowing use of futures and option contracts on the MMI as an effective hedging vehicle for hedging portfolios designed to track the DJIA.

Value Line Composite Index

The Value Line Composite Index (VLCI), the futures contract on which is traded at the Kansas City Board of Trade, is an example of an *equally weighted* index. The index includes more than 1,700 stocks and represents approximately 96% of the dollar value of U. S. equities. Every stock in the index is given a weight equal to the reciprocal of the number of stocks in the index. The purpose of equal weighting is to prevent large capitalization stocks from having an undue influence on the measure of overall stock market performance. The Value Line Composite Index is also computed as a geometric average as opposed to the arithmetic average that is the basis for the futures contract written on it.

RELATIONSHIPS AMONG THE INDICES

Since all stock market indices attempt to serve as barometers of stock market performance, one would certainly expect to find strong relationships among the indices over time. These relationships are measured by the correlation coefficients among the indices. Table 17.2 provides estimates of the correlation coefficients among the stock market indices discussed earlier over the period from January 2, 1988, through December 31, 1989.

Table 17.2 reveals that all the indices are highly positively correlated with each other. As might be expected, given the selection of stocks and construction of the indices, correlation coefficients vary among the indices. The very high correlation between the S&P 500 and the NYSE indicates that they are near-perfect substitutes for each other. The same is true for the MMI and DJIA. This suggests that the futures and option contracts on the NYSE and S&P 500 indices can be used effectively to hedge broad-based portfolios, whereas the MMI futures and option contracts can be used effectively to hedge portfolios consisting largely of

TABLE 17.2   Correlation between Stock Market Indices
(1/2/88–12/31/89)

	Correlation Coefficients				
	S&P 500	NYSE	DJIA	MMI	VLCI
S&P 500	1.000	.990	.956	.943	.742
NYSE	.990	1.000	.960	.945	.750
DJIA	.956	.960	1.000	.961	.709
MMI	.943	.945	.961	1.000	.727
VLCI	.742	.750	.709	.727	1.000

Note: All correlation coefficients are based on one-week percentage changes in the indices.

blue-chip stocks. On the other hand, the lower correlation of the VLCI with the other indices suggests limited applicability futures contract as an effective hedging vehicle.

STOCK INDEX FUTURES CONTRACTS

Futures contracts written on stock market indices are known as stock index futures contracts. As of the present writing the most actively traded futures contracts on stock market indices is the S&P 500 futures contract.

The major distinction between stock index futures and futures contracts written on commodities and most financial instruments is, as mentioned earlier, the concept of cash settlement. When stock index futures expire they are settled in cash based on the closing value of the underlying index. This is unlike most other futures contracts where delivery of the underlying commodity could occur. This distinction is important because collecting the various stocks in the required proportions to satisfy delivery is, in most cases, impossible. In cases where possible, the cost would be overwhelming. Cash settlement allows for enormous efficiency in transactions, thus permitting wide use of the contracts for meeting investment objectives.

The concept of cash settlement requires the exchanges to define the cash value of the contract so that investors may compute gains/losses on their positions as the index changes. Table 17.3 compares the cash value of each of the most actively traded stock index futures on August 23, 1990.

TABLE 17.3 Stock Index Futures Contract Values on August 23, 1990

Futures Contract	Multiplier	Futures Price	Contract Value
S&P 500	$500	306.25	$153,125
NYSE Composite	500	168.25	84,125
MMI	250	507.75	126,938
VLCI	500	234.30	117,150

Note: The futures price is for September 1990 delivery.

USING STOCK INDEX FUTURES

Stock index futures can be used in a variety of ways by individual investors and portfolio managers for risk management as well as for outright speculation.

The speculative potential is enormous because of the leverage afforded by the contracts. The margin required for participating in stock index futures contracts is around 10% to 15% of the contract's value. This is far below the margin of around 50% required for purchases of individual securities. Suppose, for example, an investor, after a careful appraisal of the markets, feels that a sharp advance is expected over the next month. He can buy index futures. If correct, he can earn a return far in excess of that from the purchase of a fund that matches the underlying index. The following example shows the profits from one such purchase in the S&P 500 futures contract.

S&P 500 Index	S&P 500 Futures
Today	
Index Level = 300	Futures Price = 304
	Buy Five Futures Contracts
	Value of Purchase = 304 × 500 × 5
	= $760,000
	Margin Posted = 0.15 × 760,000
	= $114,000
One Month Later	
Index Level = 315	Futures Price = 317
	Sell Five Futures Contracts
	Value of Sale = 317 × 500 × 5
	= $792,500

Profit from Transaction = Value of Sale − Value of Purchase
= $792,500 − 760,000
= $32,000

Return on Investment = Profit from Transaction/Margin Posted
= $32,500/$114,000
= 0.2850 (28.50%)

The profit from the transaction can be computed alternatively as:

Change in Futures × $500 × Number of Contracts
= (317 − 304) × $500 × 5 = $32,500

The leverage afforded by transacting in the futures market is seen by comparing the 28.50% return to that which would have been achieved by investing in a fund that replicated the S&P 500 Index. In the latter case the return would have been 5% [(315 − 300)/300]. If the purchase was undertaken with a 50% margin, the return would have doubled to 10%, not including the interest paid on the margin. Naturally, if the market moved in a direction opposite to what the investor forecasted the losses would be large.

It has long been argued that one of the major contributions of futures trading in any commodity or financial instrument is the opportunity it provides for hedging. In fact, it often has been suggested that if a futures market does not offer hedgers the opportunity to use it effectively for hedging, then the survival of the market itself will be threatened. Hence, we turn to the use of stock index futures for hedging.

HEDGING WITH STOCK INDEX FUTURES

Stock index futures contracts offer portfolio managers enormous opportunities for managing the risks of their portfolios with unmatched economy and efficiency. To understand how the markets can be used to tailor the risks of portfolios to satisfy the needs of investors it is important first to disaggregate the total risk of a portfolio into its component parts— hedgeable risk and nonhedgeable risk. For this we turn to portfolio theory.

According to portfolio theory, the total risk of any security consists of two components: a market risk component and a nonmarket risk component. The former is often referred to as *systematic risk* and the latter as *unsystematic risk*. The concept underlying systematic and unsystematic risk is simple.

The systematic risk of a security derives from economywide factors that affect the prices of all securities, though to different degrees. For example, inflation will clearly affect the prices of all securities. However, the prices of securities of companies that can more easily pass on costs to consumers will be less affected by inflation than those of companies that cannot. Similarly, the onset of a recession tends to have a smaller effect on companies that deal with essential goods as compared to those that deal with nonessential goods. The cumulative effect of such economywide factors on the prices of individual securities is a measurable quantity and is captured in a quantity known as the *beta coefficient* of the security.

The beta coefficient of a security measures the sensitivity of the return on the security to the return of the market portfolio. For example, a security with a beta coefficient of 1.5 indicates that if the market portfolio increased in value by 10%, then the return on the security would be expected to increase by 15%. If the beta coefficient was 0.5 then a return of 5% would be expected on the security. Hence, the beta coefficient measures the risk of a security relative to the market. A security with a beta coefficient larger than 1.00 is exposed to risks larger than the market portfolio. The opposite is true for a portfolio with a beta coefficient of less than 1.00. Beta coefficients for securities are widely available from brokerage houses and data banks. They also can be estimated through regression analysis.

The unsystematic risk of a security derives from factors that are largely company specific. Examples of such factors would be the death of a CEO, the departure of major personnel to a rival company, or the threat of a major lawsuit.

The various factors giving rise to systematic and unsystematic risk are, by definition, unpredictable. However, portfolio theory provides the means by which a portfolio manager can reduce exposure to this unpredictability. For instance, by appropriate selection of securities it is possible to construct portfolios whereby the unsystematic risks of individual securities cancel each other, leaving the portfolio with only the systematic risks of the individual securities. The resulting portfolio is now exposed only to economywide factors; it has only systematic or market risk, the risk that is hedgeable through stock index futures.

Measuring the Systematic Risk of a Portfolio

A portfolio of securities comprising all securities in the market, by definition, possesses only systematic risk. One example would be a portfolio consisting of all stocks in the New York Stock Exchange weighted in proportion to their market values. Its performance would match that of the NYSE Composite Index. Other examples would be portfolios that matched the S&P 500 Index, the Dow Jones Industrial Average, or the

Major Market Index. Of the four portfolios described the one that matched the NYSE Index would most closely reflect the market portfolio and, hence, could be considered devoid of unsystematic risk. However, if one chooses to define the market portfolio as either of these indices, then the systematic risk of a specific portfolio must be measured with respect to the benchmark portfolio (index) selected.

The systematic risk of a portfolio can be computed in a manner similar to measuring the systematic risk of an individual security. If the historical return of the given portfolio is regressed against the historical return on the chosen index, then the beta coefficient of the regression is a measure of the systematic risk of the portfolio. Alternatively, it could be obtained as the weighted average of the beta coefficients of the individual securities in the portfolio, the weights being equal to the ratio of the funds invested in the individual securities to the total funds invested in the portfolio.

Hedging Systematic Risk: Beta-Weighted Hedge

Prior to the beginning of trading in stock index futures it was scarcely possible to hedge economywide or systematic risks. The expectation of a decline in the stock market would have required the portfolio manager to move partly or wholly into cash, thereby entailing huge commission costs. Alternatively, the portfolio manager would have to short a large amount of the stocks held. The practical and logistical problems faced would be overwhelming. To protect the value of the portfolio, a beta-weighted hedge could be placed.

Consider a portfolio manager with a $100-million portfolio of stocks. The portfolio is well diversified with a beta coefficient of 1.35 with respect to the S&P 500 Index. The current value of the index is 323.55 and the futures contract on the index expiring in two months is selling for 328.00. The manager anticipates a fall in stock prices over the next two months and would like to protect the value of the portfolio. Now a beta-weighted hedge can be placed:

Number of
Contracts to Short = Beta × Portfolio Value/Contract Value
= (1.35 × 100,000,000)/(500 × 328)
= 823.17 or 823 contracts

Suppose the hedge was closed out at contract expiration when the market did indeed decline sharply to a value of 295.00 for the S&P 500 Index. Assume that the cash value of the portfolio simultaneously declined to $87.64 million. The net profit/loss (Hedge P/L) and realized portfolio value can be computed as follows:

Hedge P/L = [Ending Portfolio Value − Beginning Portfolio Value]
+ [Number of Contracts × $500 × (Sale Price − Purchase Price)]
= [$87,640,000 − $100,000,000] + [823 × $500 × (328 − 295)]
= $1,219,500

Realized Portfolio Value = Beginning Portfolio Value + Hedge P/L
= $100,000,000 + $1,219,500
= $101,219,500

If the portfolio were left unhedged its value would have been $87,640,000. Hence, the hedge provided effective protection against the decline in the market. Not including the dividends that portfolio would have generated over the two months of the hedge, the annualized return on the portfolio would be computed as follows:

Annualized Return

$$= \left[\frac{\text{Realized Portfolio Value}}{\text{Beginning Portfolio Value}} - 1 \right] \times \frac{12 \text{ Months}}{\text{Number of Months}} \times 100$$

$$= \left[\frac{\$101,219,500}{\$100,000,000} - 1 \right] \times \frac{12}{2} \times 100$$

$$= 7.317\%$$

A beta-weighted hedge recognizes that the hedged portfolio is more (or less) sensitive to economywide factors than the index on which the futures contract is written. Therefore, it provides more effective protection than a *dollar-weighted* hedge. For a dollar-weighted hedge the number of contracts required is computed exactly as shown earlier, except the beta coefficient is assumed to be 1.00.

Adjusting a Portfolio's Beta (Systematic Risk)

Stock index futures are effective tools a portfolio manager can use to increase or decrease market exposure. By buying or selling stock index futures a portfolio's beta could be increased or decreased to enhance the market timing of the exposure. Once again, the efficiency with which this is accomplished is overwhelming compared to dealing only in the cash market.

Consider a $10-million equity portfolio with a beta coefficient of 0.75 with respect to the S&P 500 Index. Anticipating a rise in the market, the portfolio manager wishes to increase market exposure by increasing the beta coefficient of the portfolio to 1.50. The number of contracts he would have to buy, assuming the S&P 500 futures is at 320, is computed as follows:

$$\frac{\text{Number of}}{\text{Contracts}} = (\text{New Beta} - \text{Old Beta}) \times \frac{\text{Portfolio Value}}{\$500 \times \text{Futures Price}}$$

$$= (1.50 - 0.75) \times \frac{\$10,000,000}{\$500 \times 320}$$

$$= 46.875 \ (47 \ \text{contracts})$$

ARBITRAGE WITH STOCK INDEX FUTURES

Arbitrage trading exists to take advantage of profitable opportunities that arise out of the relative mispricing of securities. If the relative prices of securities appear to be "out of line" when compared to historical pricing relationships, arbitrageurs enter the markets to take advantage of the apparent mispricing. They sell (purchase) one security and simultaneously buy (sell) the other security. The profit is realized by unwinding the positions when the prices of the securities get properly aligned.

Opportunities for arbitrage in stock index futures often exist—both between one index future and another, as well as between a particular index future and its underlying index. In the first case the opportunity arises when a particular group of stocks on which a futures contract exists is believed to lead all other stocks during major market moves. A case in point would be the blue-chip stocks of the Major Market Index leading the stocks in the S&P 500 Index or the NYSE Composite Index. Here, the placing of an intermarket spread would provide opportunities for profit. In the second case, if the index future is believed to be "out of line" with the theoretical futures price, then the sale (purchase) of the futures contract and the simultaneous purchase (sale) of the underlying stocks would result in arbitrage profits.

Intermarket Spreads

Spread trading, in general, is a less risky activity than taking naked positions in securities. As a result, the margin requirement for spreading is much smaller than for either long or short positions in the futures contracts. Successful intermarket spreading, however, requires a thorough understanding of the long-term price relationship between securities and the reasons why short-term discrepancies may occur.

The case for intermarket spreading opportunities can be made, for example, by comparing the correlation coefficients between the MMI and

TABLE 17.4 Correlation between MMI and
Other Indices for Varying Intervals

	Correlation Coefficients		
	S&P 500	NYSE	VLCI
MMI			
1-day	.909	.926	.581
1-week	.943	.945	.727
2-week	.944	.939	.748
4-week	.955	.947	.766

other stock index futures measured over different intervals of time in Table 17.4. Note the increase in the correlation coefficient between the MMI Index and the NYSE Index, the S&P 500 Index, or the VLCI Index as the time interval increases. The increase in the correlation coefficients with the size of the measurement interval suggests that pricing discrepancies between the MMI and the other indices may exist over short intervals of time and tend to disappear as the time interval increases.

Here is an example of how to profit from placing an intermarket spread with the MMI futures contract and the S&P 500 futures contract. Suppose a spread trader strongly believes the market is poised for a sustained upward move, and the rally will be led by the blue-chip stocks. Consequently, he places an intermarket spread—long the MMI futures and short the S&P 500 futures. Since the dollar values of the contracts are different, a *spread ratio* needs to be computed as shown in the following equation. The computation assumes the MMI futures is at 505 and the S&P 500 futures is at 306.

$$
\begin{aligned}
\frac{\text{Spread Ratio}}{\text{(MMI versus S\&P 500)}} &= \frac{\text{Dollar Value of S\&P 500 Futures}}{\text{Dollar Value of MMI Futures}} \\
&= \frac{\$500 \times 306}{\$250 \times 505} \\
&= 1.212
\end{aligned}
$$

A spread ratio of 1.212 translates into approximately five MMI futures for four S&P 500 futures. Hence, the spread trader would be long five MMI futures and simultaneously short four S&P 500 futures.

If the rally did materialize with the blue chips in the lead, then the spreader would realize a profit. One such scenario is shown on the following page.

MMI Futures	S&P 500 Futures
Today	
Buy Five MMI Futures @ 505	Sell Four S&P 500 Futures @ 306
Later	
Sell Five MMI Futures @ 525	Buy Four S&P 500 Futures @ 310
Profit	
$250 × (525 − 505) = $5000	$500 × (306 − 310) = −$2000

$$\text{Net Profit} = \$5000 - \$2000$$
$$= \$3000$$

In the above example, the start of the market rally pushed the MMI up by 20 points while the S&P 500 advanced only 4 points—a much higher percentage gain for the former compared to the latter. If the rally continues, the likelihood is high that the S&P 500 will ultimately catch the MMI in percentage gains as suggested by correlation coefficients displayed in Table 17.4. This will erode the profits hereby gained, so the timing of unwinding the spread is just as crucial as the timing of its placement.

Index Arbitrage

Opportunities for index arbitrage arise when the futures contract on the index is believed to be "out of line" with the theoretical futures price. In such a case, profits can be made by buying (selling) the index futures and simultaneously selling (buying) the stocks comprising the index.

The logic underlying index arbitrage is as follows. The theoretical futures price should equal that of a portfolio of stocks composing the index plus the net cost of carrying the stocks until delivery. If the futures price exceeds the price of the portfolio by the net cost of carry, it would be profitable for the arbitrageur to buy the index portfolio and sell futures against it. The reverse transaction would be undertaken if the difference between the futures price and the portfolio was less than the net cost of carry.

In theory, index arbitrage seems a straightforward exercise to carry out. In practice, though, there are formidable obstacles. Aside from the commissions involved in buying and selling the underlying stocks, the task of creating the portfolios by collecting the stocks in requisite proportions to mirror the index is enormous, particularly in the case of the S&P 500 Index or the NYSE Composite Index. This problem has been alleviated to a certain extent by the ability to create proxies of the index portfolios with a smaller number of stocks. In this regard, the Major

Market Index with its small 20-stock portfolio would seem to possess a decided advantage over the S&P 500 Index or the NYSE Composite Index as a candidate for index arbitrage.

PORTFOLIO INSURANCE

The term *portfolio insurance* refers to an investment strategy that prevents the value of a portfolio from dropping below a prespecified minimum value while at the same time keeping its upside potential intact.

The prospect of reducing or eliminating losses below a prespecified floor would seem attractive to a wide set of institutional investors with low levels of tolerance for risk. Also, the notion that portfolios that have achieved large gains recently could be prevented from losing them in a sudden market downturn would certainly seem attractive to almost any portfolio manager. As with any insurance, though, the price to be paid for the protection is a major factor in the decision to insure.

Conceptually, insuring a portfolio against loss is equivalent to the purchase of a protective put on the portfolio. The strike price of the put less the put premium may be viewed as the prespecified minimum value of the portfolio. The price paid for the put is analogous to the insurance premium. If the value of the portfolio falls below the strike price, the put is exercised, thereby ensuring the minimum value of the portfolio. If the value of the portfolio increases, the put expires worthless, but the value of the portfolio will exceed the prespecified minimum value.

Table 17.5 displays the results from buying puts to protect a $100-million portfolio of securities. The puts cost 1% of the value of the port-

TABLE 17.5 Portfolio Insurance Using Protective
Put Options

Portfolio Value	Put Value	P/L Portfolio	P/L Put	Net P/L	Net Portfolio Value
$ 90	$8	($10)	$7	($3)	$ 97
94	4	(6)	3	(3)	97
98	0	(2)	(1)	(3)	97
102	0	2	(1)	1	101
106	0	6	(1)	5	105
110	0	10	(1)	9	109

folio with a strike price of $98 per $100 of the portfolio's value. Hence, the minimum value of the portfolio is $97 million.

The purchase of protective puts against a portfolio is the simplest way to illustrate the portfolio insurance concept. In actual practice, however, put options for the myriad different portfolios are scarcely available, let alone the puts with the requisite strike prices. Therefore, the major task in portfolio insurance is to create a synthetic put option that will afford the desired protection.

Creating a Synthetic Put Option on a Portfolio

Option-pricing theory has revealed that the price of an option (put or call) on a security depends only on the riskless rate of interest and on the characteristics of the security itself. The theory also suggests that the option and its underlying security can always be combined in well-defined proportions to create a portfolio that is riskless. This is an important result because given any two of the three securities (the option, the underlying security, and the riskless asset), it should be possible, in principle, to create the third security. The key to creation of the third security (in this case, the put option) is the delta ratio—the ratio of options to hold versus the portfolio such that the combination portfolio is riskless.

There are at least two different methods by which the synthetic put can be created. The first method is the dynamic asset allocation method, a strategy that utilizes only cash market securities to simulate the put option. The second method uses index futures and/or option contracts to prevent losses below the floor level of return.

Dynamic Asset Allocation Strategy

In the dynamic asset allocation strategy, the investor must allocate a portion of the portfolio to the risky securities and the remainder to the riskless security. The proportion allocated to the riskless security depends on the amount of protection required and the assumed volatility of the portfolio. It is a measurable quantity based on the delta ratio of the put option. The greater the protection required or the greater the assumed volatility, the larger the fraction that must be invested in the riskless security. Just as important, as the prices of securities change, thus altering the value of the portfolio, the allocations between the riskless security and the risky securities also change. The proportion invested in the risky security increases as the market moves up and declines as the market moves down. Hence, a continuous rebalancing of funds between the risky securities and the riskless security simulates the effect of the protective put.

The dynamic asset allocation strategy has several costs a potential user needs to be apprised of. The obvious one is the commissions involved in rebalancing the portfolio between the risky security and the riskless security. Moreover, the investor is always buying at asked prices and selling at bid prices. Thus, every round-trip transaction involves a loss of the bid-ask spread. Additionally, a highly volatile market creates the potential of being whipsawed, not once but several times. Also, the estimate of volatility of the risky portfolio is a crucial determinant of the allocation fractions. An overestimate of volatility has the effect of paying higher prices for the synthetic put option or a higher insurance premium. This will result in a lower realized return. On the other hand, an underestimate of volatility has the effect of underhedging, thereby putting the achievement of the floor level of return at risk. In summary, the dynamic asset allocation strategy may work effectively in theory, but in practice, though, achieving the goal of a minimum floor return is no simple task.

Index Futures Strategy

The principle underlying the use of index futures to insure portfolios against losses below a given floor level is a simple one. Imagine a portfolio manager considering insuring a $100-million dollar portfolio. The portfolio is partly invested in risky securities and partly in riskless securities. It has a beta coefficient of 1.25 and a yield of 5%. The investment horizon is one year. The floor level of the portfolio is set at $95 million. Hence, the prespecified minimum floor return is 0% (i.e., at worst a $5-million capital loss will be offset by the $5 million in income).

The guaranteed floor level of $95 million requires that as the value of the portfolio begins dropping below $100 million the manager should start shorting index futures contracts. The shorting of futures contracts lowers the beta coefficient of the portfolio (see earlier example on adjusting the beta of a portfolio). The shorting will continue such that at a portfolio value of $95 million the effective beta coefficient of the portfolio is reduced to zero. At this point the portfolio is essentially riskless. Any drop in value below $95 million should be offset by gains in the short futures positions.

The schedule for shorting futures as the value of the portfolio declines can be computed. It is essentially a function of the assumed volatility of the portfolio and the size of insurance deductible (portfolio floor value) desired. The greater the volatility or lower the deductible, the larger the premium. The premium is paid through the give-up in upside potential caused by being short the futures contracts. For example, in the extreme case of a floor value of $100 million (current portfolio value), the number of futures contracts to be shorted would be that number that would make the beta of the portfolio currently equal to zero. Any rise in the value of the portfolio would be offset by losses in the futures position, thus resulting in no net gain. Further rises, though, would result in some gains because the futures positions would start being unwound. A sustained rally would ultimately result in the repurchase of the entire futures position. From this point on, all gains would accrue to the portfolio.

The portfolio insurance strategy using index futures has some significant advantages over the dynamic asset allocation strategy. A major one is that it can be undertaken independently of the fund manager. For example, the fund manager can continue to seek value in underpriced securities without being overly concerned with the general economic situation. The latter becomes the purview of the insurance strategist, who continuously monitors the beta of the portfolio and, as need be, assumes futures positions to afford the desired protection. The trading costs of the strategy are much lower because of the enormous leverage offered by futures contracts and the relatively low commission charges. Also, the ease of execution in futures markets because of very high liquidity makes them particularly attractive to the portfolio insurer.

There are some disadvantages, however, to implementing insurance strategies with futures contracts. First, the inevitable basis risk exists when hedging with futures contracts. What this means is that the beta coefficient of zero that is desired when the portfolio value reaches the floor value will seldom be achieved without some error. This must necessarily result in the realized return being different from the specified floor return. The extent of the error depends on the amount of basis risk. Second, transacting in futures markets requires the posting of margin and variation margin. However small this may be, it results in a drain of funds that could otherwise be invested more productively. Third, the longer the investment horizon the greater the likelihood that the futures positions have to be rolled over, resulting in additional transactions costs. Finally, the futures positions need to be continuously monitored and updated as the market moves significantly in either direction.

Index Options Strategy

The use of exchange traded option contracts on stock market indices or on futures contracts on the indices is the most direct approach to implementing a portfolio insurance strategy. The purchase of put options with a strike price equivalent to the desired floor value of the portfolio will achieve the insurance objective. The price paid for the protection equals the put premium. Alternatively, call options can be sold against the portfolio to obtain the equivalent protection.

The principle underlying the use of option contracts is similar to that of futures contracts. As the portfolio approaches and finally reaches the floor value you would want the losses in the portfolio to be increasingly offset by gains in the option positions.

If call options are used, then close monitoring of the call position is required as the portfolio changes in value. The delta ratio, that is, the ratio of change in the option price relative to changes in the portfolio value, declines sharply as the value of the portfolio begins to decline below the strike price. This requires additional calls to be sold or the entire call position to be rolled over into calls with a lower strike price. As the portfolio rises in value the delta ratio increases, requiring calls to be repurchased so that any additional gains accrue to the portfolio.

If a put option strategy is used, the monitoring requirements are far less. As the portfolio declines in value, losses in the portfolio are increasingly offset with gains in the put positions, especially when the portfolio's value declines below the prespecified minimum (or the strike price of the option).

The lower monitoring requirements give the put options strategy an obvious tactical advantage over the call option strategy. However, this advantage does not come without cost. The cost for the put strategy arises from the payment of the put premium. The call strategy, on the other hand, results in the receipt of the call premium. Since option premiums include a premium for time (to expiration), the passage of time works in favor of the call strategy. The choice of one strategy over the other rests, to some extent, on the trade-off between the premiums received (paid) versus the higher (lower) costs of monitoring each strategy.

Some additional issues need to be addressed when using an option strategy (calls or puts) in portfolio insurance. First, since the insured portfolio is likely to be different from the index on which the option contract is written, the extent of the protection will depend on how well diversified the portfolio is. The lower the unsystematic risk, the better the protection.

Second, the strike prices as well as the expiration months of the options are limited. This restricts the choice of the prespecified floor level of return and the time horizon for protection. With exchange traded options, only insurance programs of less than one year are possible. However, the longer the horizon the greater the problems associated with liquidity.

Third, since the prices of options heavily depend on estimates of volatility, the likelihood of overpricing or underpricing the options exists. Overpricing hurts in the case of the put strategy but helps in the case of the call strategy.

Last, there is always the choice of using longer-term options versus a sequence of shorter-term ones. Longer-term options may offer better long-term protection but will tend to have a larger interim volatility. This is because of their lower sensitivity to changes in the cash portfolio. For any fixed investment horizon they tend to be cheaper than a sequence of short-term options. A sequence of short-term options, by definition, requires a rollover of option positions. This necessitates incurring additional transactions costs. However, the advantage gained is better interim protection and greater flexibility in highly volatile markets. Finally, a sequence of shorter-term options allows for greater upside profit potential. But at the same time they require a lower floor level of return. Hence, the choice of the option term boils down to a trade-off between cost, flexibility, and protection, something only the portfolio manager can properly decide.

PROGRAM TRADING

The expression *program trading* refers to the execution of index arbitrage by highly sophisticated computers that place buy and sell orders simultaneously on index futures, index options, and stocks in the index portfolios. As mentioned earlier, discrepancies in pricing between index futures and the underlying stocks could create profitable opportunities. However, such profits could only be realized through fast execution of trades, something only a computer could accomplish. Timing is of the essence in program trading.

Since the index portfolios require the holding of large numbers of securities (except for the MMI Index), efficient execution of program trading requires the creation of the proxy portfolio—the portfolio that mirrors the index. The very creation of this portfolio suggests the extent to which the changes in the price of each stock will influence changes in the index. It provides the information on the size of transactions required for individual securities. Since the price discrepancies on which an arbitrageur operates are small, program trading tends to occur on a large scale. Literally hundreds of millions of dollars of securities need to be bought or sold simultaneously, a task suited mostly to institutional investors.

Program trading tends to peak around the date, or more specifically the time, at which the index options and futures contracts expire. The *triple witching hour*, the final hour of trading prior to expiration of the index option and futures contracts, is the scene of the most dramatic changes in security prices. The reason for this is that at expiration the futures price must equal the spot index. Any discrepancies between the two magnifies the profit opportunities and, thus, leads to large-scale trading in the underlying securities and the futures and option contracts.

A huge controversy has developed over the use of program trading, especially after the huge sell-off of stocks starting the week prior to the stock market crash on Monday, October 19, 1987. A major share of the blame for the debacle in stock prices was heaped on program trading and portfolio insurance.

One of the arguments offered was that on Monday following the sharp sell-off in stocks the previous Friday, portfolio insurers sold an unusual amount of stock index futures to hedge against further declines in their equity portfolios. The sale of index futures caused a decline in futures prices relative to stock prices, thereby triggering a huge amount of index arbitrage via program trading. Index arbitrageurs sold stocks through the NYSE's Designated Order Turnaround (DOT) automated execution system and simultaneously bought futures. This prompted a decline in stock prices, which led to further sales of index futures by the portfolio insurers, which, in turn, led to further sales of stocks and purchases of index futures by the index arbitrageurs. The heavy selling pressure on index futures by the portfolio insurers should have been matched, in principle, by purchases of the index futures by the index arbitrageurs, thereby providing stability to the markets. However, at some point during the process the stock market got effectively disconnected from the futures markets, and the markets lost their joint stabilizing influence. Panic set in and stocks went into a free fall. By the end of trading on Monday, October 19, 1987, the Dow Jones Industrial Average had fallen 508 points or approximately 23% of its value on a trading volume of 604 million shares.

The U.S. equity markets saw what was probably the worst single day in their history. The shock waves of the collapse on Wall Street were felt all over the world as stock markets from London to Hong Kong to Tokyo plunged.

Numerous commissions were set up to analyze the reasons for the crash. An official presidential task force was appointed by then President Reagan and headed by Nicholas Brady. The report is known popularly as the Brady Commission Report. The CFTC and the SEC also undertook studies of their own.

One of the major conclusions reached by the task force was that there was a lack of any evidence to suggest that the crash was due to willful manipulation of the markets. Many recommendations were made to reduce the possibility of such a crash reoccurring. Among the more important recommendations was the institution of a *circuit breaker* mechanism, which gets triggered if the market rises or falls by a prescribed amount. The circuit breaker mechanism essentially entails the imposition of a coordinated trading halt. Another suggestion was to reevaluate the margin requirements on stocks relative to those for stock index futures. Additionally, improved oversight by the monitoring agencies such as the CFTC, the SEC, and the Federal Reserve Board was suggested.

One of the important outcomes of the crash (and subsequent task force report) was the institution of a type of circuit breaker by the NYSE. If the DJIA changes by more than 50 points, a circuit breaker is triggered whereby the NYSE orders index arbitrage via its DOT system to cease for the day. The Chicago Mercantile Exchange also has imposed a 30-point limit on daily moves in its S&P 500 futures contract. For the MMI futures contract at the Chicago Board of Trade there is an 80-point limit for daily price moves. Additionally, coordinated trading halts occur when the contract price falls by 20, 50, and 80 points below the previous day's settlement price.

CONCLUSION

The initiation of trading in stock index futures could be viewed as a major change in the concept of futures trading. For many years it was deemed essential that actual delivery of the commodity underlying the futures contract be possible. Delivery may not have taken place, and seldom did, but the very possibility of delivery was believed to inextricably link prices determined in the futures markets to those in the cash market. If this linkage did not exist, the futures market was considered essentially speculative, and hence of no social or economic value. The introduction of stock index futures with its concept of cash settlement changed all that.

Cash settlement simply means that at contract expiration the buyer and seller of a futures contract will settle in cash the difference between the price of the futures contract originally agreed upon and the price of the underlying commodity. The acceptance of the concept of cash settlement recognized that the primary functions of a futures market are to facilitate price discovery and hedging. If it can be shown that the initiation of trading in a new contract will encourage both, then the contract has justified its existence. The details of how the contract is settled at contract expiration should not be allowed to detract from the fundamental purpose of the markets.

As a medium for hedging, stock index futures appear to have held their own. They provide ample opportunities to a wide cross section of users to use the markets effectively for hedging. At the same time, stock index futures have provided new avenues for speculation—an activity deemed critical to effective hedging. Now a speculator can act on his forecast of the direction of the market as a whole. Prior to the initiation of stock index futures a speculator would have to buy the securities composing the index or, alternatively, a basket of securities that mirrored the index. In either case the cost would have been prohibitive, more so in the case of the former than the latter. Additionally, stock index futures have accelerated the creation of many new funds designed to track the various indices, and also the creation of entirely new indices on commodities and other financial instruments.

A major hedging opportunity provided by stock index futures is the ability to hedge overall market risk. Portfolio managers can now buy or sell stock index futures to adjust the market exposure of their portfolios with unmatched economy and efficiency. Utilizing the concept of portfolio insurance, they can act to reduce the likelihood of losses below prespecified minimum values. By placing intermarket spreads they can act on their belief that one segment of the stock market leads another segment of it. If an index future is priced too low or too high relative to its underlying stocks, index arbitrage can be undertaken to exploit price differences. These are some of the many hedging applications of stock index futures. Opportunities would multiply if futures trading on the many new indices spawned by the currently traded stock index futures is ever initiated.

Do stock index futures facilitate price discovery? The answer to this question is somewhat troubling because one is not really sure what price discovery means in the context of an index of securities. Should security prices be discovered via the index or should the index value be discovered via security prices? Or should value be discovered via both? An index is, after all, a barometer that reflects the overall performance of the securities underlying the index. In a very broad sense the index reflects the effect of economywide factors on the prices of individual securities. However, this information gets filtered into the index via the securities. The index takes its cue from the changes in prices of the securities and not from independent sources. It is the securities that make up the index and not the other way around.

Prior to the initiation of trading in stock index futures there was no doubt that the index found its value via the prices of individual securities. Now it is increasingly suggested that index trading has more than a cursory effect on the pricing of individual securities.

There is no inherent problem in the spot market pricing off the futures market. In fact, this is the case in almost every commodity futures market, where spot prices are quoted in the form of discounts (or premiums) from the futures price, with enormously beneficial consequences. The economic justification here is that commodity futures markets bring together many buyers and sellers into a centralized marketplace where the combined knowledge of overall supply and demand can be brought to bear more fully on price. These centrally determined prices can then be used as a benchmark to price commodities in distant and diverse locations.

In the case of common stocks, individual security prices are already widely publicized and competitively determined. These prices reflect the combined knowledge of economywide and company-specific factors on the value of individual securities. This knowledge gets embodied in macro form in the index. Trading in stock index futures facilitates a reversal of this process. The open question is whether it is possible to bring superior information to bear on the value of the index, independently of information reflected in the prices that result from the millions of shares traded in the individual securities. Further, does it matter if the answer is no?

18

The Options Market

INTRODUCTION

Trading in option contracts has been conducted in the United States on an intermittent basis for more than a century. History has shown that whenever prices have entered a period of great volatility, shrewd operators who sell options on commodities emerge. Sometimes these operators have had legitimate interest in the commodities themselves. In many instances, though, commodity options were a favorite playground for scam operators.

In 1936, there was a charge that options played a role in a particularly blatant—and successful—attempt to manipulate the grain markets at the Chicago Board of Trade. Congress held hearings on the matter and subsequently passed the Commodity Exchange Act, which barred all trading in options under the regulation of the Commodity Exchange Authority.

In 1974, and again in 1982, during hearings to revise the Commodity Exchange Act, Congress once again addressed the issue of allowing options to be traded on regulated exchanges. After extensive testimony extolling the economic virtues of commodity options, Congress decided to leave the decision to the Commodity Futures Trading Commission.

The Commission, after a good deal of study and debate, decided to permit the trading of options on commodities and options on futures on organized exchanges in the United States for an initial three-year test period. This pilot program was to provide a means by which the commercial usefulness of options and their impact on the underlying futures and cash prices could be studied. The success of this pilot program is evidenced by the explosion in options trading currently occurring in major exchanges around the country.

As of the present writing options trading on organized exchanges takes place on common stock, stock indices, commodities, interest rate instruments, and futures contracts on a variety of underlying instruments.

In general, trading in options is a complex topic. Volumes have been written on it. Treatment of the subject has extended from the highly sophisticated and mathematical to the essentially descriptive. The approach taken here attempts to straddle these extremes. The focus, however, is on the potential user of the option. What does the user need to know about options? What opportunities do they offer, either as pure investment vehicles, or as devices to manage risk? How do they differ from other securities, futures contracts for instance, in achieving similar objectives? In short, how does one use options to assist in meeting one's investment goals?

The topic of options will be covered in two chapters. This chapter introduces the security and familiarizes a potential user with the language typical in the trade. We then move to option-pricing basics and provide a simplified illustration of how an option is priced. The fundamental factors affecting options prices are discussed together with some important differences between options written on physicals as compared to options written on futures contracts. Several examples of the use of options for hedging are next provided. The chapter closes with a comparison between option contracts and futures contracts. The following chapter deals exclusively with illustrating strategies utilizing options.

THE LANGUAGE OF OPTIONS TRADING

A good place to begin the discussion of options is with an overview of the language typical in options trading.

Definition of an Options Contract

A call (put) option gives its holder the right, but not the obligation, to buy (sell) a fixed quantity of an asset at a fixed price at any time until a prespecified date.

The fixed price is termed the *exercise price* or *strike price* of the option. The prespecified date is called the *maturity* date or the *expiration* date of the option. The price of the options is referred to as the option *premium*. Following are two quotes of option premiums taken from the *Wall Street Journal* of August 13, 1990.

Corn 230, Dec Puts @ 2½
T-bonds 86, Dec Calls @ 5³/₆₄

The corn put option gives its holder the right to sell one December futures contract on corn at $2.30 a bushel until December 14, 1990. The option premium is 2½ cents a bushel. Since the futures contract calls for delivery of 5,000 bushels of corn, the total price of the put option is $125.00 ($0.025 × 5000).

The T-bond call option gives its holder the right to buy one December futures contract on T-bonds at a price of $86 per $100 of face value until November 23, 1990. The option premium is $5³/₆₄ per $100 of face value. Since the futures contract is based on a face value of $100,000, the total price of this call option is $5046.87 ($5³/₆₄ × 1,000).

An option is said to be *exercised* if the holder exchanges the option for the underlying asset. A *European* option is exercisable only at expiration of the contract. An *American* option can be exercised at any time during the option's life. Since an American option provides its holder the advantage of early exercise, it cannot sell at a price less than that of an equivalent European option. Usually it will sell for more. The extra amount may be termed as an early exercise premium. Most options traded on the U.S. exchanges are of the American type.

An option is said to be *at-the-money* if the price of the underlying asset equals the strike price of the option. The call (put) option is said to be *in-the-money* if the price of the underlying asset is greater (less) than the strike price. The call (put) option is said to be *out-of-the-money* if the price of the underlying asset is less (greater) than the strike price.

An option *margin* is the sum of money that must be deposited—and maintained—by the option seller to provide protection to both parties to the trade. The margin is required only if the sale undertaken is a *naked* sale, that is, the seller does not possess the underlying asset. If the option seller is in possession of the underlying asset, then the sale of the option is referred to as a *covered* sale, and no margin is required. The exchange establishes minimum margin amounts. Brokerage firms often require margin deposits that exceed the exchange minimums. In turn, the brokerage houses post and maintain these margins with the Clearing Corporation. Buyers of options need not post any margin because their risk is limited to the option premium paid.

Margin calls are additional funds the seller of a naked position in the option is called upon to deposit if there is an adverse change in the price of the underlying asset, or if margin requirements are increased.

An option *spread* refers to a simultaneous long and short position in two or more options of the same type (i.e., puts or calls); for example, buying a call with one strike price and selling another call with a different strike price. An option *straddle* is a simultaneous position in a put and a call option. The *writing* of a call or a put option refers to the sale of the option in an opening transaction.

OPTION-PRICING BASICS

An option contract, like a futures contract, is a derivative instrument, meaning its price is largely driven by the asset underlying it. The two contracts are, however, significantly different from each other. The difference arises primarily from the rights and/or obligations of the holder of each of the contracts.

In the case of a futures contract the buyer is obligated either to take delivery of the underlying asset at contract expiration or to resell his contract at or prior to contract expiration. This requirement guarantees that the futures contract will trade at a price close (theoretically equal) to the spot price of the asset at contract expiration. It also implies that the price of a futures contract will closely track the price of the underlying asset prior to contract expiration.

In the case of an option contract (say a call option), the buyer has the right, but not the obligation, to take delivery of the underlying asset at the prespecified strike price. Obviously, if the actual market price of the asset exceeds the strike price, the call option will have equal value to, at least, the difference between the market price of the asset and the strike price—the option's *intrinsic value*. If the market price of the asset is less than the strike price, the option will have no intrinsic value but will have *time value*. Hence the price of an option, or the option premium, can be viewed as consisting of two components: an intrinsic value component and a time value component.

$$\text{Option Premium} = \text{Intrinsic Value} + \text{Time Value}$$

Intrinsic Value of an Option

The intrinsic value of an option is the dollar amount that would be received if the option were excercised immediately. It is computed as follows for the call and the put option.

Intrinsic Value	= Spot Price − Strike Price	. . . if Spot > Strike
(Call Option)	= 0	. . . otherwise
Intrinsic Value	= Strike Price − Spot Price	. . . if Strike > Spot
(Put Option)	= 0	. . . otherwise

The intrinsic value represents the floor price at which the option will trade at any time during the option's life. In reality the option will trade at a price higher than its intrinsic value. The differential is called the time value of the option. It is the difference between the actual market price of the option less the option's intrinsic value. For example, if a security is currently selling for $105 and a call option on it with a strike price of $100 is selling for $6.50, then the intrinsic value of the option is $5.00 ($105 − $100), and the time value of the option is $1.50 ($6.50 − $5.00).

Time Value of the Option

An option has time value because the longer the time left to contract expiration the greater the possibility that the price of the underlying asset will exceed the strike price as the option ages to its expiration date. The time value of the option is primarily a function of the volatility of the price of the asset underlying the option contract, and the level of interest rates. The greater the volatility of the asset, or higher the interest rate, the greater is the time value and, hence, the option premium.

Figures 18.1 and 18.2 are visual representations of call and put option premiums on T-bond futures with a strike price of 90.00, at a given point in time. The dashed line represents the intrinsic value of the option. Note how the intrinsic value is equal to zero when the price of the T-bond future is less than the strike price for the call option, and when the price of the T-bond future is greater than the strike price for the put option.

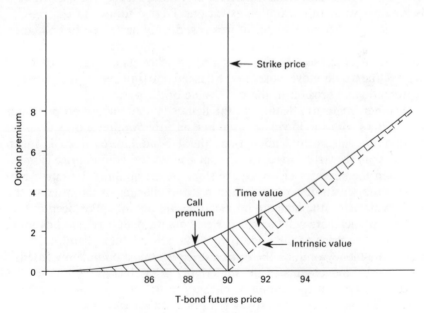

FIGURE 18.1 Call option premium.

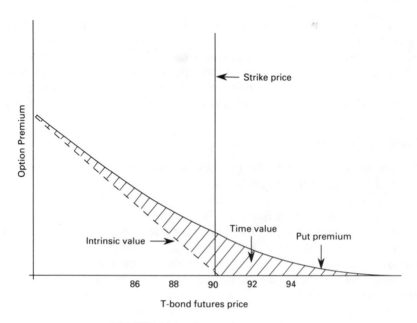

FIGURE 18.2   Put option premium.

The curved line represents the actual premium. Hence, the shaded area
is the time value of the option at various T-bond futures prices.

If the volatility of T-bond futures is suddenly perceived to be higher,
then the curved line would move up, thereby widening the shaded area
(time value increase). As the option approaches its expiration date the
curved line would move closer to the dashed line (intrinsic value), thereby
representing an erosion in the time value of the option.

Another interesting feature in the figures is how the option premium
line merges with the intrinsic value line as either option moves deep-in-
the-money; that is, for call options the T-bond futures price is much
greater than the strike price, and for put options the T-bond price is much
less than the strike price. Since the slope of the option price curve represents the sensitivity of the option price to changes in the price of the
underlying asset, the hedging implications are obvious. For deep in-the-
money options there will be near-perfect comovement between the option
price and the price of the underlying asset. On the other hand, for deep
out-of-the-money options the option price is almost completely insensi-
tive to price movements in the underlying asset. Just as important, the
price sensitivity of the option to changes in the price of the underlying
asset will change continuously as the price of the asset changes.

Calculation of the Option Premium—A Simplified Illustration

The logic underlying option pricing is riskless arbitrage. Since option contracts derive their value primarily from the assets underlying them it should be possible, in principle, to construct a portfolio with options, and its underlying asset, that is risk-free. If a risk-free portfolio does not provide a return equal to the riskless rate, then profitable arbitrage opportunities will exist. The two major option-pricing models widely used today—the *Black and Scholes Option-Pricing Model* and the *Binomial Option-Pricing Model*—utilize the concept of creating the riskless portfolio to derive equilibrium put and call option premiums. The premiums are shown to depend on the current price of the asset, the asset's volatility, the strike price, level of interest rate, and time to expiration. The Black-Scholes formula for obtaining the premiums is described in Appendix B.

Among the more interesting features of both option-pricing models is that the option price does not depend directly on the expected return on the asset nor on the risk preferences of the market participants. All investors, whether bullish or bearish on the market, should agree that option prices derived from the models are correct with respect to the underlying asset. These features allow us to provide a simplified example of how an option premium is derived. The example will be for a call option.

At contract expiration a call option will have value only if the market price of the underlying asset exceeds the strike price of the option. Hence, given a probability distribution of prices of the underlying asset at contract expiration it is possible to compute the expected profit from the option. This expected profit is the expected call price (at expiration). To obtain the current price simply discount the expected profit at expiration at the riskless rate. Following is the example.

Consider the pricing of a call option under the probability scenarios for the projected prices of the asset at expiration of the contract displayed in Table 18.1. Under both scenarios the expected price of the asset at expiration is expected to be the same ($100). However, under Scenario 2 prices are more volatile than under Scenario 1.

Table 18.2 calculates the expected option premium for the call option at contract expiration for a strike price of $100 under Scenario 1. If the riskless borrowing cost is assumed to be 10%, and there are 90 days to expiration of the contract, then the current option premium is computed as the present value of the expected premium.

$$\text{Option Premium} = \text{Present Value of Expected Premium}$$
$$= \$3/(1 + .10)^{90/365}$$
$$= \$2.93$$

TABLE 18.1   Probability Distribution of Asset
Prices under Alternative Scenarios

	Prices of Asset	
Probability	Scenario 1	Scenario 2
20.00%	90.00	80.00
20.00	95.00	90.00
20.00	100.00 ·	100.00
20.00	105.00	110.00
20.00	110.00	120.00
Expected Price =	100.00	100.00

TABLE 18.2   Calculation of a Call Option Premium under
Scenario 1 (Strike Price = 100)

Probability	Spot Price	Difference* (Spot less Strike)	Probability × Difference
20.00%	90.00	0.00	0.00
20.00	95.00	0.00	0.00
20.00	100.00	0.00	0.00
20.00	105.00	5.00	1.00
20.00	110.00	10.00	2.00
		Expected Option Premium =	3.00

*Difference = 0 if spot price is less than the strike price.

Fundamental Factors That Affect the Option Premium

Option premiums are affected by several factors. The fundamental ones
are as follows:

1. The current price of the underlying asset.
2. The strike price of the option.
3. Time left to expiration.
4. Volatility of the underlying asset.
5. Interest rates.
6. Income from the assets.

The influence of the first three factors is obvious and needs little explanation. The higher the current price of the asset relative to the strike

price, the higher is the call premium and the lower the put premium. The longer the time to expiration the greater is the probability that the price of the asset will fall below or exceed the strike price. Hence, both put and call premiums must be positively influenced by time to expiration. The last three factors are more involved and are often viewed as key determinants of option value. Hence, we consider each of them separately.

Volatility and the Option Premium

The greater the volatility of an asset the greater is the possibility that the price of the asset will exceed or fall below the strike price at contract expiration. This must result in higher call, as well as, put premiums.

Consider the valuation of a call premium under Scenario 2 in Table 18.1. Clearly the asset is much more volatile under Scenario 2 than under Scenario 1. The effect on the option premium is shown in Table 18.3. The option premium is once again computed as:

$$\text{Option Premium} = \text{Present Value of Expected Premium}$$
$$= \$6/(1 + .10)^{90/365}$$
$$= \$5.86$$

Note that the option premium under Scenario 2 is twice that under Scenario 1 in response to doubling of the volatility of the underlying asset.

There can be no disagreement that an increase in volatility must increase option premiums—both puts and calls. However, there can be substantial disagreement on the estimate of volatility to use to determine the option premium. Different estimates of volatility will result in different estimates of option premiums, and hence different conclusions as

TABLE 18.3 Calculation of a Call Option Premium under Scenario 2 (Strike Price = 100)

Probability	Spot Price	Difference* (Spot less Strike)	Probability × Difference
20.00%	80.00	0.00	0.00
20.00	90.00	0.00	0.00
20.00	100.00	0.00	0.00
20.00	110.00	10.00	2.00
20.00	120.00	20.00	4.00
		Expected Option Premium =	6.00

*Difference = 0 if spot price is less than the strike price.

to whether options are overpriced or underpriced. This, in turn, could lead one to undertake trades in order to exploit the apparent mispricing.

One useful outgrowth of the belief that the Black and Scholes and the Binomial option-pricing models correctly price an option contract is the concept of *implied volatility.*

Given the option premium quoted in the market, the volatility of the underlying asset implicit in the quoted price can be extracted from the option-pricing formula. It is referred to as the asset's implied volatility. The estimate of implied volatility is useful because it may be viewed as the market's consensus of the volatility of the asset. If a portfolio manager's estimate of volatility differs from the market consensus estimate, then a basis for executing transactions to exploit mispricing is established.

Interest Rates and the Option Premium

The interest rate prevailing in the market at any time has an influence on the option premium. In general, the higher the interest rate the higher the option premium. This seems counterintuitive following the examples shown earlier where the current premium paid for the option is the discounted value of the expected premium at expiration. However, if the expected premium at expiration is itself positively influenced by the level of interest rates, then the interest rate effect will materialize. The following example shows the interest rate effect.

Consider an asset currently priced at $100. The level of interest rates prevailing in the market must affect the expected return on the asset if investors are to be rewarded for taking on risk. The higher the interest rates the higher should be the expected return on the asset, and vice versa. Table 18.4 shows two possible sets of probability distributions of prices for the asset at the end of one year. In the first set the asset is expected to return 10%. In the second set the return is expected to be 20%.

Assume, for expositional purposes, that 10% and 20% are, respectively, the two different levels of interest rates under each expected return scenario. Hence, we assume a world of risk-neutral investors—an assumption made only for ease of exposition. The two option-pricing models mentioned earlier have proved that option premiums are independent of the risk preferences of investors and so the assumption has no effect on the option premiums derived.

Utilizing the technique for computing the option premium described earlier, the option premium under each interest rate scenario is displayed in Table 18.5 for various strike prices.

Table 18.5 confirms the influence of the interest rate on call option premiums. The higher the interest rate the higher the premium, and vice versa. However, this interest rate effect should not be confused with the

TABLE 18.4 Probability Distribution of Asset under Alternative Interest Rate Scenarios (Current Price of Asset = $100)

Probability	Prices of Asset for Varying Interest Rate Scenarios	
	10%	20%
20.00%	100.00	100.00
20.00	105.00	110.00
20.00	110.00	120.00
20.00	115.00	130.00
20.00	120.00	140.00
Expected Price =	110.00	120.00
Expected Return =	10.00%	20.00%

TABLE 18.5 Call Option Premiums under Varying Interest Rate Scenarios and Strike Prices

Strike Price	Option Premiums for Varying Interest Rate Scenarios	
	10%	20%
100.00	9.09	16.67
105.00	5.05	13.33
110.00	2.73	10.00
115.00	0.91	7.50
120.00	0.00	5.00

fact that often in a rising interest rate environment call option prices may fall instead of rise. The fall in call option prices in a rising interest rate environment may occur because asset prices fall. Falling asset prices must naturally have an overwhelming influence in lowering call option prices.

Income and the Option Premium

Other things being equal, income from an asset should lower call premiums and raise put premiums, particularly in cases where income from the asset does not accrue. A case in point is options on a dividend paying stock. On the date a stock goes exdividend, the price of the stock tends to drop by an amount equal or close to the dividend. This fall in price works in favor of the holder of a put option and against the holder of a call option. Obviously the larger the dividend the larger the influence on the option premiums.

In the case of income from assets where the income does accrue, as in the situation with bonds, an income effect will exist but it operates a little differently. This can be seen by comparing two bonds with different coupons selling at similar yields. The holder of a lower coupon bond should expect to receive a larger percentage of return through price appreciation than the holder of the higher coupon bond. This, in turn, implies that the lower coupon bond will be subject to larger percentage changes in price than the higher coupon bond for a given change in interest rates. This larger volatility for the lower coupon bond should result in higher option premiums than those for the higher coupon bonds at strike prices equal to their current market prices.

Table 18.6 summarizes the effect of each of the key variables that affect the price of a put and a call option.

Other Factors Influencing Option Premiums

Several other factors, besides the major ones discussed, influence option premiums. One that needs particular mention is the prospect of early exercise. Most options traded on the U.S. exchanges are American options—options that permit exercise at any time during the option's life. As mentioned earlier, this feature cannot have a negative value. However, this does not necessarily imply that the feature *must* have a positive value. For example, if it can be shown that it never makes sense to exercise an option prior to expiration, then the early exercise feature

TABLE 18.6 Influence of Key Variables on the Price of the Call and Put Option

Variable	Call	Put
Increase In		
Time to Expiration	Increase	Increase
Strike Price	Decrease	Increase
Volatility	Increase	Increase
Interest Rates	Increase	Decrease
Asset Income*	Decrease	Increase
Asset Price	Increase	Decrease

*Only for income that does not accrue.

is worthless—and so American options will trade at prices identical to European options.

There are, however, instances where early exercise is not only possible, but also likely. The case of a dividend paying stock is an example. Dividends on stock do not accrue like interest on bonds. As a consequence, holders of call options on common stock often find it worthwhile to exercise their options around the en-dividend date of the stock in order to capture the dividend. Another example is the case of deep in-the-money put options. If deep in-the-money put options are exercised, the proceeds can be invested to earn an extra return until contract expiration. If the put holder feels the prospect of the asset falling in price by an amount that will exceed the extra return is remote, he will be motivated to immediately exercise the option. Yet another example is when the asset underlying the option contract is a futures contract rather than the physical asset. Early exercise is likely for a call option. This is discussed in more detail a little later.

Some other factors that affect option premiums are of an institutional nature, such as taxes, margin requirements, transactions costs, and so on. Their effects are small, however. Their influence is seen primarily in the extent to which they inhibit trading in the contracts, which in turn tends to impair the viability of the markets.

OPTIONS ON PHYSICALS VERSUS OPTIONS ON FUTURES

The basics of option pricing discussed so far did not concern itself with whether the instrument underlying the option contract was the actual physical asset or a futures contract on the physical asset. Hence, the major concepts underlying the pricing of the contract apply equally to both types of options. However, there are some important differences to be aware of when the deliverable instrument happens to be a futures contract rather than the physical asset.

When an option on a futures contract is exercised, a transfer of a futures contract takes place at the exercise price. Because of the mark-to-market feature of futures trading, an immediate cash settlement between the buyer and seller of the option contract must take place when the option is exercised. For example, suppose the holder of a September T-bond futures call option at a strike price of 86.00 exercised the option when the September T-bond futures is selling for $90^{28}/_{32}$. On exercise the holder of the call option will have a long position in September T-bond futures. Marking-to-market would result in an immediate transfer of \$4875.00 ($90^{28}/_{32} - 86 = 4^{28}/_{32}$ @ 31.25 per $^1/_{32}$) from the seller of the call to the buyer of the call. This contrasts significantly with exercising a call option on a physical asset.

When a call option on a physical asset is exercised, there is a net transfer of funds equal to the exercise price from the buyer of the call option to the seller. This distinction is important because the net transfer of funds from the buyer of the call on physicals to the seller provides a disincentive for early exercise. On the other hand, the net transfer of funds from the seller to the buyer in the case of a call option on futures encourages early exercise, particularly if the option is deep in-the-money. The proceeds from early exercise can be invested to earn an extra return until expiration of the futures contract.

The likelihood of early exercise for call options on futures clearly works in favor of the buyer of the option rather than the seller. Hence, the buyer should be willing to pay an additional amount for the early exercise feature. However, this fact does not necessarily translate into a call option on futures always selling for more than a call option on the physicals with the same strike price, because the futures prices are almost invariably different from the spot price of the physicals. If the futures price is higher than the spot price, the call option on futures should sell for more than the call option on the physical asset. If the futures price is lower than the spot price, the call option on futures should sell for less than the call option on the physicals. The reverse is true for put options.

HEDGING WITH OPTIONS

Options can be used in a variety of ways in portfolio management. In a manner similar to the buying of futures contracts to lock in high yields, an investor can similarly purchase a call option on a fixed income security to accomplish the same objective. To protect a portfolio against possible loss in value due to rising interest rates, put options can be purchased to effect the same result as the selling of futures contracts. In many other ways options provide opportunities similar to those offered by futures contracts. Later we discuss the differences between the two securities and their contributions to meeting investment objectives. At present it is worthwhile to consider how call and put options can be used in some important applications.

Purchasing a Call Option as an Alternative Investment

Suppose an investor feels that yields currently being offered by Treasuries are high and wishes to lock them in. Funds are not available today but will be forthcoming in one year. The following alternatives are available:

Alternative I: Buy the securities today and finance them for one year.

Alternative II: Buy a call option on the security.

Consider the outcome from implementing each alternative under the following conditions:

Security: 10%, 15-Year U.S. Treasury bond selling at par
               (ytm = 10%)
Call Option: Strike Price = 100; Expiration = 1 Year;
               Premium = $3; Borrowing Cost = 12%

Under Alternative I the investor purchases a security that will provide a negative cash flow of $2 in the first year (coupon less financing cost), and $10 per year for the remaining 14 years. The negative cash flow in the first year has the effect of purchasing the bond at the end of the year for approximately $102, or a yield of 9.73%.

Under Alternative II the purchase of the call option at $3 has put a ceiling of $103 on the price of the bond or a floor of 9.61% on its yield. Hence, compared to Alternative I the yield disadvantage is 12 basis points if interest rates remain the same or fall. However, this 12 basis point yield disadvantage permits the investor to gain substantially if rates happen to rise. Table 18.7 shows the effective price and the effective yield obtained under various interest rate (yield) scenarios under Alternative II.

Purchasing Put Options to Protect an Existing Portfolio

Put options can be used to protect portfolios against erosion in value in a rising interest rate environment leaving their upside potential intact. This protection against loss is the reason why the insurance analogy is

TABLE 18.7 Effective Yield Via Option Investment under Various
Interest Rate Scenarios

Yield	Price of Bond	Option P/L	Effective	
			Price	Yield
8.00%	116.66	13.66	103.00	9.61%
9.00	107.87	4.87	103.00	9.61
10.00	100.00	−3.00	103.00	9.61
11.00	92.93	−3.00	95.93	10.56
12.00	86.59	−3.00	89.59	11.51

Note: Option P/L = Price of Bond − Strike Price − Option Premium.
Effective Price = Price of Bond − Option P/L. The cost of financing and option premium is ignored.

often invoked in discussions relating to put options. Following is an example of how a put protects a portfolio against loss.

Consider the same 10%, 15-Year U.S. Treasury bond in the previous example. A put option with a strike price of $100 and one year to expiration is available at a price of $3. The bond is selling at par. The price of $3 places a floor on the value of the bond to the investor of $97 (strike price less put premium) at the end of one year. Table 18.8 shows how this protection works under different interest rate scenarios.

An alternative way to look at the protection provided by the put would be to determine the yield of the portfolio if the profits (losses) on the put option were amortized over the remaining life (14 years) of the portfolio. This is done in Table 18.9. The amortized option P/L is computed as the semiannual cash flow that would be obtained if the option P/L were invested over the remaining 14 years at the prevailing interest rate. This semiannual cash flow is added to the semiannual coupon and multiplied by two to provide the yield.

TABLE 18.8   Purchase of a Put Option to Protect the Value of an Investment

Interest Rates	Bond Price	Option P/L	Effective Price
8.00%	$116.67	($ 3.00)	113.67
9.00	107.87	(3.00)	104.87
10.00	100.00	(3.00)	97.00
11.00	92.94	4.06	97.00
12.00	86.59	10.41	97.00

TABLE 18.9   Purchase of a Put Option to Protect the Yield of an Investment

Interest Rates	Bond Price	Option P/L	Semiannual Income		Portfolio Yield
			Amortized Option P/L	Coupon Income	
8.00%	$116.67	($3.00)	($0.18)	$5.00	9.64%
9.00	107.87	(3.00)	(0.19)	5.00	9.62
10.00	100.00	(3.00)	(0.20)	5.00	9.60
11.00	92.94	4.06	0.15	5.00	10.29
12.00	86.59	10.41	0.39	5.00	10.77

Put-Call Parity and the Creation of Synthetic Securities

One very useful applicaton of option contracts is the ability to create synthetic securities, that is, replicas of existing cash market securities or entirely new ones. The logic underlying the creation of synthetic securities is the *put-call parity* relationship.

The put-call parity relationship essentially states that since the profit/loss from holding a security can be replicated through put and call options on the seurity, the three securities should be priced so as to prevent arbitrage profits. The put-call parity relationship is formally represented in the following equation.

$$\text{Call Price} - \text{Put Price} = \text{Bond Price} - \text{Present Value of Exercise Price}$$

If market prices violate the above relationship, then appropriate positions can be taken in three securities and the riskless security to realize arbitrage profits. For example, suppose a bond is currently selling for $100. Puts and calls on the bond with a strike price of $100 are selling for $2.55 and $5.00, respectively. The options have three months to expire, and the riskless borrowing (and lending) rate is 8%. Using this information the following are values for the left-hand side and the right-hand side of the put-call parity relationship.

$$\begin{aligned}\text{Call Price} - \text{Put Price} &= \$5.00 - \$2.55\\ &= \$2.45\end{aligned}$$

$$\begin{aligned}\text{Strike Price}&\\ -\text{ PV of Exercise Price} &= \text{Cost of Financing Security}\\ &= 100 \times .08 \times (^3/_{12})\\ &= \$2.00\end{aligned}$$

The apparent violation of the put-call parity suggests that the call is overpriced and/or the put is underpriced. In either case an arbitrage opportunity exists and can be exploited by undertaking the following transactions.

1. Write one call at $5.00.
2. Buy one put at $2.55.
3. Finance the purchase of the bond ($100) at 8% for three months.

Table 18.10 shows the profits that would be realized at contract expiration by undertaking the above positions. If the put-call parity relationship is violated in the opposite direction, a reverse of all transactions specified earlier would result in arbitrage profits.

In practice, the implementation of an arbitrage strategy to exploit mispricing could be restrained by several factors. Among them are transactions costs, margin requirements, taxes, cash flow from the security, and

TABLE 18.10 Arbitrage Profits Resulting from the Violation
of the Put-Call Parity Relationship

Security Price	Profit From			Net Profit
	Security Position	Call Position	Put Position	
110.00	8.00	($5.00)	($2.55)	$0.45
105.00	3.00	0.00	(2.55)	0.45
100.00	−2.00	5.00	(2.55)	0.45
95.00	−7.00	5.00	2.45	0.45
90.00	−12.00	5.00	7.45	0.45

Note: Cost of financing security = $2.00. Investment income from the net cash flow from the call and put option is ignored.

the inability to use the entire proceeds from a short sale. Also, the need to hold the positions until expiration of the options requires that none of the option positions be exercised prior to contract expiration. This condition may not be reasonable as we have seen. Nevertheless, the possibility of realizing arbitrage profits from mispricing locks the prices of the options and the underlying security into a relationship that is defined to a large extent by the requirement of put-call parity.

One very useful application of the put-call parity relationship is the possibility, in principle, to use put and call options to create synthetic securities. The application is best explored graphically. In the examples to follow, any reference to the cash security should not be interpreted strictly as a cash market security. The cash security is meant to be the security underlying the option contract. Hence, the analysis applies equally to futures contracts on which options exist.

Consider the following profit/loss (P/L) diagrams for the cash security, and the put and call options shown in Figure 18.3.

Panels A and B, respectively, show the P/L in a long and short position in the cash market security currently priced at 100. Panels C and D shows the P/L of a long and a short position in a call option, respectively. Panels E and F show the P/L in a long and a short position in a put option, respectively. All options have a strike price of $100 and are currently priced at $1.

It is straightforward to see how appropriate positions in the call and the put option can create a P/L picture identical to the positions in the cash market security. For example, a long position in the call option and simultaneous short position in the put option have an identical P/L as being long in the cash market security. Similarly, a short position in the

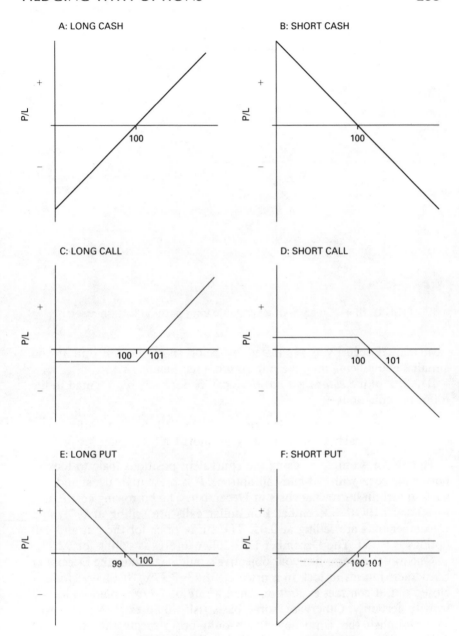

FIGURE 18.3 Profit/Loss (P/L) for naked positions.

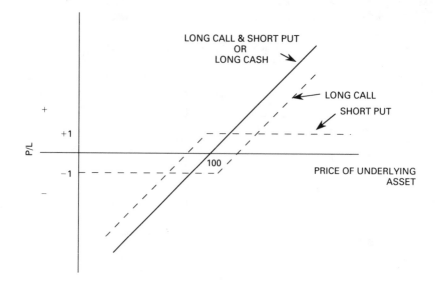

FIGURE 18.4 Creation of a synthetic long position in cash asset.

cash market security is replicated by being short the call option and simultaneouly being long the put option. (See Figure 18.4.)

The P/L of the *equivalent positions* can be formally represented in the following equations:

Long Cash Market Security = Long Call + Short Put
Short Cash Market Security = Short Call + Long Put

Here is an example of using the equivalent positions logic to lock in borrowing costs with put and call options. It is presently August and you wish to lock in borrowing costs in December. The borrowing cost is tied to 90-day LIBOR. December Eurodollar calls are selling at 0.71, and December puts are selling at 0.05. The strike price for the put and call options is 91.50. The December Eurodollar futures is selling for 92.23.

One way to accomplish your objective would be to short the December Eurodollar futures to lock in a price of 92.23 (7.77%). If this position is closed out at contract expiration, then a rate of 7.77% would be locked in with certainty. Otherwise, some basis risk would exist. Another way to accomplish the same objective would be to create the equivalent position with options. Remember the equivalent of a short position in the underlying security would be to short the call option and take a simultaneous long position in the put option. If these positions were taken in the options then the equivalent futures price would be computed as follows:

$$\text{Equivalent Futures Price} = \text{Strike Price} + \text{Call Premium}$$
$$- \text{Put Premium}$$
$$= 91.50 + 0.71 - 0.05$$
$$= 92.16$$

Hence, the lock-in price with the option contracts is 92.16 (7.84%). Table 18.11 shows that no matter where futures prices may go, if the option contracts are closed out at expiration, the price of 92.16 will be obtained.

Equivalent Positions and Arbitrage

The existence of equivalent positions invites arbitrage opportunities if any of the three securities (put, call, and underlying security) are not priced properly with respect to each other. It should be remembered that the equations representing P/L of the equivalent positions are those that will materialize at contract expiration. Prior to contract expiration the going interest rate should lock the prices of the three securities into a relationship that should prevent arbitrage profits. Consider the following example.

Suppose the cash market security is a 10% coupon bond selling at par. A three-month put and call option with a strike price of $100 are selling at $2.00 and $2.50, respectively. Assume a borrowing cost of 9%. What would be the investor's P/L if the following positions were simultaneously taken?

TABLE 18.11   Using Put and Call Options to Lock in
Borrowing Costs

Futures Price	Put Profit	Call Profit	Realized Futures Price
89.00	2.45	0.71	92.16
90.00	1.45	0.71	92.16
91.00	0.45	0.71	92.16
91.50	−0.05	0.71	92.16
92.00	−0.05	0.21	92.16
93.00	−0.05	−0.79	92.16

Note: Realized Futures Price = Futures Price + Put Profit + Call Profit.

1. Long cash security and financed at 9% for three months.
2. Short call option and long put option.

Investment	= Long Cash + Short Call + Long Put
	= −$100 + $2.50 − $2.00
	= −$99.50
	= Amount Borrowed
Interest Earned	= 0.10 × $100 × 3/12
	= $2.50
Borrowing Cost	= 0.09 × 99.50 × 3/12
	= $2.24
Profit	= Interest Earned − Borrowing Cost
	= $2.50 − $2.24
	= $0.26
Risk	= None

The investor who executes the positions in the three securities would make a profit of $0.26 on a zero net investment (since investment was financed by borrowing) if the positions were held until expiration. The investment would be riskless because the P/L on the cash position would be exactly offset by the P/L on the option positions. If the computed profit were negative, a reversal of the positions would yield a positive profit.

Do such profit opportunities exist? If they do, then barely so. Probably a small enough profit exists to attract only dealers in the cash market securities to undertake such transactions. Furthermore, the possibility of early exercise on the short call position does introduce risk, however small. Nevertheless, any existence of such arbitrage opportunities will encourage market participants to undertake the requisite transactions resulting in the ultimate elimination of the opportunities.

Using Options to Hedge Portfolios—Delta Hedging

Options can be used like futures to hedge individual securities or portfolios of securities. The principle of offsetting gains/losses in the cash position with losses/gains in option positions applies equally well to options as it does to futures. Any change in the prices of the securities must cause changes in the prices of options written on them.

The hedge ratio in options is often referred to as the *delta ratio*. It is the ratio of the change in price of the option to the change in price of the security hedged. For fixed income securities it could be defined as follows:

$$\text{Delta Ratio} = \frac{\text{Price Value per Basis Point of Option}}{\text{Price Value per Basis Point of Underlying Instrument}}$$

If the instrument being hedged is not the one underlying the option contract then the denominator of the delta ratio needs to be adjusted by a *relative yield volatility* factor.

$$\text{Relative Yield Volatility} = \frac{\text{Price Value per Basis Point of Hedged Instrument}}{\text{Price Value per Basis Point of Underlying Instrument}}$$

Since it is typical to define the hedge ratio in futures hedging as the relative price sensitivity of the instrument hedged to that of the hedging vehicle, then for the sake of consistency the hedge ratio in options hedging is defined as:

$$\text{Options Hedge Ratio} = \frac{\text{Price Sensitivity of Instrument Hedged}}{\text{Price Sensitivity of Option Contract}}$$

$$= \frac{\text{Relative Yield Volatility}}{\text{Delta Ratio}}$$

The delta ratio in an options hedge is very sensitive to the level of price of the instrument underlying it. For example, for options that are deep in-the-money the delta ratio is very close to 1.00. For options deep out-of-the-money the delta ratio is close to zero. For options that are at-the-money the delta ratios are close to 0.5.

The conceptual reasoning behind this behavior of the delta ratio is as follows: If the option is deep in-the-money, the option is almost certain to be exercised. The certainty of exercise will cause the option price to closely track the price of the underlying instrument—a one for one hedge will create a perfect offset between profits/losses in the option position and its underlying instrument.

For deep out-of-the-money options exercise is all but impossible. This fact causes the option price to change very little in response to changes in the price of the underlying instrument. Hence, a huge position in options would be required to offset a small change in the cash price.

For options at-the-money there is a 50-50 chance that the price of the underlying instrument will either rise or fall, thus requiring the delta ratio to be close to 0.50.

Hedging with Put or Call Options

If hedging is undertaken to offset cash price changes with those of the option contract, then conceptually either call option or put options can be used. However, the position (long or short) taken will depend on which option is used.

Consider, for example, the choice of the put or the call option that is presently at-the-money. The delta ratio in either case is close to 0.50. If the cash position hedged is a long one, the hedge can be accomplished by either being short two call options (1/Delta Ratio) per unit of the cash position or long two put options per unit of the cash position. Which one should the hedger prefer?

From a pure price offset point of view both options are equally good. However, the sale of call options provides an inflow of cash, in the form of the call premium, to the hedger. The put option route, on the other hand, requires the hedger to pay the put premium. If prices do not change, the hedger gains the "time value" component in the call premium and loses the same in the put premium. In this case hedging with calls would be preferred.

However, if the hedger is primarily concerned with downside risk—a likely possibility—then the put option would provide better protection. Falling prices of the cash instrument are better offset by rising prices in the long put position than falling prices in the short call position. In either case, however, the positions in the options will have to be adjusted as prices change.

OPTIONS VERSUS FUTURES

There are some important differences between an options contract and a futures contract. A futures contract is a bilateral contract requiring action by both parties and obligating both the buyer and the seller to fulfill the conditions by delivery and payment. An option contract, on the other hand, is a unilateral contract. Unlike a futures contract, the buyer and the seller of the option do not have an equivalent obligation to perform. The purchaser of an option has the right but not the obligation to require the seller to perform under the contract, and the seller is obligated to do so only if the buyer exercises his right. The converse, however, is not true. The seller of an option cannot require the purchaser to exercise. Only the buyer has the right to require fulfillment of the contract terms.

Perhaps the most distinguishing feature of an option contract is the limited liability of the purchaser. The potential loss to an option purchaser is limited to the "premium" that he pays to the seller at the time of the purchase of the option. The potential for gain, theoretically, is limited only by the extent of the price movement of the underlying contract. In contrast, on the futures contract, the holder of either a long or a short futures position remains liable to margin calls as long as his position remains open.

In short, therefore, the purchaser of an option contract can lose at a maximum only the amount paid for the option. This is so because, if the price does not move in the purchaser's favor, he fails to "exercise" his option and, instead, simply abandons it. An analogy can be drawn with an insurance contract. The writer of the insurance policy receives the premium for undertaking the risk but has to stand ready in the future to make any payments due the person who bought the insurance if that person submits a valid claim. If the person does not submit the claim, the insurance company still keeps the premium.

One major advantage of options over futures markets for the business person is that, when prices are extremely volatile, options can reduce the demands on cash flow. For example, if you have purchased a futures contract and it declines, you will have to pay in more margin, which, of course, must be paid in cash. If, on the other hand, you have purchased a call option, you will have a one-time payment; no matter how far price falls, you will not be asked to post more money. The converse of this is, of course, also true. If prices go up, the futures position will yield cash to you while no such thing will happen with the option. Options thus provide more certainty in planning cash flow exposure.

Options permit a range of investment and resource management strategies not available from futures. Options used in conjunction with futures and actual inventories of a product afford a wide range of strategies for a merchandiser, producer, or processor in managing inventories. They can provide greater control with lower capital requirements than do futures alone.

To a large extent, options are substitutes for stop orders on futures. You can attempt to limit your risk on a futures position by placing a stop loss order at whatever level you choose. Then, if the market touches that level, your broker would automatically offset the futures contract at the price stipulated or at the next possible price.

In essence, the purchase of an option serves the same purpose as the stop loss order serves in the futures contract. They are both there to limit losses. The difference between the two, however, is:

1. A stop loss order may not always be exercised at the price stimpulated, so the loss cannot be absolutely fixed in advance. The size of the option premium, however, is fixed in advance, and the loss cannot exceed the size of the premium.
2. A poorly disciplined trader may decide not to use stop loss orders and to met margin calls when he should not, thus sticking with a losing position in the hope that the market will reverse. This can lead to very large losses. An option, on the other hand, does not give that discretion to the holder. Once he buys the option, the marketplace decides whether it will be profitable to exercise it. The holder has no more decisions to make if the market moves against him.

3. One can get whipsawed in a market using stop loss orders. The market can set off a stop order, causing the offset of the futures contract, and then the market could turn around and go the opposite direction. Due to the offset, you would be without a position in the market and unable to take advantage of the price move.

In sum, the option is a more certain way of limiting losses. The value of this certainly has to be weighed against the size of the premium paid. It may be a very high price to pay for the luxury of not having to exercise the self-discipline in using stop loss orders or for the potential that you will get whipsawed.

Other differences between options and futures will become apparent as you read some of the strategies for trading options discussed in the next chapter.

19
Options Strategies—Illustrated

This chapter illustrates the rich variety of strategies available for foreign currency traders, stock index traders, or interest rate futures traders. The strategies illustrated apply equally well in all areas and to both options on futures and options on actuals.

1. Buy Put Options

Assume you are anticipating an increase in long-term interest rates and a corresponding decrease in futures prices. To take advantage of your expectations, assume you buy a Treasury bond March 76 put at a premium cost of $2000, reflecting an interest rate on long-term bonds of about 11%. If, by expiration in March, the interest rate has increased to 12%, the futures price will have decreased to 70–00 and you should be able to sell the option at a difference in value of $6000. Your profit on this transaction will be $4000 ($6000 less your $2000 premium) minus transactions costs.

If by the time March rolled around, interest rates had decreased to approximately 10.5%, the futures would be selling for about 79–00 and your put option with a strike price of 76–00 would expire worthless. You would have lost the entire $2000 paid for the option.

In many cases, you might decide not to wait until expiration to close out your position. If, in the above example, interest rates started falling with expiration a month or so away, you might have decided to sell the option before it reached a value of zero. By selling the option at say $500, you would reduce your loss to only $1500 ($2000 premium minus $500), plus the transaction costs.

2. Buy Call Options

If you anticipate an increase in prices, your strategy should be to purchase call options. A call option, as just noted, gives you, the buyer, the right to buy the underlying futures contract at the specified strike price. You will realize a profit if the intrinsic value of the option at expiration is greater than the premium you paid for the option. For example, assume it is June and you expect the S&P 500 Stock Index to be higher in September. Assume you pay a $2000 premium to buy a September 140 call option. If, when September rolls around, the S&P Index has risen to 150, the futures price should have increased to 150 also. You should then be able to sell the call option at its intrinsic value of 10 ($5000). Your net profit would be $3000 less the transaction costs.

Suppose, however, that when September rolled around, the futures price was 130 or below. In that case your call would expire worthless and you would lose the entire $2000. If, on the other hand, the futures price is at 140, your call would be worth the same price you paid for it. If the futures price has increased to 160, your call should be valued at 20, to yield an $8000 net profit.

3. Sell (Write) Call Option in Anticipation of Lower Prices

Writing (selling) options involves risks and rewards that are the exact opposite of the risk and rewards involved in buying options. The option writer assumes unlimited risk with the prospect of limited reward, whereas the option buyer assumes limited risk, with the prospect of potentially unlimited reward; hence, one who enters into the writing of options wants to do so with great caution.

An option writer must be ready to respond promptly to any adverse change in the futures price. The prudent option writer will decide in advance the futures price at which he will "buy back" the option to avoid or limit a loss if expectations on price turn out to be wrong.

When writing uncovered or naked call options, investors need to take account of their price expectations and their tolerance for risk at the time the call is written. Investors have several alternative strategies to follow with regard to their tolerance for risk. They can write at-the-money calls, in-the-money calls, or out-of-the-money calls.

Writing an at-the-money call is probably most appropriate for investors who feel strongly that prices are likely to remain flat during the life of the option, or, if any change occurs, that it will be in the direction of a slightly upward-trending price. If investors are right in this expectation, their call options will expire without being exercised and they will retain the premium received from writing it. For example, assume that in June, an investor sells a September 70 call option on Treasury bonds at a premium of $2000. If, when September comes, the futures price is 70–00 or below, the option will not be exercised and the investor will retain the $2000 premium. As an option seller, he had to post margin at the clearing-house. Had the required margin deposit on the call been $2000, the $2000 premium would amount to a 100% return on the original investment. The risk, however, is that the investor will incur a net loss. For example, if the futures price in September when the option expires is above 72–00, the loss will exceed the $2000 earned from writing the option.

If our investor, however, decided to write an out-of-the-money call, the premium that can be earned by writing such an option will be smaller, thus providing a greater margin for error in anticipating correctly the direction of prices. Let us assume that at a time when the futures price is 70–00, the investor earns a premium of only $1000 by writing a call option with a strike price of 74–00 for the Treasury bond futures. Unless the futures prices at expiration is above 74–00, the option will not be exercised and the investor, as the writer of the call, will retain the full $1000 premium, a 50% profit on the original $2000 margin deposit. The break-even point with this transaction is 75–00. If the futures price is above 75–00, the loss when the option is exercised will exceed the $1000 premium earned.

If our investor decided to write an in-the-money call, he will undoubt-edly receive a correspondingly higher premium because the premium will reflect the combination of the intrinsic value and the time value of the option. Let us assume in this case that the call writer receives a premium of $3000 on an in-the-money call with a strike price of 68–00 at a time when the futures are at 70–00. If the futures price is 68–00 or lower when the option expires, the investor will retain the full $3000 premium. How-ever, should the futures price decline only to 69–00, the call with a 68–00 price will be exercised at a $1000 loss, and the investor will have a net profit of $2000. He will have an unlimited potential loss, however, if the futures price when the option expires is above 71–00, because the loss on the option will then exceed the $3000 premium received.

4. Writing Put Options in Anticipation of Higher Prices

Writing put options is the opposite strategy to writing call options. It is the strategy to follow when an investor has at least a mildly bullish outlook on prices. If the futures price stays above the exercise price of the put that has been written, the option is unlikely to be exercised and the writer will retain the full amount of the option premium. A note of warning, however, just as with writing calls, the profit and risk considerations in writing puts for investment income are identical. There is great profit potential and unlimited risk.

Let us assume an investor expects stock prices to be either flat or slightly upward-trending over a coming period of time. Let us also assume that on the basis of his expectations, he decides to write puts on the NYSE Stock Index Futures. Assume the investor writes an at-the-money put at a premium of, say, $2000, and deposits the initial margin of $3500 with a broker. In this case, if the option expires without being exercised, he will retain the $2000 premium and reap a net return on the investment of about 57.1%. Just as with the writing of call options, the writer of put options can adjust potential risk/reward ratios by writing at-the-money puts, in-the-money puts, or out-of-the-money puts, and by judicious selection of the maturity of the option. For example, an option with only three months until expiration is less likely to be exercised than an otherwise identical option with six months until expiration. That lower risk will be reflected in a lower premium. An out-of-the-money option will also have lower risk and is likely to carry a smaller premium.

5. Sell Futures and Buy Call Options

The purchase of a call option in conjunction with a short futures position effectively creates a put, thereby making it possible to limit the otherwise unlimited risk involved in selling futures contracts. In effect, the call option provides insurance against major loss.

For example, suppose you were expecting higher interest rates and you sold a September U.S. Treasury bond futures contract at the price of 70–00. At the same time, to protect yourself against major losses that could result if futures prices rise, you might decide to pay a $2000 premium for the purchase of a September 70 call option. The most that you could lose if futures prices rise instead of falling is the $2000 cost of the call option. A summary of how this transaction could turn out under various scenarios is shown on the following page.

A major advantage of this strategy is the "staying power" it can provide—that is, these two transactions provide the ability to maintain a futures position despite adverse short-term price movements. The idea is to survive in order to maintain the potential for the position to eventually become profitable.

In the absence of the protection provided by the call, you might be faced with a large margin call on your futures position. If such a margin requirement can't be met, you would be forced to liquidate the futures position at a loss. The call protects against that because, as the futures position loses value, the call increases in value. The call acts as a hedge against major losses.

Scenario Summary of Sell Futures–Buy Call Option

Sell Sept. T-bond futures @		70–00
Buy Sept. 70 T-bond		$2000
futures call @	P or L at Expiration	
Futures rise to 76–00		
Buy futures @ 76–00		$6000 Loss
Sell call @ 76–00		$4000 Gain
		$2000 Net Loss
Futures do not change		
Buy futures @ 70–00		No Gain–No loss
Sell call @ 0		$2000 Loss
		$2000 Net Loss
Futures fall to 68–00		
Buy futures @ 68–00		$2000 Gain
Sell call @ 0		$2000 Loss
		0 Net
Futures fall to 62–00		
Buy futures @ 62–00		$8000 Gain
Sell call @ 0		$2000 Loss
		$6000 Net Gain

6. Buy Futures and Buy Put Options
(A Guaranteed Stop Order)

Options can work as guaranteed stop orders in the futures markets; except compared with placing a stop order at a particular price, the purchase of the put option offers the advantage of staying power. For example, assume the purchaser of a NYSE Index Futures Contract has a position in which there has been a substantial gain. He may anticipate a continuing rise in stock prices but be reluctant to risk losing the existings profit should the market suddenly turn down. Among alternatives would be to place a stop order to liquidate the futures position if the price drops to a particular level. An alternative and potentially more attractive strategy could be to purchase a put option. In that case, if an unexpected or temporary price decline should occur, he would be protected by the put but still have the staying power to remain in the market and profit if and when the market resumes its upward course. Had he placed a stop order, on the other hand, and the futures position been liquidated, he would no longer have had an opportunity to benefit from the subsequent price increase.

To illustrate: Assume an NYSE Stock Index Futures Contract was purchased at a price of 70.00, and the price has since risen to 82.00; thus the investor has a profit of $6000. By paying, say, $600 for an out-of-the-money put with an exercise price of 80, and three months to expiration, the investor can achieve protection against any decline below 80.00. At the same time, he retains the opportunity to realize additional futures profits should the stock price continue to climb. This is a most useful technique to use in a futures hedging program.

7. Buy Futures and Write Call Options to Increase Return

Let us suppose that you were mildly bullish on prices. You expect prices to be at least flat and probably slightly upward-trending. One trading strategy to consider would involve taking a long position in the futures and simultaneously writing a call option. The objective is to earn a potentially high rate of return on a relatively small investment (the amount of the margin deposit required to buy the futures contract). Investors following such a strategy should recognize that the potential loss, however, is unlimited. The greater the decline in the futures price, the greater the loss; hence, any investor employing a Buy/Write Strategy should consider also placing stop loss orders to liquidate the long futures position if the price drops beyond a certain level.

To illustrate this strategy, assume an investor buys an NYSE Stock Index futures contract and posts a margin of $3500, and earns a $1750 premium by writing an at-the-money call option with an exercise price of 76.

If the futures price climbs above 76.00, the call will be exercised, meaning the writer of the call will now have a short futures position at a price of 76.00. That new futures position will offset previously purchased long futures position purchased at 76.00. The investor's gain will be the option premium of $1750, a 50% return on the original margin deposit.

If the futures price remains at exactly 76.00, however, the option will expire worthless and, again, the investor will have a 50% gain equal to the $1750 premium.

If on the other hand, the futures price falls below 76.00, the option will expire worthless and, depending on the extent of the price decline, the loss on the futures position will reduce or exceed the option premium received when he wrote the call.

8. Sell Futures and Write a Put

This strategy is exactly the reverse of the one just described; instead of going long with futures and writing a call option, it involves going short with the futures and writing a put option. This strategy, instead of being most appropriate when the investor's market outlook is bullish, is most appropriate when its outlook is bearish. The objective, however, is the same—a potential high rate of return from the option premium on a relatively small investment reflected in the margin deposit on the futures. The risk is also the same—a potentially unlimited loss on the short futures position if there is an unexpected increase in futures prices. If the futures price increases, the option will not be exercised, but the loss on the short futures position will reduce or could exceed the option premium received. Note that the potential loss is unlimited.

PRICES STABLE—USING OPTION SPREADS AND STRADDLES

With the introduction of options on futures, traders now have a strategy to take advantage of stable prices—selling option straddles. An option straddle involves being long *or* short *both* a put and a call at the same strike price for the same expiration date. This strategy effectively locks in a trading range equal to the strike price, plus and minus the option premiums paid or received before commissions; thus, a trader anticipating stable prices would sell both the put and the call, hoping to pocket both premiums at expiration. On the other hand, a trader anticipating a dramatic price movement, but not sure of which direction, would buy the straddle, that is, buy the put and the call, hoping for futures prices to move in one direction or another—but in excess of the two premiums paid.

1. Buying Put/Call Straddles

An investor anticipating a sharp movement in the level of stock prices during the months ahead, but uncertain of what the direction of movement will be, would buy a put option and a call option. This strategy will produce a net profit if either of the options can ultimately be sold at a price higher than the total premium cost. There is a known and limited risk whichever way stock prices move. If stock prices drop, the put option will be profitable to exercise. To whatever extent the gain in the option that's exercised exceeds the total premium cost of the straddle, the investor will realize a net profit. On the other hand, the investor's maximum loss is the cost of the straddle, that is, the total of the premiums paid.

Assume NYSE Index futures are trading at 76.00 and an investor expects stock prices to move sharply higher or sharply lower over the next six months; assume he pays a $2000 premium to buy an at-the-money call and a $2000 premium to buy an at-the-money put. Each $1.00 change in the NYSE Index equals $500. For the investor to recover the $4000 total premium cost and to realize a profit, the NYSE Index at expiration must be either below 68.00 or above 84.00. It must move more than eight points below or above the exercise price of 76.00.

If the futures climb to 86.00, the call option will have an intrinsic value of $5000, yielding the investor a $1000 profit on the investment. Similarly, if the futures decline to 66.00, he will have a $1000 net profit on the put option to be sold or exercised. Unless the futures price at expiration is exactly equal to the options' exercise price of 76.00, one or the other of the options will be worthwhile to exercise and the investor will recover at least a portion of the investment.

In the example above, the buyer of the put/call straddle expected prices to change in one direction or the other but had no opinion as to the most probably direction. An investor who considered a change in one direction somewhat more likely than a change in the other direction may wish to purchase a put/call combination in which the put and the call have different strike prices. The lower premium cost will increase net profit if he is right about the most probable direction. A combination such as this enables an investor to adjust the break-even parameters of transactions as well as to reduce the maximum potential loss.

2. Writing Put/Call Combinations

Another straddle technique would involve writing both a put and a call. An investor who employed this technique would be one who does not expect any substantial change in the level of prices during the coming months. As long as the futures price remains within a range, the investor will normally realize a profit because the total option premiums received will exceed the loss incurred on whichever option is exercised; hence, this strategy is employed when one expects relatively flat prices.

To illustrate, assume the NYSE Index futures contract is at 76.00 and assume also the investor earns a $2000 premium by writing an at-the-money call and an additional $2000 premium by writing an at-the-money put; therefore, the total premium income is $4000.

If the futures price remains at exactly 76.00, neither option will be exercised and the investor will retain the full $4000. As long as the futures price remains above 68.00 and below 84.00, the investor will retain at least a part of the $4000 premium. If the index futures at expiration were at 70.00, the put would be exercised at a loss of $3000 and the investor's profit would be reduced to $1000.

If the futures contract at expiration has risen to 86.00, the call option with the 76 exercise price will be exercised at a $5000 loss. Since this is greater than the $4000 premium received, the investor will incur a $1000 net loss.

From the foregoing, it should be evident that the break-even parameters of a straddle can be readily calculated. Specifically, the writer of a straddle will not incur a loss unless the futures price at expiration is outside the range of the strike prices by more than the amount of the premium received when the straddle was written. One who engages in this type of trading must pay close and continual attention to futures prices and be prepared to act promptly to liquidate one or both of the options. Otherwise substantial losses could be obtained if prices change dramatically. The risk of loss from price changes with this strategy is unlimited.

3. A Neutral Calendar Spread

Suppose you expect that prices will remain relatively flat over the next few months. One potentially profitable trading strategy with such expectations involves writing a call option with a near-term expiration and buying a call option with the same strike price but a longer period of time until expiration. This strategy capitalizes on the fact that the time value for a near-term option erodes more rapidly than the time value for a more distant option.

For example, assume in June that an investor anticipates that long-term interest rates during the summer months will remain essentially unchanged. Assume also that he pays a premium of $2700 to buy a December 76 T-bond call and receives a premium of $1900 by writing a September 76 call. The net difference between these two premiums is $800. If, when the September option expires, the futures price is at 76.00, the September call will expire unexercised and the December call can be sold for its remaining time value. Suppose it can be sold for $2000; in such an instance, the investor's net profit will be the $2000 proceeds received from the sale, less the initial $800 cost of the spread—a net of $1200. In no case, even if interest rates were to sharply increase or decrease, can the investor lose more than the $800 net cost of the spread.

Even if interest rates should happen to increase or decrease slightly, this strategy will still yield some net profit, provided that, at the time the September call expires, the premium difference between the September and December options is greater than the initial net cost of the spread. The maximum net loss will occur only if the December call no longer has time value when the September call expires.

This will happen only if it is so far out of the money that no market exists for it, or so far in the money that its premium is totally a reflection of its intrinsic value.

It should be noted that although the maximum possible loss can be determined exactly, and is equal to the net cost of the spread, the maximum potential profit can only be approximated—it depends on the time value differential between the two options at the time the near-term option expires.

4. A Bear Call Spread

During a period of declining prices, you may find a strategy known as a "bear call spread," or a vertical bear spread, attractive. It offers clearly defined and potentially attractive risk/reward (because the investor can know in advance and to the dollar the maximum net profit possible and the maximum net loss possible). A bear call spread, meaning the investor is bearish on prices, involves buying a call option with a high strike price and writing or selling a call with a lower strike price. The maximum net profit possible in this transaction is the net premium received on the sale of the call option. The maximum net loss is the difference between the strike prices of the two options less the net premium received.

For example, assume an investor is expecting higher interest rates and lower bond prices at a time when the December futures price is at 66–00. To profit from this scenario, assume the investor buys a December 66 call at a premium of $1900 and sells a December 60 call at a premium of $6200. The maximum net potential profit is the net premium received of $4300 ($6200 minus $1900). The maximum potential loss is $1700 (the strike price difference of $6000 less the net premium received of $4300).

In order to realize the maximum profit, the futures price at expiration must be below or equal to the strike price of the option sold. If it isn't, the option should be exercised and the investor's resulting profit or loss will depend on whether the value of the option at expiration is smaller or greater than the net premium received. For example, had the futures price in this illustration above declined to 65–00, the $5000 loss when the September 60 call is exercised will exceed the $4300 net premium and the investor will have lost $700. However, if the futures price declined to 62–00, the investor would have a $2300 profit—the difference between the $4300 net premium received and the $2000 loss when the Sept. 60 call is exercised.

An investor interested in modifying the risk/reward arithmetic of a bear call spread can do so by careful selection of the options bought or written. For example, if the investor in the preceding illustration had bought a December 60 call at a premium of $6400 and written a September 58 call at a premium of $8100, the maximum profit would have been $1700—the difference in the premiums. The maximum loss, however, would be only $300 (the $2000 strike price difference less the $1700 net premium received).

5. A Bear Put Spread

If you expect declining prices for stocks, you could profit by purchasing a put option with a high strike price and selling or writing a put option with a low strike price. The maximum net profit is the difference in the strike prices less the net cost of the two options. The maximum loss is the net cost of the two options.

For example, suppose in June you expect that the NYSE Composite Stock Index will rise in price through the month of September. Assume the September futures price is at 88.00. To profit from your expectations, let us say you buy a September 88 put for a premium of $2000 and you sell a September 82 put and collect a premium of $1000. Your net cost is $1000.

If the future's price in September turns out to be 82.00 or lower, your profit will be $2000, the difference between the strike price of the options ($3000 less the net premium cost of the two options: $1000). If, on the other hand, futures prices at expiration are at 88.00 or above, both options will expire worthless and you will suffer your maximum loss of $1000.

6. Bull Put Spreads for Rising Prices

This strategy is designed for the investor who believes prices will be rising during a coming time period. The strategy consists of purchasing a put option with a low strike price and selling or writing a put option with a high strike price. The maximum profit possible is the premium difference between the two options. The maximum loss possible with this strategy is difference in strike prices minus the net premium received.

For example, let us suppose that in June, the September Treasury bond futures price is 66–00. To profit from an expected decline in interest rates and, therefore, an increase in the futures price, assume an investor pays a premium of $2000 to buy a September 66 put and collects a premium of $6300 by writing a September 72 put. The net premium received is $4300. If the futures price at expiration is 72–00 or above, neither put will be exercised and the investor's net profit will be the $4300 net premium received. A maximum loss of $1600 will occur if the futures price at expiration is 66–00 or below.

7. A Bull Call Spread

Perhaps a more conservative approach to a situation where you expect interest rates to decline and bond prices to rise would be one known as a vertical bull spread. With such a strategy, you would know in advance the exact maximum net profit you could possibly make, and the exact maximum net loss possible on the transaction.

Like all spreads, bull call spreads (meaning the investor is bullish on bond prices) involves buying one option and writing or selling another option. In this case, you would buy a call option with a low strike price and sell a call option with a high strike price.

Your maximum net loss potential is the net premium cost, or the difference between the premium you pay for the call you buy and the premium you receive for the call you sell.

The maximum net profit you can make in this transaction is the difference between the strike prices of the two options less the net premium cost.

For example, suppose in March you expect lower interest rates and higher bond prices and you find that the June futures price is trading at 66–00. Suppose, further, you buy a June 66 call at a premium of $2000 and sell a June 72 call at a premium of $500. The maximum net profit would be $4500, the strike price difference of $6000 less the net premium cost of $1500, and your maximum net loss would be $1500, the net premium cost. To realize maximum profit, the futures price at expiration must be equal to or above the strike price of the option written, in this case 72.00. If it isn't, the investor's resulting profit or loss will depend on whether the value of the purchase option at expiration is more or less than the premium cost.

Scenario Summary
Bull Spread—Call Options

	Paid	Received
Buy June 66–00 call	$2000	
Sell June 72–00 call		$500
Net premium	$1500	
P or L Summary		
Futures at 72–00		
Sell June 66 call		+$6000 Gain
Buy June 72 call		0
Net premium cost		−$1500
		$4500 Net Gain
Futures at 66–00		
Sell June 66 call		0
Buy June 72 call		0
Net premium cost		$1500
		$1500 Net Loss
Futures at 69–00		
Sell June 66 call		$3000
Buy June 72 call		0
Net premium cost		$1500
		$1500 Net Gain

TABLE 19.1 Summary of Option Strategies under Various
Price Scenarios

Price Expectation	Possible Strategy	Price Expectation	Possible Strategy
Declining prices	Buy put options	Rising prices	Buy call options
Declining prices	Sell futures and buy call options	Rising prices	Buy futures and buy put options
Declining prices	A "bear" call spread	Rising prices	A "bull" call spread
Declining prices	A "bear" put spread	Rising prices	A "bull" put spread
Steady to slightly lower prices	Sell futures and write put options	Steady to slightly higher prices	Buy futures and write call options
Steady to slightly lower prices	Write call options	Steady to slightly higher prices	Write put options
Relatively flat prices	A "neutral" calendar spread	Prices will be highly volatile, could change in either direction	Buy a put-call straddle
Relatively flat prices	Write a put-call straddle		

Note: Interest rates and bonds, T-bills, GNMAs, etc., move in opposite directions. So the above strategies for rising prices (falling prices) should be considered when interest rates are expected to fall (to rise).
Source: Chicago Board of Trade.

OPTION STRATEGIES UNDER VARIOUS PRICE SCENARIOS

As is obvious from the foregoing, the number and variety of trading strategies that can be employed using options and futures, singly or in combination, is large. In general, one can now tailor a limited risk trading, or hedging, strategy to almost any price trend (or nontrend) scenario that could occur. Table 19.1 has been compiled to help the reader better understand the variety of strategies available and the situation in which they should be used.

Part Five

Hedging and Arbitrage

20
The Concept of Hedging

Several years ago the CFTC decided it was time to develop a modern definition of the term "hedging." A casual perusal of the statistics on users of futures markets had revealed that many corporations who could hedge were not doing so. A little reflection revealed why.

The traditional and "textbook" concept of hedging was so narrow as to severely limit the use of futures markets for risk-shifting purposes. The older definition simply precluded many legitimate uses of the market for managing price risk. For example, unless one had the nearly identical product in the cash market as was reflected in the futures market, it was frequently not considered a hedge by the federal government. Boards of directors of major corporations were regularly advised by their legal counsel that unless their use of futures markets coincided directly with the narrow definition used by the federal government, their futures transactions would not be considered as hedges by the IRS. Thus, the legal definition of hedging was severely hampering the opportunity the futures markets provided the business community to use hedges for the purpose for which they had been developed.

To satisfy the niceties of the law and to assure that the proper technical expertise would be brought to bear in developing the new definition, the CFTC held a series of hearings around the United States titled "What Is Hedging?" Scholars of all sorts, chief executive officers of major corporations, experienced commercial users of futures markets, professional commodity speculators, and others were invited to these meetings to speak their minds and to provide answers to the question raised. After hundreds of hours of hearings, thousands of pages of testimony, and dozens of days spent in analyzing the information, the new definition was ready. Following is the new definition:

(1) *General Definition.* Bona fide hedging transactions and positions shall mean transactions or positions in a contract for future delivery on any contract market, where such transactions or positions normally represent a substitute for transaction to be made or positions to be taken at a later time in a physical marketing channel, and where they are economically appropriate to the reduction of risks in the conduct and management of a commercial enterprise, and where they arise from:

(i) The potential change in the value of assets which a person owns, produces, manufactures, processes, or merchandises or anticipates owning, producing, manufacturing, processing, or merchandising.

(ii) The potential change in the value of liabilities which a person owes or anticipates incurring, or

(iii) The potential change in the value of services which a person provides, purchases or anticipates providing or purchasing.

Notwithstanding the foregoing, no transactions or positions shall be classified as bona fide hedging for purposes of section 4a of the Act unless their purpose is the offset price risks incidental to commercial cash or spot operations and such positions are established and liquidated in an orderly manner in accordance with sound commercial practices and unless the provisions of paragraphs (2) and (3) of this section and sections 1.47 and 1.48 of the regulations have been satisfied.

(2) *Enumerated Hedging Transactions.* The definition of bona fide hedging transactions and positions in paragraph (1) of this section includes, but is not limited to, the following specific transactions and positions.

(i) *Sales* of any commodity for future delivery on a contract market which do not exceed in quantity:

(A) Ownership or fixed-price purchase of the same cash commodity by the same person; and

(B) Twelve months' unsold anticipated production of the same commodity by the same person provided that no such position is maintained in any future during the five last trading days of that future.

(ii) Purchases of any commodity for future delivery on a contract market which do not exceed in quantity:

(A) The fixed-price sale of the same cash commodity by the same person;

(B) The quantity equivalent of fixed-price sales of the cash products and by-products of such commodity by the same person; and

(C) Twelve months' unfilled anticipated requirements of the same cash commodity for processing, manufacturing, or feeding by the same person, provided that such transactions and positions in the five last trading days of any one future do not exceed the person's unfilled anticipated requirements of the same cash commodity for that month and for the next succeeding month.

(iii) Sales and purchases for future delivery described in paragraphs (2)(i) and (2)(ii) of this section may also be offset other than by the same quantity of the same cash commodity, provided that the fluctuations in value of the position for future delivery are substantially related to the fluctuations in value of the actual or anticipated cash position, and provided that the positions in any one future shall not be maintained during the five last trading days of that future.

(3) *Non-Enumerated Cases.* Upon specific requests made in accordance with section 1.47 of the regulations, the Commission may recognize transactions and positions other than those enumerated in paragraph (2) of this section as bona fide hedging in such amounts and under such terms and conditions as it may specify in accordance with the provisions of §1.47. Such transactions and positions may include, but are not limited to, purchases or sales for future delivery on any contract market by an agent who does not own or who has not contracted to sell or purchase the offsetting cash commodity at a fixed price, *provided* that the person is responsible for the merchandising of the cash position which is being offset.

In short, a bona fide hedge requires the futures position to be economically related to the cash position and designed to reduce the risk of the cash enterprise.

This chapter deals with the concept of hedging, starting with an overview of how the concept has evolved over time. We then provide answers to some important questions related to the making of the hedging decision. The concept of the *basis* is next introduced and explored in-depth, because it plays a major role in the performance of hedges. Exploration of the concept of the basis leads to discussions regarding cross-hedging, basis risk, and the understanding of basis relationships. Since most hedges in futures markets tend to be cross-hedges, the concepts of *dollar equivalency* and *cheapest to deliver* are introduced. They play important roles in the decision of how many contracts to buy or sell when hedges are placed. Next we discuss the structure of futures prices and how they relate to case prices. The concept of the *cost of carry* is introduced. This concept allows us to identify whether futures contracts are priced either cheap or expensive relative to the cash market. Another important concept, *convergence*, is discussed, as it provides clues to which contract month to use in placing hedges. The chapter closes with some examples of basic hedges.

HEDGING THEORY

Hedging theory has changed considerably over time. Three relatively distinct strains of the theory have marked its evolution. How one views the purpose and functions of futures markets leads one to favor one theory over the others. The three theories are:

1. Traditional Theory.
2. Working's Arbitrage Theory.
3. Portfolio Theory.

Traditional Theory

Traditional theory emphasizes the risk avoidance potential of futures markets. Hedgers are envisioned as taking futures positions equal and opposite to positions they have (or intend to have) in the cash market. For example, a holder of $10 million of Treasury bonds would protect himself against a decline in price by selling short the equivalent amount of Treasury bond futures. When the cash position is liquidated, the futures contracts are repurchased, canceling the short position. Similarly, an investor intending to invest $10 million in 90-day Treasury bills would purchase an equivalent amount of Treasury bill contracts. On the date of the intended purchase of the cash bills, the futures contracts would be sold, canceling the previously held long positions.

In both of the preceding examples the number of contracts purchased or sold exactly matches the underlying cash position. This equal and opposite matching of cash with futures positions is based on the argument that cash and futures prices generally move in parallel, so gains (losses) in the cash market will be offset by losses (gains) in the futures market. The emphasis on risk avoidance is obvious. In terms of the *basis*, defined as the difference between the cash price and the futures price, a stable basis is critical to the realization of a perfect hedge. A hedge is deemed as perfect, or completely effective, if there is no change in the basis over the life of the hedge.

This risk avoidance view of hedging was challenged by Holbrook Working, considered by many as the dean of economists in the area of futures trading and hedging.

Working's Arbitrage Theory

In direct contrast to traditional theory, Working argued that rather than being risk avoiders, most hedgers are, in fact, arbitrageurs who hedge on the expectation of making a profit. Instead of expecting cash and futures prices to move together (a stable basis), Working posited that most hedging is done on the expectation of a favorable change in the basis. Hedgers act much like speculators. Instead of speculating on changes in cash prices, they speculate on changes in the cash-futures relationship—the basis. Hedging is, in effect, *speculating on the basis*.

Working's critique of traditional theory stemmed from the theory's unreasonable assumption of basis stability as a measure of the effectiveness of hedging. Since futures prices must converge to cash prices as the expiration date of the contract is approached, futures prices, by definition, cannot parallel cash prices. In other words, the basis must change over time. No hedger can reasonably expect it not to. Hence, the conventional practice of illustrating the effectiveness of hedging with a hypothetical example, in which the price of the futures contract bought or sold rises or falls by the exact amount as the spot price, is a seriously mistaken notion.

Working's arbitrage approach to hedging has often been interpreted as an "expected profit maximization" approach, particularly by the proponents of yet a third theory—portfolio theory.

Portfolio Theory

Portfolio theorists argue that if traditional theory emphasizes risk avoidance and Working emphasizes profit maximization, a middle approach that trades off profit against risk must exist. Hedgers buy and sell futures for the same risk-return reasons that one buys or sells any other asset. Hence, it is not only possible, but also likely, that hedgers will intentionally hedge only a portion of their stocks of a commodity. The fraction of stocks hedged depends on the degree of risk aversion of the hedger.

The major difference between the portfolio theory approach to hedging compared to Working's arbitrage theory is in how each theory views the relationship between cash and futures prices. Working views a futures transaction as a temporary substitute for a cash transaction. As a consequence the difference between cash and futures prices (the basis) represents an arbitrage opportunity that plays a critical role in the decision to hedge or not to hedge. In portfolio theory, on the other hand, cash and futures are not viewed as substitutes. Consequently, the basis between cash and futures prices plays no explicit role (at least theoretically) in the hedging decision. In actual practice, though, hedgers recognize that the size of the basis does represent an important measure of hedging cost (or profit) and do factor it into the hedging decision.

WHO HEDGES AND WHY

The purpose of hedging in interest rate futures is to establish in advance a particular rate of interest for a specific period of time. Borrowers may seek to establish a specific cost of money to protect themselves from higher interest costs and to enhance the success of business decisions involving factors sensitive to interest rates. Lenders seek protection against lower rates.

Portfolio managers and holders of fixed income securities can hedge to protect the value of their assets from erosion during periods of rising interest rates. Lenders and investors with cash can hedge against declining rates by buying futures at current high yields.

Hedging provides portfolio managers with a great deal of flexibility in investment choices and in timing purchases and sales. This is especially pertinent for investment managers operating under a corporate policy of not selling a security that has a current principal loss, as the futures profit helps offset the decline in asset value, and thus significantly broadens the portfolio manager's available alternatives.

Mortgage bank and savings and loan institutions can use the MBS futures market to hedge both the mortgages they plan to hold and the mortgages they currently hold.

Builders can lock in construction loan costs and protect themselves from higher mortgage rates through the use of futures.

Corporations can use futures to protect against higher borrowing costs and higher sinking fund costs while at the same time smoothing out their cash flow.

MAKING THE HEDGING DECISION

Hedging should be looked upon as a process of risk management that involves decisions as to whether, when, and how to utilize the futures markets. As with any tool, its benefits hinge on the skill with which it is used. To do an intelligent and informed job of hedging one must consider two fundamental criteria: the economic outlook and the economic practicability of a hedge. The following questions will aid one in making the hedging decision. These questions, while traversing the same ground we covered earlier in the chapter on foreign exchange, provide a slightly different view and apply whether one is hedging in the forward markets or the futures markets; hedging lumber, wheat, or interest rates.

Question 1. What is the risk exposure?

The objective in answering this question is to quantify the loss that would be incurred if there were no hedge. To answer this question one needs to go far beyond the simple accounting calculation of how much money is involved. The answer also includes analysis of the outlook for interest rates, the estimation of the size of the rate change, and the probability of its occurrence.

Once the determination has been made as to the probably direction and size of the rate change and the probability of its occurrence, one can plug the numbers into a simple mathematical expectation model and arrive at a quantification of risk exposure associated with not hedging.

Question 2. Is the risk affordable?

Frequently one will find that the answer to Question 1 on risk exposure will be such that one can bear the risk without hedging. That decision should be based on the relative size of the risk compared to the capital of the entity taking the risk. If the risk is small and the capital of the firm is large, management may decide that it is a risk not worth covering. On the other hand, if the risk is quite large relative to the capital of the firm, the banker may insist that the firm hedge.

Question 3. Is the risk hedgeable in futures markets?

The answer to this question is found largely through analysis of the correlation between the yields on the cash instrument hedged and that of the instrument underlying the futures contract. If the cash instrument hedged closely resembles the one underlying the futures contract in both quality and maturity, the probability is high that the futures contract will be effective in reducing risk. The computed correlation coefficient will be high. For example, CD yields will correlate highly with LIBOR but less so with T-bills, thus making the Eurodollar contract a better hedging vehicle than the T-bill contract in reducing risk.

Whether the appropriate correlation for a reasonable hedge is 0.80 or 0.90 depends on the discretion of the individual manager. It is possible that a manager may conclude that a .70 correlation provides a high enough probability for risk transfer to make the hedge worthwhile. For example, if it is normal for commercial paper to trade within a range of 25 to 150 basis points over T-bills, one might think that the T-bill contract would be a poor hedging vehicle to hedge commercial paper. However, if the volatility of commercial paper rates is such that a 300 basis point change is possible, then one could see that a hedge reducing the risk exposure to, say, 150 basis points may be well worthwhile.

Question 4. What is the basis relationship?

The *basis* is easily the single most important concept in hedging. As previously defined, it is the difference between the price of the instrument hedged and the price of the futures contract.

All successful hedgers know and understand the basis. They study how and why it changes and make their decisions to hedge or not to hedge depending on the expected change in the basis. Basis is explored in greater depth later in this chapter. Suffice to say here that one cannot do an effective job of hedging without understanding the behavior of the basis.

Question 5. What are the costs of hedging?

Hedging costs can be grouped into two major categories: explicit costs and implicit costs. Explicit hedging costs are transactions costs such as commissions paid to brokers and the interest foregone on money posted as margin requirements. These costs are generally minor or can be covered through tailing the hedge, i.e., adjusting the number of futures contracts to reflect the cost of money for margin.

The more important category of costs are the implicit ones. The first of these are execution costs. They are reflected in the size of the bid-ask spread for prices in the market For example, if one bought a contract and sold it immediately, one would incur a cost equivalent to the bid-ask spread. This cost becomes important when trades are made in illiquid markets. For example, the bid-ask spread in the T-bill futures market is larger than that in the Eurodollar market. Also, trading in distant contracts results in bid-ask spread costs substantially larger than those in the nearby contracts. The second aspect of implicit costs is built into the basis. This cost is only fully realized when the hedge is closed out. Hence, it is often referred to as the cost of incurring basis risk. If the basis changes adversely, the hedge may turn out to be less effective than predicted. For example, if a borrower expected to lock in a borrowing cost of, say, 10% but ended up realizing 10.05%, then the additional cost due to basis risk is .05%.

Question 6. What are the tax implications of the hedge?

This question highlights the importance of having an accountant helping to devise the hedging and strategy plan. Generally, all monies made or lost on hedges are considered ordinary income. But because of the complexity of the IRS codes and the fundamental questions surrounding the definition of a "hedge," it is most important that your accountant provide an opinion on whether a particular transaction qualifies under the IRS code as a hedge. If it does, the income or loss could be considered ordinary. A number of instances may arise, particularly in the "cross-hedge" situation, where the IRS may question the validity of the transaction as a hedge. In order to put the best light on the transaction for tax purposes, the accountant should set forth the criteria necessary to assure the IRS that the transaction does qualify as a hedge.

Once one has reviewed each of these aspects, one can put all the variables into a decision-making framework and quantify some of the uncertainties.

THE CONCEPT OF THE BASIS

Basis refers to the difference between the price of the cash instrument being hedged and the price of the futures contract. Depending on one's perspective, it represents either a profit opportunity or a price to be paid for risk reduction. The following examples highlight the role played by the basis in realizing this profit or cost. For expositional purposes the instrument hedged is assumed to be the one underlying the futures contract.

Suppose the rate on 90-day LIBOR is currently quoted at 10% and the Eurodollar contract is priced at 89.75 (10.25%). Hence, the (yield) basis between the Eurodollar contract and 90-day LIBOR is 25 basis points (10.25%–10%). This means that a potential borrower in the LIBOR market could guarantee himself a rate of 10.25% to take down a loan on the expiration date of the Eurodollar contract. The premium (or cost) he is willing to pay for risk reduction is the basis (25 basis points). On the other hand, a potential investor in the LIBOR market would view the basis as a profit opportunity. The investor could lock in a profit of 25 basis points above that currently offered in the LIBOR market for an investment to be made on the date of expiration of the Eurodollar contract.

The reason why the borrower and the investor will realize the rate of 10.25% is that the basis must necessarily converge to zero as contract expiration is approached. For example, suppose at contract expiration the yield on 90-day LIBOR happened to be 10.75%, thus implying a yield of 10.75% on the Eurodollar contract. The investor in the preceding example would actually be able to invest funds at the going rate of 10.75%. However by hedging, he would incur a loss in the futures position of 0.50% (50 basis points), bringing the net investment yield down to 10.25% (10.75% − 0.50%). The borrower, on the other hand, would actually borrow at 10.75%. This cost would be reduced by a futures profit of 0.50%, resulting in a net borrowing cost of 10.25%.

Basis Risk

In the previous examples the hedgers were able to fully realize the rate of 10.25% that was anticipated at hedge initiation. The reason for this was that the hedges were assumed to be lifted at contract expiration when the basis, by definition, is known with certainty. For any other hedge lifting date the outcome is not exactly predictable because *basis risk* necessarily exists.

Basis risk may be strictly defined as the deviation of the basis from its predicted value. A hedge is considered riskless if the actual basis equals the expected basis. Otherwise the hedge is risky. Note the difference between this definition of a riskless hedge and the one often used in many texts and brochures on hedging. In the latter, hedging is often defined as highly effective (riskless in the extreme) if price changes of the hedged instrument are exactly offset by price changes in the futures contract; that is, the basis is stable over the life of the hedge. Excellent tracking of cash and futures prices or basis stability is seen as a requirement for effective hedging. This appears to be too strong a requirement for effective hedging primarily because the notion of basis stability is unrealistic. The basis cannot be stable because cash and futures prices must converge to each other over time necessitating a gradual shrinkage in the basis. Nevertheless, after taking convergence between cash and futures prices into account, good tracking between cash and futures prices is an essential ingredient for successful risk reduction.

CROSS-HEDGES

If every financial instrument in the cash market had a futures contract that exactly mirrored its characteristics, futures markets would provide the opportunity to yield very good hedges. In the real world hedging must often be accomplished by using futures contracts on different deliverable instruments. Such hedges are called *cross-hedges*.

An example of a cross-hedge is the use of the T-bill or the Eurodollar contract to hedge another money market instrument—CDs, BAs, commercial paper, prime rate, and so on. Another example would be the use of the Treasury bond futures contracts to hedge a different long-term asset or liability, such as corporate bonds, permanent construction financing, or other long-term investments and loans.

Basis Risk in Cross-Hedges

Cross-hedges are generally considered riskier than hedging the instrument underlying the futures contract, because of the additional dimension to basis risk—the predictability of the spread between prices of the cash instrument being hedged and the one underlying the futures contract. However, this dimension of basis risk could be reduced through the appropriate choice of the hedging vehicle. For example, since CDs and commercial paper have credit risks closer to LIBOR than T-bills, one might expect better risk reduction for CDs and commercial paper with the Eurodollar contract than with the T-bill contract, thus making the Eurodollar contract the hedging vehicle of choice. Additionally, basis risk could be effectively managed through good hedge ratio design. Taken together, the choice of the optimal hedging vehicle and good hedge ratio design would result in hedges with a much smaller risk than not being hedged at all.

Correlation and Basis Risk

Hedges can be very effective if basis risk is low. The potential efficiency of a hedge can be measured through correlation analysis. If the price of the instrument being hedged in the cash market is highly correlated with an instrument for which a futures contract exists, one could expect to be able to create effective hedges. The reason for this is that high correlation implies strong comovement between the prices (low basis risk), which in turn implies effective risk reduction possibilities. The fact that interest rates, even after allowing for credit quality differences, are highly correlated suggests that extensive risk management opportunities exist with the futures contracts presently available.

UNDERSTANDING BASIS RELATIONSHIPS

In financial futures, basis relationships should be analyzed from two standpoints: the group context and the individual context.

The group context is important because certain groups of securities, such as AAA industrial bonds, have price characteristics that may be either highly correlated or not so highly correlated with an instrument for which a futures contract exists. Armed with this information one could then proceed to determine the basis relationship for an individual issue of AAA industrial bonds.

ANALYZING GROUP BASIS CHANGES

There are a number of factors that cause the basis to change on individual issues as a result of group influence. Among them are:

1. *General Economic Conditions.* Securities of different credit quality will fluctuate differently under the same economic conditions. In periods of increasing rates, securities with lower credit ratings will decline faster than securities with higher credit ratings. They will also rise faster in easy money or declining-rate markets. Therefore, before you enter into your cross-hedge, study how the different periods of past economic conditions influence the general basis for groups of securities with different quality ratings.

2. *Cyclical Effects.* Some securities perform differently from others as one moves through the interest rate cycle. In a "boom" economy federal government borrowings should decline as tax revenues increase and budget deficits run to relatively smaller levels. During tight money, however, organizations issuing debt instruments operate in different ways. They develop new types of debt instruments to fund expansion and they switch emphasis among different types of issues to raise money in the most effective way. One therefore needs to look carefully at the relative supply of the new securities being issued and whether they will cause fundamental changes in rate relationships.

3. *Institutional Segmentation of Markets.* This situation is also a key consideration in calculating group basis. Different industry groups rely on different types of securities for raising money. As a result, the economics of a particular industry can cause the securities that industry relies on to perform differently. For example, MBS futures may react sharply in periods of disintermediation whereas corporate bonds react very little. During a liquidity squeeze commercial banks may demand large amounts of money through the CD markets, whereas the T-bill market may be very attractive to foreign central banks. Thus, one needs to know which institutional investing groups are most likely to have an impact on the price of the cash instrument being hedged *and* the instrument represented in the futures contract.

4. *Administered Rates Versus Free Market Rates.* It is important to note that the prime rate is an administered rate. It may change significantly while the T-bill and commercial paper rates—which are fundamentally free markets—remain relatively unchanged. So if one is trying to use the T-bill market for hedging the prime rate, one needs to be aware of the effect of the difference between administered rates and free market rates. GNMAs may experience severe distortions, when base minimum lending rates for FHA and VA mortgages lag behind changes in conventional mortgages, for the same reason. The FHA and VA mortgage rates are administered rates, whereas the GNMA rate is mostly a free market rate.

Individual Basis Changes

Basis changes in the individual context are important because, after all, it is an individual commitment that is being hedged and not the group. The following factors need to be considered:

1. *Credit Worthiness.* If the credit rating of the cash instrument hedged is not as high as the credit worthiness of the instrument reflected in the futures contract, the correlation in price movement will be reduced, resulting in higher basis risk.

2. *Maturity.* The maturity of the instrument being hedged relative to the maturity of the instrument reflected in the futures contract is important. The closer their maturity, the more they reflect the same time value judgments.
3. *Liquidity.* The liquidity of the cash instrument and the liquidity of the futures market are both meaningful. If both markets are highly liquid, the less basis variation one can expect.
4. *Supply and Demand Factors.* If a cash instrument has a limited supply, the chances are that the basis relationship will be less stable. Similarly, certain cash instruments have peculiarities in their demand factors that are not present in the futures market, resulting in increased basis variation.

In analyzing basis changes in the individual context one must be aware that many of the individual factors are also reflected in the group context. For example, if one is hedging a new issue of AAA bond, and one does not know how it will correlate with, say, the Treasury bond contract, then the best guide to use is the historic correlation between the group (e.g., an index of AAA bonds) with a similar index of Treasury bonds. If it is a seasoned issue with a good price history, one may use its own price history to determine the correlation. However, one should be aware that even if an issue trades with much better correlation to the futures than does the group, over any given period of time the group influence may dominate.

Armed with an understanding of what causes basis to change, one is ready to consider more fully the concept of dollar equivalency hedging.

DOLLAR EQUIVALENCY

Dollar equivalency refers to the process of structuring a hedge whereby one gets equivalent movement in cash and futures positions. The need for this structuring arises primarily because the cash position being hedged does not have the same maturity as the instrument underlying the futures contract. The longer the maturity of the cash position relative to the instrument underlying the futures contract, the more the dollar principal risk exposure of the cash position per basis point change in yield.

For example, a one basis point (0.01%) change in yield results in a $25 change in price in the Eurodollar contract. The same one basis point change in yield for a 180-day CD results in a price change of $50 per $1 million face value. Therefore, if one were hedging a $1 million face value 180-day CD with the Eurodollar contract, one would use two contracts to create a dollar-equivalent hedge.

When hedging liabilities one frequently finds that the maturity of the loan (liability) being hedged frequently does not match the maturity of the instrument deliverable on the futures contract. This mismatching can be adjusted for by increasing or reducing the number of futures contracts to be sold. Consider the following example. Assume a $1-million floating rate loan for one year, with the rate tied to 90-day LIBOR. Further, assume that this loan is repriced every three months at the then prevailing 90-day LIBOR. This loan could be hedged with the Eurodollar contract. If one were to use dollar equivalency hedging, one would find that a one basis point change in the yield on the Eurodollar contract would result in a $25 change in its price. For the loan, a one basis point change in yield results in a $100 change in price. Thus, one would need a 4-to-1 hedge ratio to exactly offset gains (losses) in the loan position to losses (gains) in the futures position—at the start of the hedge.

On the day the loan is taken down, one contract is repurchased to reflect the fact that repricing risk exposure now exists for only three repricing dates. Until the first repricing date the liability hedged is a 270-day loan, which has a price sensitivity of $75 per basis point change in yield; hence, the need for being short only three contracts—a 3-to-1 hedge ratio. When the first repricing occurs another contract is repurchased to reflect the fact that the risk exposure is now related to a 180-day loan, which has a price sensitivity of a $50 per basis point change in yield. The hedge ratio is now 2-to-1. Contracts are repurchased in this manner at each repricing date to maintain the dollar equivalency of the declining maturity loan with that of the futures contract.

The principle underlying dollar equivalency is to match the dollar movement of the cash position to the dollar movement in the futures position to obtain as close an offset as possible. The principle applies to all types of hedges—on assets or liabilities. In the case of assets or liabilities that carry a coupon, a minor modification is required in how dollar equivalency is computed.

Weighting a Coupon Hedge

When hedging a coupon-bearing instrument, the size of the coupon itself has an effect on the price sensitivity of the instrument for a given change in yield. Consider, for example, hedging with the Treasury bond (T-bond) futures contract. The T-bond contract calls for delivery of an 8% coupon bond with at least 15 years left to maturity or call, whichever is nearer. Even though bonds with coupons other than an 8% can be delivered on the contract, a complication that is discussed later, the price sensitivity of the deliverable 8% coupon bond will be very different from that of a different coupon bond with the same maturity. For instance, an 8%,

15-year bond priced at par has a price sensitivity per basis point change in yield of $86.41 (per $100,000 face value). On the other hand, a 13%, 15-year bond selling at a yield of 8% has a price sensitivity of $112.64 per basis point change in yield. To compensate for this different price sensitivity arising from different coupons requires a (coupon) weighting scheme for the hedge. In this example the weight would be 1.3036 (112.64/86.41), that is, approximately 1.3 contracts to be bought or sold per $100,000 face value of the 13% bond being hedged.

A quick method of determining the weighting ratio is to use the conversion factor furnished by the exchange on which the contract is traded. There is a conversion factor for all bonds with a specific coupon and maturity.

In summary, it is crucial to remember that, in order to obtain efficient hedges, one needs to obtain the dollar-equivalent change in the cash position versus the futures position for a given change in yield.

THE STRUCTURE OF FUTURES PRICES

What determines the price of a futures contract? And how is it related to prices in the cash market? The answers to these questions are important for several reasons. Knowing how a futures contract is priced provides the understanding of what will cause its price to change. Since the futures contract is used for hedging, knowledge of what causes prices to change is extremely valuable in designing effective hedges. Second, if a futures contract is to be used as a temporary substitute for a cash transaction, its value relative to cash must be ascertained to determine whether it is worthwhile using it as a substitute for the cash transaction. Finally, at any time, trading in futures simultaneously exists for delivery in several different months. How do prices differ based on different delivery months? The answer to this question will influence the choice of which contract month to use as the most effective hedge.

Futures Prices and the Cost of Carry

The expression *cost of carry* refers to the net cost of owning an investment over a stipulated time period. It is similar to the concept familiar to traders in storable agricultural commodities such as wheat or corn, where cost of carry includes storage, insurance, interest, and transactions cost associated with holding the commodity.

In the case of financial instruments, such as T-bills or T-bonds, cost of carry is the net interest differential between interest earned on the instrument less the cost of financing the purchase of the instrument. Following is an example of the cost of carry.

Suppose one can borrow money for 90 days at 10% per annum. If 90-day T-bills are selling at a (simple interest) yield of 12%, the cost of carry is +2% (per annum). The investor can thus earn 2% over the borrowing cost. On the other hand, if the 90-day T-bills are selling at a yield of 8%, the cost of carry is −2%. Financing the purchase of 90-day T-bills with borrowed money in this case would result in a net loss of 2%.

Determining the correct rate to use as the borrowing cost is obviously critical in determining the true cost of carry. Normally one uses the repo rate as the borrowing cost. Repos are "sale and repurchase agreements." It involves the sale of an instrument, such as a 90-day T-bill, under an agreement to repurchase it later at a prespecified price. The buyer, and later reseller, of the bill in effect makes a loan to the original owner of the bill for the time stipulated in the repo transaction. The difference between the buying price and the predetermined resale price of the bill represents the financing cost in the repo transaction. This cost is usually stated as an interest rate and is called the *repo rate.*

Repo transactions normally span very short periods of time, such as overnight to five days. Nevertheless, 30-day repos are not unusual. Regular quotes on them are available. Repos covering periods longer than 30 days are also available but must be requested of dealers.

As a substitute for using repo rates as a means of estimating the cost of carry, one can use the cash yield curve. If it is normal, that is, upward sloping to the right, the cost of carry is positive. If it is downward sloping, the cost of carry is negative.

Once one knows the cost of carry for a cash market instrument, one can determine whether the futures contracts are cheap or expensive relative to each other or to the cash market alternative. If the net cost of carry is positive, the futures contract should sell at a discount relative to cash. Conversely, if the net cost of carry is negative, the futures contract should sell at a premium relative to cash. The logic underlying this pricing is seen in the following example.

Consider a normal upward-sloping yield curve where a 90-day and a 180-day T-bill are yielding 10% and 12%, respectively. This is an indication of a positive carry market. Suppose a T-bill futures contract expiring in 90 days is also available. The investor has at least two options available for a 180-day investment. He can buy the 90-day T-bill today plus one futures contract (Option 1). At the end of 90 days he takes delivery of a 90-day T-bill (via the futures contract). Or, the investor can simply buy the 180-day T-bill (Option 2). If the futures contract is priced correctly, that is, to prevent riskless arbitrage profits, then the profit from both transactions should be identical.

$$\text{Profits from Option 1} = (\text{90-day T-bill Yield} + \text{Futures Yield}) \\ \times 90/360 \\ = (0.10 + \text{Futures Yield}) \times 90/360$$

$$\text{Profits from Option 2} = (\text{180-day T-bill Yield}) \times 180/360 \\ = (0.12) \times 180/360$$

To prevent riskless arbitrage:

$$\text{Profits from Option 1} = \text{Profits from Option 2}$$

Hence,

$$(0.10 + \text{Futures Yield}) \times 90/360 = (0.12) \times 180/360$$

Or,

$$\text{Futures Yield} = 0.12 \times 2 - 0.10 = 0.14 \ (14\%)$$

The futures should sell at a discount (or its yield at a premium) relative to cash 90-day T-bills in a positive carry market. In this example the futures yield is 14% while the cash yield is 10%. If the futures yield were above 14%, riskless arbitrage opportunities would exist via being long Option 1 and simultaneously being short Option 2. If the futures yield were below 14%, the exact reverse would take place. In actual practice, though, restrictions on the use of the proceeds of short sales, as well as the ability to borrow funds at rates low enough to execute the arbitrage transactions, may cause the futures contract to sell at a yield slightly different from 14%.

An alternative way to obtain a theoretical futures price and to show whether it is cheap or expensive to the actual futures price is to determine it via a specific cost of carry. The following procedure can be used:

Step 1. Determine the net cost of carry for the cash instrument being considered. This is obtained by subtracting the cost of financing for the holding period from the bond equivalent yield on the cash security.

Step 2. Convert the net cost of carry to a dollar value by multiplying it by the face value of the security and the fraction of the year the security is held.

Step 3. Obtain the dollar price adjustment by dividing the dollar value of the net cost of carry by the value of a basis point. In the case of T-bonds or GNMAs, divide the net income by the value of 1/32, or $31.25.

Step 4. Add the appropriate dollar price adjustment to the current cash price of the security to obtain the theoretical futures price. Or, alternatively, subtract the dollar price adjustment from the yield of the cash security to get the futures yield.

Step 5. Compare the theoretical futures price to the actual futures price.

An illustration of this evaluation would be:

Step 1. A 180-day bill has a yield of 10.25% and a bond equivalent yield of 10.85%. There are 45 days to expiration of the T-bill futures contract. Financing can be obtained at 10.5%.

Net Cost of Carry (%) = 10.85% − 10.50% = 0.35%

Step 2. Net Cost of Carry ($) = 0.35% for 45 Days
= 0.0035 × (45/365) × $1,000,000
= $431.50

Step 3. Dollar Price Adjustment = Net Cost of Carry/Value of a Basis Point
= $431.50/$25
= 17.26 Basis points

Step 4. Theoretical Futures Yield = 10.25% − 0.1726%
= 10.0774%

Step 5. An actual futures yield greater than 10.0774% reflects an undervalued futures contract. A yield less than 10.0774% reflects an overvalued futures contract.

This system of evaluation must be tempered by two considerations: first, when contracts are evaluated over long periods of time the financing costs are difficult to lock in; it may even be difficult to get a reliable quote on what they should be. Second, in further out contract months the market will begin to anticipate different financing rates and expectations begin to play a larger role in futures prices. These expectations become more dominant as longer-term financing becomes difficult to obtain. Nevertheless, by plugging in the appropriate numbers to the formulas, one has a means to compare futures to futures and futures to cash, and in this way identify potentially cheap or expensive futures prices.

In summary, you would be willing to pay more for a futures contract if it helped offset an income loss arising from a negative (yield) carry. You would also pay less for a futures contract that would not earn the positive carry received by owning the cash market security.

EXPECTATIONS

The cost of carry is a convenient technique for estimating the value of a particular futures contract compared to cash market instruments or to other futures contracts. However, often futures markets react to forces other than the cost of carry. One of those forces is *expectations*. As mentioned earlier, expectations will play a larger role in the pricing of more distant contracts because of the difficulty of obtaining longer-term financing. Using shorter-term financing necessarily involves a certain amount of speculation regarding the rate of refinancing at the various rollover dates. Nevertheless, it is possible to get a sense of relative value for futures contracts for different delivery months by comparing the cash yield curve with the futures yield curve.

If the futures yield curve lies above the cash yield curve, a positive carry market exists. If the futures yield curve lies below the cash yield curve, a negative carry market exists.

CONVERGENCE BETWEEN CASH AND FUTURES PRICES

Futures prices must converge to cash prices as contract expiration is approached. This is known as the phenomenon of *convergence*. The closer a futures contract is to its delivery date the less the futures price will deviate from the spot price. In fact, the price of an expiring futures contract will equal the price of the deliverable cash market security at the close of trading on the contract expiration date. This effect does have a substantial impact on the performance of a hedge that attempts to offset cash price changes with futures price changes. Figure 20.1 shows the impact of convergence on a hedge in a positive carry market (i.e., a downward-sloping price curve or an upward-sloping yield curve).

The top curve represents futures prices in September. The curve shifts downward over the next three months to the bottom curve (December). Over the three months the cash price of the 90-day T-bill dropped from A to B. A short hedge in the December contract would produce a profit of C − B. This profit is insufficient to offset the cash market loss (A − B). On the other hand, if the hedge were placed in the March contract, a better offset would have been obtained because the March contract is on the flatter portion of the curve. The rate of convergence declines in the more distant contracts as the price curve flattens out. Thus, short hedges in nearby contracts in a positive carry market produce are less effective in offsetting futures gains (losses) with cash market losses (gains) than the more distant contracts. Convergence works against the short hedger in a positive carry market.

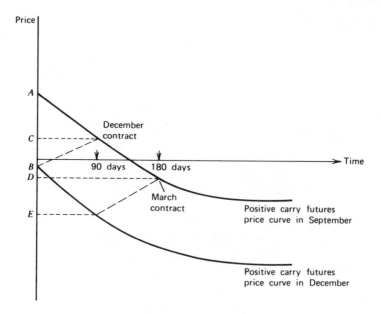

FIGURE 20.1 Yield curve for futures. *A–B*, loss in cash; *C–B*, profit from hedge if December contract is used; *A–C*, net loss using December hedge; *D–E*, profit from hedge if March contract is used; (*A–B*) − (*D–E*), net loss using March hedge.

On the other hand, convergence works in favor of the long hedger in positive carry markets. In negative carry markets the role played by convergence is exactly reversed for the short and long hedger. It favors the short hedger as opposed to the long hedger.

This simple example illustrates the importance of convergence and how it can work for or against the hedger (short or long). The example was for a parallel shift in the price (yield) curve. For a nonparallel shift, the final shape of the curve will be critical in determining how convergence will influence the choice of the preferred contract for each hedger.

CONTRACT SPECIFICATIONS AND HEDGING EFFICIENCY

Once a futures contract has been selected as a hedging vehicle, one should carefully study the contract's specifications to carefully determine if there are any provisions that may make it trade differently from cash. In this type of study there are two major areas of concern.

First, does the contract have specifications for a "market basket" delivery, whereby the deliverable item could be any security within a broad spectrum of maturities? For example, for the T-bond contract any Treasury bond with a maturity or call date of 15 years or more, as of the expiration date of a futures contract, is eligible for delivery. Often this allows for more than 20 different T-bonds with varying coupons and maturities to meet delivery specifications. This wide range of deliverable bonds adds a new dimension to basis risk because of the uncertainty regarding which particular bond the futures contract may be pricing off. If there is a change in the cash market security the futures prices off, it could play havoc with the hedge ratio calculations, which in turn will affect hedging efficiency.

Second, is the contract written to facilitate delivery? The answer to this question is very important. Some contracts will have severe aberrations from the cash market due to their contract delivery specifications. If the contract has restrictive delivery specifications, it could be technically influenced by the supply of securities eligible for delivery. So when possible, use a contract that does not present the added risk of delivery distortions.

Cheapest to Deliver

Since it is always in the interest of the seller of a futures contract to deliver the cheapest available grade deliverable on the contract, futures prices will tend to reflect the *cheapest to deliver* grade. Therefore, it is important to be able to identify that issue which is cheapest to deliver and to track its price in the cash market in order to develop an effective hedging strategy.

The most precise technique for identifying the cheapest to deliver is to determine the "holding period return" or the "implied repo rate," the rate that determines a trader's break-even financing cost for cash-futures arbitrage. These transactions keep prices "in line," because traders buy cash securities and sell futures contracts if the return on the combined transaction is greater than the cost of financing the cash security until the delivery date. Because this method considers the accrued interest earned during the holding period it is more accurate than simply dividing a deliverable issue's cash price by the conversion factor.

The implied repo rate reflects break-even financing costs. Hence, the cheapest to deliver will generally, though not always, have the highest repo rate. To calculate the implied repo rate for deliverable coupons:

1. Multiple the futures price by the conversion factor.
2. Add the accrued interest on the deliverable security up to the delivery date. This equals the futures invoice amount.
3. Subtract the securities total cost—current cash market price plus accrued interest until delivery from the futures invoice amount.

4. Divide the difference by the securities total cost and annualize; the result is the implied repo rate.

$$\text{Implied Repo Rate} = \frac{(\text{Total Cost} - \text{Invoice Price})}{\text{Total Cost}} \times \frac{365}{\text{Days to Deliver}}$$

EXAMPLES OF BASIC HEDGES

For expositional purposes hedges are categorized by positions taken in the futures markets—a short hedge and a long hedge.

The Short Hedge

Consider a bank facing the following situation on September 1. It plans to sell 90-day CDs a month later, on October 1. Current 90-day CDs can be sold at 10%. The December Eurodollar contract is selling at 89.70 (yield = 10.30%), while current 90-day LIBOR is quoted at 10.15%. Given this information, what rate should the bank expect to lock in on its CD sale and how should it hedge to achieve that rate?

Setting the Target (Lock-in) Rate and Placing the Hedge

Since the Eurodollar contract is selling at a yield 15 basis points above current 90-day LIBOR (the contract's deliverable instrument), the bank should expect to sell its 90-day CDs at a rate higher than the 10% currently prevailing on 90-day CDs. Assuming that convergence between 90-day LIBOR and the Eurodollar contract will take place evenly over the next three months (to delivery), the bank should expect the basis between 90-day LIBOR and the Eurodollar contract to decline by five basis points (opening basis/3 = 15/3). This five basis point decline in the basis should be viewed as a *premium* the bank is willing to pay to get rid of the risk of sharply rising interest rates over the next month. Hence, the bank should set itself a target rate of 10.05% (current CD rate + premium).

To achieve this target rate of 10.05%, the bank should sell one Eurodollar contract per $1 million face value of CDs on October 1 and repurchase them on November 1 when the CDs are actually issued.

Calculating the Realized Rate on the Hedge

Suppose on November 1 rates have risen sharply. 90-day CDs are selling at 10.50%, 9-day LIBOR at 10.65%, and the December Eurodollar contract at 10.77% (price = 89.23). The realized rate on the newly issued CD after adjusting for profits/losses on the hedge would be 10.03%, computed as follows:

$$\begin{aligned}
\text{Futures P/L (\$)} &= (\text{Sale Price} - \text{Purchase Price}) \times 100 \\
&\quad \times \$25 \text{ per BP} \\
&= (89.70 - 89.23) \times 100 \times 25 \\
&= \$1175
\end{aligned}$$

In terms of yield on a 90-day instrument, this $1175 profit is equivalent to 47 basis points, calculated as follows:

$$\begin{aligned}
\text{Yield P/L} &= \frac{\text{Futures P/L (\$)}}{\text{Value of 1 BP for Hedged Instrument}} \\
&= \$1175/\$25 \\
&= 47 \text{ Basis Points (0.47\%)}
\end{aligned}$$

The realized yield on the new 90-day CD after adjusting for futures P/L is given by:

$$\begin{aligned}
\text{Realized CD Yield} &= \text{Cash CD Yield} - \text{Yield P/L} \\
&= 10.50\% - 0.47\% \\
&= 10.03\%
\end{aligned}$$

Measuring the Performance of the Hedge

The performance of the hedge should be measured with reference to the target rate the hedge was attempting to lock in. In this example the target rate was 10.05%. The realized rate was 10.03%. The hedge was off by only two basis points (in this case better than the target rate). The hedge was very effective, based on how close the realized rate was to the target. The fact that a much lower rate was achieved by hedging compared to not hedging should not be used as a measure of hedging effectiveness. After all, if rates had fallen instead of risen; the realized rate might have been higher than the unhedged rate.

The Long Hedge

A long hedge can be used to protect against falling yields. If a money manager believes that yields in the futures markets will exceed yields forecasted for the cash market, a long hedge could be used to lock in those higher yields. Consider the following example.

An investor wishes to lock in the high yields currently prevailing on long-term government bonds. Two options are available. He can either purchase them directly in the cash market and finance them for six months or purchase a T-bond futures contract for delivery in six months.

Which option should the investor choose? Assume the following hypothetical prices in March.

U.S. 10%, 20-year bond selling at par (yield = 10.00%)
September T-bond future @ 83⁹/₃₂ (yield = 10.20%)
Financing cost = 9.00%
Conversion factor for U.S. 10%, 20-year bond = 1.1979

The implicit futures price for the cash bond is obtained by multiplying the September futures price by the conversion factor; that is, 83.2813 × 1.1979 = 99²⁴/₃₂.

If the cash bond is purchased at par and financed at 9% for six months, the positive carry of 1% (10% − 9%) would provide the investor an additional $500 over six months per $100,000 of face value (.01 × $100,000 × ⁶/₁₂). This $500 effectively reduces the price of the bond by ¹⁶/₃₂ or 99¹⁶/₃₂. Since this price is less than the implicit futures price, the cash market option is preferred to the futures option.

However, if either the September futures were lower or the financing cost were higher, it is likely that the futures route might turn out to be the preferred alternative.

Consider, for example, a financing cost of 9.5%. The positive carry in this case is 0.5%. Over six months this positive carry provides the investor an additional $250, which is equivalent to a price reduction of ⁸/₃₂ or 99²⁴/₃₂. Since this price exceeds the futures price, the futures route is preferred.

CASH FLOW IMPLICATIONS OF HEDGING

Cash flow considerations are important factors that can work for or against the hedger. The cash flow implications of hedging arise because of the daily cash settlement procedures of the clearinghouse, wherein each day the losses from the previous day are collected from the losers and passed on to the gainers. For example, when a mortgage banker sells production into the futures market and interest rates rise, the mortgage banker will have a positive cash flow as he receives the profit daily on the short futures position. This occurs because the clearinghouse marks-to-market daily and pays all profits in cash on the next day. The value of the cash thus received from the clearinghouse makes the futures market an attractive alternative in rising rate markets. In declining interest rate markets, the sale of the futures contract would have adverse effects on cash flow. The loss in value would have to be paid daily by the mortgage banker to the clearinghouse as interest rates declined. In the cash and forward markets, profits are not realized on a cash basis until settlement and delivery of the physical securities. Thus, cash flow considerations are negligible in the cash market.

The futures market hedger will recoup this variation margin when the cash transaction is consummated. But the use of cash will be lost until settlement day and this constant cash flow outflow could cause cash flow problems. The "losses" on the actual cash securities are paper losses to the hedger. The total profit or loss earned on the transaction for the hedger comes from the difference between the price paid for futures and the price received or paid for cash securities.

This concept of cash flow gain or loss applies to all futures market contracts and is an important consideration in evaluating the cost of hedging. The practice of "tailing" a hedge is used to adjust the hedge position in order to compensate for these cash flow costs.

INTERNAL ORGANIZATION FOR HEDGING

The internal organization of the decision-making machinery for a firm is quite important. The hedge decision should be a part of a firm's total management strategy. It's important that the top people in the firm, including the president and the board of directors, be aware of how and why the futures market is being used for hedging. If they understand the theory of hedging and that hedges do not always work out perfectly, the chances of futures trading becoming an integral and useful part of the management decisions of the firm are much greater.

Some firms establish committees to review the basic economic data, estimate risk exposures, set the hedge policy, and monitor the results. The actual implementation of the hedge is often delegated to an individual.

In all cases there should be a close liaison between the comptroller of the firm and the person having responsibility for the hedging, because hedging is basically a financial operation and, as we have seen, can have an important effect on the cash flow of the firm. It can also be used advantageously for tax purposes. The internal organization and record-keeping aspects of a hedging program are discussed in greater detail in Chapter 22.

In summary, hedging cash market financial commitments can reduce interest rate risk, create more certainty in business planning, and optimize the use of money, either for a borrower or for a lender/investor. Depending on the forecast for the direction of interest rates, hedging with futures can increase the profitability of your money management efforts.

21

Hedging Strategies for Various Industries

FINANCIAL CORPORATIONS

The very essence of financial institutions is that they are leveraged corporations that borrow money to invest in financial instruments or to reloan at higher rates of return. The difference between the cost of money and the rate of return on assets, minus operating expenses, is the firm's profit. This spread between cost and return is the lifeblood of the financial institution and must be maintained if the corporation is to survive. This profitability depends partly on the firm's ability to forecast cost of money and rates of return in advance and position the corporation to take advantage of, or avoid being harmed by, changes in interest rates that affect that spread. Financial futures can be used to protect one or both sides of their transactions.

Financial futures offer a unique opportunity to hedge the fluctuations in the value of fixed income securities caused by changes in interest rates. Interest rates have risen to record levels in recent years, eroding the value of investment portfolios and increasing the cost of borrowing money. No business operates without firsthand knowledge of the cost, or value, of money. It is imperative that they know the cheapest place to get money—whether from banks, the credit markets, or the equity market—and, conversely, the best place to invest excess cash. Financial futures offer a method of assuring, usually within a small range of error, interest rates at a specific level. Through interest rate futures, a rate of return on investments can also be established, again within some small margin of error.

This chapter looks at some basic strategies for hedging. For simplicity, industry groups, where they have the widest application, are used to illustrate various strategies and concepts of hedging. However, many of the strategies used in one industry group are applicable to other groups.

COMMERCIAL BANKS

Commercial banks are the epitome of financial corporations. Their business is to borrow large sums of money from their depositors and reloan the money to others at higher rates. A bank may loan money to the public in the form of business loans or consumer loans, or it may loan the money to governmental bodies through the purchase of Treasury notes, bonds, or bills.

A bank gets in trouble when its borrowers default on loans, or the cost of money borrowed from depositors is more than the return from its loan portfolios. The latter problem usually occurs when a bank mismatches the maturity of its fixed income assets with the average maturity for deposits. Usually, in these cases, banks purchase assets that have maturities longer than the average life of its liabilities. As rates rise, the liabilities mature and are reissued to the same or a different depositor at a higher cost to the bank. The return on the investment portfolio thus remains fixed while the cost of "rolling over" the liability increases, causing a decrease in the profit spread. If rates continue to rise, and the maturity of the assets is too long, the spread will become negative and the bank will begin losing money. Likewise, if a bank makes fixed-rate loans, it is subject to the risk that the spread will go against it unless it locks in a cost of money to fund the fixed-rate loans. A fixed rate of return on an asset could be especially costly if funded by a variable rate liability. A bank should use financial futures to hedge that portion of its balance sheet that is mismatched in maturity between assets and liabilities, or that portion of its balance sheet that is fixed in terms of rate of return.

A bank may also wish to hedge the spread between assets and liabilities when the spread difference is changing because of different market forces operating in different money markets. Banks sometimes find the cost of funds increasing faster than the rates of returns on assets. This differential in rates of change can also be hedged.

A bank must be very careful, however, not to increase its risk through hedging. This can happen when a bank's assets and liabilities are matched naturally by maturity and liquidity. A hedge may disturb this natural match and cause an imbalance. Many banks have a great portion of their balance sheets already in a natural hedge. For example, short-term variable rate commercial loans are balanced against short-term variable rate liabilities, such as demand deposits and certificates of deposits. Any hedge that would lock in, or sterilize, one side of the balance sheet without affecting the other side of the balance sheet could be creating more risk than it is averting. Hedging should be practiced when the hedge evens out the maturity differences between the asset and the liability, or evens out liquidity.

Hedging Assets

When a bank finds itself with a portfolio of fixed-rate assets and financing costs that are rising, it may wish to hedge those assets. Two ways of doing so are to hedge the cost of financing or to hedge the portfolio from further price erosion. Since the bank cannot always easily identify the exact source of funds used to finance a portfolio, it often chooses to hedge the asset itself.

The fixed income securities in a portfolio can be hedged by shorting an appropriate amount of interest rate futures contracts. As the level of interest rates increases, the price of the fixed income securities will decline. The offsetting short position in the futures market should show a similar price decline, but this price decline will generate a profit because the bank was short futures contracts that declined in value. The profit from the hedge is then used to adjust the cost of the fixed income asset to a lower cost (higher yield). The higher yield on the asset then works to maintain the spread between the cost of funds and the return on assets.

For example, assume a bank owns $10,000,000 worth of 30-year U.S. government Treasury bonds, 10.375% coupon with a maturity of 11/15/09. Assume the bank purchased these bonds at par and wishes to protect them from a price decline as interest rates rise. To hedge, the bank should short 100 U.S. Treasury bond contracts against the 10 million 10.375% Treasury bonds. We have assumed:

Long	Short
$10,000,000 10.375% T-bonds 11/15/09	100 U.S. T-bond contracts Sept. 1980 CBT Price $82.10
Price 100 Book yield 10.375%	

Interest rate rise for long bonds to 11.5%

Price of 10.375 $900,000	Price of futures $72.10
Loss on 10.375 $100,000	Profit on futures $100,000

Adjust book value of 10.375% 11/15/09 by $100,000 profit from futures.

In this example the bank has effectively *unlocked* the return on a fixed asset, thus matching the unlocked cost of liabilities that finance this asset.

In this simple example we illustrated a perfect hedge—U.S. Treasury bond futures contracts versus cash Treasury bonds—with no basis change. It is unusual for hedge situations to be so clean and to work out so well. (See Chapter 20 for discussions on basis, dollar equivalency, and convergence.)

In hedging a bank's spread it may be easier to hedge the cost of money than to hedge particular assets. Hedges against the cost of liabilities can be carried out using Eurodollar and T-bill futures contracts, since they more closely coincide with the nature of a bank's liabilities.

Locking in the Cost of Funds

In hedging liabilities a bank is attempting to protect itself against a rise in the cost of funds. When a bank begins to experience an increasing cost of money and is concerned that liability costs are rising faster than asset returns, it may choose to protect its spread.

For example, assume there is a bank with $50 million of negotiable certificates of deposit having an average maturity of 90 days. Assume also that at the end of that 90 days the portfolio would normally be rolled over into new certificates at the then current rate. If the bank fears that it will not be able to roll into 90-day paper at favorable prices, it could hedge to establish today its liability prices for that 90-day period between the maturity of the liability and the maturity of its assets. To accomplish this the bank would short fifty 90-day Eurodollar (ED) futures contracts. If rates rise 100 basis points equally in the cash and ED futures markets, the profit from the futures will offset the increased cost of rolling over the liabilities for 90 more days.

CD rates on day 1	Futures prices on day 1
15.00%	86.50
CD rates on day 90	Futures prices on day 90
16.00%	85.50
Increased cost of writing $50 million of 90-day CDs on day 90 versus day 1 = $125,000	Profit on short position in 50 ED futures contracts = $125,000

The profit from the ED futures contract would lower the book cost of the liability, thus maintaining the spread.

This same technique is applied when hedging the total liability portfolio of the bank. A short futures position taken against a "long" money position will effectively lock in that cost of money for as long as the hedge is maintained—if the buying basis and the selling basis remain constant. As the basis (the price difference between the futures contract and the liability) changes, the number of contracts shorted should be increased or decreased depending on the amount necessary to maintain dollar equivalency. If liability costs begin to rise in yield faster than CDs, more contracts would have to be shorted to maintain dollar-for-dollar gains and losses between the cash and future sides of the hedge.

Hedging When Rates Are Falling

Commercial banks usually make nice profits as rates rise, because the rates of return on many of their assets (prime rate commercial loans) are administered higher on a same-day basis. Although the return on assets goes up on day one, the cost of liabilities does not change until the liability matures and is refunded at the new higher rates. This lag in timing between price changes usually allows a healthy bank a windfall profit. The longer the average life of a liability portfolio in rising rate markets, the greater the windfall.

However, when the market turns down, the rates at which the liabilities roll over does not fall as fast as, say, the prime rate, which is administered down. Therefore, banks need to hedge their liabilities by "unlocking" the fixed cost of their liabilities as they lower the return on their variable rate assets.

To unlock the costs of the liability portfolio a banker would purchase futures contracts that coincide with the maturity of the existing portfolio of CDs or other variable rate liabilities. As rates move lower, the profit on the futures contract would offset the cost of being in higher rate CDs as the return on prime rate assets decreases.

For example, assume a bank with a CD portfolio of $50,000,000 and an average maturity of 180 days. When rates begin to decline, and the prime is being lowered, the banks would purchase 90-day ED futures contracts. (If the average maturity on the liabilities were to decline, the number of contracts should also decline; if the average maturity were to remain at 180 days, the number of contracts would remain unchanged. This adjustment is done to maintain dollar equivalency in the two positions.) This would effectively unlock the maturity of the portfolio and give it a floating rate cost based on the daily price of the 90-day ED contract. This type of hedge unlocks the costs of funds, opening the portfolio to immediate lowering of costs if rates go lower; but it also precludes any opportunity profits if rates go higher, because the "cheap" money

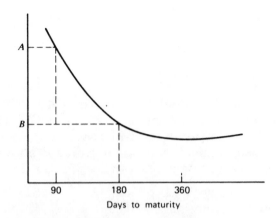

FIGURE 21.1 Yield curve with an inverse slope.

already purchased would be offset by the loss on the long position in ED futures.

Another strategy can be employed when rates are expected to peak in the near future. For example, liability managers shun the longer-term liabilities and attempt to keep the maturity of their liability portfolio as short term as possible when rates are expected to decrease in the near future. This preference usually causes the yield curve to have an inverse slope with near-term rates being considerably higher than longer rates. (See Figure 21.1.)

Banks don't want to buy the longer-term money and lock in higher liability costs for long periods of time as rates begin to fall. Therefore, they tend to bunch their purchases of money into the shorter maturities, causing short-term money to be bid for very aggressively by banks. To take advantage of this type of yield curve a bank would buy the longer term money—180 days in Figure 21.1—and pay price *B* for it. This would be substantially cheaper than buying the 90-day money at price *A*. It then purchases 90-day ED futures in an equal amount. The short position of the 180-day CDs versus the long position in 90-day ED futures in effect reduces the exposure of the banks CD position to 90 days while allowing it to pay the lower 180-day rate. If rates were to go lower, the profit from the futures contract would be applied to the difference between 90-day CD rates on day number 90 of the hedge, minus the 180-day rate from day one. To illustrate, consider the following:

Assume that on day one, 90-day CD rates are 16.00% and 180-day CD rates are 15.00%.

Step 1. Purchase the money for 180 days by selling $10,000,000 in certificates of deposit.

Saving 1% for 90 days on $10,000 equals $25,000.

Step 2. Buy 90-day ED futures contracts.

Assume that rates do indeed move sharply lower 90 days later and that the new 90-day CD rate is now 13.75%.

Since the CDs purchased earlier are locked in at 15.00% for another 90 days, they cannot be rolled into another 90-day CD. Thus, the opportunity cost is $31,250 for the next 90 days.

However, if the CD futures have also improved in price by 125 basis points, the profit on the long position will be $31,250. To summarize:

Saving on original CD position	+$25,000
Opportunity loss after 90 days	−$31,500
Profit on CD futures position	+$31,500
Net saving	$25,000

(*Note:* The assumption made in this example was that the basis did not change—a rather unrealistic assumption, as mentioned several times before. Nevertheless, as also noted, the variation in the basis is likely to be a lot less than the variation in absolute price.)

The important concept just illustrated is that a hedger can take what the yield curve gives and then use the futures market to tailor the maturity of the liability to fit his or her needs. This concept works equally well with asset hedging.

Another use of interest rate futures is in pre-refunding existing assets when rates are falling. Many times a bank will have securities maturing over the next six months and would like to reinvest those monies at current rates rather than at rates that might prevail at the time of maturity. The bank portfolio manager has three choices. First, the bank could sell the securities now and reinvest in longer maturities at current rates. This is possible only if the bank is willing to take the losses on the income statement in the current quarter. Second, the bank could borrow the money in the federal funds market or the CD market, or purchase longer-term securities and finance them until the maturity of the current assets. This alternative has some possible disadvantages, however. In financing a new position, the bank could end up paying a higher reserve requirement for a marginal purchase that it financed. Also, the bank's limits on portfolio size may limit new purchases and, finally, the longer security could be at a negative carry versus the cost of short-term money used to finance the longer asset. Third, the bank could purchase interest rate futures. If the bank picks this alternative, it should decide on the maturity range. Then it should pick a futures contract or contracts that would give the same dollar value price appreciation if rates move lower. If rates go lower between the time the hedge is put on and reinvestment, the hedger's profit on the futures helps lower the cost of investments. If rates go higher the investors do not receive the benefits from reinvesting at higher rates, as the losses on the futures would offset any increase in income from higher rates and lower prices at reinvestment.

All of these examples are straightforward strategies designed to illustrate various basic concepts in the use of futures contracts for hedging. Although not specifically noted in each case, each example assumes that the correlation between the cash and futures positions are high (so that the risk of basis change is low) and that the hedger uses the correct dollar equivalency factors in matching cash and futures positions.

There are many other variations in the uses of futures by a bank for hedging. As readers apply the concepts explained here and in the other chapters on strategies, they will begin to see the other applications, and the basic elements of hedging will become more apparent.

THRIFT INSTITUTIONS

As a group, thrift institutions have generally relied on savings deposits as a main source of borrowed money. Their assets tend to be longer-term investments in mortgages with relatively small, highly liquid portfolios of short-term investments. This type of asset and liability mismatch, short-term borrowing and long-term investment, is a classic textbook formula for financial disaster.

As short-term interest rates have risen since the early 1970s, deposits have moved out of thrift institutions and into the money market funds or other short-term investments. As thrift institutions began losing savings deposits, they devised new methods of attracting deposits to fund their long-term loans. After supplying their depositors with toasters and electric drills, there was nothing left to do but compete for deposits by matching the higher interest rates being paid by alternative investments. Regulatory authorities cooperated by allowing thrift institutions to raise rates to regular depositors, create new types of savings instruments, and allow NOW accounts or demand deposits that pay interest.

The new savings instruments have had a significant long-run impact on the thrift institutions. They were very well received by the public and their use became widespread. However, because they locked thrift institutions into a bidding war with other financial institutions for short-term deposits, in the final analysis this new solution only added to the mismatch of assets and liabilities. Unlike other financial institutions, as interest costs on short-term borrowing rise the return on the existing assets remains constant. As short-term interest rates rise, the profit spread between investments and borrowing narrows and eventually becomes negative, due in large part to the increasing costs of the variable rate borrowings that have been made. Thrift institutions could use the financial futures market to hedge these variable borrowing costs and lock in a cost of funds for their fixed-rate assets and protect their profit spread.

How Issuers Can Hedge Money Market Certificates

The money market certificate pays a varying interest rate. Every week the issuer changes the interest rate paid, based on the average price paid for 180-day T-bills at the most recent weekly auction of bills. As T-bill rates increase, the cost of borrowing money through the sale of money market certificates increases proportionately.

This type of commitment lends itself to effective hedging through the T-bill futures contracts. It can be almost a direct hedge, except that T-bill futures are based on 90-day T-bill rates whereas the money market certificate is based on 180-day bill rates. This creates two problems. A change in the price of a 90-day bill will return only half as many dollars as the same change in the price of 180-day bills. And, second, the basis between 90-day T-bill futures and six-month T-bills is not always constant.

Taking these facts into consideration, a savings bank or S&L could hedge against the risk of higher interest costs by shorting twice as many 90-day T-bill contracts as it has millions of dollars of certificates outstanding. This would establish, within a small margin, the cost of interest in advance of the adjustment on the certificate. As the interest rate on T-bills in the cash market rises, the price of T-bill futures should decline. The profit from the short position in futures will help offset the increased cost of borrowing when the money market certificates are repriced.

For example, assume a savings bank has $25 million in money market certificates outstanding. If bill rates go higher between now and when those certificates are repriced, the bank will have to pay the higher rate for the next six months. Assume that it is November, and the $25 million worth of money market certificates yield 12% and are due May 1, 1991. If the interest rate rises between November and May to say, 13%, the savings bank, when it reprices its money market certificates, would sustain an increased cost of borrowing for the next six months of $125,000. Assume, however, the savings bank had sold short fifty 90-day Treasury bill contracts on November 1 at 12%, and that interest rates climbed 100 basis points for a profit of $125,000 on the short position. As long as the savings bank leaves its short position intact in the futures market, it has locked in the 12% rate that was prevailing at the time the hedge was transacted. The gain on the T-bill futures short position offsets any increase in borrowing costs, but not on a one-for-one basis because of commissions on the futures transaction.

What if interest rates moved in the opposite direction? What if they fell to 11% on 180-day T-bills instead of climbing to 13%? In this situation the savings bank would have lost $125,000 on its short position in the futures market. But on May 1 it would have repriced the money market certificates at 11%, reducing the interest cost by $125,000. In effect, the costs for the second six-month period would have been the same as for the original six-month period. The bank avoided the risk of having to pay 13% or more and also gave up the opportunity for a windfall gain if rates fell. At any time during the intervening period between November 1 and May 1, the savings bank cold have lifted the hedge by buying back fifty 90-day T-bill futures contracts for the same months it had previously sold. This would unlock the interest rate level previously fixed and allow the new rate to decline from that date forward. Of course, this sort of selective hedging leaves the savings bank at risk again.

Hedging Other Savings Banks Liabilities

Another important source of funding for thrifts has been the "jumbo" certificate of deposit. This is a certificate of deposit of at least $100,000. The rates of these certificates are administered by the savings banks in much the same way as a commercial bank administers the rate paid on its certificates of deposit. To attract money for these types of certificates, the banks must pay a rate that is at least as good as and often better than most commercial banks for similar maturities. The higher rates are sometimes necessary because the thrift institutions usually have less capital than commercial banks and the secondary market for their certificates is usually less liquid.

The rate paid on jumbos is not directly related to T-bill rates as in the previous example. It is more closely related to the rate paid by other savings banks and commercial banks for certificates of deposit. Thus, the secondary CD market is a better barometer of interest costs for jumbo certificates than is the T-bill market. Therefore, the hedging of jumbos would be done in ED futures. Similar to the preceding hedge, this type of hedge would be a short hedge; that is, a hedge in which the futures market side of the hedge results in a short position and the cash market part of the hedge results in a long position. The savings bank is long money. The contract month shorted would be the one that best coincides with the maturity of the CDs anticipated to be written. It is conceivable that the interest rates on CDs will rise more than interest rates on ED futures. In this situation, because the hedge is a cross-hedge, the cost of writing new CDs may not be completely offset by the profits on the futures contract. In other words, there could be some basis risk. If changes in the basis are not anticipated or are inadequately compensated for through adjustments in the number of futures contracts shorted, the hedge will not be efficient.

PENSION FUND MANAGERS AND THE FINANCIAL FUTURES MARKETS

Chapter 17 covered the basics on stock index futures and their use for hedging by pension fund managers and portfolio managers. This section provides a more robust look at the many other ways pensions may use futures and options, including their consideration as a separate asset class.

Pension fund managers in recent years have become more active in the management of the assets under their control. There are several uses of the futures market that enable them to increase the return on their assets and to increase the liquidity of the portfolios that they manage. Let's look first at increasing the return on pension investments through the use of futures.

Many times in the recent past the yield curve has been negatively sloped. That is, higher rates have been paid on the shorter end of the market than on the longer end of the market. This is characterized by a downward-sloping yield curve. If pension fund managers have money to invest, they are faced with difficult decisions. Do they make long-term investments at lower rates, where they might have potentially greater appreciation in price in the future, or do they maximize immediate return by purchasing shorter-term money market instruments? By using the futures market pension fund managers can have the best of both worlds. They can invest cash in short-term money market certificates earning a higher current yield, but not lose the advantage of capital appreciation available in the long-term market. They can do this through the simultaneous purchase of long-term bond futures contracts and high-yield short-term cash investments. The purchase of the long-term futures contracts locks in today's current prices on long-term bonds. When this is coupled with the purchase of money market securities, portfolio managers have the luxury of having a high short-term return on current investments and, through the futures market, the benefit of capital appreciation if long-term rates decline. Money managers are assuming that sooner or later the inverted yield curve will return to a normal yield curve and as it does they will gain on both ends of the portfolio.

There is one important drawback to this type of strategy. In a market with a negatively sloped yield curve the prices for futures contracts will be higher than prices on similar securities in the cash market. Thus, unless managers assume they will have a stable basis, they have to compare the premium paid to purchase securities through a futures contract against the extra current income earned on the short-term investment.

For example, if 90-day certificates of deposit offer the investor 17% and long-term bonds are yielding 13%, an investor could earn 4% more income in the CD than in long-term bonds. But if long-term rates were to decline and the basis were to change accordingly while the investor was in the CDs, the higher prices paid later for long-term bonds could quickly wipe out or even exceed the short-term return differential between CDs and bonds. Four percent per million for 90 days is worth $9863.00 per million in extra income. If the premium on a Treasury bond future 90 days from settlement is less than $9863 ($31/32$), it would make sense to pursue this type of strategy. If the premium paid for futures was greater than $31/32$, it would be better to buy long Treasury bonds in the cash market and avoid the short-term investment.

Assume, however, that futures prices are below $31/32$ premium and the investor purchases 90-day certificates of deposit and goes long Treasury bond futures. If during the time of this hedge long-term rates actually declined, the investor would make a profit on the Treasury bond futures contract. But because of lower long-term rates, the investor would have to pay more for long-term fixed-income securities. The profit from the futures would be applied to the new purchase price, thus lowering it back toward the level that existed on the day the futures position was initiated.

If long-term interest rates were to rise during this period, the investor would lose money on the futures contract. The loss wold be no greater than the loss would have been if a cash purchase of long bonds had been made assuming a stable basis. The investment prices will be lower at the end of 90 days when this strategy ends and this lower reinvestment price will offset the loss on the futures position.

This technique actually reduces total loss because the extra income earned on the short-term investment will partially offset any losses that might occur when interest rates rise.

A slight variation of this strategy is to sell an exiting portfolio in the cash market, purchase higher yielding short-term investments, and re-purchase the equivalent of the original position in the futures market. This strategy allows a portfolio manager to increase current return and still hold a portfolio of longer-term investments, which over time he or she feels will be good investments. All of the basis and dollar equivalency risks described in previous chapters are inherent in this strategy, however. And the manager has to ask, Does the short-term pickup in yield make up for the premium paid on the futures contracts, plus any transaction costs? Further, the implications of gains or losses on the sale of the existing portfolio need to be considered.

This strategy of using the futures market to alter the maturity of a portfolio works best with a portfolio of long-term Treasury bonds provided that the Treasury bonds are of a factor type contract that equalizes the prices of all potential delivery items is used. It should be noted that with this strategy one need not actually take delivery of the securities purchased through the futures contract. Instead the futures contract is used as a temporary substitute to guarantee an investment price at the maturity of the short-term investment.

If the cash portfolio is composed of securities other than U.S. Treasury bonds (say corporate bonds), then one has a cross-hedge situation and an increase in basis risk. As noted earlier, picking the proper contract, the correct number of contracts, and the correct month are most important in reducing basis risk. Thus, if corporate bonds were sold from the portfolio or their purchase delayed, one would need a good understanding of the nature and extent of the price relationship between Treasury bond futures and the corporate bond market. If the spread between corporates and government bonds were to change during the short-term investment period, the futures position would not give you the same return as holding the original position in corporate bonds.

The futures market can also be used to increase the liquidity of a long-term investment portfolio and to cut the time lag between decision processes and the execution of those decisions. Market conditions do not always allow the portfolio manager sufficient time to quickly and efficiently execute the strategies she or he has devised. Often a portfolio manager may decide to purchase a block of a certain type of security but will find that security unavailable in the market at that time. Even if the securities were available in the market, the size he or she desires to purchase may affect the prices.

A simple method of overcoming this problem is to purchase futures contracts that are closely correlated in price movement with the security the manager wishes to buy in the cash market. This allows the manager time to accumulate the securities in the cash market without being subject to the full risk of a change in market prices. As the cash securities are purchased, the manager would sell the futures contracts that he or she had previously purchased. The profit and loss from those futures contracts would then be applied to offset the change in the purchase price of the cash market securities. In this way the portfolio manager can reduce the time between decision and execution and be more efficient in the cost-effectiveness of cash market purchases. In short, the manager uses the futures as a temporary substitute for cash market transactions.

The same strategy would apply when a portfolio manager wished to sell from a fixed income portfolio. On the date the decision to sell was made the portfolio manager would sell futures contracts into the market. Then as he or she was able to sell off the securities the futures contracts would be covered. This type of strategy might be especially applicable when the securities to be purchased or sold are not actively traded. Note however, that once again, this strategy involves a cross-hedge. Most of the time the securities being purchased or sold would not be the securities that underlie the corresponding futures contracts. Therefore, it would be important to know the basis and the beta and to monitor it to maximize the efficiency of the hedge.

Commodities and Asset Allocation for Pensions

The magazine *Pensions and Investments Age* reported recently that 40.5% of the top two hundred pension fund sponsors, measured by dollars under management, and 18.9% of the bottom 800 sponsors were using futures and options as part of their investment management activity. (See Figure 21.2.)

These pension managers are using the full range of financial futures and options, that is, foreign currency, Eurodollar, Treasury bond, Treasury note, Treasury bill, and stock index. They are using them for hedging, arbitrage, portfolio insurance, creation of synthetic securities, implementing asset allocation strategies, facilitating manager restructuring, and as a separate asset investment class specifically designed to add value to fund performance. It is this latter activity that we focus on in this section.

Until very recently, any pension manager who suggested using futures as an investment to add value would probably have received a cold re-

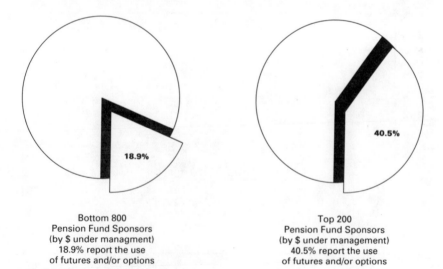

Bottom 800
Pension Fund Sponsors
(by $ under managment)
18.9% report the use
of futures and/or options

Top 200
Pension Fund Sponsors
(by $ under management)
40.5% report the use
of futures and/or options

FIGURE 21.2 Pension fund use of futures. (Data used to construct these charts was provided by Pensions & Investment Age. © Crain Communications, Inc. Source: FIA Review Jan/Feb 1991.)

ception from his trustees. But more and more institutions are finding that money invested in professionally managed futures products can act as an important risk diversification technique. Eastman Kodak, AMP, Inc., and the Virginia State Employee's Pension Fund, as well as a handful of others, have put small portions of their pension monies in commodity investment. Kodak's pension fund took the lead in this regard in 1987 when it made a $50 million trial investment in a commodity fund. They have since upped the investment to over $200 million. As an experiment, AMP, Inc. invested $10 million of its plan's assets in two commodity futures funds. Their returns were extraordinary in the first few months and, more importantly, they found that the returns were negatively correlated with returns for the Dow Jones Industrials and the S&P 500.

In short, in recent months, financial institutions, and pensions in particular, have begun to realize that they cannot afford to ignore an entire asset class. Commodity fund managers now recognize they can obtain significant reductions in overall portfolio risk through diversification into commodity futures. They find that the "efficient frontier" (the optimal mix of investments that represents the highest expected return for each level of risk) shifts in their favor when professionally managed commodity investments are added to their portfolio of stock investments. (See Figure 21.3.) Studies indicate that the returns on commodity funds are negatively

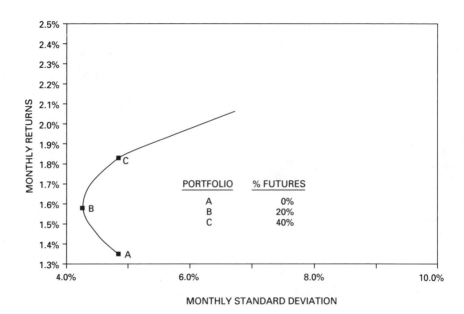

FIGURE 21.3 Portfolio return—Risk tradeoffs.

or very poorly correlated with returns on their other investments such as stocks, bonds and real estate. (See Figures 21.4 and 21.5.)

Financial engineering techniques such as have been described in other sections on portfolio insurance, options, arbitrage, and so on, have allowed the development of new investment vehicles for people interested in trading commodity futures. Pension funds need and desire investments that have particular risk, reward, and cash flow characteristics. Futures and options, in combination with traditional investments, allow these products to be custom designed to the pension manager's needs.

All of this has resulted in the carving out of a new niche in the managed money field—one created out of sudden demand by institutions for instant expertise in selecting and monitoring CTAs, who are the ones pension managers would rely on to make trading decisions.

These new "manager of managers" perform an important role in locating CTAs, both experienced and new, handling the marketing and legal support issues, creating the investment product, allocating and distributing capital among the CTAs, monitoring their performance, and providing general administrative and consulting services to the pension investor. In short, they act as special consultants to the pension investor providing management expertise.

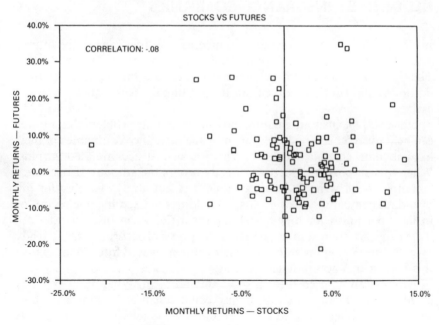

FIGURE 21.4 Correlation diagram.

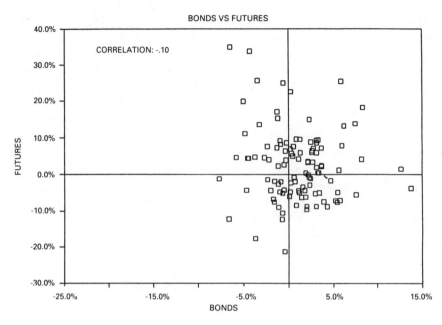

FIGURE 21.5   Correlation diagram.

HEDGING BY INSURANCE COMPANIES

Insurance companies that have fixed income securities can use the futures market to hedge the depreciation of their assets as interest rates go higher. They can also use the futures market to increase the liquidity of their portfolios and cut down execution times using the techniques explained earlier.

However, *life* insurance companies have a unique problem that futures can help overcome. Any losses taken by life insurance companies in their fixed income portfolios must be charged against accumulated surplus. When this surplus is reduced it directly lowers the amount of insurance a company can write. Because of this, it is not always feasible for life insurance companies to swap existing holdings of fixed income securities in their portfolios for higher yielding securities when interest rates are increasing. As interest rates go higher the prices of securities they already own decline. Swapping into the higher coupons would force them to take this loss against accumulated surplus.

Futures can be used to help solve this problem. When rates begin to go higher, a life insurance company could sell futures contracts short against its existing portfolio. As rates continued to move higher the profits from the short portion in futures contracts would help offset the losses on the existing cash position. When swaps of lower coupon securities for higher yielding coupons became attractive they could be transacted with no net loss charged against surplus. As cash securities were sold and loss taken, futures short positions would be covered. This strategy allows insurance companies to improve the yields of their fixed income portfolios in periods of higher interest rates.

In this type of hedge program it should not be necessary to identify futures contracts to be used for each particular cash position. The overall exposure of the portfolio should be analyzed by categorizing the securities into their major groups. See Table 21.1 for an example of a grouping of securities for a hedge program.

Once the issues are grouped by maturity, the average quality of each group would need to be determined, as well as the average maturity. Once these two factors are known one is then in a position to do the correlation studies and begin the process of calculating basis and dollar equivalency ratios.

TABLE 21.1 Breakdown of a Fixed Income Portfolio in Hedgeable Groups

Maturity	Type of Instrument	Type of Futures
0–2 years	U.S. Treasury bills U.S. Treasury notes and bonds U.S. ageny issues Commercial paper Bank liabilities	90-day Eurodollar deposits 90-day Treasury bills
2–6 years	U.S. Treasury notes and bonds U.S. agency issues Corporate bonds and notes	U.S. 2-year Treasury note U.S. 5-year Treasury note
7–12 years	U.S. Treasury notes and bonds Corporate debt U.S. agency issues MBSs	U.S. Treasury note
12–30 years	Corporate debt U.S. agency issues U.S. Treasury bonds	U.S. Treasury bond

Failure to go through these steps could result in overhedging a portfolio and create great risk for the portfolio manager.

After the portfolio was properly hedged and when attractive, yield improvement swaps became possible, the manager would select the issues to be sold and unwind the futures contracts that coincided with that particular security group.

MORTGAGE BANKERS

Mortgage bankers can use the futures market in a variety of ways to hedge the financing cost of warehousing mortgages, to hedge the selling price of mortgage production, and to hedge the cost of mortgages in the pipeline.

The hedging of mortgages is not an easy task nor is it necessarily low risk. This is because most mortgages have a number of "embedded options" allowing the mortgagee the choice (option) to prepay a mortgage if it is economically advantageous to do so. Also many mortgages contain interest rate caps and interest rate floors, all of which affect the economic incentive for the mortgagee to prepay. This prepayment option dramatically affects the value of the mortgage and the rate of change in the value of the mortgage as interest rates rise or fall. This makes the process of hedging, which is designed to achieve equal dollar value changes in the futures position and the cash position, difficult and complex. Hence, anyone attempting to use Treasury bond or Treasury note futures as a vehicle for hedging mortgages should be aware that there is a high risk of the hedges being ineffective under certain circumstances. The key element in controlling that risk is correct forecasting of the prepayment rate on the mortgages. Forecasting prepayment rates is not an exact science.

Hedging the Finance Cost of Warehousing

Mortgage bankers who are collecting mortgages with a view toward creating a pool and originating a GNMA usually need to finance part of the mortgages until the closings of all the mortgages. During the period prior to completion of a pool, the mortgage banker borrows money to finance mortgages already purchased. These loans are usually made by commercial banks at a rate based upon the prime rate.

When interest rates keep moving higher, the mortgage banker's costs of warehousing keep increasing. To protect against this, the banker can hedge by selling Eurodollar futures or 90-day T-bill futures, whichever provides the most efficient basis against the bank loan. As short-term rates work higher the short futures position should offset the increased financial costs.

Sell Production

When a mortgage banker has accumulated a pool of mortgages and wishes to originate a GNMA pass-through and then sell that pass-through, he or she can use the futures market as a temporary substitute, and as an alternative marketplace if later it should be more economical to give delivery. The futures market offers a mortgage banker advantages not available in other marketplaces. When the GNMA is sold, the mortgage banker need not be concerned that the buyer will be able to honor the commitment, as the exchange clearinghouse stands behind the purchase. The futures contract is standardized, so terms of sale do not fluctuate from dealer to dealer.

INDUSTRIAL CORPORATIONS

Nonfinancial, or industrial, corporations can use the futures markets to hedge the cost of borrowed money. Bank loans, commercial paper, and long-term borrowing costs can be established in advance at acceptable levels. This can work to lower the cost of borrowing and increase certainty in business decisions by reducing a very important uncertainty—interest costs.

Hedging the Prime Rate

A variable prime rate loan can be hedged over long periods of time to protect against changes in interest rates. Correlation studies show that the best contracts to use are the Eurodollar contracts. There are some difficulties and risk (especially accounting risk) in doing so, however. One reason for the difficulty is the fact that the prime rate is not always highly correlated with futures price movements; the prime rate is administered, but futures prices are not. Another reason is that the futures contract and the cash asset may not mature at the same time. This uncertainty in basis and lack of coincidence in maturity of the cash and futures positions presents significant problems.

Both of these problems can be compensated for by (1) selling a series of consecutive contract months and retiring the contracts as the loan approaches maturity or (2) selling an adequate amount of one futures month that matures after the loan matures and retiring contracts as the loan ages. The first technique helps to smooth basis change risk because the futures contracts cover a wide maturity range. The second is sometimes preferable because it reduces transaction costs and in rising rate markets the longer-term contract will outperform shorter-term contracts. Each technique is illustrated below.

The Multicontract Technique of Hedging

Assume that, as a result of correlation studies, Eurodollars have been picked as the best vehicle for hedging a variable rate bank loan against a rise in rates. If the price spreads between various ED futures contracts had been fluctuating sharply, it might be difficult to pick one contract month to short and maintain a good basis relationship. In such a case a string of different months could be shorted to average out the maturity of the futures contract.

The following is an example of this type of hedge. (This concept was introduced earlier in our discussion of spreads, but it's important enough to bear repeating.)

On August 15, a corporation borrows $10 million for one year at the prime rate. The corporation expects the prime rate to rise over the next year, or at least part of that year. The loan agreement stipulates that the interest rate of the loan changes on the same day the lender changes its posted prime rate.

The key consideration is that the amount of money owed will depend not only on changes in the prime rate, but on *when* those changes occur. If the bank raises the rate on the 10th day of the loan, the borrower must pay the increased rate for the next 355 days. If the rate changes on day 150, the borrower pays the higher rate for only 215 days. The trick is to be fully hedged, but not overhedged, for every day of the life of the loan. This calls for the hedger to establish dollar equivalency at the outset, and then maintain it by reducing the size of the short position in futures proportionately over the life of the loan.

To accomplish this, the corporation should, on day one of the loan, short five times (assume a 1.2 beta) as many millions of dollars worth of 90-day Eurodollar contacts as they have millions of prime-rate loan dollars. Each 0.01% increase in one 90-day T-bill futures contract returns only $25, while each 0.01% increase in cost of a one-year loan is $100 per million. As the loan moves toward maturity, the value of each 0.01% change in the futures contract remains $25, while the dollar value of a .01% change in loan interest declines. Table 21.2 shows these values for the loan. The five contracts sold on day one of the loan would be covered on a proportional basis with the declining maturity of the loan.

On August 15, when the loan was made, the corporation would short 13 September futures contracts, 13 December contracts, 12 March con-

TABLE 21.2 Dollar Value per 0.01%

Time Left to Maturity	Cost per $1 Million of Loan
90 days	$ 25
180 days	50
270 days	75
360 days	100

tracts, and 12 June contracts. Just prior to the settlement of each contract month, the corporation would roll that contract month into the next contract month. During the periods between rollovers the corporation would cover the shorts to match the declining maturity, always covering them in the closest contract month. The corporation would liquidate the last 10 contracts over the time remaining between the last contract month and the maturation date of the loan. Hence, between August and September the hedger should offset four September futures, buying one every seven days (every seven days because 50 contracts must be retired over 365 days, and $365/50 = 7.03$ days). On September 19, just prior to the September contract settlement, the hedger would roll the remaining September contracts into the December contract by purchasing September contracts and shorting more December contracts. This process of retiring contracts every seven days will keep the proper balance until the loan matures, assuming there is no basis change.

The Single Month Method

A single contract month of EDs could also be used to hedge the loan. The hedger could short 50 September ED futures contracts and retire one of the contracts every seven days. Near the middle of September, the remaining contracts must be rolled forward into the December contract. This could increase the basis risk. If the spreads between months are changing rapidly, the September futures contracts could outperform or underperform the rest of the market, causing severe basis problems.

However, there are two times when such a one-month strategy pays off. First, when the cash market yield curve is negatively sloped and futures prices are at considerable premiums to cash, it makes sense to lump all shorts into the nearby futures contract, because the convergence of the premium to spot will work in favor of the short. This positive aspect more than overcomes the problem of concentration. It does, however, increase commission cost as the remaining short positions must be rolled into the next contract month more frequently.

A second type of single contract month hedge is to short the closest month following the maturity of the loan. The contracts would be retired proportionately until maturity of the loan. There are two advantages to this strategy. First, the strategy precludes the necessity of rolling into new contract months. This not only reduces brokerage commissions but also cuts down operational expenses and bookkeeping expenses. Second, if the market rallies on a short-term basis, the more distant futures months often will gain less than the front months. This can reduce the opportunity costs of the hedge. In other words, the basis may be more stable, or more likely to work in the hedger's favor.

Hedging the Prime at Different Stages of the Business Cycle

There is no "right" technique to hedge variable rate bank loans, but market volatility and the stage of the business cycle must be taken into consideration. There is also no "right" type of futures contract to use as the short side of the hedge. Often Eurodollar futures will be the best type of futures contracts to short; at other times T-bill contracts are best, because they will correlate better with prime-rate changes.

The keys to picking between EDs and bills lie in two fundamental considerations. First, corporate liquidity is very important. In the early stages of an increasing rate cycle, corporate liquidity is usually high and ED rates will not always correlate with the prime-rate changes. In the later stages of a cycle corporations get squeezed for cash and ED and prime-rate loans tend to follow one another closely. During this time bank loans are taken down as an alternative to commercial paper loans. Second, T-bills and T-bill futures are investment vehicles, and investor expectations play a large role in their pricing structure. Therefore, in the first stages of a rising interest cycle, T-bills will usually decline as fast as or faster than the prime rate, as a result of investor expectations of higher rates. However, toward the last stages of an interest rate upswing, investors often anticipate the actual peak and drive the prices of T-bills higher while the prime rate remains unchanged.

In general, Treasury bill futures therefore make better hedge vehicles in the beginning and middle stages of a rising interest rate cycle, and Eurodollar futures make better vehicles in the later stages of the cycle.

Hedging Commercial Paper Costs

Commercial paper costs can be hedged in much the same way a commercial bank hedges the costs of certificates of deposit. It may actually be easier to hedge commercial paper costs than CDs, because commercial paper is often better correlated with Eurodollar futures than CDs. The techniques of hedging would be the same as for CDs, but caution must be used because these are still cross-hedges.

Smoothing out Seasonal Cash Flows and Increasing Returns on Investments

The futures market can be used by the corporate treasurer to even out the investment returns of excess cash. Usually a corporation is limited to the rates extant in the money market at the time the cash is on hand. Also it is subject to the vagaries of the market when it must sell securities whose maturities are longer than the period the case is available. This either limits the maturity of the investment to the life of the cash or opens the corporation up to security losses.

Lock-in Rates for Future Dates

The corporation that knows when it will be receiving cash may invest at any time prior to actually receiving the cash by purchasing futures contracts. The purchase of futures fixes the return at today's futures rates. When the cash arrives and investments are made in the cash market, their performance is adjusted by the profits or losses from futures. A corporation need not take delivery of a security purchased by a long commitment in a futures contract. It is looking for the price appreciation *as if* it had made the cash investment on the day the futures contract was purchased.

The opposite is true for the corporation that has a portfolio and wishes to sell today because of an expected market decline. The corporation may not want to realize the loss on its books, and also may not need the cash at this time. It could instead sell futures contracts against the cash position. As the futures prices declined, the profit from the short would offset the loss in value of the portfolio from the day the hedge was placed.

Increasing the Return of Short-Term Investments

Corporate treasurers often have money for specific periods of time and are limited to making investments for that specified period of time. By using interest rate futures along with cash investments, the treasurer can increase this return for the period held. This can be accomplished by taking the best possible yield in the cash market, then tailoring the maturity of that investment to match the life of the cash. This is very similar to the technique of the liability manager of a bank using the yield curve for CDs to his or her advantage.

If the highest short-term yield available were 180 days but the corporation had cash for only 90 days, it could purchase the 180-day instrument and sell short a 90-day CD contract. If at the end of 90 days prices in the money market had declined, the corporation would lose money on selling the 180-day investment to raise cash. However, to the extent that prices in the futures market declined equally, the corporation would earn an equal profit to offset the loss. If prices were to increase over the 90-day period, the profit from the cash sale would similarly offset the loss in the futures position. The outcome of both possibilities would be a higher return for the 90-day period than if the money were invested in lower yielding 90-day spot instruments.

The same logic applies when shorter-term rates are higher than longer-term rates—an inverse yield curve. A corporation with 180-day money might find 90-day rates more attractive than 180-day rates. The problem with this type of yield curve is that there is no guarantee that at the end of the original 90-day investment interest rates will be equally as high for the next 90 days. However, futures could be used to "lock in" a rate for the last 90 days of a 180-day program. In this strategy the investor would maximize return by buying 90-day paper and also buying a 90-day futures contract. If the whole yield curve has shifted lower at the end of the first 90 days, the profit from futures would effectively increase the yield for the last 90 days. If rates were to go higher, the higher reinvestment rate for the last 90 days will be partially or entirely offset by the loss in the futures.

Hedging Long-Term Interest Rates

Corporations may wish to hedge the cost of long-term borrowing when the time between the decision to borrow and the actual process of borrowing is protracted. For example, corporations who have planned to borrow in the future may wish to lock in today's futures market rates. This can often be the case when corporations contract to have capital goods built. The construction process is financed by short-term borrowing, but after completion of construction long-term debt is sold to finance the asset. When the period of construction is lengthy the corporation may not want to pay both short-term borrowing and long-term borrowing costs, particularly if it does not wish to risk paying higher long-term rates at a later time.

To hedge such a risk the borrower can establish her or his rate today by shorting T-note futures contracts. To accomplish this the hedger should do the following:

1. Complete a correlation study to find which futures contract provides the most constant basis relationship with the debt that will be eventually sold.

2. Study changes in the size of the basis, including those caused by credit differences. A mathematical function can be statistically derived through regression analysis of past relationships.
3. Adjust for changes in rate resulting from differences in maturity.
4. On a present value basis, using the expected coupon rate of the bond for a compounding factor, calculate the amount of money that must be made on the futures to cover increased interest costs.
5. Calculate the duration ratio between the futures and the corporate bond.

Once these five steps have been taken the appropriate number of contracts should be shorted. If interest rates increase between hedge date and bond-sale date, the profits from futures would be added to the proceeds of the bond sale to reduce interest costs of the sale. In effect, the corporation would be receiving a premium for its bonds. To illustrate this process consider the following.

Hedging Corporate Bond Issuance

A company with a single-A bond rating currently foresees the need to issue $50,000,000 of debt six months from now. Believing that rates will increase, the company wishes to hedge against any rate rise.

The company can now issue 20-year debt at a coupon rate of 10%. If rates were to rise 1%, the added cost over 20 years will be $50,000,000 × 0.01 × 20 = $10,000,000. The present value of this potential future cash outflow is $4,289,772, which is determined from the equation

$$PV = \sum_{i=1}^{N} \frac{\text{PMT}}{(1 + R)^i}$$

where

$N =$ the number of semiannual payments
$PMT =$ the amount each semiannual payment will increase per 1% rise in interest costs
$R =$ semiannual discount factor, which is the current semiannual rate
$PV =$ the present value of a 1% increase in rates

Once the additional cost of a 1% change in rates is known, the number of T-bond contracts needed to hedge this potential increase in costs should be determined. For now, it is assumed that when corporate bond rates increase 1%, so will T-bond rates. This assumption will be relaxed later on.

Assume the CBT's cheapest deliverable bond is the 11¾% of 2010 maturities cash T-bond. The futures market will trade in tandem with this issue. A 1% change in yield in the cash bond can be represented by an $8^{22}/_{32}$ price movement.

The CBT's contract specifies that the futures price (for invoicing delivery purposes) be multiplied by a delivery factor. As the price of the cash bond changes, the futures price movement can be represented by

$$\text{Futures Price} = \frac{\text{Cash Price}}{\text{Delivery Factor}}$$

Assuming December delivery and the delivery factor is 1.3974 for $11^{3}/_{4}$. The price change in the futures market for a 1% change in yield will be

$$\text{Futures price } \Delta = \frac{\text{Cash Price } \Delta \text{ per 1\% Yield Change}}{\text{Current Delivery Factor}}$$

Plugging values into this equation, the futures price change per 1% yield change will be $6^{7}/_{32}$, or $(8^{22}/_{32}) \div 1.3974$.

Thus for a 1% yield change, we now know that the futures price will move $6^{7}/_{32}$, with a value of $6218.75. Still assuming that a corporate yield change will be equally matched by an equivalent move in government bond yields, the $6218.75 should be divided into $4,289,772 to determine how many contracts should be used:

$$4,289,772 \div 6,218.67 = 690 \text{ contracts}$$

Assume historical data show that single A rated, 20-year corporate bond yields move at a rate of 1.02 to 1.00 against yields on 20-year government bonds. Because of this, when rates are rising, the company's interest rates will rise faster. Earlier it was assumed that the rates moved at an equal rate. To adjust for this differential, the corporate hedger should use (1.02 × 690 contracts =) 703 contracts to most efficiently hedge against rates rising on a 20-year $50,000,000 debt issue.

HEDGING WITH THE INTEREST RATE SWAP CONTRACT

The introduction of the 3- and 5-year interest rate swap futures contracts by the Chicago Board of Trade (CBOT) marks the most recent innovation in the interest rate futures markets. These contracts were developed in response to the rapid growth of the interest rate swap market. As a tool for hedging, the interest rate swap contracts offer swap dealers and corporate treasurers the opportunity to manage the interest risk exposure of their cash market positions. For speculators, the contracts offer the opportunity to speculate on the level and direction of interest rates in the medium- to long-term private credit markets.

The interest rate swap market developed in the early 1980s in response to the efforts of Japanese investors to circumvent restrictions on the kinds of foreign assets they could own. The success of the market is seen in its phenomenal growth—from a few millions dollars in 1981 it has grown to exceed $1.5 trillion as of 1990. In economic terms, interest rate swaps permit borrowers with a comparatively good standing in the fixed-rate debt market to benefit by exchanging debt obligations with borrowers that have a comparatively good standing in the variable rate market. Hence, the market may be viewed as a mechanism that serves to improve the efficiency of risk allocation.

What Is an Interest Rate Swap?

An interest rate swap is an agreement between two parties to exchange interest payments on a fixed (notional) amount of debt. In its standard (generic) form, one party to the swap agrees to pay a fixed interest rate in exchange for receiving a variable (floating) rate on the swap's notional amount. The reverse position is taken by the counterparty. Typically, the floating rate side of the swap is tied to 3- or 6-month LIBOR (London Interbank Offer Rate).

As an example, consider Party A and Party B enter into a 3-year swap agreement. Assume Party A can borrow in the variable rate market at more favorable terms than it can in the fixed rate market and the reverse is true for Party B. Given such a situation, both parties borrow the notional principal amount in the market favorable to them, and then swap interest payments. Party A pays the fixed rate obligation of Party B, and Party B pays the variable rate obligation of Party A. The net effect of such an arrangement is that both parties are able to borrow at terms more favorable than either could obtain on its own. It is important to note that in a swap transaction the notional principal amount is not exchanged between the parties to the swap, only the interest on it is.

Role of the Swap Dealer

The swap dealer plays a role similar to that of dealers in other financial markets and takes the opposite position in the swap until a suitable counterparty can be found. In so doing, the dealer is exposed to the risk that the spread between the fixed and the floating rate could change prior to the completion of the search for the counterparty. The CBOT contract provides the opportunity to manage such risk.

Characteristics of the Interest Rate Swap Futures Contract

The CBOT 3- and 5-year interest rate swap futures contracts are quoted on the basis of 100 minus the yield on the fixed rate portion of a generic 3- and 5-year interest rate swap versus the floating rate on 6-month

LIBOR. The fixed rate is the all-in cost for a generic $25 million swap quoted to prime credit U.S. swap dealers for settlement on the third Wednesday of the contract month.

The final settlement price of the expiring contract is determined on the last trading day of the contract at 3:30 P.M. London time (9:30 A.M. Chicago time). The final settlement price is determined by randomly selecting at least seven reference dealers from an approved list of swap dealers. The bid-ask quotes from each dealer on the fixed rate payments on a $25 million interest rate swap is averaged, and the median of the resulting average will be the settlement yield. (See Appendix A for more details on contract specifications.)

There is an important difference between the quote on the interest rate swap contract compared to those of the T-bond or T-note contracts. The trading unit for the swap contract is not $25 million but rather the yield that would be quoted on a swap with a notional principal amount of $25 millon. By contrast, the trading unit for the T-bond and the T-note contract is $100,000. The dollar value of a one basis point change in yield on the contract is fixed at $50, and the value of one tick (minimum price move) is equal to one half basis point, or $25. As a consequence, the variable in the contract is the notional value of the swap contract changes as yields change. It is computed as follows:

$$\text{Notional Value of Swap Contract} = \frac{\text{Face Value of Instrument}}{\text{BPV of Instrument}} \times \text{BPV of Swap Contract}$$

where: BPV (basis point value) is the dollar change for a one basis point change in yield of a $100 face value instrument

The BPV for an instrument with a face value of $100 is computed as follows:

$$\text{BPV} = \sum_{i=1}^{N} \frac{\$100 \times 0.0001/(\text{Number of Payments per Year})}{(1 + \text{Yield/Number of Payments per Year})^i}$$

where N = Number of payments on transaction

The following is an example of a BPV calculation on a 5-year, $100 face value instrument selling at a yield of 8%.

$$\text{BPV} = \sum_{i=1}^{10} \frac{\$100 \times 0.0001/2}{(1 + 0.08/2)^i}$$
$$= 0.0405545$$

Hence the notional value of the 5-year swap contract selling at a yield of 8% is:

$$\text{Notional Value of Swap Contract} = \frac{\$100}{0.0405545} \times \$50$$

$$= \$123,290.88$$

Table 21.3 provides the notional principal amount of the 3- and 5-year swap contract as yields change.

The prices at which the swap contract trades should be affected by the same variables that affect 3- to 5-year treasury yields and the credit spread between corporate and treasury yields. In fact, the spread between the yields on treasuries and those of the swap contract could be viewed as a medium-term TED (treasury bill to Eurodollar) spread.

Hedging with the CBOT Swap Contract

The swap contract provides the opportunity for dealers to hedge the fixed rate portion of their swap position, and hence lock-in the spread between the fixed and floating rate in the swap. Currently this is typically accomplished either through a strip of Eurodollar contracts, or the T-note contract. The problem with the Eurodollar strip is the poor liquidity and costs of trading in the distant contract months. The problem with the T-note contract, on the other hand, is the risk it exposes the dealer to changes in the credit spread. For dealers concerned with either, or both, of these shortcomings, the swap contract provides an alternative opportunity to manage the risks of their swap positions. The following is an example of how a swap dealer may use the swap contract to lock-in the spread between the fixed and floating rate in a swap.

Consider a swap dealer who holds a $100 million swap position in which he receives a fixed rate of 9.00% semiannually for five years and pays 6-month LIBOR semiannually. Assume he would earn a profit of 5 basis points on the fixed rate portion of the swap if a counterparty could be found to immediately offset the swap position at a level of 8.95%. Because short-term rates are volatile, the trader is concerned that the profit margin will erode. Consequently, the trader decides to place a hedge in the 5-year swap contract until the counterparty is found. Assume the 5-year swap contract is selling at 91.08 (yield = 8.92%).

$$\text{Number of Contracts Required} = \frac{\text{BPV of Swap Position}}{\text{BPV of Futures}}$$

$$= \frac{\$39612.26}{\$50}$$

$$= 792 \text{ contracts}$$

TABLE 21.3 Swap Yields and the Notional Value of 3-Year and 5-Year Interest Rate Swap Futures

Swap Yields	Notional Value of 3-Year Swap Futures	Notional Value of 5-Year Swap Futures
1.00%	$169,595	$102,771
1.50	171,069	104,171
2.00	172,551	105,582
2.50	174,034	107,003
3.00	175,525	108,434
3.50	177,022	109,876
4.00	178,527	111,326
4.50	180,034	112,787
5.00	181,551	114,258
5.50	183,073	115,741
6.00	184,601	117,231
6.50	186,130	118,731
7.00	187,670	120,240
7.50	189,211	121,761
8.00	190,763	123,291
8.50	192,319	124,830
9.00	193,877	126,379
9.50	195,442	127,938
10.00	197,017	129,505
10.50	198,594	131,082
11.00	200,176	132,668
11.50	201,767	134,264
12.00	203,364	135,868
12.50	204,964	137,482
13.00	206,569	139,103
13.50	208,182	140,736
14.00	209,798	142,377
14.50	211,416	144,026
15.00	213,042	145,686
15.50	214,680	147,354
16.00	216,314	149,029

Source: CBOT Swap Futures Reference Guide.

Suppose five days later a counterparty is found when the fixed rate yield equals the breakeven yield of 9.00%. Assume the futures contracts are repurchased at 91.03.

If no hedge was placed, the dealer would have suffered an opportunity loss of $198,060 (5 basis points in 5-year yields over 5 years on $100 million). By hedging, the dealer was able to offset this loss by a gain on the futures contracts of $198,000 (10 ticks × $25 per tick × 792 contracts). Hence, the profit on the swap contracts substantially offset the opportunity loss.

There are other potential hedging uses of the interest rate swap contract in addition to its obvious use to swap dealers. Since the contract is basically pricing credit risks in the medium-term debt market, corporate treasurers and corporate note underwriters should be able to use it as a proxy for a corporate note contract. Further, the contract should offer bond portfolio managers the opportunity to hedge the price risks of corporate bonds held in their portfolios. Additionally, the contract should open up arbitrage and spreading opportunities against Eurodollar strips and corporate debt issues. However, all of these uses, including its primary use by swap dealers, hinges on the markets achieving a reasonable degree of liquidity. Liquidity has a direct impact on lowering hedging costs. With hedging costs sufficiently low, substantial hedging interest could develop.

22

Internal Record Keeping and Corporate Control Systems for the Hedge

As in many things, success in hedging depends on having good people and good records. Once the decision has been made to establish a hedging program, immediate attention should be paid to the internal record keeping, control, audit, and accounting procedures. This section deals with the record keeping, control, and internal audit aspects.

In establishing a system of internal control, an organization must give due consideration to the risks involved and to the costs of maintaining the system. Therefore, the system will differ between hedging organizations, depending on such things as the volume of trading and the sophistication of the system needed for covering the trading activity. Nevertheless, every system should include the following:

1. A definition of the authority and responsibility of the personnel to be involved in the hedging decisions.
2. Segregation of duties such that no one individual has simultaneous control of both the trading activity and the record-keeping activity.
3. The establishment of independent checks and balances against which transaction details can be checked.
4. The use of after-the-fact internal audit devices to check the accuracy and propriety of recorded transactions and accounting and operating data.

PROCEDURES

In most instances firms establish procedures relating to the trading and the documentation necessary for record keeping. This facilitates both internal audits and the reporting procedures for top management.

Generally the record-keeping procedures include:

1. A listing of the authorized brokers with whom the firm will trade.
2. A statement of the trading limits and the description of the procedures to be followed if the limits are exceeded by any one trader.
3. A description of the accounting records to be used to control and monitor the activity.
4. A description of the documents to be received from the broker with whom the trading is being conducted.
5. A description of the various reports that are to be generated for senior management.

In establishing trading limits, the hedger should consider setting them at three levels—totals for the entire organization, for each trader individually, and for each contract maturity. These three limits should be referenced to the cash position.

As each trade is made, the trader should prepare a trade ticket that becomes the starting point for the accounting information flow. Trade tickets should contain all essential information, such as the date of the trade, whether it is a buy or sell, contract description, quantity, price, trader's name, and the description of the cash position being hedged. The accuracy of the trade ticket is the responsibility of the trader and as a verification the trader should "balance out" nightly with the broker with whom he is dealing.

Although the form of the records varies from one hedger to another, a corporation typically develops ledgers segregated according to the various futures contract maturities that coincide with their cash market activity. Thus, an independent ledger is kept to include trade date, trader, reason for trade, whether buy or sell, quantity, price, and commmission expense. Such a ledger provides detail for preparing the following:

1. A general ledger memorandum reflecting total futures positions.
2. A record reflecting commission expenses.
3. A trial "balance" of futures positions.
4. Reports to management on trading activity and positions taken by each trader.

It is also advisable that daily margin runs be prepared by the hedger's broker and received by someone independent of the trading and the record-keeping function. This individual should verify the open positions and contract prices as well as the margin balance to assure that they are correct and to assure that the appropriate debit or credit tickets are prepared for recording losses and gains.

Keeping records in such detail as outlined above assures that the hedger will properly manage its money and the cash flow between it and its brokers.

REPORTING TO MANAGEMENT

The primary objective of the procedures mentioned above is to ensure that all trades are properly recorded in both the general ledger and the supporting subsidiary ledgers. But it also forms the basis for generating reports to senior management that provide an overall evaluation of the entire trading and hedging operation. Generally, reports should be required weekly by top management. Such reports should reflect all open positions and the related income effects of both realized and unrealized gains or losses. These reviews allow management to determine whether the policies they've established are being followed. Further, the reviews highlight the financial effect on current operations and the economic impact of the overall hedging operation.

23
Arbitrage and Spreading Strategies

One of the most intellectually challenging and potentially rewarding trading strategies is one designed to take advantage of the temporary discrepancies that occur in price relationships between markets or between securities. These discrepancies occur frequently, arising because of temporary supply and demand imbalances or time lags in the market response for various securities.

These price discrepancies disappear rather quickly and the prices move back to their natural equilibrium because sharp traders quickly recognize the situation and immediately buy the cheap instrument or contract and sell the more expensive, causing the lower-priced instrument to rise and the higher-priced instrument to fall in price.

When this process of simultaneous buying and selling involves two different markets—such as the cash and futures market, or two different securities on the same yield curve such as T-bills and T-bonds—it is referred to as arbitrage. When it is conducted within the same marketplace or between different futures months of similar securities, it is called spreading. Hence, a position of long December T-bill futures and short March T-bill futures is a spread. This chapter provides a brief explanation of the concepts of arbitrage and spreading.

ARBITRAGE

Although both the spread trade and arbitrage attempt to profit from relative price changes that might occur as market conditions are changing, spread trading makes a statement about the spreader's attitude on which way the market is going to move, while arbitrage does not.

To illustrate this point let's look at the hypothetical yield curve shown in Figure 23.1. The arbitrageur would study the market and note the yield difference between the various issues, A through G. He or she would look at the comparison between security D and security E, for example, and realize that D was cheaper than normal in comparison to the yield curve, and that E was expensive relative to the yield curve.

The arbitrageur would also consider the characteristics of the two securities in assessing their relative prices, including:

1. *The credit rating.* Different credit ratings would cause the issues to trade at different relative values.
2. *The interest rate coupon of each security.* Differences in coupons would cause securities to trade differently under changing market conditions.
3. *The maturities of the two securities.* An arbitrageur would seldom be in risk in the transaction. A position of long security A and short security G would reflect expectations of long-term rates rising faster than short-term rates. An arbitrageur does not "ride" the yield curve or bet on yield curve changes in this fashion. He or she expects that securities D and E, however, since they have the same maturity, will eventually trade at even prices regardless of changes in the yield curve. He or she concentrates on these.
4. *Liquidity.* Good arbitrage opportunities require that the liquidity of the two securities be roughly comparable.

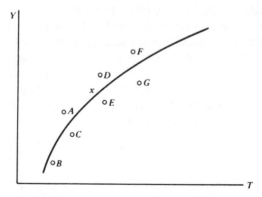

FIGURE 23.1 Hypothetical yield curve.

If the arbitrageur found that the characteristics of D and E were similar, she or he would purchase security D and sell E. The anticipated profit would be the gain on D as it moved down to the yield curve (point x), and the gain on E as it moved up to the yield curve. In this arbitrage the investor seeks to make a profit on both securities. This type of trade would not necessarily be affected by a shift in the yield curve or any changes in general market conditions.

Cash and Futures Arbitraging

Cash/futures arbitrage involves simultaneous transactions in the two markets for securities of the same credit, coupon, and maturity. Arbitrageurs are trying to profit only from price discrepancies. They are not interested in taking on the additional risks associated with different securities. Until recently, liquidity in the futures market was a problem in doing cash/futures arbitrage. But recently this has been of less concern as long as one stays in the nearest three futures contract months. Liquidity in the more distant futures is still a concern and must be carefully considered when arbitraging longer futures contracts. The lack of liquidity can cause transaction costs to rise and frequently masks dangerous trading situations as apparent arbitrage opportunities.

The Essence of Cash/Futures Arbitrage

In cash/futures arbitrage, comparisons are not of similar securities on a common yield curve but are of similar securities on different yield curves. One, the cash market, is an existing yield curve. The other, the futures market, is an expected yield curve. The comparison is between prices for securities in the futures market and the prices for the same security in the cash market. As explained in Chapter 11, there is a natural price differential between futures and cash based upon the spot price for money, plus or minus the net cost of carry, and the effect of investors' expectations. When the price differential between cash and futures is greater or less than the aggregate cost of carry, there is an opportunity for arbitrage.

ARBITRAGE OPPORTUNITIES

When the prices for futures, after adjustment for cost of carry, are greater than cash prices, the arbitrageur purchases cash securities and sells futures contracts. This is referred to as "long arbitrage." When the prices for futures, after adjustment for cost of carry, are less than the cash prices, the arbitrageur sells the cash market and buys the futures contract. This is referred to as "short arbitrage."

The arbitrageur usually does not hold the positions for an extended period of time. The position would normally be taken off when the price relationships return to normal. Sometimes, however, the arbitrageur will continue to hold a position if the cost of carry considerations continue to remain profitable even after the differential has been dissipated.

It is important to weigh carefully all cost and revenues in an arbitrage situation. Table 23.1 shows cost and revenues for various arbitrage possibilities.

PROFITS AND RISKS OF ARBITRAGE

Arbitrage risk arises from two sources: changes in financing costs and variations in the price of the securities and/or contracts held. In actual trading, long-cash arbitrage positions would probably outnumber short-cash arbitrage positions. This is because futures pay no interest, and financing costs are considerably higher for a short position in the cash market than for either a long cash position or a short futures position. Although the general principles outlined in this section apply to both, the following discussion of strategy will be formulated in terms of a long-cash position.

Here is a simple example of an arbitrage opportunity using T-bill futures. Suppose 180-day T-bills are selling at a discount yield of 8.20%. Term repo financing is available at 8.10% (discount basis). If a T-bill futures expiring in 90 days is selling at a price other than 91.70 (8.30%), then opportunities for riskless arbitrage exist.

To realize arbitrage profits assume the T-bill contract is selling at 91.75 (8.25%). The arbitrage strategy would be as follows:

1. Repo the 180-day bill at 8.10% for 90 days.
2. Sell one T-bill contract at 8.25% and repurchase at expiration.

The following scenarios are examples of the profit/loss (P/L) at contract expiration:

Scenario 1: Yield on T-bill Futures at Expiration = 8.50%

Interest from Repo = 8.20% − 8.10% = +10 Basis Points
P/L on Cash Bill   = 8.20% − 8.50% = −30 Basis Points
P/L Futures = 8.50% − 8.25% = +25 Basis Points
Net Gain   = Interest + P/L Cash Bill + P/L Futures
              = +5 − 30 + 25
              = +5 Basis Points
              = +$125 (@ $25 per Basis Point)

TABLE 23.1 Costs and Revenues for Various Arbitrage Possibilities

Revenues	Costs
Long Cash/Short Futures	
Interest income earned on the cash position.	Interest cost of financing the cash position, or the opportunity cost of money used to purchase the cash position.
Price appreciation of the cash position and price depreciation of the futures position.	Price appreciation of the futures contract and price depreciation of the cash security.
The value of cash that may be received from the clearinghouse if the futures position depreciates in value and cash is paid to the trader.	Cost of execution: brokerage fees and transaction costs. Transaction costs include the market movement caused by the execution of an order on the exchange. Cash market reflects the difference between the bid and ask.
	The opportunity cost of negative cash flow as a result of maintenance margin calls if the futures appreciate.
Short Cash/Long Futures	
Interest income on cash securities used to collateralize borrowing of cash positions, or interest earned on the reverse repurchase agreement entered into to obtain the cash security for delivery on the short sale.	Accrued interest paid on the cash security sold in the market.
Price appreciation of the futures position and price depreciation on the cash security.	Price depreciation of the futures contract and price appreciation of the cash contract.

(continued)

TABLE 23.1 (Continued)

Revenues	Costs
	Short Cash/Long Futures
Value of cash received from the clearinghouse if the futures position appreciates in value.	Any borrowing fees incurred if the cash security is borrowed to fill the short sale delivery (usually .5%).
	Transaction costs: brokerage fees. Difference between bid and ask and execution cost of the exchange.
	Opportunity cost of negative cash flow as result of maintenance margin call if the futures market depreciates.

Scenario 2: Yield on T-bill Futures at Expiration = 8.00%

Interest from Repo = 8.20% − 8.10% = +10 Basis Points
P/L on Cash Bill = 8.20% − 8.00% = +20 Basis Points
P/L Futures = 8.00% − 8.25% = −25 Basis Points
Net Gain = Interest + P/L Cash Bill + P/L Futures
     = +10 + 20 − 25
     = +5 Basis Points
     = +$125 (@ $25 per Basis Point)

If the futures contract was selling at a yield greater than 8.30%, a reversal of the above strategy would yield arbitrage profits.

In general, the formula for calculating arbitrage profits per $1 million of face value using T-bill futures is as follows:

$$\text{Profit} = [(D - RP)h/360 + 90\ d/360] \times \$1{,}000{,}000$$

where: D = Discount yield on deliverable cash bill
    RP = Term repo rate
     h = Term of repo (holding period)
     d = Change in T-bill futures yield over holding period.

The first term, $(D - RP)h/360$, is the carry on the position, and the second term, $90\ d/360$, is the expected arbitrage pickup valued at \$25 per basis point. The equation reveals that the profits are inversely related to the repo rate and directly related to the forward discount discrepancy. The earnings from carrying the position are directly proportional to the holding period, but the arbitrage pickup is fixed. As long as the position yields a positive carry, total earnings will increase with the length of the holding period.

To evaluate an arbitrage, the following four principles must be considered:

1. The spread between the bid and asked quotations in the cash market imposes an immediate turnover cost when the position is acquired.
2. The cash discount does not remain fixed, but is permitted to converge gradually to the implicit forward level during the period remaining until contract settlement. The higher the futures rate premium relative to spot rates, the smaller the earnings on the cash security.
3. The repo charge is levied against the current discounted market value of the bill, not its maturity value.
4. Brokerage and clearing fees for the futures transaction must also be deducted as an expense.

A sample run of the profit projection incorporating these four revisions into the preceding profit equation produces the characteristic time pattern of daily profits shown in Figure 23.2. In the early days of the arbitrage, profits are dominated by the fixed arbitrage pickup, which in this illustration more than offsets the transaction costs. As the holding period is lengthened, the fixed arbitrage pickup diminishes on a daily basis and eventually becomes overshadowed by the position's carry as a source of profit.

Market Price Fluctuations

The normal variability of interest rates presents a twofold problem. First, a change in the cash bill discount will not necessarily be accompanied by an equivalent basis point change in the associated futures discount. Second, a given basis point change in the cash discount may translate into a different dollar value than an identical change in the futures discount.

Imperfect Basis Offset. To the extent that the market correctly discounts an impending movement in interest rates, the expected change, when it arrives, will tend to have a more pronounced impact on the spot market than on the forward market. With efficient money market pricing,

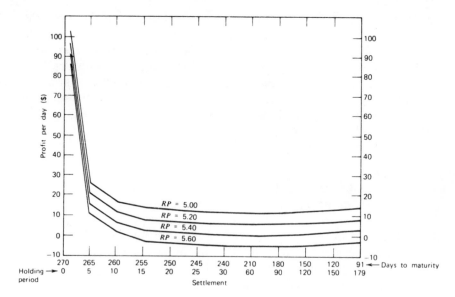

FIGURE 23.2   Profit per day.

one might expect this type of movement to occur more frequently than the converse possibility—a change in forward rates in excess of the movement in spot rates. Nevertheless, futures have a history of overreacting to economic events, and this nervous behavior may lead to transitory swings in the forward rate of much greater extent than the corresponding movements in spot rates.

If a long arbitrage position were held, its value would appreciate in response to a fall in the cash bill discount if not offset by an equivalent fall in the forward discount. The arbitrageur would tend, *ceteris paribus*, to shorten the holding period in order to realize the gain. On the other hand, if either the forward discount fell further than the cash discount, or the cash discount advanced more than the forward discount, the arbitrageur would suffer a loss. Supposing the dollar value of a basis point to be roughly the same in the two markets; the arbitrageur would be inclined to extend the holding period to allow convergence of the two markets to proceed.

Long-term arbitrage allows for convergence of the spot and forward discounts; it is only *unanticipated* interim gyrations in these markets prior to settlement that pose a market risk. Although it is known that a dollar hedge would be achieved by locking in a trading profit or loss amounting to the difference between the cash price and futures prices (if the position were retained until settlement), this provides no assurance of particular gains or losses prior to settlement.

Basis Point Bias. T-bill futures that call for delivery of a 90-day bill are uniformly valued at $25 per basis point, but this is not true of cash bills. In fact, the particular T-bill deliverable against a given contract, the "underlying bill," will have a higher dollar value per basis point than the contract until the day of settlement arrives. (Technically, on the settlement date the underlying bill would ordinarily have a 91-day maturity, for a basis point value of $25.277.) Thus, even if perfect basis point offset existed for all market variations, these differences would still produce a greater dollar change on the cash side of the arbitrage than on the forward side. This, of course, would prove advantageous if the market changed in the arbitrageur's favor. If the market moved adversely to his or her position, he or she might be forced to retain the position until contract settlement to effect a full dollar hedge, thereby increasing exposure to the possibility of higher financing expenses. In some cases, more than one futures contract must be used to obtain the dollar equivalency.

FINANCING

In choosing between overnight and term repos, it is doubtful if any invariant rule can be specified, since each type of financing has advantages and disadvantages. Overnight financing seems preferable whenever flexibility is particularly desired—in newly acquired positions where a quick arbitrage pickup is anticipated, positions close to a contract settlement date, or positions showing a trading profit that might be realized prior to an inversion point. Term financing is the superior method when an increase in the repo rate appears imminent, or when a trading loss is to be deferred until an inversion point.

SPREADING IN FINANCIAL FUTURES

Spread trading in financial futures is a method of speculation for the trader who wishes to assume slightly less risk than occurs in owning a one-sided or "net" position. Spread trading comprises the simultaneous buying and selling of two different futures contracts. The purpose of the trade is to anticipate the potential change in the *relative* values of two different contracts. In financial futures there are two different types of spreads: intracontract and intermarket.

INTRACONTRACT SPREADS

This is the most common type of spread. It consists of buying and selling different settlement months of the same contract. The intent is to purchase the month that will increase in value and sell the month that will decrease. To be successful at this type of spreading the trader must fully understand what makes the price differentials between delivery months. This was discussed earlier. However, those same concepts can be used to explain the two basic intracontract spread trades, the bull spread and the bear spread.

The Bull Spread

The "bull" spread is so named because it is put on in anticipation of bullish conditions in the money markets. When short-term financing costs are decreasing and security prices are on the rise, nearby financial futures contracts tend to gain on the more distant contracts. The bull spreader therefore buys a nearby contract and simultaneously sells a distant contract against it, looking for the *relative* change in their prices to earn spread profits. (This is also called "buying" the spread, or going "long" on the spread. Conversely, if the nearby position is the short side of the spread, the spreader is considered to have "sold" or be "short" the spread.) In a general sense spreads "bull" because the *net cost of carry* is becoming positive or more positive.

In the following example the trader has bought the spread at 120 points premium to December:

	Price	Price difference
Long—June 90-day T-bills	90.00	
Short—December 90-day T-bills	91.20	1.20

Let's further assume the spread changes to 100 basis points:

	New price	Price difference	Profit (loss)
Long—June 90-day T-bills	90.20		+$500
Short—December 90-day T-bills	91.20	100	—
			$500

In this example the trader was long the June/December T-bill spread. As the long side gained 20 points on the short side, the trader realized a

$500 profit for each spread he or she was long, before deducting commissions.

Bull spreads can be put in any financial future by buying a nearby contract and selling a distant contract.

Assume 90-day T-bills are trading at 10%, and the price of T-bills does not change; if the cost of financing is 12%, the price curve for T-bill futures would be P_1 (see Figure 23.3). However, if financing costs change to 8%, the price curve will change to P_2. If a June/December bull spread in T-bills had been purchased prior to the change in rates, the trader would have lost money on the June bill equal to $A-B$, and the profit on the short in December T-bills would have been $C-D$. Because $C-D$ is greater than $A-B$, the bull spread would have shown a profit of $(C-D) - (A-B)$.

In the real world, what would most likely happen is that spot price would sharply increase in this situation. For example, in Figure 23.4 the price increased as the yield went from 10% to 8%.

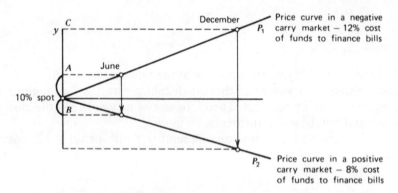

FIGURE 23.3 Price curve.

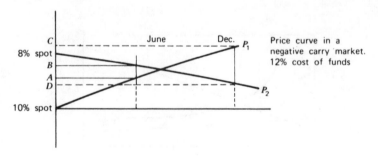

FIGURE 23.4 Price curve in a negative market, 12% cost of funds.

In this case, profits in the long position are $A-B$ and the December position also profits to the extent of $C-D$. Total profit is therefore $(A-B) + (C-D)$.

In summary, bull spreads work when financing costs decline relative to investment yields on the underlying contract securities. What happens is that the futures market moves from a "premium" market, where each further-out contract month sells at a higher price, toward a "discount" market, where each month sells at a discount to its more nearby contracts. This type of price behavior usually occurs when the yield curve for cash securities moves and becomes a "normal" or positively sloped market.

An example of this would be when the yield curve switches from Y_1 to Y_2 (see Figure 23.5). In Y_1, short-term interest rates are higher than long-term rates, therefore the futures market would be a premium market. In Y_2 the short-term rates are lower than long-term rates, giving the investor a positive cost of carry and thereby a discount futures price curve. If traders put bull spread on when the yield curve was Y_1 and took them off when it was Y_2, they would be wealthy traders.

The Bear Spread

The "bear" spread is just the opposite of the bull spread. In this type of spread the trader is speculating that the distant contract will gain ground relative to the nearby contract. Therefore, she or he would sell the closer contract and purchase the further-out contract.

Let's once again assume the June/December T-bill spread at 120 basis points premium to December:

	Price	Price difference
Short June T-bill futures	90.00	
Long December T-bill futures	91.20	1.20

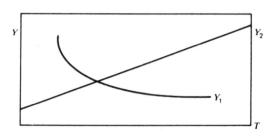

FIGURE 23.5 Yield curve.

If financing costs were to go higher, the price curve would move to a higher premium and the spread would change to reflect this:

	New price	Price difference	Profit
Short June T-bill futures	90.10		−250
Long December T-bill futures	91.40	+1.30	+500
			+250

In this case the bear spread profited $250 (gross) because the price differential moved from 120 points to 130 points (10 points × $25 = $250). What happened in this spread is that the price curve shifted upward as negative carry became greater.

In summary, spreads tend to "bear" when the cost of financing goes higher on the yield curve because cash securities become more negative. Remember the key to spread trading is the forecasting of repurchase agreements, or the cost of financing securities.

INTERMARKET SPREADS

Intermarket spreads comprise the simultaneous buying and selling of different interest rate futures contracts. An example would be to sell MBS futures and buy U.S. Treasury bond futures. The purpose of the spread is the same—to take advantage of relative price changes between two futures contracts. Intermarket spreads can also be either bull or bear spreads.

Spread Changes Due to Yield Curve Changes

This type of spread is profitable when the trading correctly forecasts changes in the yield curve for fixed income securities. To take advantage the trader would buy the portion of the yield curve that should be relatively strong and sell the weaker portion of the curve. An example of this is the T-note/T-bond intermarket spread. Let's assume the yield curve for the cash market is shaped like Y_1 in Figure 23.6. If the spreader anticipates that the yield curve will change to Y_2, then the trader would sell the U.S. T-bond issue, which trades off the 30-year bond market, and purchase the 10-year T-note futures contract. If the curve does move to Y_2, then the yield on 30-year bonds will increase and the price will decline, creating a profit in the short position in U.S. T-bond futures. If the yield and price of notes remain constant, the spread would be profitable. The following illustrates this:

	Price Y_1	Price difference
Long position, June note	78	
Short position, June T-bond	80	+2 points

The yield curve shifts to Y_2:

	Price Y_2	Price difference	Profit spread
Note future, June note	78		—
T-bond future, June T-bond	77	−1 point	+$3000
			$3000

In the jargon of the futures business, if the spreader is *long* the T-bonds and short the notes, he or she is said to be *long* the intramarket. When the T-bond futures position is *short* and the note futures contract is the long position, then the spreader is short the intramarket. As in intra-market spreads a trader *buys* or goes long the spread, or sells or goes short the spread.

RISK AND SPREAD TRANSACTIONS

Spreading may be touted as the most conservative form of futures trading, but as anyone who followed news reports during recent years is aware, some spreads can lead to very large losses. It seems that customers of one large brokerage house were encouraged to establish a spread position

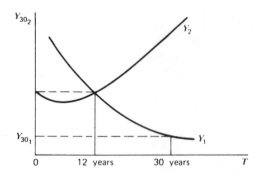

FIGURE 23.6 Cash yield curve.

in which they would be short Treasury bond futures and long Ginny Mae futures. (GNMA futures are no longer active.) The assumption was that with interest rates falling, both Treasury bonds and Ginny Mae futures would rise in value. Falling interest rates always make existing yield curves more attractive, just as rising yields make older and lower-yielding securities less desirable. Because Ginny Mae futures were selling well below Treasury bonds, it was assumed that they would rise faster, thus generating profits.

What happened in reality, however, is that Treasury bond futures soared in price while Ginny Maes moved up only modestly. For example, Ginny Mae futures rose from 64 to 69 and $8/32$s, while the Treasury bond futures jumped from 66 to 76 and $17/32$s. Each thirty-second of a point represented \$31.25 on contracts with a \$100,000 face value, and both with 8% coupon. The result was that during this time period the Treasury bond futures, which had been sold, lost about \$10,531, while the Ginny Mae side of the spread gained only \$5,250. This meant a net loss of \$5,281 on each spread, not counting the commissions.

The major error made in this transaction was that someone overlooked a fundamental fact with respect to the contract specifications and the workings of the markets in the two securities.

To put it simply, the futures contract for Ginny Maes and for Treasury bonds allows the seller to select the instrument that she or he wishes to deliver within the terms of the contract. In the case of both futures, at delivery the deliverable instruments are adjusted in price to equal the 8% coupon. All that matters is that the short seller delivers certificates with the face value of \$100,000 at a price equivalent to an 8% coupon regardless of whether the actual instruments are selling at a premium or discount to their face value.

In the specific case at hand of the Ginny Maes, the average life of a mortgage was assumed to be $12\frac{1}{2}$ years, but, because of a prolonged period of high rates, many Ginny Mae certificates had been issued with much higher coupons than 8%. When interest rates fall, Ginny Mae mortgages tend to be prepaid as homeowners refinance at lower rates. Hence, the higher premium and interest coupon, the shorter expected life there is for a Ginny Mae. Investors do not like to hold mortgages that can be prepaid because it reduces the yield or return on investment. The marketplace recognized these drawbacks to owning high coupon Ginny Maes and priced them accordingly; that is, at lower levels. The sellers of futures found that high coupon issues were the cheapest to deliver and it was exactly those issues that buyers did not want to receive. For that reason, the spread between Ginny Maes and T-bonds did not narrow, but rather widened.

Causes of Yield Curve Changes

The causes of yield curve changes are many and often misunderstood. The best explanation rests on two fundamentals.

First, changes in expectations of future yield curve shape are generally believed to be the chief mover of the yield curves. This occurs because future yield curve expectations are really the market's perception of the future supply and demand of and for debt securities. These expectations of supply and demand of debt securities are based on what investors think the general level of economic activity will be in the near future. Once the investing public guesses what the economy will be doing, they then know what type of yield curve to expect. When they expect a curve to be a certain way they usually force it to meet that expectation. A trader makes money in intermarket spreads by being able to understand the psychology of the market and what that psychology will do to the yield curve. If we assume the economy is in the late stages of an expansionary business cycle, the yield curve usually will be shaped similar to Y_1 in Figure 23.7. This environment usually is characterized by high interest rates, high inflation, and large demands for short-term credit. Under these conditions the Federal Reserve usually pursues a tight credit policy. These conditions and these types of yield curves existed in 1982, 1979, 1973, and 1968.

If the public assumes the expansion has come to an end and the economy is going into a downturn, they can expect the yield curve to switch to Y_2. This happens because economic activity slows, demand for short-term credit declines, the Federal Reserve eases, and credit becomes easier.

The spread trader would see this basic change taking place and sell the intermarket spread, selling 30-year maturities and buying futures contract in MBSs, Treasury notes, or even Treasury bills. To take advantage of this type of spread the correct leverage or dollar equivalency must be used.

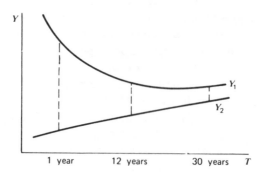

FIGURE 23.7   Yield curve showing late stages of expansionary economy.

Fluctuations in short-term supply are the second fundamental cause of changes in yield curves. For the active trader who wishes to be in the market more frequently than when fundamental economic changes are occurring, trading the intermarket on a relative supply basis may be profitable.

Assuming no changes in basic economic conditions, intermarket spreads often react sharply to periods of heavy temporary supply in the cash market. When the supply of a specific type of cash security expands faster than other cash securities, underwriters of the cash security sell the futures to hedge their commitments and investors demand discounts for these securities. The prices of these securities then become depressed, in relative terms, until a distribution of the cash security takes place.

The following are the three most common supply-induced intermarket spread opportunities.

1. Quarterly Treasury refundings occur every February, May, August, and November. During these refunding dates the Treasury almost always sells a large number of long-term Treasury bonds. This causes the long-term Treasury bond market to be temporarily more heavily supplied than another market, which has no sudden influx of supply. Therefore, it is often profitable to sell intermarket spreads some weeks before the actual refunding period and unwind it a few weeks after the refunding.
2. Housing starts are a good indicator of the future supply of mortgages and eventually MBSs. When housing starts fall or rise sharply the market frequently begins to discount the relative supply of MBSs versus T-bonds, causing the spread to change. All other factors being constant, on low housing starts buy MBS futures and sell Treasury bond futures.
3. Large temporary buildups in the corporate bond market's new financing calendar often puts pressure on the long Treasury bond market while having much smaller relative impact on the MBS market. This occurs because corporate offerings usually tend to be of a long-term nature, and underwriters use the Treasury bond futures market to hedge underwriting commitments.

Shifts in the Yield Curve

Shifts in the yield curve also take place frequently and offer trading opportunities to the active market participant. Unlike the yield curve changes discussed earlier, the trader does not need to forecast fundamental changes in the yield curve shape, only shifts up or down in the curve. This can be illustrated by comparing Figure 23.8a with 23.8b.

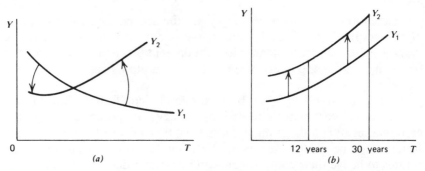

FIGURE 23.8   (a) Change in the yield curve; (b) shift up in the yield curve.

Figure 23.8a shows a change in the yield curve, and 23.8b shows a shift up in the yield curve.

To take advantage of price movements in Figure 23.8b, the trader is really taking advantage of dollar equivalency. As the yield curve shifts up and down equally, money can be made by having equal numbers of different futures contracts in spread position.

Intermarket Bull Spread.   If the spreader feels the curve will not change its basic shape, but only shift lower in yield, he or she would want to buy the intermarket, or go long T-bond futures and short MBS futures. As yields move proportionately lower, T-bond futures prices will rise faster than MBS futures prices.

Intermarket Bear Spread.   An equal shift upward in the yield curve causes prices to decline as yields rise. The correct strategy is to sell the spread, short T-bonds, and purchase MBSs. As yields go higher prices of MBSs will drop less than T-bond prices because of the maturity difference.

The Combination Spread.   To achieve maximum return on the bull and bear intermarket spread the spreader would not always sell the same month in T-bonds and MBSs. As discussed earlier, in rising price markets nearby contracts usually outperform further-out contracts. Therefore, when putting on a bull spread in the intermarket it often pays to go long a close T-bond contract and short a further-out MBS futures contract; for example, purchase June Treasury bonds and sell December MBS futures. This would offer two profit possibilities:

1. The profit from the shift in the cash yield curve as shown in Figure 23.8b.

2. The profit from a shift in the futures price curve as shown in Figure 23.8*a*.

When bear spreading the intermarket, sell longer T-bond contracts and purchase nearby MBS futures. However, be very careful with this combination: Greater potential return also means greater risk.

24

Hedging and Accounting Issues

This chapter attempts a cursory review of some of the major hedge accounting issues that arise. As such it ignores many important nuances and elements unique to particular industries or company circumstances. Anyone seriously interested in operating a hedging program should consult in advance with their auditors and accountants to establish the proper policies, procedures, and interpretations.

ACCOUNTING FOR HEDGE RESULTS

Hedging is a relatively complex activity. Accounting for hedge results is even more complex. Although accounting literature on hedging abounds, definitive guidance is not available in the literature. Application of the accounting literature requires interpretation and judgment, both of which assume a sound understanding of hedge theory, transactions, and techniques.

The guiding document for accounting for futures contracts is Financial Accounting Standards Board Statement 80 (FASB-80), entitled "Accounting for Futures Contracts." The intent of FASB-80 is to permit hedge or deferral accounting to an entity that reduces its interest rate risk through the effective use of financial futures contracts. The essence of Statement 80 attempts to distinguish the hedger from the speculator.

There are four major criteria reflected in FASB-80 that must be met in order for a transaction to be eligible for hedge accounting. First, there must be a demonstration of enterprise risk. Second, the transaction must be designated as a hedge at the onset of the hedge. Third, the futures contracts must reduce the enterprise's exposure to risk as measured by substantial offset of market or price changes between the cash item being hedged and the hedging instrument. This measurement must be made through correlation analysis before the onset of the hedge so that a presumption of offset can be made. And it must be made on an ongoing basis during the hedge to assure continuing offset. Fourth, there must be adequate documentation maintained on the first three steps.

If the hedge activity is meant to hedge an anticipated transaction, then the timing and the terms of the anticipated transaction must be predictable, and there must be a reasonable probability that the transaction will indeed occur. If these conditions are met, then the entity is presumed entitled to defer losses and is required to defer gains from its futures activity.

Basically then, Statement 80 distinguishes the hedger from the speculator and requires that daily changes in the market value of futures contracts be recognized immediately in income, unless the contracts qualify as hedges. Put another way, the daily cash settlements on futures contracts represent income or expense to an enterprise unless the contracts qualify for deferral under the hedge provisions of FASB-80, and to qualify for deferral, the transaction must meet the requirements stated above.

ENTERPRISE RISK

As noted, Statement 80 requires that the item being hedged expose the enterprise to price or interest rate risk if the transaction is to be eligible for hedge accounting. Generally, enterprise risk will be measured at the balance sheet level, for a financial institution, or at the business unit level if the enterprise can not assess risk for the enterprise as a whole. This may occur especially if the enterprise conducts its risk management activities on a decentralized basis.

The enterprise risk test essentially means that a financial institution has to conduct an exposure analysis of its balance sheet matching its assets and liabilities in various time periods over a time horizon, reflecting at least the period it desires to have the hedge in place. The matching of the assets and liabilities coming due for repricing in each time period and the accumulation of those net differences over a given time horizon provide a static measure of the enterprise risk or net exposure that could be eligible for hedging. The word "static" in the preceding sentence is important because that matching process provides only a snapshot of the balance sheet at any point in time and does not reflect the dynamics of risk exposure associated with the rollovers of instruments at future time periods. So one should go the next step and accumulate the impact of rollovers.

Clearly, one question that arises in the conduct of exposure analysis and in the application of FASB-80 is the length of time that must be considered in conducting enterprise risk measurement. As with most other things, there are no hard and fast rules. The enterprise is not required to consider any minimum or maximum time period. It must only show that under whatever period it is considering, the enterprise is exposed to risk. It also must consider whether commitments, or anticipated transactions, that will occur in time periods not considered will affect the risk inherent in the period that is considered.

CORRELATION

The second major condition of FASB-80 requires that the enterprise establish that there is a "high" correlation between the price, or interest rate, movements of the item being hedged, and the futures contract selected for accomplishing the hedge. High correlation in this context is usually considered to be .80, or better.

Correlation analysis is a statistical technique for expressing the degree of association (strength and direction) of the relationship between any two series of numbers (price or interest rates) over a specific period. For a graphic presentation of correlation analysis see Figure 24.1. A correlation coefficient of + 1.0 indicates that the prices are perfectly correlated or 100% correlated; that is, they tend to move in the same direction at the same time. If the correlation coefficient were a − 1.00, it would indicate that each pair of prices is perfectly negatively correlated; that is, they tend to move in opposite directions. And a correlation coefficient of .00 signifies that there is absolutely no tendency for the prices to move in anything except a random relationship to each other. Obviously, for effective hedging, you want positive correlation coefficients as close to 1.00 as possible.

Sometimes correlation coefficients are developed from a statistical technique called regression analysis. Regression analysis is a higher form of correlation analysis and helps explain the relationship between the two variables. The R-squared factor generated from regression analysis provides the correlation coefficient. Specifically, the R-squared factor is the square of the correlation.

It has been said that if you torture data long enough, it will confess to almost anything. If one wants to achieve a correlation of .80 or better,

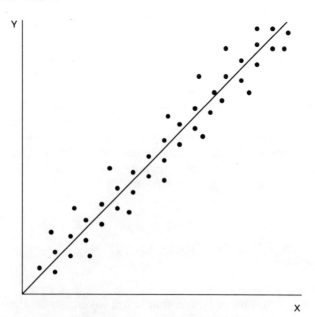

FIGURE 24.1 A scatter diagram.

one can easily do that by manipulating the time period over which the data is selected, or by adjusting the frequency with which the data observations are selected (daily, weekly, monthly), or by cleaning the data to discard unusual observations. It is important that the hedge manager establish a correlation policy regarding the time period to be covered, the frequency of the observations selected, and the circumstances under which abnormal data points are to be ignored. Generally, correlation, or regression analysis, should cover a minimum time period of 40 to 50 observations. If the observations are selected daily, then this would suggest 40 or 50 consecutive days of data. If weekly, it would suggest almost a year's worth of data. Second, since futures contracts are settled daily at the clearinghouse, it is generally best to use daily observations and, last, individual data points should be excluded only in exceptional circumstances where it is clear that the data represent aberrations from the general relationships. Such an event might occur on a day in which unusual market activity due to rumors (e.g., the President being shot), or some other short-term phenomena occur.

One of the most troublesome aspects of the criteria for hedge accounting deals with the maintenance of continual correlation during the life of the hedge. As noted above, FASB-80 requires an ongoing demonstration that high correlation exists. This test is met through measurement of offsetting dollars associated with the change in value of the instrument being hedged and the results of the futures activity. If that offset does not approximate more than 80% and less than 125% (the reciprocal of 80%), then the hedge has not met the high correlation test and the enterprise must (1) cease hedge accounting and (2) recognize gains and losses in income to the extent the futures results have not been offset by the changes in value on the hedge item since inception of the hedge.

If high correlation has been lost, one should determine whether the loss is due to unusual circumstances, and, therefore, only temporary, or whether it represents a fundamental change, before deciding to discontinue hedge accounting. Generally, ongoing correlation determinations should be made a couple times per month.

LIFO (LAST IN FIRST OUT) ACCOUNTING AND HEDGING

Gains or losses on futures contracts that hedge inventory are considered adjustments to the cost of the hedged inventory and should be recognized in income when the inventory is sold. A unique situation arises, however, when the hedged inventory is carried on the LIFO basis. In this case, the hedged LIFO inventory in theory would not be sold unless sales exceeded purchases, causing a decrease in the LIFO base. This could result in the permanent deferral of the hedge gains or losses and that would be unrealistic. So, when LIFO inventory is hedged, it is appropriate to consider the hedge applying only to the actual flow of inventory rather than the theoretical flow under the LIFO concept. This also points up the potential redundancy there is in using hedging in conjunction with the LIFO basis. In such cases, one would be hedging only the inventory flows, not the core inventory.

When an asset is carried at lower of cost or market, a change in the market value of the futures contract qualifies as a hedge of the existing asset and should be reported as an adjustment of the carrying amount of the asset. Deferred gains and losses are generally recognized in income at the same time as the other components with a carrying amount of the hedged asset.

If assets are carried at amortized cost, the gains and losses on the futures contracts are reflected as adjustments of the carrying value of the asset. These adjustments must be amortized as adjustments of interest income over the expected remaining life of the instrument, which may be different from its stated maturity; for example, Ginnie Mae-backed securities with a 25- to 30-year stated maturity historically have a much shorter life because of unscheduled prepayments.

CBOT 30-Day Interest Rate Futures

Trading Unit	$5 million
Tick Size	In .01 of 1 percent of $5 million on a 30-day basis ($41.67 per basis point)
Price Basis	100 minus the monthly average overnight fed funds rate
Daily Price Limit	150 basis points
Contract Months	First seven calendar months and the first two months in the March, June, September, December cycle following the last spot month
Trading Hours	7:20 A.M. to 2 P.M. (Chicago time)
Last Trading Day	Last business day of the delivery month
Delivery	The contract is cash settled against the average daily fed funds rate for the delivery month. The daily fed funds rate is calculated and reported by the Federal Reserve Bank of New York.

IMM Three-Month Eurodollar Futures

Trading Unit	Eurodollar Time Deposit having a principal value of $1 million with a three-month maturity
Tick Size	Multiples of .01 ($25 per contract)
Daily Price Limit	No limit
Contract Months	March, June, September, December, spot month
Trading Hours	7:20 A.M. to 2 P.M. (Chicago time), except on the last trading day of an expiring contract, when trading closes at 9:30 A.M. (3:30 P.M. London time). The market will close earlier on or preceding certain holidays. Contact the exchange for further details.
Last Trading Day	The second London bank business day immediately preceding the third Wednesday of the contract month
Delivery Days	The last trading day. Cash settled.

FASB-80 also specifies that amortization should begin no later than when a futures contract is closed, regardless of any rollover of futures contracts to more distant delivery dates.

If a futures contract qualifies as a hedge of a firm commitment, changes in the market value of the contract should be deferred on the balance sheet and ultimately included in the transaction when the commitment is recorded. This same treatment should be followed in the case of an anticipated transaction. In other words, the results of the futures contracts are reflected in the balance sheet as deferred gains and losses until the transactions actually occur.

SUMMARY

In summary, FASB-80 requires all futures contracts be marked-to-market. An exception to this are transactions that meet the specificied hedge criteria. If a futures contract can be classified as a hedge, then the net gains or losses from the futures transactions can generally be deferred and become part of the completed transaction when it is recorded.

APPENDIX A

Contract Specifications for Financial Futures and Options Contracts on Maj U.S. Exchanges

Chicago Board of Trade (CBOT)	International Monetary Market (IMM) Division of the CME	Index and O Market (IO Division of the

MidAmerica Commodity Exchange (MidAm)	Kansas City Board of Trade (KCBT)	Financial Instru Exchange (FINE Division of the NY

New York Futures Exchange (NYFE)	Philadelphia Board of Trade Inc. (PBOT)

Information obtained from *The Commodity Trading Manual*, Chicago Board of Trade © 1989.

FASB-80 also specifies that amortization should begin no later than when a futures contract is closed, regardless of any rollover of futures contracts to more distant delivery dates.

If a futures contract qualifies as a hedge of a firm commitment, changes in the market value of the contract should be deferred on the balance sheet and ultimately included in the transaction when the commitment is recorded. This same treatment should be followed in the case of an anticipated transaction. In other words, the results of the futures contracts are reflected in the balance sheet as deferred gains and losses until the transactions actually occur.

SUMMARY

In summary, FASB-80 requires all futures contracts be marked-to-market. An exception to this are transactions that meet the specificied hedge criteria. If a futures contract can be classified as a hedge, then the net gains or losses from the futures transactions can generally be deferred and become part of the completed transaction when it is recorded.

APPENDIX A

Contract Specifications for Financial Futures and Options Contracts on Major U.S. Exchanges

---

Chicago Board of Trade (CBOT)	International Monetary Market (IMM) Division of the CME	Index and Option Market (IOM) Division of the CME

MidAmerica Commodity Exchange (MidAm)	Kansas City Board of Trade (KCBT)	Financial Instrument Exchange (FINEX®) Division of the NYCE®

New York Futures Exchange (NYFE)	Philadelphia Board of Trade Inc. (PBOT)

Information obtained from *The Commodity Trading Manual*, Chicago Board of Trade © 1989.

CBOT 30-Day Interest Rate Futures

Trading Unit	$5 million
Tick Size	In .01 of 1 percent of $5 million on a 30-day basis ($41.67 per basis point)
Price Basis	100 minus the monthly average overnight fed funds rate
Daily Price Limit	150 basis points
Contract Months	First seven calendar months and the first two months in the March, June, September, December cycle following the last spot month
Trading Hours	7:20 A.M. to 2 P.M. (Chicago time)
Last Trading Day	Last business day of the delivery month
Delivery	The contract is cash settled against the average daily fed funds rate for the delivery month. The daily fed funds rate is calculated and reported by the Federal Reserve Bank of New York.

IMM Three-Month Eurodollar Futures

Trading Unit	Eurodollar Time Deposit having a principal value of $1 million with a three-month maturity
Tick Size	Multiples of .01 ($25 per contract)
Daily Price Limit	No limit
Contract Months	March, June, September, December, spot month
Trading Hours	7:20 A.M. to 2 P.M. (Chicago time), except on the last trading day of an expiring contract, when trading closes at 9:30 A.M. (3:30 P.M. London time). The market will close earlier on or preceding certain holidays. Contact the exchange for further details.
Last Trading Day	The second London bank business day immediately preceding the third Wednesday of the contract month
Delivery Days	The last trading day. Cash settled.

IOM Options on Three-Month Eurodollar Futures

Trading Unit	Option to buy, in the case of the call, or to sell, in the case of the put, one Eurodollar time deposit futures contract
Tick Size	One basis point, or .01 IMM index point ($25 per contract). A trade may occur at a price of .005 IMM Index point ($12.50) if it results in the liquidation of positions for both parties to the trade.
Strike Prices	Stated in terms of the IMM Index for the Eurodollar time deposit futures contract that is deliverable upon exercise of the option and shall be at intervals of .25.
Daily Price Limit	None
Contract Months	March, June, September, December
Trading Hours	7:20 A.M. to 2 P.M. (Chicago time), except on the last day of an expiring contract, when trading closes at 9:30 A.M. The market will close earlier on or preceding certain holidays. Contact the exchange for further details.
Last Trading Day	Same date and time as the underlying futures contract
Exercise Days	Any business day that the option is traded

IMM Three-Month U.S. Treasury Bill Futures

Trading Unit	Three month (13-week) U.S. Treasury bills having a face value at maturity of $1 million
Tick Size	Multiples of .01 ($25 per contract)
Daily Price Limit	No limit
Contract Months	March, June, September, December
Trading Hours	7:20 A.M. to 2 P.M. (Chicago time), except on the last trading day of an expiring contract, when trading closes at 10 A.M. The market will close earlier on or preceding certain holidays. Contact the exchange for further details.
Last Trading Day	Futures trading in the lead month shall terminate on the business day immediately preceding the first delivery day
Delivery	Delivery shall be made on three successive business days. The first delivery day shall be the first day of the spot month on which a 13-week Treasury bill is issued and a 1-year Treasury bill has 13 weeks remaining to maturity.

IOM Options on Three-Month U.S. Treasury Bill Futures

Trading Unit	Option to buy, in the case of the call, or to sell, in the case of the put, one three-month U.S. Treasury bill futures contract
Tick Size	One basis point, or .01 IMM Index point ($25 per contract). A trade may occur at a price of .005 IMM Index point ($12.50) if it results in the liquidation of positions for both parties to the trade.
Strike Prices	Stated in terms of the IMM Index for the three-month Treasury bill futures contract that is deliverable upon exercise of the option and shall be at intervals of .50 for IMM Index levels below 91.00 and at intervals of .25 of IMM Index levels above 91.00
Daily Price Limit	None
Contract Months	March, June, September, December
Trading Hours	7:20 A.M. to 2 P.M. (Chicago time). The market will close earlier on or preceding certain holidays. Contact the exchange for further details.
Last Trading Day	The business day nearest the underlying futures contract that meets the following two criteria: (1) the last day of trading shall be the last business day of the week and (2) the last trading day shall precede by at least six business days the first business day of the underlying futures contract month
Exercise Days	Any business day that the option is traded

MidAm U.S. Treasury Bill Futures

Trading Unit	$500,000 face value U.S. Treasury bills within 90 days until maturity
Tick Size	One basis point ($12.50 per contract)
Daily Trading Limit	None
Contract Months	March, June, September, December
Trading Hours	7:20 A.M. to 2:15 P.M. (Chicago time), except on the last trading day of an expiring contract, when trading closes at 10:15 A.M.
Last Trading Day	The second day following the third weekly Treasury bill auction in the contract month
Delivery	Settled in cash at the settlement price of the corresponding International Monetary Market T-bill contract

FINEX® U.S. 5-Year Treasury Note Futures

Trading Unit	U.S. Treasury notes with a face value at maturity of $100,000
Tick Size	Percentage of par in increments of ½ of ¹⁄₃₂ of a point ($15.625 per contract)
Daily Price Limit	None
Contract Months	March, June, September, December
Trading Hours	8:20 A.M. to 3 P.M. (New York time)
Last Trading Day	1 P.M. (New York time) on the eighth last business day of the delivery month
Delivery	Federal Reserve book-entry system

Options on FINEX® U.S. 5-Year Treasury Note Futures

Trading Unit	One FINEX® five-year Treasury note futures contract
Tick Size	¹⁄₆₄ of one point
Strike Prices	Intervals of ½ of one FINEX® five-year Treasury note futures point
Daily Price Limit	None
Contract Months	March, June, September, December
Trading Hours	8:20 A.M. to 3 P.M. (New York time)
Last Trading Day	The Friday that is at least the fifth business day prior to the first notice day of the expiring month

CBOT U.S. 10-Year Treasury Note Futures

Trading Unit	$100,000 face value U.S. Treasury notes
Tick Size	¹⁄₃₂ of a point ($31.25 per contract)
Daily Price Limit	Three points ($3,000) per contract above or below the previous day's settlement price
Contract Months	March, June, September, December
Trading Hours	7:20 A.M. to 2 P.M. (Chicago time), Monday through Friday Evening trading hours are from 5 to 8:30 P.M. (Chicago time), or 6 to 9:30 P.M. (central daylight saving time), Sunday through Thursday
Last Trading Day	Seven business days prior to the last business day of the delivery month

CBOT U.S. 5-Year Treasury Note Futures

Trading Unit	$100,000 face value U.S. Treasury notes
Tick Size	Prices are quoted in increments of 1/32 of a point; minimum price fluctuation is 1/2 of 1/32 ($15.625 pe contract)
Daily Price Limit	Three points ($3,000 per contract) above or belov the previous day's settlement price (expandable t 4 1/2 points)
Contract Months	March, June, September, December
Trading Hours	7:20 A.M. to 2 P.M. (Chicago time)
Last Trading Day	The eighth to last business day of the delivery month
Deliverable Grades	Any of the four most recently auctioned 5-year Treasury notes. Specifically, U.S. Treasury notes th; have an original maturity of not more than 5 years and 3 months and remaining maturity of not less than 4 years and 3 months as of the first day of th delivery month.
Delivery	Federal Reserve book-entry wire-transfer system

MidAm U.S. Treasury Note Futures

Trading Unit	$50,000 face value U.S. Treasury notes
Tick Size	In percentage of par in minimum increments of 1/32 of a point, or $15.62 per tick (e.g., 91-01, or 91 points and 1/32 of a point)
Daily Price Limit	96/32 ($1,500 per contract) above or below the previous day's settlement price
Contract Months	March, June, September, December
Trading Hours	7:20 A.M. to 3:15 P.M. (Chicago time), except on the last trading day of an expiring contract, when trading closes at noon
Last Trading Day	The eighth to last business day of the delivery month
Deliverable Grades	U.S. Treasury notes maturing not less than 6 1/2 years or more than 10 years, from the first day of the delivery month
Delivery	Federal Reserve book-entry wire-transfer system. Invoice price on delivery is adjusted to a standard 8 percent and actual term to maturity.

Deliverable Grades	U.S. Treasury notes maturing at least 6½ years, but not more than 10 years, from the first day of the delivery month. Coupon based on an 8 percent standard.
Delivery	Federal Reserve book-entry wire-transfer system

Options on CBOT U.S. 10-Year Treasury Note Futures

Trading Unit	One $100,000 face value CBOT U.S. Treasury note futures contract
Tick Size	1/64 of a point ($15.63 per contract)
Strike Prices	Integral multiples of one point ($1,000) per T-note futures contract to bracket the current T-note futures price. If T-note futures are at 92-00, strike prices may be set at 89, 90, 91, 92, 93, 94, 95, etc.
Daily Price Limit	Three points ($3,000) per contract above or below the previous day's settlement premium
Contract Months	March, June, September, December
Trading Hours	7:20 A.M. to 2 P.M. (Chicago time), Monday through Friday Evening trading hours are from 5 to 8:30 P.M. (Chicago time), or from 6 to 9:30 P.M. (central daylight saving time), Sunday through Thursday
Last Trading Day	Options cease trading prior to the delivery month of the underlying futures contract. Options cease trading at noon on the first Friday preceding by at least five business days the first notice day for the corresponding T-note futures contract. For example, the last trading day for December 1988 T-note options is November 18, 1988.
Expiration	10 A.M. (Chicago time) on the first Saturday following the last trading day

CBOT U.S. Treasury Bond Futures

Trading Unit	$100,000 face value U.S. Treasury bonds
Tick Size	1/32 of a point ($31.25 per contract)
Daily Price Limit	Three points ($3,000) per contract above or below the previous day's settlement price
Contract Months	March, June, September, December

Trading Hours	7:20 A.M. to 2 P.M. (Chicago time), Monday through Friday Evening trading hours are from 5 to 8:30 P.M. (Chicago time), or 6 to 9:30 P.M. (central daylight saving time), Sunday through Thursday
Last Trading Day	Seven business days prior to the last business day of the delivery month
Deliverable Grades	U.S. Treasury bonds maturing at least 15 years from the first day of the delivery month, if not callable; if callable, not so for at least 15 years from the first day of the delivery month. Coupon based on an 8 percent standard.
Delivery	Federal Reserve book-entry wire-transfer system

CBOT 3-Year Interest Rate Swap Futures

Underlying Instrument	The yield on the fixed-rate side of an interest swap. This fixed-rate yield is based on a generic 3-year $25 million interest rate swap versus a floating rate of six month LIBOR, priced to settle on the third Wednesday of the contract month.
Price Quotation	100 minus the fixed-rate yield on a generic 3-year interest rate swap. For example, a 7.875 percent yield equals a price of 92.125.
Tick Size	$25 per one-half basis point
Daily Price Limit	100 basis points ($5,000 per contract) above or below the previous day's settlement price, expandable to 150 points
Contract Months	March, June, September, and December
Last Trading Day	The Monday preceding the third Wednesday of the contract month
Delivery Method	Cash settlement. The final settlement price will be determined on the last day of trading at 9:30 A.M. (Chicago time) by surveying at least seven reference dealers randomly selected from an approved list who will provide bid and ask quotes on fixed-rate payments on 3-year $25 million generic interest rate swaps. Each dealer's bid and ask quotes will be averaged and the median of the resulting average will be the settlement yield.
Delivery Day	The last day of trading in the delivery month

Trading Hours	7:20 A.M. to 2:00 P.M. (Chicago time), Monday through Friday. On the last trading day of an expiring contract, trading in that contract closes at 9:30 A.M.

CBOT 5-Year Interest Rate Swap Futures

Underlying Instrument	The yield on the fixed-rate side of an interest rate swap. This fixed-rate yield is based on a generic 5-year $25 million interest rate swap versus a floating rate of 6-month LIBOR, priced to settle on the third Wednesday of the contract month.
Price Quotation	100 minus the fixed-rate yield on a generic 5-year interest rate swap. For example, a 7.875 percent yield equals a price of 92.125.
Tick Size	$25 per one-half basis point
Daily Price Limit	100 basis points ($5,000 per contract) above or below the previous day's settlement price, expandable to 150 basis points
Contract Months	March, June, September, and December
Last Trading Day	The Monday preceding the third Wednesday of the contract month
Delivery Method	Cash settlement. The final settlement price will be determined on the last day of trading at 9:30 A.M. (Chicago time) by surveying at least seven reference dealers randomly selected from an approved list who will provide bid and ask quotes on fixed-rate payments on 5-year $25 million generic interest rate swaps. Each dealer's bid and ask quotes will be averaged and the median of the resulting average will be the settlement yield.
Delivery Day	The last day of trading in the delivery month
Trading Hours	7:20 A.M. to 2:00 P.M. (Chicago time), Monday through Friday. On the last trading day of an expiring contract, trading in that contract closes at 9:30 A.M.

Options on CBOT U.S. Treasury Bond Futures

Trading Unit	One $100,000 face value CBOT U.S. Treasury bond futures contract
Tick Size	1/64 of a point ($15.63 per contract)

Strike Prices	In integral multiples of two points ($2,000) per T-bond futures contract to bracket the current T-bond futures price. For example, if T-bond futures are at 86-00, strike prices may be set at 80, 82, 84, 86, 88, 90, 92, etc.
Daily Price Limit	Three points ($3,000) per contract above or below the previous day's settlement premium
Contract Months	March, June, September, December
Trading Hours	7:20 A.M. to 2 P.M. (Chicago time), Monday through Friday Evening trading hours are from 5 to 8:30 P.M. (Chicago time), or from 6 to 9:30 P.M. (central daylight saving time), Sunday through Thursday
Last Trading Day	Options cease trading prior to the delivery month of the underlying futures contract. Options cease trading at noon on the first Friday preceding by at least five business days the first notice day for the corresponding T-bond futures contract. For example, the last trading day for December 1988 T-bond options is November 18, 1988.
Expiration	10 A.M. (Chicago time) on the first Saturday following the last trading day

MidAm U.S. Treasury Bond Futures

Trading Unit	$50,000 face value U.S. Treasury bonds
Tick Size	1/32 of a point ($15.62 per tick)
Daily Price Limit	96/32 ($1,500 per contract) above or below the previous day's settlement price
Contract Months	March, June, September, December
Trading Hours	7:20 A.M. to 3:15 P.M. (Chicago time), except on the last trading day of an expiring contract, when trading closes at noon
Last Trading Day	The buiness day prior to the last seven business days of the delivery month
Deliverable Grades	U.S. Treasury bonds with a nominal 8 percent coupon maturing at least 15 years from delivery date if not callable; if callable, not so for at least 15 years from delivery date
Delivery	Federal Reserve book-entry wire-transfer system. Invoice price on delivery is adjusted for coupon rates and term to maturity or call.

CBOT Municipal Bond Index Futures

Trading Unit	$1,000 times *The Bond Buyer*™ Municipal Bond Index.* A price of 90-00 reflects a contract size of $90,000.
Tick Size	1/32 of one point ($31.25 per contract)
Daily Price Limit	Three points ($3,000 per contract) above or below the previous day's settlement price
Contract Months	March, June, September, December
Trading Hours	7:20 A.M. to 2 P.M. (Chicago time)
Last Trading Day	The eighth to last business day of the delivery month
Delivery	Municipal Bond Index futures settle in cash on the last day of trading. Settlement price on the last trading day equals *The Bond Buyer*™ Municipal Bond Index* value on that day.

*Copyright 1983, *The Bond Buyer*™ and the Chicago Board of Trade. All rights reserved.

Options on CBOT Municipal Bond Index Futures

Trading Unit	One CBOT Municipal Bond Index futures contract deliverable during the months of March, June, September, December
Tick Size	1/64 of a point ($15.63 per contract)
Strike Prices	Integral multiples of two points ($2,000) to bracket the current muni-bond futures price
Daily Price Limit	Three points ($3,000) per contract above or below the previous day's settlement premium
Contract Months	March, June, September, December
Trading Hours	7:20 A.M. to 2 P.M. (Chicago time)
Last Trading Day	Options on Municipal Bond Index futures cease trading at 2 P.M. (Chicago time) on the last day of trading in the Municipal Bond Index futures of the corresponding month
Expiration	8 P.M. (Chicago time) on the last trading day

CBOT Mortgage-Backed Futures

Trading Unit	$100,000 par value
Coupons Traded	Each month, the exchange will list a new coupon four months in the future. The coupon for that month will be the current Government National Mortgage Association coupon; trading nearest to par (100) but not greater than par.

Tick Size	$\frac{1}{32}$ of a point ($31.25 per contract)
Daily Price Limit	Three points ($3,000 per contract) above or below the previous day's settlement price (expandable to 4½ points)
Contract Months	Four consecutive months
Trading Hours	7:20 A.M. to 2 P.M. (Chicago time)
Last Trading Day	At 1 p.m. on the Friday preceding the third Wednesday of the month
Delivery	In cash on the last trading day based on the mortgage-backed Survey Price; the Survey Price shall be the median price obtained from a survey of dealers

Options on CBOT Mortgage-Backed Futures

Trading Unit	One CBOT mortgage-backed futures contract of a specified delivery month and coupon
Tick Size	$\frac{1}{64}$ of a point ($15.625 of $15.63 per contract)
Strike Prices	Multiples of one point ($1,000)
Daily Price Limit	Three points ($3,000 per contract)
Contract Months	Four consecutive months
Trading Hours	7:20 A.M. to 2 P.M. (Chicago time)
Last Trading Day	Options cease trading at 1 P.M. (Chicago time) on the last day of trading in mortgage-backed futures in the corresponding delivery month
Expiration	8 P.M. (Chicago time) on the last day of trading; in-the-money options are exercised automatically

IOM Standard & Poor's 500 Stock Price Index Futures

Trading Unit	$500 times the Standard & Poor's 500 Stock Price Index
Tick Size	.05 index points ($25 per contract)
Daily Price Limit and Trading Halts	Coordinated with trading halts of the underlying stocks listed for trading in the securities markets. For complete details of this rule, contact the Chicago Mercantile Exchange Research Division.

Opening Price Limit	During the opening range, there shall be no trading at a price more than five index points above or below the previous day's settlement price. If the primary futures contract is limit bid or offered at the five index point limit at the end of the first 10 minutes of trading, trading shall terminate for a period of two minutes, then reopen with a new opening range.
Contract Months	March, June, September, December
Trading Hours	8:30 A.M. to 3:15 P.M. (Chicago time)
Last Trading Day	The business day immediately preceding the day of determination of the final settlement price
Delivery	Cash settlement to the final settlement price, determined by a special quotation of the Standard & Poor's Stock Price Index based on the opening prices of the component stocks in the index on the third Friday of the contract month

IOM Options on Standard & Poor's 500 Stock Price Index Futures

Trading Unit	Option to buy, in the case of the call, or to sell, in the case of the put, one Standard & Poor's 500 Stock Price Index futures contract
Tick Size	.05 index points ($25 per contract), except that trades may occur at a price of .025 index points ($12.50) if such trades result in the liquidation of positions for both parties to the trade
Daily Price Limit	All S&P 500 options series close when the S&P 500 futures lock limit
Strike Prices*	Stated in terms of Standard & Poor's 500 Stock Price Index futures contract, which is deliverable upon exercise of the option and shall be an integer divisible by 5 without remainder, e.g., 110, 115, 120, etc.
Contract Months	Serial month listings include options in the March quarterly cycle (March, June, September, December) and options not in the March quarterly cycle (January, February, April, May, July, August, October, November)
Trading Hours	8:30 A.M. to 3:15 P.M. (Chicago time)
Last Trading Day	The same date and time as the underlying futures contract for March quarterly months and on the third Friday of the contract month in those months other than those in the March quarterly cycle

Exercise Days	Any business day that the option is traded
Delivery	A long or short position in the underlying futures contract. In the absence of contrary instructions to the clearinghouse, expiring March quarterly cycle in-the-month options are automatically exercised and settled in cash to the final settlement price of the underlying futures contract.

*The CME has proposed 10.00 index point exercise price intervals fro the third-nearest contract month in the March quarterly cycle, e.g., 110, 120, 130, etc. Proposed rule is pending CFTC approval.

NYFE NYSE Composite Index Futures

Trading Unit	$500 times NYSE Composite Index (e.g., $500 times 135.00 = $67,500; 135.00 represents recent index level)
Tick Size	Five basis points, or .05, e.g., 135.05, 135.10, 135.15 ($25 per contract)
Daily Price Limit	None
Contract Months	March, June, September, December cycle (four months traded at all times)
Trading Hours	9:30 A.M. to 4:15 P.M. (New York time)
Last Trading Day	The Thursday preceding the third Friday of the month; if that day is not a NYFE and NYSE business day, the last trading day will be the preceding such business day
Delivery	Settlement at contract maturity is by cash payment; final settlement is based upon a special calculation of the third Friday's opening prices of all the stocks listed in the NYSE Composite Index

Options on NYFE NYSE Composite Index Futures

Trading Unit	One NYSE Composite Index futures contract
Tick Size	Five basis points, or .05 ($25 per contract); however, if an option transaction liquidates an existing position, the minimum fluctuation can be one point ($5) if the price is less than five points
Strike Prices	Integers that are evenly divisible by two (e.g., 152.00, 154.00). Minimum of nine exercise prices at all times: four in-the-money, one at-the money, four out-of-the-money.
Daily Price Limit	None

Contract Months	The current calendar month, the two months following the current calendar month, the next month in the calendar quarterly cycle (four options months traded at all times). The futures contract underlying the noncalendar quarterly cycle months is the next futures contract following the option expiration.
Trading Hours	9:30 A.M. to 4:15 P.M. (New York time)
Last Trading Day	For the calendar quarterly cycle months (March, June, September, December), the last day of trading is the last trading day of the underlying futures contract (the business day preceding the third Friday of the expiration month; except that if the third Friday is not a NYFE and NYSE business day, the last trading day shall be the business day preceding the business day immediately preceding the third Friday). For the noncalendar quarterly cycle months, the last day of trading is the third Friday of the expiration month; except that if the third Friday is not a NYFE and NYSE business day, the last trading day shall be the business day immediately preceding the third Friday.

CBOT Major Market Index Futures

Trading Unit	$250 times the value of the Major Market Index, e.g., at 472.00, the value of the MMI futures contract is $118,000 ($250 times 472.00)
Tick Size	.05 of an index point ($12.50 per contract)
Daily Price Limit	80 index points above the previous day's settlement price; initial limit of 50 index points below the previous day's settlement price*
Contract Months	The first three consecutive months and the next three months in the March, June, September, December cycle
Trading Hours	8:15 A.M. to 3:15 P.M. (Chicago time)
Last Trading Day	Third Friday of the delivery month
Delivery	Major Market Index futures are marked-to-market daily according to the closing MMI futures prices and are settled in cash at the closing value of the Major Market Index on the last trading day

*For prices below the previous day's settlement price, coordinated price limits and trading halts will be based on 250- and 400-point declines in the Dow Jones Industrial Average. See CBOT Rules and Regulations for detailed plan.

KCBT Mini Value Line Average Stock Index Futures

Trading Unit	$100 times the Value Line Arithmetic Index
Tick Size	.05 point ($5 per contract)
Daily Price Limit	Consult the exchange for current information
Contract Months	March, June, September, December
Trading Hours	8:30 A.M. to 3:15 P.M. (Kansas City time)
Delivery	Settlement: actual Value Line Arithmetic Index at the close on the last trading day of the contract month

KCBT Value Line Average Stock Index Futures

Trading Unit	$500 times the Value Line Arithmetic Index
Tick Size	.05 point ($25 per contract)
Daily Price Limit	Consult the exchange for current information
Contract Months	March, June, September, December
Trading Hours	8:30 A.M. to 3:15 P.M. (Kansas City time)
Delivery	Settlement: actual Value Line Arithmetic Index at the close on the last trading day of the contract month

PBOT National Over-the-Counter Index™ Futures

Trading Unit	$500 times futures price
Tick Size	.05 point ($25 per contract)
Daily Price Limit	None
Contract Months	Consecutive and cycle months, such as February, March, April, June, September
Trading Hours	9:30 A.M. to 4:10 P.M. (Philadelphia time), except on the last trading day of an expiring contract, when trading closes at 4 P.M.
Last Trading Day	At 4 P.M. (Philadelphia time) on the third Friday of the contract month
Delivery	Cash settled: OX futures contracts will be settled in cash based on the difference between the value of the XOC Index as disseminated by the exchange at 4 P.M. on the last trading day of the OX futures contract and the closing value of the OX futures contract on the day preceding the last trading day
Final Settlement	On the first business day following the last trading day in the contract month

IMM Australian Dollar Futures

Trading Unit	100,000 Australian dollars
Tick Size	.0001 per Australian dollar ($10 per contract)
Daily Price Limit	Opening price limit between 7:20 and 7:35 A.M. of 150 points. There are no price limits after 7:35 A.M.
Contract Months	January, March, April, June, July, September, October, December, spot month
Trading Hours	7:20 A.M. to 2 P.M. (Chicago time), except on the last trading day of an expiring contract, when trading closes at 9:16 A.M. The market will close earlier on or preceding certain holidays. Contact the exchange for further details.
Last Trading Day	9:16 A.M. on the second business day immediately preceding the third Wednesday of the contract month
Delivery	Delivery shall be made on the third Wednesday of the contract month
Delivery Points	Delivered in the country of issurance at a bank designated by the clearinghouse

PBOT Australian Dollar Futures

Trading Unit	100,000 Australian dollars
Tick Size	$0.0001 per Australian dollar, commonly referred to as one point ($10 per contract)
Contract Months	March, June, September, December, two additional near months
Trading Hours	4:30 A.M. to 2:30 P.M. (Philadelphia time), Monday through Friday Evening trading hours are from 6 to 10 P.M. (Philadelphia time), or from 7 to 11 P.M. (daylight saving time), Sunday through Thursday
Last Trading Day	Friday before the third Wednesday of the month

IOM Options on Australian Dollar Futures

Trading Unit	Option to buy, in the case of the call, or to sell, in the case of the put, one Australian dollar futures contract

Tick Size	One point, or $0.0001 per Australian dollar ($10 per contract). A trade may occur at a price of .00005 ($5) if it results in the liquidation of positions for both parties to the trade.
Strike Prices	Stated in terms of U.S. dollars per Australian dollar at intervals of 1 cent
Daily Price Limit	Option ceases trading when corresponding futures lock limit at the opening price limit
Contract Months	Serial month listings include options in the March quarterly cycle (March, June, September, December) and options not in the March quarterly cycle (January, February, April, May, July, August, October, November)
Trading Hours	7:20 A.M. to 2 P.M. (Chicago time). The market will close earlier on or preceding certain holidays. Contact the exchange for further details.
Last Trading Day	Second Friday immediately preceding the third Wednesday of the contract month. If this date is an exchange holiday, trading shall terminate on the immediately preceding business day.
Exercise Days	Any business day that the option is traded
Delivery	A long or short position in the underlying futures contract

IMM Swiss Franc Futures

Trading Unit	125,000 Swiss francs
Tick Size	.0001 per franc ($12.50 per contract)
Daily Price Limit	Opening price limit between 7:20 and 7:35 A.M. of 150 points. There are no price limits after 7:35 A.M.
Contract Months	January, March, April, June, July, September, October, December, spot month
Trading Hours	7:20 A.M. to 2 P.M. (Chicago time), except on the last trading day of an expiring contract, when trading closes at 9:16 A.M. The market will close earlier on or preceding certain holidays. Contact the exchange for further details.
Last Trading Day	9:16 A.M. on the second business day immediately preceding the third Wednesday of the contract month
Delivery	Delivery shall be made on the third Wednesday of the contract month

Delivery Points	Delivered in the country of issuance at a bank designated by the clearinghouse

PBOT Swiss Franc Futures

Trading Unit	125,000 Swiss francs
Tick Size	$0.0001 per Swiss franc, commonly referred to as one point ($12.50 per contract)
Contract Months	March, June, September, December, two additional near months
Trading Hours	4:30 A.M. to 2:30 P.M. (Philadelphia time), Monday through Friday Evening trading hours are from 6 to 10 P.M. (Philadelphia time), or from 7 to 11 P.M. (daylight saving time), Sunday through Thursday
Last Trading Day	Friday before the third Wednesday of the month

MidAm Swiss Franc Futures

Trading Unit	62,500 Swiss francs
Tick Size	$0.0001 per Swiss franc ($6.25 per contract)
Daily Price Limit	None
Contract Months	March, June, September, December
Trading Hours	7:20 A.M. to 2:15 P.M. (Chicago time), except on the last trading day of an expiring contract, when trading closes at 9:31 A.M.
Delivery	The currency shall be deliverable in the country of issuance at a bank approved by the clearinghouse

IOM Options on Swiss Franc Futures

Trading Unit	Option to buy, in the case of the call, or to sell, in the case of the put, one Swiss franc futures contract
Tick Size	One point, or $0.0001 per Swiss franc ($12.50 per contract). A trade may occur at a price of .00005 ($6.25) if it results in the liquidation of positions for both parties to the trade.
Strike Prices	Stated in terms of U.S. dollars per Swiss franc at intervals of 1 cent
Daily Price Limit	Option ceases trading when corresponding future locks limit at the opening price limit

Contract Months	Serial month listings include options in the March quarterly cycle (March, June, September, December) and options not in the March quarterly cycle (January, February, April, May, July, August, October, November)
Trading Hours	7:20 A.M. to 2 P.M. (Chicago time). The market will close earlier on or preceding certain holidays. Contact the exchange for further details.
Last Trading Day	Second Friday immediately preceding the third Wednesday of the contract month. If this date is an exchange holiday, trading shall terminate on the immediately preceding buiness day.
Exercise Days	Any business day that the option is traded
Delivery	A long or short position in the underlying futures contract

IMM Canadian Dollar Futures

Trading Unit	100,000 Canadian dollars
Tick Size	.0001 per Canadian dollar ($10 per contract)
Daily Price Limit	Opening price limit between 7:20 and 7:35 A.M. of 100 points. There are no price limits after 7:35 A.M.
Contract Months	January, March, April, June, July, September, October, December, spot month
Trading Hours	7:20 A.M. to 2 P.M. (Chicago time), except on the last trading day of an expiring contract, when trading closes at 9:16 A.M. The market will close earlier on or preceding certain holidays. Contact the exchange for further details.
Last Trading Day	9:16 A.M. on the second business day immediately preceding the third Wednesday of the contact month
Delivery	Delivery shall be made on the third Wednesday of the contract month
Delivery Points	Delivered in the country of issuance at a bank designated by the clearinghouse

PBOT Canadian Dollar Futures

Trading Unit	100,000 Canadian dollars
Tick Size	$0.0001 per Canadian dollar, commonly referred to as one point ($10 per contract)

Contract Months	March, June, September, December, two additional near months
Trading Hours	4:30 A.M. to 2:30 P.M. (Philadelphia time)
Last Trading Day	Friday before the third Wednesday of the month

MidAm Canadian Dollar Futures

Trading Unit	50,000 Canadian dollars
Tick Size	$0.0001 per Canadian dollar ($5 per contract)
Daily Price Limit	None
Contract Months	March, June, September, December
Trading Hours	7:20 A.M. to 2:15 P.M. (Chicago time), except on the last trading day of an expiring contract, when trading closes at 9:31 A.M.
Delivery	The currency shall be deliverable in the country of issuance at a bank approved by the clearinghouse

IOM Options on Canadian Dollar Futures

Trading Unit	Option to buy, in the case of the call, or to sell, in the case of the put, one Canadian dollar futures contract.
Tick Size	One point, or $0.0001 per Canadian dollar ($10 per contract). A trade may occur at a price of .00005 ($5) if it results in the liquidation of positions for both parties to the trade.
Strike Prices	Stated in terms of U.S. dollars per Canadian dollar at intervals of ½ cent
Daily Price Limit	Option ceases trading when corresponding future locks limit at the opening price limit
Contract Months	Serial month listings include options in the March quarterly cycle (March, June, September, December) and options not in the March quarterly cycle (January, February, April, May, July, August, October, November)
Trading Hours	7:20 A.M. to 2 P.M. (Chicago time). The market will close earlier on or preceding certain holidays. Contact the exchange for further details.
Last Trading Day	Second Friday immediately preceding the third Wednesday of the contract month. If this date is an exchange holiday, trading shall terminate on the immediately preceding business day.

Exercise Days	Any business day that the option is traded
Delivery	A long or short position in the underlying futures contract

IMM Deutsche Mark Futures

Trading Unit	125,000 deutsche marks
Tick Size	.0001 per mark ($12.50 per contract)
Daily Price Limit	Opening price limit between 7:20 and 7:35 A.M. of 150 points. There are no price limits after 7:35 A.M.
Contract Months	January, March, April, June, July, September, October, December, spot month
Trading Hours	7:20 A.M. to 2 P.M. (Chicago time), except on the last trading day of an expiring contract, when trading closes at 9:16 A.M. The market will close earlier on or preceding certain holidays. Contact the exchange for further details.
Last Trading Day	9:16 A.M. on the second business day immediately preceding the third Wednesday of the contract month
Delivery	Delivery shall be made on the third Wednesday of the contract month
Delivery Points	Delivered in the country of issuance at a bank designated by the clearinghouse

PBOT Deutsche Mark Futures

Trading Unit	125,000 deutsche marks
Tick Size	$0.0001 per deutsche mark, commonly referred to as one point ($12.50 per contract)
Contract Months	March, June, September, December, two additional near months
Last Trading Day	Friday before the third Wednesday of the month
Trading Hours	4:30 A.M. to 2:30 P.M. (Philadelphia time), Monday through Friday Evening trading hours are from 6 to 10 P.M. (Philadelphia time), or 7 to 11 P.M. (daylight saving time), Sunday through Thursday

MidAm Deutsche Mark Futures

Trading Unit	62,500 deutsche marks

Tick Size	$0.0001 per deutsche mark ($6.25 per contract)
Daily Price Limit	None
Contract Months	March, June, September, December
Trading Hours	7:20 A.M. to 2:15 P.M. (Chicago time), except on the last trading day of an expiring contract, when trading closes at 9:31 A.M.
Delivery	The currency shall be deliverable in the country of issuance at a bank approved by the clearinghouse

IOM Options on Deutsche Mark Futures

Trading unit	Option to buy, in the case of the call, or to sell, in the case of the put, one deutsche mark futures contract
Tick Size	One point, or $0.0001 per deutsche mark ($12.50 per contract). A trade may occur at a price of .00005 ($6.25) if it results in the liquidation of positions for both parties to the trade.
Strike Prices	Stated in terms of U.S. dollars per deutsche mark at intervals of 1 cent
Daily Price Limit	Option ceases trading when corresponding future locks limit at the opening price limit
Contract Months	Serial month listings include options in the March quarterly cycle (March, June, September, December) and options not in the March quarterly cycle (January, February, April, May, July, August, October, November)
Trading Hours	7:20 A.M. to 2 P.M. (Chicago time). The market will close earlier on or preceding certain holidays. Contact the exchange for further details.
Last Trading Day	Second Friday immediately preceding the third Wednesday of the contract month. If this date is an exchange holiday, trading shall terminate on the immediately preceding business day.
Exercise Days	Any business day that the option is traded
Delivery	A long or short position in the underlying futures contract

IMM Pound Sterling Futures

Trading Unit	62,500 pounds sterling (British pounds)
Tick Size	.0002 per pound ($12.50 per contract)

Daily Price Limit	Opening price limit between 7:20 and 7:35 A.M. of 400 points. There are no price limits after 7:35 A.M.
Contract Months	January, March, April, June, July, September, October, December, spot month
Trading Hours	7:20 A.M. to 2 P.M. (Chicago time), except on the last trading day of an expiring contract, when trading closes at 9:16 A.M. The market will close earlier on or preceding certain holidays. Contact the exchange for further details.
Last Trading Day	9:16 A.M. on the second business day immediately preceding the third Wednesday of the contract month
Delivery	Delivery shall be made on the third Wednesday of the contract month
Delivery Points	Delivered in the country of issuance at a bank designated by the clearinghouse

PBOT British Pound Futures

Trading Unit	62,500 British pounds sterling
Tick Size	$0.0001 per British pound ($6.25 per contract)
Contract Months	March, June, September, December, two additional near months
Trading Hours	4:30 A.M. to 2:30 P.M. (Philadelphia time), Monday through Friday Evening trading hours are from 6 to 10 P.M. (Philadelphia time), or from 7 to 11 p.m. (daylight saving time), Sunday through Thursday
Last Trading Day	Friday before the third Wednesday of the month

MidAm British Pound Futures

Trading Unit	12,500 British pounds
Tick Size	$0.0002 per British pound ($2.50 per contract)
Daily Price Limit	None
Contract Months	March, June, September, December
Trading Hours	7:20 A.M. to 2:15 P.M. (Chicago time), except on the last trading day of an expiring contract, when trading closes at 9:31 A.M.
Delivery	The currency shall be deliverable in the counry of issuance at a bank approved by the clearinghouse

IOM Options on Pound Sterling Futures

Trading Unit	Option to buy, in the case of the call, or to sell, in the case of the put, one pound sterling futures contract
Tick Size	Two points, or $0.0002 per pound sterling ($12.50 per contract). A trade may occur at a price of .0001 ($6.25) if it results in the liquidation of positions for both parties to the trade.
Strike Prices	Stated in terms of U.S. dollars per pound sterling at intervals of 2½ cents
Daily Price Limit	Option ceases trading when corresponding future locks limit at the opening price limit
Contract Months	Serial month listings include options in the March quarterly cycle (March, June, September, December) and options not in the March quarterly cycle (January, February, April, May, July, August, October, November)
Trading Hours	7:20 A.M. to 2 P.M. (Chicago time). The market will close earlier on or preceding certain holidays. Contact the exchange for further details.
Last Trading Day	Second Friday immediately preceding the third Wednesday of the contract month. If this date is an exchange holiday, trading shall terminate on the immediately preceding business day.
Exercise Days	Any business day that the option is traded
Delivery	A long or short position in the underlying futures contract

IMM Japanese Yen Futures

Trading Unit	12,500,000 Japanese yen
Tick Size	.000001 per yen ($12.50 per contract)
Daily Price Limit	Opening price limit between 7:20 and 7:35 A.M. of 150 points. There are no price limits after 7:35 A.M.
Contract Months	January, March, April, June, July, September, October, December, spot month
Trading Hours	7:20 A.M. to 2 P.M. (Chicago time), except on the last trading day of an expiring contract, when trading closes at 9:16 A.M. The market will close earlier on or preceding certain holidays. Contact the exchange for further details.

Last Trading Day	9:16 A.M. on the second business day immediately preceding the third Wednesday of the contract month
Delivery	Delivery shall be made on the third Wednesday of the contract month
Delivery Points	Delivered in the country of issuance at a bank designated by the clearinghouse

PBOT Japanese Yen Futures

Trading Unit	12,500,000 Japanese yen
Tick Size	$0.000001 per Japanese yen, commonly referred to as one point ($12.50 per contract)
Contract Months	March, June, September, December, two additional near months
Trading Hours	4:30 A.M. to 2:30 P.M. (Philadelphia time), Monday through Friday Evening trading hours are from 6 to 10 P.M. (Philadelphia time), or from 7 to 11 P.M. (daylight saving time), Sunday through Thursday
Last Trading Day	Friday before the third Wednesday of the month

MidAm Japanese Yen Futures

Trading Unit	6,250,000 Japanese yen
Tick Size	$0.000001 per Japanese yen ($6.25 per contract)
Daily Price Limit	None
Contract Months	March, June, September, December
Trading Hours	7:20 A.M. to 2:15 P.M. (Chicago time), except on the last trading day of an expiring contract, when trading closes at 9:31 A.M.
Delivery	The currency shall be deliverable in the country of issuance at a bank approved by the clearinghouse

IOM Options on Japanese Yen Futures

Trading Unit	Option to buy, in the case of the call, or to sell, in the case of the put, one Japanese yen futures contract

Tick Size	One point, or $0.000001 per Japanese yen ($12.50 per contract). A trade may occur at a price of .0000005 ($6.25) if it results in the liquidation of positions for both parties to the trade.
Strike Prices	Shall be stated in terms of U.S. dollars per Japanese yen at intervals of $0.0001
Daily Price Limit	Option ceases trading when corresponding futures lock limit at the opening price limit
Contract Months	Serial month listings include options in the March quarterly cycle (March, June, September, December) and options not in the March quarterly cycle (January, February, April, May, July, August, October, November)
Trading Hours	7:20 A.M. to 2 P.M. (Chicago time); the market will close earlier on or preceding certain holidays. Contract the exchange for further details.
Last Trading Day	Second Friday immediately preceding the third Wednesday of the contract month. If this date is an exchange holiday, trading shall terminate on the immediately preceding business day.
Exercise Days	Any business day that the option is traded
Delivery	A long or short position in the underlying futures contract

IMM French Franc Futures

Trading Unit	250,000 French francs
Tick Size	.0005 per franc ($12.50 per contract)
Daily Price Limit	Opening price limit between 7:20 and 7:35 A.M. of 500 points. There are no price limits after 7:35 A.M.
Contract Months	January, March, April, June, July, September, October, December, spot month
Trading Hours	7:20 A.M. to 2 P.M. (Chicago time), except on the last trading day of an expiring contract, when trading closes at 9:16 A.M. The market will close earlier on or preceding certain holidays. Contact the exchange for further details.
Last Trading Day	9:16 A.M. on the second business day immediately preceding the third Wednesday of the contract month
Delivery	Delivery shall be made on the third Wednesday of the contract month

Delivery Points	Delivered in the country of issuance at a bank designated by the clearinghouse

PBOT French Franc Futures

Trading Unit	500,000 French francs
Tick Size	$0.00005 per French franc, commonly referred to as five points ($25 per contract)
Contract Months	March, June, September, December, two additional near months
Trading Hours	4:30 A.M. to 2:30 P.M. (Philadelphia time)
Last Trading Day	Friday before the third Wednesday of the month

FINEX® U.S. Dollar IndexSM Futures

Trading Unit	$500 times the U.S. Dollar IndexSM
Tick Size	.01 of one U.S. Dollar IndexSM point ($5 per futures contract)
Daily Price Limit	None
Contract Months	March June, September, December
Trading Hours	8:20 A.M. to 3 P.M. (New York time)
Last Trading Day	Third Wednesday of the expiring contract month
Delivery	Cash settlement

Options on FINEX® U.S. Dollar IndexSM Futures

Trading Unit	U.S. Dollar IndexSM futures contract
Tick Size	.01 of one U.S. Dollar IndexSM point ($5 per contract)
Strike Prices	Intervals of two U.S. Dollar IndexSM trading points (200 ticks)
Daily Price Limit	None
Contract Months	March, June, September, December
Trading Hours	8:20 A.M. to 3 P.M. (New York time)
Last Trading Day	Two Fridays before the third Wednesday of the expiring contract month

FINEX® European Currency Unit Futures

Trading Unit	ECU 100,000
Tick Size	$0.0001 per ECU ($10 per contract)
Daily Price Limit	None
Contract Months	March, June, September, December
Trading Hours	8:20 A.M. to 3 P.M. (New York time)
Last Trading Day	Two business days prior to the third Wednesday of an expiring contract month
Delivery	Physical delivery of ECU

PBOT European Currency Unit Futures

Trading Unit	125,000 European Currency Units
Tick Size	$0.0001 per European Currency Unit, commonly referred to as one point ($12.50 per contract)
Contract Months	March, June, September, December, two additional near months
Trading Hours	4:30 A.M. to 2:30 P.M. (Philadelphia time)
Last Trading Day	Friday before the third Wednesday of the month

APPENDIX B
Formulas

MONEY MARKET FORMULAS*

Calculating Dollar Discount and Price on Discount Securities with Rate of Discount Given

Let

D = discount from face value in dollars
F = face value in dollars
d = rate of discount (decimal)
t_{sm} = days from settlement to maturity
P = price in dollars

Then

$$D = dF \frac{t_{sm}}{360}$$

and

$$P = F - D = F\left(1 - \frac{dt_{sm}}{360}\right)$$

---

* Formulas adapted from *Money Market Calculations*, by Marcia Stigum, Dow-Jones Irwin (Homewood, Illinois, 1981).

Calculating the Rate of Discount on Discount Securities with Dollar Discount or Price Given

Let

D = discount from face value in dollars
F = face value in dollars
d = rate of discount (decimal)
t_{sm} = days from settlement to maturity
P = price in dollars

Then

Case I: Discount in dollars given:

$$d = \frac{D}{F} \frac{360}{t_{sm}}$$

Case II: Price in dollars given:

$$d = \left(1 - \frac{P}{F}\right)\frac{360}{t_{sm}}$$

Solving for Equivalent Bond Yield (Coupon Yield Equivalent) on a Discount Security

Let

d = rate of discount (decimal)
d_b = equivalent bond yield (decimal)
t_{sm} = days from settlement to maturity

Case I: Security has 6 months (182 days) or less to run:

$$d_b = \frac{365d}{360 - dt_{sm}}$$

Case II: Security has more than 6 months (182 days) to run:

$$d_b = \frac{-\dfrac{2t_{sm}}{365} + 2\sqrt{\left(\dfrac{t_{sm}}{365}\right)^2 - \left(\dfrac{2t_{sm}}{365} - 1\right)\left(1 - \dfrac{1}{P}\right)}}{\dfrac{2t_{sm}}{365}} - 1$$

Value of an 01 (a Basis Point) on a Discount Security

Let

v_{01} = Value of an 01 per $1 million of face value on a discount security

Then

$$v_{01} = 0.0001(1,000,000)\frac{t_{sm}}{360}$$

which reduces to

$$v_{01} = \$0.277778t_{sm}$$

A useful number to remember is that on a 90-day bill, with a $1 million face value

$$v_{01} = \$0.277778(90)$$
$$= \$25$$

Approximating the Tail on a Discount Security Financed with Term Repo

Let

d = rate of discount at purchase (decimal)
d = approximate *break-even* sale rate
r_t = term repo rate
t_{is} = days from issue (or purchase) to settlement, which is taken to be the day the term repo comes off
t_{sm} = days from settlement to maturity

Then

$$d = d + (d - r_t)\frac{t_{is}}{t_{sm}}$$

BASIC CD FORMULAS

Let

c = coupon rate
y = yield at which the security is traded
P = price per $1 of face value, accrued interest *included*
t_{im} = days from issue to maturity
t_{is} = days from issue to settlement
t_{sm} = days from settlement to maturity
a_i = accrued interest

I. Yield given price:

$$y = \left(\frac{1 + c\,\dfrac{t_{im}}{360}}{P} - 1 \right) \frac{360}{t_{sm}}$$

II. Price given yield:

$$P = \left(\frac{1 + c\,\dfrac{t_{im}}{360}}{1 + y\,\dfrac{t_{sm}}{360}} \right)$$

III. To break P into accrued interest and principal, note

$$a_i = c\,\frac{t_{is}}{360}$$

and

$$\text{Principal} = P - a_i$$

Calculating Yield Earned on a CD Sold Before Maturity

Let

i = Simple interest return earned over the holding period

Case I: The CD is purchased at issue: Let

y = sale rate
c = coupon rate
t_{im} = days from issue to maturity
t_{is} = days from issue to settlement
t_{sm} = days from settlement to maturity

then

$$i = \left(\frac{1 + c\,\dfrac{t_{im}}{360}}{1 + y\,\dfrac{t_{sm}}{360}} - 1 \right) \frac{360}{t_{is}}$$

Case II: The CD purchased in the secondary market:

Let

y_1 = purchase rate
y_2 = sale rate
t_1 = days from purchase to maturity
t_2 = days from sale to maturity

then

$$i = \left(\frac{1 + y_1 \dfrac{t_1}{360}}{1 + y_2 \dfrac{t_2}{360}} - 1 \right) \frac{360}{t_1 - t_2}$$

Figuring the Tail on a CD Hung Out on Term Repo

Let

y = break-even sale rate
c = coupon rate
r_i = term repo rate
t_{im} = days from issue to maturity
t_{is} = days from issue to settlement
t_{sm} = days from settlement to maturity

Case I: CD is RPed at issue:

$$y = \left(\frac{1 + c \dfrac{t_{im}}{360}}{1 + r_t \dfrac{t_{is}}{360}} - 1 \right) \frac{360}{t_{sm}}$$

Case II: A secondary CD is RPed:

Let

y = yield at which security is purchased
t_1 = days from purchase to maturity
t_2 = days from purchase to sale

Then

$$y = \left(\frac{1 + y \dfrac{t_1}{360}}{1 + r_t \dfrac{t_2}{360}} - 1 \right) \frac{360}{t_1 - t_2}$$

MEASURES OF BOND PRICE VOLATILITY: DURATION AND CONVEXITY

$$P = \frac{C}{(1 + y)^1} + \frac{C}{(1 + y)^2} + \ldots + \frac{C}{(1 + y)^n} + \frac{M}{(1 + y)^n}$$

where

P = price of the bond
C = *semiannual* coupon interest (in $)
M = maturity value (in $)
n = number of semiannual periods (number of years $\times$ 2)
y = one-half the yield to maturity or required yield

Macaulay duration

$$= \frac{\dfrac{1\,C}{(1 + y)^1} + \dfrac{2\,C}{(1 + y)^2} + \ldots + \dfrac{n\,C}{(1 + y)^n} + \dfrac{n\,M}{(1 + y)^n}}{P}$$

$$\text{Modified duration} = \frac{\text{Macaulay duration}}{(1 + y)}$$

$$\text{Dollar duration} = -(\text{Modified duration})\,P$$

Approximating the Percentage Price Change Using Modified Duration

$$\frac{dP}{P} = -\text{ Modified duration} \times dy$$

Approximating the Dollar Price Change Using Dollar Duration

$$dP = -(\text{Dollar duration})\,(dy)$$

Calculation of Macaulay Duration and Modified Duration for 9%, 5-Year Bond Selling to Yield 9%

Coupon rate = 9.00%
Term (years) = 5
Initial yield = 9.00%

Period (t)	Cash Flow*	PV of $1 0.045	PV of CF	t × PVCF
1	$ 4.50	0.956937	4.306220	4.30622
2	4.50	0.915729	4.120785	8.24156
3	4.50	0.876296	3.943335	11.83000
4	4.50	0.838561	3.773526	15.09410
5	4.50	0.802451	3.611030	18.05514
6	4.50	0.767895	3.455531	20.73318
7	4.50	0.734828	3.306728	23.14709
8	4.50	0.703185	3.164333	25.31466
9	4.50	0.672904	3.028070	27.25262
10	104.50	0.643927	67.290443	672.90442
Total			100.000000	826.87899

*Cash flow per $100 of par value.

$$\text{Macaulay duration (in half-years)} = \frac{826.87899}{100.000000} = 8.27$$

$$\text{Macaulay duration (in years)} = \frac{8.27}{2} = 4.13$$

$$\text{Modified duration (in years)} = \frac{4.13}{1.0450} = 3.96$$

CONVEXITY

$$\text{Convexity} = \frac{\sum_{t=1}^{n} \dfrac{t \times (t+1)(c)}{(1+y)^t} + \dfrac{n(n+1)M}{(1+y)^n}}{(1+y)^2 \times 2 \times 2 \times P}$$

$$\text{Dollar Convexity} = \text{Convexity} \times P$$

Calculation of Convexity for a 9%, 5-year Bond

Coupon Rate = 9%
Term = 5 years
Yield to maturity = 9%
Price = 100

Period (t)	t(t + 1)	Cash Flow	PV of Cash Flow (PVCF)	t(t + 1) × PVCF
1	2	4.50	4.31	8.62
2	6	4.50	4.12	24.72
3	12	4.50	3.94	47.28
4	20	4.50	3.77	75.40
5	30	4.50	3.61	108.30
6	42	4.50	3.46	145.32
7	56	4.50	3.31	185.36
8	72	4.50	3.16	227.52
9	90	4.50	3.03	272.70
10	110	104.50	67.29	7401.90
		Total	100.00	8497.12

$$\text{Convexity} = \frac{8497.12}{(1.045)^2(2)(2)(100)} = 19.45 \text{ (in half-years)}$$

Dollar Convexity = 19.45 × 100 = 1945.

OPTION-PRICING FORMULAS

$$\text{Call Price } (C) = S(1 - d)^t N(d_1) - E(1 + r)^{-t} N(d_2)$$

$$d_1 = \frac{[S(1 - d)^t / E(1 + r)^{-t}] + 1/2\sigma^2 t}{\sigma\sqrt{t}}$$

$$d_2 = d_1 - \sigma\sqrt{t}$$

$$\text{Put Price } (P) = C - S(1 - d)^t + E(1 + r)^{-t}$$

where:

S = Price of stock or instrument underlying option contract
E = Exercise or strike price
r = Annualized risk-free rate
σ = Annualized standard deviation of return
t = time to expiration
$N(\ )$ = Cumulative normal density function
d = Annualized dividend yield

$$\text{Option Delta} = \frac{\Delta\text{Option Price}}{\Delta\text{Stock Price}}$$

Delta (Call) = $(1 - d)^t N(d_1)$
Delta (Put) = $(1 - d)^t [N(d_1) - 1]$

$$\text{Option Gamma} = \frac{\Delta\text{Delta}}{\Delta\text{Stock Price}}$$

$$\text{Gamma (Call)} = \text{Gamma (Put)} = \frac{(1 - d)^t N'(d_1)}{S\sigma\sqrt{t}}$$

where:

$$N'(d_1) = \frac{1}{\sqrt{2\pi}} e^{-d_1^2/2}$$

$$\text{Option Vega} = \frac{\Delta\text{Option Price}}{\Delta\text{Volatility}}$$

$$\text{Vega (Call)} = \text{Vega (Put)} = (1 - d)^t S\sqrt{t}\, N'(d_1)$$

$$\text{Option Theta} = \frac{\Delta\text{Option Price}}{\Delta\text{Time to Expiration}}$$

Theta (Call) $= \frac{1}{2}(\text{Gamma})\sigma^2 S^2 + S\,\text{Delta (Call)} \times [\log(1 + r) + \log(1 - d)] - \log(1 + r) \times C$

Theta (Put) $= \frac{1}{2}(\text{Gamma})\sigma^2 S^2 + S\,\text{Delta (Put)} \times [\log(1 + r) + \log(1 - d)] - \log(1 + r) \times p$

Example

$S = 50;\ E = 48$

$r = 5.5\%;\ d = 3.55\%$

$\sigma = .2627;\ t = 44/365$ (44 days to expiration)

$\qquad = .1205$

$$d_1 = \frac{\ln[50(1 - .0355)^{.1205}/48(1.055)^{-.1205}] + (.5)(.2627)^2(.1205)}{(.2627)\sqrt{.1205}} = .5162$$

$$d_2 = .5162 - .2627\sqrt{.1205} = .4250$$

$C = 50(1 - .0355)^{.1205}.697 - 48(1.055)^{-.1205}.6646 = 3.00$

Delta (Call) $= (1 - .0355)^{.1205}.697$

$\qquad\qquad = 0.6939$

$$N^1(d_1) = \frac{1}{\sqrt{2 \times 3.1415}} e^{-(.5162)^2/2} = .3492$$

$$\text{Gamma (Call)} = \frac{(1 - .0355)^{.1205}.3492}{50(.2627)\sqrt{.1205}} = .0762$$

Vega (Call) $= (1 - .0355)^{.1205} 50\sqrt{.1205}\ .3492$

$\qquad\qquad = 6.03$ per 100% change in volatility

Theta (Call) $= \frac{1}{2}(.3476)(.2627)^2(50)^2 + 50(.6939) \times [\log(1.055) + \log(1 - .0355)] - \log(1.055) \times 3.00$

$\qquad\qquad = 30.42$ per year

Index